Miranda Seymour is the author of several widely admired biographies including *Ottoline Morrell: Life on the Grand Scale*, twelve times selected as Book of the Year for 1992; *Robert Graves: Life on the Edge*, recently re-issued by Scribner; and *Mary Shelley*. Her latest book is the highly acclaimed *The Bugatti Queen*, a life of the pioneer racing driver Hellé Nice. Miranda Seymour also writes novels and children's books. She lives in London.

A *Ring of* *Conspirators*

HENRY JAMES
and his literary circle
1895–1915

Miranda Seymour

Scribner

First published in Great Britain by Hodder & Stoughton in 1988
This edition published by Scribner in 2004
An imprint of Simon & Schuster UK Ltd
A Viacom company

Scribner and design are trademarks of Macmillan Library Reference
USA, Inc., used under license by Simon & Schuster, the publisher of this work.

1 3 5 7 9 10 8 6 4 2

Simon & Schuster UK Ltd
Africa House
64–78 Kingsway
London WC2B 6AH

Simon & Schuster Australia
Sydney

www.simonsays.co.uk

A CIP catalogue for this book is available
from the British Library.

ISBN: 0-7432-3220-8

Printed and bound in Great Britain by
Bookmarque Ltd, Croydon, Surrey

In memory of Howard Sturgis

CONTENTS

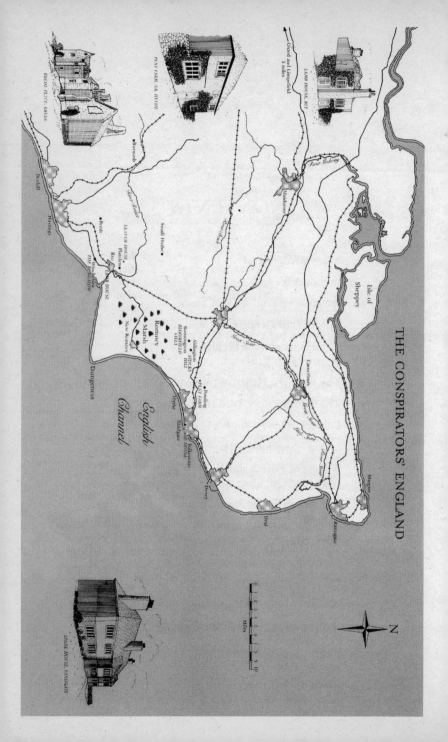

THE CONSPIRATORS' ENGLAND

ACKNOWLEDGEMENTS

Anyone writing about Henry James would wish first to thank Professor Leon Edel, who has devoted his life to the subject, to the benefit of us all and who, in his biography and his editions of the letters and notebooks, has provided James's admirers with an unfailing source of pleasure and information.

I would like to thank the Authors' Foundation for a grant which was both welcome and useful. Professor Inga-Stina Ewbank and Professor John Dixon Hunt showed me new ways to look at James and were always encouraging and helpful. Without them, this book could never have been written. My editor, Ion Trewin, has been patience itself while giving me the benefit of his wise ideas and suggestions. Maria Rejt and Carol Johnson have been invaluable advisers, and special thanks are due to Hazel Bell, who spared me from the trauma of compiling an index. I am most grateful, too, to Anthony Goff for keeping my spirits up and for keeping a very necessary eye on my progress, and to Felicity Bryan for her support and enthusiasm. Dr Richard Luckett, too, has my warmest thanks for his ideas, his help and his investigations on my behalf. Merlin Sinclair deserves a special place in this group for his good-humoured tolerance of a mother who was rather too wedded to the typewriter and her notes to give him all the attention he deserved and never demanded while this book was being written. I am also especially grateful to my American cousins for responding magnificently to all my questions about James and Howard Sturgis and I would like, in this connection, to mention Mrs Armistice P. Rood, Mrs Katherine Sturgis Goodman and Dr and Mrs Edwin Cole. My parents, too, are to be thanked most warmly for all their suggestions and recollections, and for some very rewarding researches in the family albums, diaries and letters in connection with my great-great-uncle, Howard Sturgis.

Thanks for courteous help and permissions are due to Alexander James, Barrett College, University of Virginia, the Berg Collection, New York, the Bodleian Library, Oxford, the British Library Manuscript Department, London, to the Master and Fellows of Magdalene College, Cambridge for allowing me to quote from Arthur Benson's diaries, to the Houghton Library, Harvard, the Humanities Research Center, Texas, Cornell Uni-

ACKNOWLEDGEMENTS

versity Library, New York, to the Cambridge and Harvard University Presses, the Pierpont Morgan Library, New York, the Alumnae Association of Smith College, Massachusetts, and to all the staff of the London Library.

I would like to express my grateful thanks to those literary editors who kept me handsomely supplied with new books relating to James and his literary neighbours and to Lucy Abel-Smith for some very helpful ideas which resulted from delivering Chapter 3 as a lecture organized by her at Oxford. I am last, but far from least, grateful to the following for suggestions, hospitality and information. It has been one of the great pleasures of writing this book to have been met on all sides with such generous kindness and enthusiasm. Thanks, then to: The staff of Spade House, Sir Brian Batsford, Barbara Belford, Alan Jenkins, Sir Rupert Hart-Davis, Mrs Viola Bayley, Miss Veronica Powles, Mrs Diana Bazalgette, Charlie Brookes, Percy Hooker, Mrs Enid Sills, Mrs Nancy Steeper, Thomas Seymour, Mrs Elizabeth Divine, and James Fergusson. John Saumerez Smith of Heywood Hill Bookshop did a splendid job in tracking down books which were out-of-print. Mr Montgomery Hyde, in his *Henry James at Home*, provided me with many a good trail to follow, as did Iain Finlayson in his *Writers of the Romney Marsh* and Nicholas Delbanco in his *Group Portrait*.

The mistakes, of course, are all my own.

M.S.

INTRODUCTION

An achievement in art or in letters grows more interesting when we begin to perceive its connections; and, indeed, it may be said that the study of connections is the recognized function of intelligent criticism.

'Pierre Loti', Henry James, 1888

Edward Gordon Craig's design for Henry James's personal bookplate, used for his Lamb House library. The 1902 woodcut shows the mulberry tree in the Lamb House garden which was brought down by winds shortly before Henry James's death.

INTRODUCTION

When a man has neither wife nor mistress and leads a life which is both orderly and prudent, he does not invite the conventional biographical approach. Henry James was such a man. The richness of his life lies in his words and in his relationships.

James's character was full of contradictions. He was witty and melancholy, formidable and vulnerable, suavely brutal and imperiously kind. He was fiercely private and exuberantly sociable, guarded in many of his friendships, overt and demonstrative in his passions.

A man of such a fascinatingly complex character provoked conflicting reactions among those who knew – or thought they knew – him well. My aim has been to uncover and reconcile the many facets of his nature by looking at him through their eyes – and at them through his. The portrait emerges from the mass of evasions, omissions, misunderstandings and misrepresentations which surrounded James in his later life and to which he himself contributed.

Chronology imposes a convenient discipline on the biographer but one which tends to keep him at a distance from the mind of his subject. Our minds conduct a constant war against the ordering years. We remember life, not as a neat sequence of events, but in the context of friendships, hopes and disappointments, significant events. The shifting time-schemes and perspectives of a novelist often prove more successful in bringing a character to life. I have borrowed a little of this larger freedom given to the maker of fictions, disposing with a neat chronological thread while working in a time-frame of 1895–1915, the last twenty years of James's life in England. The authoritative position of the biographer is deliberately diminished by this method of approach. The readers are left free to draw their own conclusions about James.

The reasons which led me to concentrate on the last two decades of James's life were several. Mindful of the axiom that it is wiser to write of what you know than what you do not, I wanted, as an

English author, to concentrate on the period when James transferred his allegiance from America to England. He did not become a British subject until 1915, the last year of his life, but his decision in 1897 to exchange the life of an urban bachelor for the life of a country gentleman living at Lamb House in Rye marked the opening of his most English period, the years in which he was delighted to hear himself referred to as a 'squire' and to speak, with his tongue in his cheek, of 'his people'. A second subjective reason for choosing this period was that it would allow me to write about the Qu'Acre circle. Qu'Acre, a handsome Victorian house on the edge of Windsor Great Park, was the home of my great-great-uncle, Howard Sturgis, one of James's closest friends. Sturgis, although he was born and bred in England, was a New Englander by descent and his home became a meeting point and open hotel to Americans like James and Edith Wharton who had strong attachments and links with New England. 'A ring of foreign conspirators' might seem a very adequate description of this wealthy group of witty and intelligent American anglophiles in which James was most thoroughly at home.

The phrase also has a more precisely literary origin. H. G. Wells coined it to describe the group of writers who were his neighbours in East Sussex at the turn of the century. Henry James was not the only novelist to be attracted to this lovely and unspoilt region in the 1890s. Ford Madox Ford, who had known the area since childhood, returned to it in his twenties with his young wife, Elsie Martindale. Nomadic though Ford was in his shifts of home during his ten years as a Kent and Sussex smallholder and amateur farmer, he was never more than a few miles from Rye and the lonely marshes of Romney which he loved. Joseph Conrad, with his naval days behind him and at the beginning of his remarkable career as a foreign master of English prose, rented Pent Farm at Postling from Ford and, with him, embarked on one of the most famous literary collaborations of the time, one which James and Wells viewed with jaundiced misgiving. Stephen Crane, fresh from the transatlantic success of his war-novel, *The Red Badge of Courage*, was persuaded to exchange his role as dare-devil journalist and wild boy for the more sober guise of an English country squire. Brede Place, a dilapidated Tudor house six miles inland from Rye, offered ample scope for a part which Crane, briefly, played with uncommon zest. Wells, the only true-blue Englishman among them (Conrad was Polish and Hueffer, who had not then changed his name to Ford, was half-German), was recommended to the coast for his health, undermined by the almost superhuman rate at which he had been pouring out his early works of science-fiction. He came to Sandgate, a quiet little town on the coast two or three miles west of Folkestone and, after a humble start at 2, Beach Cottages, commissioned an architect to build him Spade House, a fine new home on top of the cliff. It was on this circle of writers that I wanted to concentrate.

Words like 'circle' or 'group' are apt to be misleading in this context. James, Ford, Crane, Conrad and Wells were neighbours and colleagues in a common craft. Only by topography and date can they be neatly yoked together as sharers in a common cause. They had no such united purpose as one finds in the Imagists under Ezra Pound's leadership or in the Vorticists with Wyndham Lewis as their guiding spirit. The nearest they came to it was when Conrad, Wells and Ford were briefly joined together in 1908 by the wish to create a magazine which would have, in Ford's words, 'the definite design of giving imaginative literature a chance in England'. The *English Review*, under Ford's brief but inspired administration until Sir Alfred Mond bought the magazine and sacked the editor, did give a new and identifiable face to one of England's richest literary periods; the first issue contained contributions by Conrad, Galsworthy, Hardy, Hudson, James and Wells.[1]

Had there been a group ready to follow his banner, Ford would have been the man willing to lead them. But Ford in 1900 was too much of a juvenile to raise a standard which James or Wells would have stooped to follow. Defer to a bumptious twenty-seven-year-old with a few fairy tales, a thin volume of poems and a biography of an illustrious relation to his credit? (Ford had recently published a life of his grandfather Ford Madox Brown, the great Pre-Raphaelite painter.) It was all they could do to stomach the thought of Ford exercising his intellectual muscles at the expense of Conrad's 'wonderful oriental style'. Crane, the last of the five to arrive in the area and the most defiantly anti-intellectual, was the least likely to provide them with a literary manifesto, although hindsight enables us to link him to Conrad and Ford by the impressionistic uses of colour in his narratives.

Wells, looking back in 1934 on his early years in Sussex, was inclined to think that he could have been the one to organize them and to orchestrate their thoughts. The problem, as he remembered it, was that they were incapable of being subdued.

> Instead of being based on a central philosophy, they started off at a dozen points; they were impulsive, unco-ordinated, wilful. Conrad, you see, I count uneducated, Stephen Crane, Henry James, the larger part of the world of literary artistry . . . The science and art of education was not adequate for the taming and full utilization of these more

powerfully receptive types and they lapsed into arbitrary inconsistent and dramatized ways of thinking and living. With a more expert and scientific educational process all that might have been different.[2]

Might James have succeeded where Wells had failed? While ranking mortifyingly far below Wells in terms of commercial success, he stood head and shoulders above him in terms of literary reputation. As Ford engagingly puts it, he 'bulked enormously in polite advanced circles in London'. James had not yet published the sonorous Prefaces which, however misleading as the introductions to his novels they profess to be, contain the core of his literary belief. The basic articles of his faith had already been established in the critical essays, in the precociously assured study of Hawthorne and in the diverse but stylistically consistent novels of his early and middle years. He had constructed and developed his singular creed long before his arrival in Rye. He used it as a measuring stick by which to evaluate and judge the works of his fellow-novelists, but he was not a Pound, a Lewis or a Wordsworth looking for kindred spirits with whom to unite. Social to a formidable degree – few writers can have dined out with such debilitating regularity – he was nevertheless a solitary worker and thinker. The muse he invoked in his notebooks with the ardent urgency of a medium summoning up a capricious spirit responded to him alone.

In the strictest sense, then, there was no group, no conspiracy. In the more lax sense, whereby creative persons will seek out and form attachments with like-minded neighbours and will privately discuss and publicly review each other's work, a group existed.

I am not the first to have been intrigued by the relationships which developed between these prestigious and disparate novelists. *Group Portrait* by Nicholas Delbanco (1982) concentrates on their work as literary collaborators, while *Writers in Romney Marsh* by Iain Finlayson (1986) offers an engagingly anecdotal history of the area with brief but vivid portraits of eight of its most celebrated authors. The difference is in my angle of approach, a circular one which encompasses the group while retaining a focus on Henry James. The chapters are arranged in such a way as to show him in his various roles, as the slightly too correct provincial gentleman who kept his finger firmly on the pulse of London society, as the family man, wearily accepting but never following the unsolicited views of his elder brother on novel-writing, delighting in the visits of his young nieces and nephews, as a celibate bachelor whose preference among females was for clever, witty, strong-minded women, although his less overt predilection was for handsome boys; their youthful admiration and affection was a more than adequate compensation for their inferior intelligence and breadth of experience of the world. The final chapter looks at James in what many hold to be his most admirable role, as the passionate patriot of his adopted country when England went to war, anxiously following the latest reports from the Front, tirelessly visiting the sick when he himself was old and infirm.

In the cause of clarity, these aspects of James have been divided into separate sections which are linked by the chapters relating to his literary friendships. A list of relevant dates attached to each chapter hopefully remedies the absence of a clear chronological structure.

Finally, the setting. An Introduction seems the appropriate place in which to offer some description of Rye and the Sussex landscape which provides the background to this book and which has been an unfailing source of pleasure and interest to me in the course of writing it, a pleasure which was only marred by the knowledge that the construction of the Channel Tunnel will inevitably spoil the face of this beautiful and hitherto unspoilt corner of England.

Among the many evocative descriptions of Rye in Henry James's day, one of the best is quoted by Leon Edel in his biography. The writer is Jonathan Sturges, a shrewdly observant New Yorker who shared his friend James's enthusiasm for the area.

> I wish I could give you a portrait of this little, red, pointed, almost medieval town with its sea-wall and its Norman relic of Ypres castle which they call here 'Wipers' – perched on a hill in the midst of the grey-green, sand-coloured waste of Romney Marsh, an Anglo-Saxon Mont St Michel, long deserted by the sea yet with the colour and scent of the sea in its quiet brown streets, a brown of the tone of fishermen's sails and nets. The blue-jerseyed retired fishermen themselves are to be found at any hour, on the deserted bastion of Ypres Castle happily armed against the French invasion a hundred years ago. They address one another with a classical 'what ho!' which seems almost too beautiful to be true, and through brass telescopes they study the sails upon the distant Channel. In sou-westerly gales one hears the roar and sees the long white *raselier**★** of the surge. The sheep huddle together upon the marsh and the fishing boats huddle with bare poles in the Rother in Rye 'Harbour', a hamlet like a Dutch picture against the wild grey sky – three miles away.

Fishermen no longer gather at Ypres Castle or address each other in such picturesque fashion but, when seen from a distance, Rye can

★ *Raselier* is a word which seems to have been invented by Sturges as it is not to be found in any French dictionary.

still excite feelings of wonder and delight. Red-tiled roofs climb up its rock to make a scarlet halo around the tall red-roofed church which dominates the town. Less fiercely solitary than Mont St Michel, Rye can transform itself from a pretty toytown of sparkling reds and russets into a whispering necropolis when, at nightfall, the housetops tower close and high and the cobbled streets echo, their corners slanting steeply away into obscure alleys and sudden drops. Ford's impression of a Georgian city of the dead which provoked in him a feeling of alarm and panic on his first nocturnal visit is as true to the town's atmosphere as E. F. Benson's later portrait of an Edwardian Cranford inhabited by genial colonels, pretentious spinsters and incorrigible gossips. Benson's brother, Arthur, visiting James at Lamb House for the first time, was struck by the Dutch trimness and bourgeois stateliness of the town, an observation which holds good today of Rye's upper streets, any one of which would look entirely at home in a painting by Pieter de Hooch. Turner, painting the town from the marshy plain below, captured its most memorable quality when, floating above a veil of mist from the sea which long ago receded from its walls, Rye ascends from prettiness to the aspect of a visionary city, ethereal as a medieval poet's dream of Jerusalem.

Anyone wishing to see Rye at its best is advised to view it as Turner did, from a distance. Lamb House, a visitable shrine of Jamesiana, has been courteously and discreetly preserved and it is still hoped that funds can be raised to recreate the pretty 'Garden Room' in which James dictated his last works and which was, sadly, destroyed in the last war. The town, however, while still delightful for the private visitor who can escape the hubbub of the summer streets, reeks of tourism and the twentieth century. The visitor in search of the past should drive away from it, out onto the grey-green flats of Romney Marsh, where the landscape is as James saw it at the turn of the century when he bowled downhill on his bicycle and out along pitted dust-tracks and leafy lanes towards Winchelsea and Brede, Sandgate and Postling.

'The world according to the best geographers is divided into Europe, Asia, Africa, America and Romney marsh?

Richard Barham Harris's nineteenth-century division of the world in *The Ingoldsby Legends* is a cheerful piece of effrontery which, nevertheless, conveys an intriguing truth. The marsh, which some would take to be a representative piece of thoroughly English landscape, would carry quite as much conviction if we were told that we were looking at a landscape in Italy, or in France. Few areas in Britain are so remarkable for their sudden variety of mood and aspect. To

James, whose affection for England was tempered by his yearning for the Roman campagna he had loved in his youth and was now growing too old to enjoy, this foreign aspect was one of the area's greatest attractions. Living in England, he could still fancy himself to be abroad.

Architecturally, this Kentish corner of Sussex is a democratic muddle. Half-timbered cottages squint round the sides of Queen Anne town houses; medieval churches preside over Georgian buildings and over the isolated parishes of the marsh itself with impartial dignity. Physically, the marsh is a slavish mirror to a restless sky, dark as a scud of storm clouds on a day when the lonely buildings flatten themselves to the ground against the screaming wind, brilliant as a Highland summer of purple and blue, peat and gold when the light shimmers over the dykes and the broad, sheep-cropped pastures. Grimness and gaiety are never further apart than the sudden sweep of a cloud across the sun.

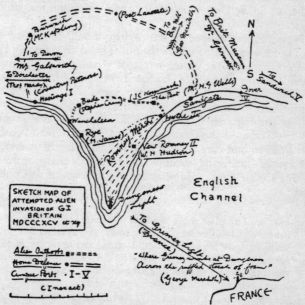

Ford's sketch of the conspirators' invasion of Romney Marsh, inspired by Wells

There are changes, of course, since the time when Wells playfully portrayed the area as a hotbed of conspiring foreigners intent on changing the course of British writing. Corrugated barn roofs loom over Pent Farm, the small and frowning red house on the edge of

Postling village where the two great raconteurs, Ford and Conrad, spun stories to each other and for each other in their collaborative friendship. Pretty straggling Aldington is already becoming a smart retreat for city-dwellers with second homes, but you can still see where Conrad lived in the dell below Aldington church in a comical little cottage with a red witch's hat of a roof and the tiny cramped rooms in which, at another period, he and his family lived above the village butcher and beer-seller. You can still climb up to Aldington Knoll where Ford stood watching shadows on the marsh before tramping home to damp and dismal Bloomfield Villa in neighbouring Bonnington. Time has certainly left its mark on Spade House, the ultra-modern – by the lights of late Victorian domestic architecture – home which Charles Voysey built for the Wellses at Sandgate. Once a restaurant and now a nursing-home, the house has no more literary atmosphere than a garage. But even here, in the small two-tiered garden looking down to a sea less murmurous than the old ladies of Spade House calling for their afternoon tea, time shrinks back.

Nothing has changed at Winchelsea, a well-buttressed hill-town two miles west of Rye where the Fords lived after renting Pent Farm to the Conrads. One visitor wrote of Winchelsea's 'stillicide'. Stand outside Ford's neat white clapboard cottage with the grand lines of St Thomas's church dictating the view, and 'stillicide' precisely captures the dreaming passivity of the broad quiet streets which still follow the regimental lines on which the town was rebuilt in the times of Edward the Confessor. Ford, better remembered for *The Good Soldier* and *Parade's End* than for his marvellous evocations of the English landscape, captured Winchelsea's charm most precisely in *The Cinque Ports*, a book about the area which was published in 1900.

> I know of no place more prodigal of pleasant impressions than this old town, which offers itself so open to the sky upon its little hill . . . The shadows have a peculiar, liquid effect, the moisture of the evening seeming to split the light up and to shower it about even in the deep shade the town casts out on to the marshes, seawards.

Brede Place, described by county historians as a perfect example of a medieval home and one of Sussex's greatest treasures, was not viewed with similar enthusiasm by Stephen Crane's friends and neighbours. Ford could not imagine why anybody should want to live in such a damp and dismal house. James, returning there shortly after Crane's death, thought it looked 'conscious and cruel'. He probably shared Ford's belief that Brede itself, damp, draughty and financially burdensome, was largely responsible for the rapidity of poor Crane's deterioration. Gutted by fire in the recent past, Brede is the place where one might most reasonably look for change. Happily, the house's present owner has confined his work of restoration – and alteration – to the interior. No trace remains of the draughty halls in which the Cranes entertained an endless stream of guests, but the leafy mile-long drive, the long view over an unspoilt valley and the house's gravely beautiful exterior are as they were. Brede today still conveys the intoxicating blend of grandeur and romance which entranced the Cranes and intrigued their neighbours.

The Cranes, by their choice of home, invited their literary neighbours to look up to them. It is not apparent that they did so in anything but a geographical sense – the house stands in a commanding position – but I see no reason why we should not remedy that here by starting the story at Brede Place, the oldest and by far the most spectacular of the houses we shall be visiting.

1

IMAGINATIVE TRUTHS: THE CRANES

The first of these four men to die was the youngest. Taken altogether they were, these four, all gods for me. They formed, when I was a boy, my sure hope in the eternity of good letters. They do still.

Ford Madox Ford,
Return to Yesterday

They (Englishmen) will believe anything wild or impossible you tell them . . .

Stephen Crane, 1897

A lie is a figurative truth – and it is the poet who is the master of these illusions.

Ford Madox Ford & Joseph Conrad,
Romance

Since there is no clear line of chronological progress, I have provided a list of dates for each chapter. These are not intended to be comprehensive. Their purpose is only to provide a framework and reference point.

1896 Henry James begins to look for a country home after renting a villa near Rye. Writes *The Spoils of Poynton*.

1896 Ford completes the biography of his grandfather, Ford Madox Brown, and lunches with James in Rye.

1896 Stephen Crane, the most celebrated of them all at this point for his remarkable war-novel, *The Red Badge of Courage*, goes to Jacksonville and falls in love with Cora Taylor.

1896 Wells, writing away for dear life, moves to Heatherley with Jane and writes *The Wheels of Chance, The Invisible Man* and *The War of the Worlds*.

1986 Joseph Conrad marries Jessie George, publishes *An Outcast of the Islands* and almost finishes *The Nigger of the 'Narcissus'*.

1897 James rents Lamb House, starts working by direct dictation on to his typewriter and completes *What Maisie Knew*.

1897 Stephen Crane and Cora arrive in England, meet Conrad and Ford and move to Ravensbrook Villa at Oxted. Crane suggests a collaboration which Conrad refuses.

1898 Henry James meets Conrad and Wells. He writes *The Turn of the Screw* and *The Awkward Age*.

1898 Ford meets Conrad, suggests the move to The Pent and begins to collaborate with him.

1898 Cora adopts the Frederic children and decides to move to Brede while Crane is away.

1898 Conrad begins work on a preliminary sketch of *Lord Jim*, and on *Heart of Darkness*, and completes *Youth*. He begins collaborating on Ford's 'Seraphina' (*Romance*).

1899 James decides to buy the freehold of Lamb House. He starts work on *The Wings of the Dove*.

1899– Wells and Jane progress from 2, Beach Cottages to Arnold House to the
1900 home built to their specifications by Charles Voysey, Spade House, in Sandgate.

1899 The Cranes give a great Christmas-New Year party at Brede, attended by Conrad and Wells. Crane collapses.

1900 James finishes *The Sacred Fount*, endures Ford's overtures and begins epistolary battle with Wells over the purpose of literature.

1900 Crane dies in the summer of 1900, at Nordracht. He was still trying to complete *The O'Ruddy*, but dictated his final thoughts to Robert Barr, who completed the book.

1900 Conrad finishes *Lord Jim*, goes on holiday with the Fords, and becomes one of Pinker's authors.

1

IMAGINATIVE TRUTHS:

THE CRANES

Henry James was not in the mood to join the noisy celebrations with which the Cranes marked the end of their first year at Brede Place and the dawn of the new century. His brother, William, never an easy guest and never less of one than when he was ill and overworked, was visiting him for Christmas with his wife, Alice. William had not yet recovered from a heart attack for which he had been recently treated in London, and Lamb House offered a brief resting-spot before he embarked for further treatment in Europe. A wild all-night party at Brede was not on the agenda for an invalid, although William might have secretly hankered for an escape from the decorous tranquillity of his brother's home. James himself was thoroughly disinclined to participate in rowdy entertainments. Keeping William cheerful was exhausting work and the prospect of entering the twentieth century filled him with gloom. It made him want to turn back to 'the warm and coloured past and away from the big black avenue that gapes in front of us'.

Conrad, while watching 'in fear and trembling another year approaching', was ready to put aside his worries about writing *Lord Jim* and his despair at trying to secure any peace with a wailing year-old son in the house, and to go to Brede to join in the fun.

It was a little more than a year since Conrad had travelled up to London to make the acquaintance of the young author of *The Red Badge of Courage* and the two men had since become firm friends. Conrad, old enough to be Crane's father, had immediately been charmed by the younger and more famous man's simplicity and directness. Ford would later describe Crane as 'an Apollo with starry eyes'. Conrad saw a slight, startlingly handsome boy with thick light-brown hair, large shining eyes and a bright unsmiling stare. Something about the face troubled him, however. It gave him a queer presentiment of misfortune.

Shortly after that first London meeting, the Cranes had taken the advice of Edward Garnett, the kindly friend and mentor to so many young writers, and had gone to live near him and his wife, Constance, the Russian translator, at a damp and draughty house on the unattractive road from Oxted to Limpsfield. It was here, at Ravensbrook, that Joseph and Jessie Conrad first met the unusual lady who Crane was doing his best to pass off as his wife.

Cora Stewart* was a big handsome warm-hearted woman, impulsive and sentimental. Her eyes were blue, her mass of blonde hair was of so vivid a colour that it was often incorrectly assumed to be dyed. Age was against her – the observant Conrads could not fail to register that she was a good deal older than Crane – but it was evident that they were a devoted couple who had in common a sense of fun, a love of adventure and a cheerful disregard for money. It is unlikely that they heard about Cora's previous history as the 'madam' of the Hotel de Dream in Jacksonville, Florida. (For a name which could have been coined by Tennessee Williams, Cora was indebted to her predecessor, Ethel Dreme.) They would certainly have heard about the couple's exploits the previous year when Cora travelled to Turkey with Crane as one of the first female war-correspondents, sending back her despatches under the nom de plume of Imogene Carter. Jessie Conrad, herself an excellent housekeeper, could find no fault with her hostess's excellent cooking but, as a woman who reckoned every halfpenny spent in the house, she was horrified by Cora's airy disregard for economy. 'Stephen and I are the same person,' Cora announced. 'We have no sense of money at all.' She did not exaggerate.

It was Cora, eager to improve her insecure social position, who decided that the best way to set about it was by becoming a lady of the manor. In June 1898 Crane was away in Cuba when Edward Garnett, knowing that they were anxious to find a new home, suggested that she might take a look at Brede Place. 'Go without expectations,' he advised, having noted the house's tumbledown state. Cora went, and was captivated. The Moreton Frewens had only recently acquired the house from Mr Frewen's elder brother with Mrs Frewen's money. As one of the three Jerome heiresses, Clara Frewen could gratify such impulses, but a couple of months at Brede had been enough to quench her enthusiasm for country life. London was a good deal more comfortable and amusing, and the Frewens were delighted to let Brede for a peppercorn rent to anyone

* Born Miss Howorth, Cora briefly became Mrs Thomas Murphy before her marriage to Captain Donald Stewart from whom she was unable to obtain a divorce. No satisfactory explanation has ever been found for the name Cora Taylor which she frequently employed before discreetly introducing herself as 'Mrs Crane', an address to which she was not legally entitled.

foolish enough to overlook howling draughts, stinking drains and bone-chilling damp. If the Cranes were prepared to undertake some repairs, keep on the servants and look after the horses, the house was theirs.

Brede Place drawn by Augustus Hare, engraved by T Sulman.

A prudent woman would have decided to stay at the dull but more manageable house. Prudence was not Cora's strongest point. Surrounded by angry creditors, she nevertheless set about planning the restoration of Brede. They might build a conservatory. The garden would have to be completely replanted. She started at once by ordering 300 roses to improve the approach.

Crane returned to England at the beginning of January 1899 and visited Brede a week later. As romantic as Cora, he viewed its evident disadvantages through rose-coloured spectacles. 'Stephen was mad over the place,' Cora reported triumphantly to Edward Garnett. 'We tramped, later, after a supper of ham & eggs beside the kitchen fire – to a cottage in the village and put up for the night there. Then spent the day at Brede. We are going to move Heaven and Earth to get there. Stephen said that a solemn feeling of work came to him there so I am delighted.'[1] Crane, whose solemn feeling had more to do with the large pile of bills which greeted him on his return to England, acknowledged that the old house was 'a pretty fine affair' which might, he thought, have been designed by Sir Walter Scott to suit Cora's dream of baronial life. The grandeur outweighed the prospect of a certain amount of physical discomfort; they had both had the experience of living rough.

The one practical attraction of the house was its size. When Crane's friend, Harold Frederic, the rumbustious London editor of the *New York Times*, died in August 1898, Cora had acted with her usual impulsiveness, taking under her wing not only Frederic's common-law wife, Kate Lyon, but Kate's niece, Edith Ritchie Jones, and the three little children. Life had been severely cramped by this sudden expansion, but Brede was large enough to house the adopted tribe and Crane's five dogs with ease.

Life at Brede sounds to have come straight out of a novel by Maria Edgeworth. In Ireland, it would have seemed nothing extraordinary, but in decorous Sussex it struck visitors as decidedly bizarre. Cora in open sandals with her hair hanging loose down her back, the cook refusing to do her job until she had been plied with large amounts of alcohol, and Crane doing nothing to stem the endless tide of guests or to discipline this life of shiftless chaos; the Conrads looked on with dismay and felt that their worst fears were being confirmed.

By the time he first saw Brede, Crane's tuberculosis had already set in – he had started to cough up blood in 1898. Recurrent fever attacks of malaria followed the move. In this low physical state, he struggled to achieve the impossible, namely, to write fast enough to keep his creditors at bay while representing himself as a rich, generous, easy-going host to the spongers who looked on his new home as a free hotel and didn't wait for invitations. In the mornings, dressed in gaucho costume, he went riding. Later in the day, he locked himself up in the dank red-walled study over the main entrance and wrote, posting the pages under the door for Cora to type before the latest masterpiece – it was always declared to be a masterpiece – was posted to Pinker with a request for immediate payment and, more often than not, for a loan against outstanding bills.

One of the first professional literary agents – all of our five Sussex-based writers used him to place their works – Pinker must have been tempted to change his profession during the seventeen months of the Cranes' residence at Brede. They demanded, they cajoled, they wrote twice a day to ask for money for stories which poor Pinker had scarcely received, let alone had time to place. The greater the need, the more imperious grew the demands, forcing him to point out that he could not be treated as their free bank. 'You telegraphed on Friday for £20,' he wrote back in answer to a spate of frantic appeals; 'Mrs Crane, on Monday, makes it £50; today comes your letter making it £150, and I very much fear that your agent must be a millionaire if he is to satisfy your necessities a week hence, at this rate.'[2] Cora's prompt response was a demand for £40 by return of post with £150 to follow as soon as possible, after which she upbraided Pinker for having dared to suggest that Crane should slow down his output because too many stories might spoil the market. How could he be so insensitive, she wished to know? 'This is a fatal thing to say to a writing man. Particularly to Stephen Crane.

And how can you think so with an utterly unspoiled and vast American market? . . . you could sell a thousand short stories of Mr Crane's there if you had them.'[3]*

Superficially, Crane was as aggressively optimistic as Cora, tireless in his assertions that each piece of work was his best yet. That, as he saw it, was salesmanship. In private, he was confident only of his ability to persist and be true to himself.

> I know that my work does not amount to a string of dried beans – I always calmly admit it – but I also know that I do the best that is in me without regard to praise or blame. When I was the mark for every humorist in the country, I went ahead; and now when I am the mark for only fifty per cent of the humorists of the country, I go ahead; for I understand that a man is born into the world with his own pair of eyes, and he is not at all responsible for his vision – he is merely responsible for his quality of personal honesty. To keep close to this personal honesty is my supreme ambition.[4]

Heavily in debt though they were by the end of their first year at Brede, the Cranes were determined to celebrate the passing of the century in style and to fill the house with people. Why should they make themselves sick with misery over the future when the present could be made so enjoyable? Cora probably took the initiative, entranced by her role as a grand hostess. Crane went along with it, eager to divert his thoughts from his increasingly bad health and the constant worry of financial pressure. He had for some time been toying with the idea of writing a play and they wanted to find a way of entertaining their guests and neighbours. Casting about for a suitable subject, he settled on a spoof about Brede's most famous ghost.

Sir Goddard Oxenbridge, a kindly old gentleman whose finest moment had been to attend Henry VIII at the Field of the Cloth of Gold, had passed into Sussex folklore as the monster of Brede, a child-eating ogre whose other agreeable pastime had been to hang his numerous wives in the Gallows Room. (An unusually broad beam in one of the halls at Brede had given rise to this gory legend.) Sir

---

* Crane was not alone in regarding Pinker as a benevolent machine for dispensing cash to needy writers. Conrad was equally ready to make use of him, requesting that he should settle the bills for school fees, furniture, medicines and even hats, and abusing him roundly if he failed to do so. The success of *Chance* in 1914 allowed Pinker to recoup his losses, but Conrad had already gone some way towards indirectly repaying him by introducing him to such lucrative authors as Galsworthy when they were in search of an agent. Ford, another writer who was not too proud to draw on Pinker's purse, also helped to swell his list of authors.

Goddard's fate, according to the stories, was to have been sawn in half by vengeful children on Groaning Bridge, where an unwary traveller might still hear the old knight crying for mercy in the late hours of the night.

Crane, not the kind of man to be intimidated by such tales, saw only a good subject for a comedy. He scribbled a rough draft of a play and sent it off to his literary neighbours with a note asking them to add whatever improvements or additions they pleased.

> We of Brede Place are giving a free play to the villagers at Christmas time in the school-house, and I have written some awful rubbish which our friends will on that night speak out to the parish.
>
> But to make the thing historic, I have hit upon a plan of making the programmes choice by printing thereon a terrible list of authors of the comedy and to that end I have asked Henry James, Robert Barr, Joseph Conrad, A.E.W. Mason, H.G. Wells, Edwin Pugh, George Gissing, Rider Haggard and yourself [the letter was to H.B. Marriott-Watson] to write a mere word, 'it', 'they', 'you' – any word, and thus identify yourself with this crime.
>
> Would you be so lenient as to give me the word in your hand writing and thus appear in print on the programme with this distinguished rabble.[5]

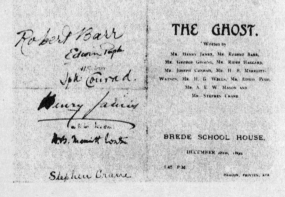

The rabble were ready to oblige so long as they did not have to suffer the embarrassment of appearing in the play. A.E.W. Mason, the only one among them with any acting experience, was the willing exception who took the part of the ghost. Conrad was brief ('This is a jolly cold world'); Gissing was facetious ('He died of an indignity caught in running after his hat down Piccadilly') and Edwin Pugh offered a demure joke ('A bird in the hand is worth two in the bush, but the birds in the bush don't think so'). James, who contributed only the name of Peter Quint from *The Turn of the Screw*, a story which may have borrowed something of its setting from haunted Brede, made his excuses and stayed at home. To the young A.E.W. Mason who stopped to pay his respects en route to Brede, James only had one word of advice – don't be caught by a pretty actress!

The revels began on the 26th of a bitterly cold December. Extra servants had been hired for the week and the bare walls of the double hall which stretched to nearly the full length of the house had been garlanded with holly and ivy. The first guests to arrive were the plump and voluble Wells with his delicately pretty little wife, eager to miss none of the fun and games which had been promised. A resourceful couple, they had taken a hint from Cora and brought their own bedding. Punctuality earned the Wellses one of the four bedrooms, but the other thirty-odd guests were not so lucky. The ladies were despatched to the 'Girls' Dormitory' for which Cora had managed to hire an assortment of truckle-beds while the men were packed off to the attics. Lewis Hind, a young editor on the *Pall Mall Gazette* who had visited Brede that summer when writing an article about Crane, remembered being put in a vast, bare room furnished only with six iron bedsteads. A.E.W. Mason, stumbling in the darkness of his privileged single room, tried to let in some light by opening the large doors which comprised one wall. He closed them again pretty hurriedly after finding they gave on to a thirty-foot drop into the family chapel: the 'bedroom' was an exalted pew! Comfort was on hand, however, in the pleasantly dangerous form anticipated by Henry James. The house was crowded with pretty American girls with whom to dance or to romp in a game devised by Wells of broomstick races across the uneven stone floors. Generously fuelled with food and wine, the house-party entered into the general spirit of foolery led by Wells, while Crane sat quietly by the great fireplace in the hall, looking on. The few guests who paused to wonder why their host was not joining in remembered that he seemed quietly amused by it all, but very silent. He looked, they thought, a little bewildered. After a late and hectic night, the morning brought a doleful awakening for the male guests, obliged to wander out into the frozen park in search of a concealing hedge or bush in lieu of a lavatory. (The only household one was reserved for the ladies of the party.)

Cora and Edith Ritchie Jones had been busy typing up the play-scripts and a rehearsal took place the next day. The performance was to be in Brede village school-house, a long mile away and all uphill.

Even the company of the sparkling American beauties could not solace Lewis Hind for the awfulness of the journey, despite the smart new vehicles Crane had hired to transport them.

> It was a pouring wet night, with thunder and lightning. The omnibuses which transported us up the hill stuck in the miry roads. Again and again we had to alight and push, and each time we returned to our seats on the top (the American girls were inside) I remarked to my neighbour, H.G. Wells, that Brede village is not a suitable place for dramatic performances.[6]

At the time of writing that in 1921, Lewis Hind could not remember anything about the play. Malice later sharpened his memory and enabled him to recall that it had been stunningly bad. Hind was being shrewish. Moreton Frewen, a great entrepreneur, suggested that it ought to be put on in London after he had read and laughed at the script which Crane sent him. Both Mason and Wells remembered it as having been performed 'with much laughter and success' in front of what was a very adequate audience, considering the atrocious weather and the prevalence of a local flu epidemic.

Crane's dramatic offering was fairly summed up by Wells as 'allusive and fragmentary'. In the play the Ogre of Brede is discovered to be still going strong in the year 1950 and is mistaken by some visiting tourists for an old servant who can guide them round the house. The Ogre answers their questions about the famous ghost with appropriately sinister hints and tells them to return at midnight if they want to see him. A light-hearted romance provides the sub-plot for Act II, after which the ghost appears and reveals his identity in Gilbert and Sullivan style song. A rousing chorus from the gratified tourists ends the piece. Mrs Wells, a very competent pianist, provided some suitably stirring accompaniment and joined the players for a generous round of applause before the audience showed their appreciation by singing 'For they are jolly good people'. 'Fellows', when most of the players were women, was thought a little ungallant.

The *Manchester Guardian*'s drama critic – writing from hearsay – was dismayed that such a remarkable work of collaboration should have been allowed 'to waste its sweetness on the Sussex air' and regretted that it was not to be published or brought to London. 'When the London theatres are so void of good plays as is the present case, it seems unkind to deprive managers of such an opportunity,' wrote the excited reviewer.[7]

It is unlikely that the manager of any London theatre would have seriously considered putting on *The Ghost* at any time, except as a tax-loss. Despite the dazzling list of authors, it is clear that the play had no greater dramatic merit than a hundred of the similar entertainments which Victorian and Edwardian houseparties devised to amuse themselves and their hosts. But we can admire Crane for taking such trouble to please and entertain his friends at a time when he was haunted by more terrible spectres than the Ogre of Brede.

The weather continued to be vile, but the guests were no longer called on to push buses and even Lewis Hind could find no fault with the hospitality. If pumpkin pies and sweet potatoes were not to everybody's taste, there were plum puddings and barrels of beer to satisfy those who preferred English fare. Champagne, claret and the newly fashionable crème de menthe were the order of the night, putting the guests in the mood for the games and dancing which usually continued until two or three in the morning when the ball-room reverted to its secondary use as the hostess's bedroom. And a very wretched makeshift kind of bedroom, thought Jessie Conrad, bidding Cora good night with a disapproving eye on the furniture stacked up anyhow around the bed and the two candles providing meagre light.

Quiet evening chats with Conrad seem to have been Crane's only reward in the week of non-stop partying. Wells, genial and rumbustious, grew bored with what he took to be a sulky aloofness in his young host. Crane was no fun. He didn't want to dance or join in broomstick races. He didn't even want to get into a good argument about books. Oh yes, he had tried to teach some of them to play poker, but where was the fun in that when you weren't allowed to talk? Surely Crane didn't expect an Englishman at Brede to behave as though he was in a New York poker saloon.

Wells's awakening to the real cause for Crane's reserved behaviour was swift and alarming. Just before dawn on the third night of their stay, Cora came into the Wellses' bedroom. She was pale and frantic with worry. Crane had had a haemorrhage. He had told her to keep quiet about it, but she was dreadfully worried. Did Mr Wells think he could possibly find a doctor prepared to come out to Brede at such an hour? Desperate to talk to somebody, she began to pour out the history of Crane's illness.

Wells had suffered from tuberculosis himself as a child. He left Cora with his reassuring and practical wife, a woman already well-versed in coping with the dramatic situations brought about by her volatile and far from monogamous husband, while he hurried to bring assistance.

There was a bicycle in the place and my last clear memory of that fantastic Brede house-party is riding out of the cold skirts of a wintry night into a drizzling dawn along a wet road to call up a doctor in Rye.[8]

Dr Skinner would later show himself to be all and more than Henry James could have hoped for in a local practitioner, but he was not equipped to grasp the severity of Crane's illness or the desperation of his circumstances. Rest was what he recommended, but rest was a luxury Crane could not afford. His own solution was to ignore the problem. When Ford drove over from Winchelsea early in the New Year, he was already shrugging aside his collapse as the result of a bout of the local flu. He cut down on his smoking and drinking and gave up his morning rides – an ominous sacrifice by somebody who was never happier than on a horse – but he was working at a more frantic pace than ever. Stories, battle articles and his 'Romance' (*The O'Ruddy*, a rollicking novel set in Ireland) were being written in tandem and sent off to Pinker with increasingly desperate requests for advances, loans, news of sales. Five days after his collapse, he was ready to promise three new chapters of the novel by the end of the week. Two days later, on 4 January, 1900, a chapter and part of a battle article were posted off with a demand for instant payment. By the next day, he was resorting to threats. 'If you cannot send £50 by the next mail, I will have to find a man who can.' But where was he going to find a man so long-suffering as Pinker? Aware that he had gone too far, he disowned the letter and assured his agent that he was 'A BENIFIT' (sic). Pinker was, and he was doing all that he could, but it was never enough.

Crane had the look of a haunted man. A friend who saw him at a party during that winter was shocked by the contrast between him and the other guests, 'all of whom were in good health and spirits. Poor Stephen had that white, worn-out restless look betokening complete nervous exhaustion. He took no tea, and did not join in general conversation, but moved about uneasily as if in search of something he could not find.'[9]

Cora was not, or did not choose to be, so observant. Soothed by Crane's constant assurances that he was on the mend, she set off on 31 March for a shopping expedition to Paris with Helen, his pretty young niece. (Helen's father, knowing that Cora sometimes wrote fashion articles, had offered to subsidize the trip if she would use her expert eye to pick out the most suitable clothes for his daughter.) They had barely arrived in the city when a telegram – sent without Crane's knowledge – brought the alarming news that he had had two more severe haemorrhages. Couture clothes and economy went out of the window. The American Embassy was called in to secure the services of London's top lung specialist, Dr Maclagen, and two trained nurses. Cora came home with Helen the next day.

Crane was as unlucky in his medical attendants as Byron at Missolonghi. Charm rather than expertise had been the foundation for Dr Maclagen's successful career. He had no more knowledge of tuberculosis than Rye's Dr Skinner. He was also a good deal more expensive. He returned to London £50 richer for declaring one lung to be perfectly healthy and for telling his patient to rest quietly at home. Dr Skinner was also ready to declare that there was nothing seriously wrong, despite the evidence of Crane's terrible weakness, his daily fevers and the agonizing abscess which opened periodically in his bowels or rectum.

The Cranes were not fooled but they did their best to fool each other. When Crane heard that somebody had been less than encouraging to Cora about his condition, he fired off an angry note. 'Please have the goodness to keep your mouth shut about my health in front of Mrs Crane hereafter. She can do nothing for me and I am too old to be nursed. It's all up with me but I will not have her scared. For some funny woman's reason, she likes me. Mind this . . .'[10] Cora, meanwhile, was withholding any letters which she felt might alert Crane to the gravity of his illness, preferring to spare him the dreadful jocularity of Wells's condolences.

> My dear Crane, I have just heard through Pinker that you are getting better and I rejoice mightily thereat. I was hugely surprised to hear of your haemorrhaging for you're not at all the hectic sort of person who does that with a serious end in view . . . From any point of view it's a bloody way of dying, and just about when you get thirsty and it bubbles difficult [sic] and they inject you with morphia, I know few, more infernally disagreeable.
>
> And confound it! what business have you in the Valley? It isn't midday yet and Your Day's Work handsomely started I admit, is still only practically started. The sooner you come out of that Valley again and stop being absolutely irrelevant to your work, the better![11]

The fact that Wells had been a witness to the haemorrhage at Christmas makes the letter all the more extraordinary.

In Crane's presence, Cora managed to seem cheerful and hopeful; in private, she gave way to despair, thrashing at her skirts with one of Crane's riding-crops as she paced up and down, blaming herself for not having allowed him more peace, for the worrying burden of debts which she as much as he had heedlessly incurred.

On 15 April, the doctors were still promising a recovery. By the 24th, Dr Skinner thought that the only chance was to get Crane to the sea, while Maclagen was still for keeping him at home in a ground-floor room from which he could be carried out to the sun. But sunshine was not to be relied on in an English April and Cora staked her last hopes on a foreign cure – but where? Crane's own idea was that they should go to St Helena and that he should cover the expenses by writing a series of articles on the Boer prisoners who had been interned there. Dr Skinner suggested Bournemouth, while Crane's family in America favoured New Mexico. The Frewens, whose kindness to their distressed tenants at Brede was unstinting during this period, thought Crane might benefit from the Nordracht treatment in the Black Forest. Their friend, the Cuban-born Duchess of Manchester who had lost two children through tuberculosis, thought that Davos in the Swiss Alps would be less painful ('It is the Nordracht treatment without the brutality') and easier to get into.

By May, Cora had decided that the Black Forest was their only chance. The cost would be horrendous – it was already well beyond their means with the doctors charging fifty guineas for each consultation. Crane would have to be taken on an airbed to Rye and from Rye to Dover in an invalid carriage with two nurses and a doctor in attendance. After two weeks' rest at Dover's best hotel, they would make the voyage to Calais where another invalid carriage would be ready to cover the journey to the Black Forest. 'A valuable life can't be saved by saving pennies and pounds,' Cora concluded after outlining her grand plan to Pinker. Nor could it now be saved by spending them, but neither Pinker nor anyone else felt ready to state the brutal truth.

Where was the money for this hopeless mission to come from? Conrad, dreadfully upset though he was, had no money to offer. He could only suggest that Crane's relations ought to help. They would not. His brother was willing to send money, but only enough for Helen's return trip to America. As to the rest, they must look elsewhere. The kind-hearted Frewens sent pleas to their influential American friends, among them J.P. Morgan, the great banker. Henry James, dismayed to hear that his friend Dr Skinner's bill had not been paid, sent £50.

Somehow, the money was raised, mostly through the efforts of Moreton Frewen, and on 15 May, the sad little party left Brede for Dover. Crane's last letter from Brede – the last he ever wrote – was typically generous, a plea to a friend to help Conrad to a place on the Civil List which would give him financial security. ('He is poor and a gentleman and proud . . . please do me the last favour.')

The Cranes spent eight days at Dover staying at the Lord Warden, shabbily grand and far from cheap. James had intended to visit, but was kept at home by editorial duties.* Conrad came over with Jessie and went away saddened by the spectacle of his friend emaciated, immobile and hardly able to speak, his eyes wistfully fixed on the ships beyond the open window. 'He goes only to please Cora,' he said afterwards to Jessie, 'and he would rather have died at home.' Wells, still aggressively confident that Crane had only to put his mind to it to achieve a full recovery, left a memorable picture of the patient from his own brief visit.

> If you would figure him as I saw him, you must think of him as a face of a type very typically American, long and spare, with very straight hair and straight features and long, quiet hands and hollow eyes, moving slowly, smiling and speaking slowly, with that deliberate New Jersey manner he had, and lapsing from speech again into a quiet contemplation of his ancient enemy.[12]

The ancient enemy, it should be explained, was not Wells but the sea which was visible through Crane's window. Wells had settled on it as a likely enemy after reading 'The Open Boat', based on Crane's own hazardous experiences at sea.

Work went on. Chapters 14 and 15 of *The O'Ruddy* had been sent to Pinker in manuscript just before Crane's collapse, and Cora's repeated requests for their return show that Crane was anxious to get on with the novel although he had recently been questioning the economic wisdom of 'abandoning my lucrative short story game for this long thing which doesn't pay (much) until the end'. Now, too weak to hold a pen, he asked his friend Robert Barr to complete it. Kipling, it was hoped, would edit. For four days, Barr sat by his bed, taking notes for a work which he felt most ill-equipped to undertake. 'I don't know what to do, for I could never work up another man's ideas,' he wrote to a mutual friend on 8 June, still haunted by the ghastly inappropriateness of scribbling comic situations beside a deathbed.

They crossed to Calais on 24 May with Crane's favourite dog lying at his side. After a brief pause at Basle, they reached the sanatorium three or four days later. (The dates have not been verified.) Crane died within the week, slipping quietly out of a life which his spirit had already left.

Cora had spent £150 on making the journey and she was not now

---

* 'A mass of proofs' to be read was the excuse James offered; he was also struggling to complete *The Sacred Fount*.

to be dissuaded by the prospect of further expense from taking the body home with her. Friends were invited to pay their last respects at the Mortuary in Baker Street and on 17 June Cora, the dogs and young Helen set sail for New York with their sad cargo after making a detour to Dieppe to avoid the quarantine laws which would have required them to leave Crane's animals behind. The journey seems to have buoyed up Cora's spirits. By the time they reached New York, she was feeling cheerful enough to giggle at the sight of herself in a nunnish mourning veil and trailing black skirts and to tell Crane's shocked relations that he would have died all over again of laughing if he could see her in such an unlikely costume.

Crane was buried – but not in the family plot – at Hillside, New Jersey. Cora returned to England to pack up their belongings at Brede and to plan a modest life in South Kensington, letting out rooms to pay the rent on her small house. Incurable optimism led her to hope that Mr Frewen would help her to make a fortune out of a canteen filter which she had invented. Like so many of Cora's grand plans – and for that matter, Mr Frewen's – the scheme came to nothing. In 1901, she abandoned her idea of settling in England and went back to America for good while the Frewens took up residence again at Brede. By the following year, Cora was back in Jacksonville again and running a similar establishment to the Hotel de Dream. She died in 1910 after what can cryptically be described as a colourful decade. (Some details can be found here on page 200.)

It was not only William's ill-health which had kept James away from the revelries at Brede. His final verdict on Cora was harsh – 'I judge her whole course and career, so far as it appeared in this neighbourhood, very sternly and unforgivingly' – but he had decided long before then to maintain a cautious distance from his eccentric neighbours and their goings-on. It was not until the Frewens and their heirs returned to Brede Place that he became a frequent visitor.

There had been no jubilation in Lamb House on the day the Cranes moved into their new home. Their determination to enter into the spirit of their role as lord and lady of the manor caused James to cringe at having to acknowledge them as compatriots. It was apparent from the start that they had no proper respect or understanding of the English way of life in which James had so successfully immersed himself, save for his tell-tale American accent. The entrance hall of Lamb House was, as Wells maliciously observed, an unwittingly comic display of the owner's anxious observation of the laws of etiquette. There was a deerstalker for the Golf Club (although he never played the game, James was no stranger to the club-room), a brown felt hat and cane for his morning stroll, a grey felt hat and a grander gold-headed cane for his afternoon calls. Crane, in contrast, had given the hall at Brede a dashing South American air by decorating the walls with swords and brightly coloured Mexican blankets. Mr James on his afternoon bicycle rides was a model of balanced dignity; Mr Crane made his excursions in cowboy costume with a pistol in his belt, riding one of the Frewens' old coach-horses. His guests were intolerably vulgar, his dogs committed the unpardonable sin of running amok among the local farmers' sheep, provoking one infuriated shepherd to string his butchered flock up on the trees shading the drive to Brede Place. James, a dog-lover himself, preferred small and unaggressive canines. The new owners of Brede were, in short, as out of place and as unconvincingly English as Conrad in his pony-cart or Ford in his vegetable-patch. Pistolshooting and rowdy parties were not what Sussex expected to associate with Brede and Crane's was not the sort of behaviour James cared to see in a fellow-American. He resolved to be cordial, but distant.

Legend – and one or two susceptible biographers have mistaken legend for truth – asserts that a close friendship did exist. It is said that James sent manuscripts to Crane for his opinion and that he enjoyed nothing more than an evening's entertainment at Brede and loved to join in an impromptu concert by whistling through a comb covered in tissue paper. It is a charming picture, but an unlikely one. James's visits were seldom recorded by him – which doesn't entirely rule out the possibility of their occurrence – and the formality of his brief letters to Cora hardly suggests that he was in the habit of dropping in on that bohemian household. He did send Crane an affectionately inscribed copy of 'In the Cage', one of his rare attempts to represent a member of the English working classes and one which he justifiably might have felt would interest the author of *Maggie: A Girl of the Streets*, Crane's first novel. It didn't. Crane 'got horribly bored half-way through and just reeled along through the rest' before passing it on to a friend, along with his reservations.

> I do not think that this girl in the cage is exactly an underclass clerk in love with a 'man about town'. Women think more directly than he lets this girl think. But notice the writing in the fourth and fifth chapters when he has really got started.[13]

We should not, however, be too hasty in concluding that there was no love lost between James and Crane. If Edith Ritchie Jones's memory is held to be trustworthy, James was a frequent informal visitor, and one who was always welcome. James's own correspondence bears witness to the fact that he spent a long and agreeable afternoon at a garden fête given by the Cranes. A photograph shows him contentedly munching one of Cora's home-made doughnuts after having his future examined by the 'gypsy' fortune-teller, Miss Ritchie Jones in suitable disguise. Ford was ready to swear that James had been agonized by the news of Crane's illness and that he had spent many hours anxiously pacing the marshes, debating whether to have a hamper of American delicacies sent to the invalid, or whether they might cause him to be homesick 'and so hasten his end. James wavered backwards and forwards between the alternatives beneath the grey walls of Rye town. He was not himself for many days after Crane's death.'[14] Ford's recollections are full of inaccuracies (he gave Lamb House stone walls, put Brede in a dank hollow and remembered Crane's 'Five Blind Mice' as the nursery-rhyme trio), but they usually contain a germ of truth. James had a kind heart. It is reasonable to suppose that he would have been upset by the wretchedness of Crane's last months.

If James was volatile in his attitude to Crane, he was not alone. Conrad, who had loved Crane and constantly expressed the most lively admiration for his work, was strangely under-praising when he came to write about him. In 1912, he went so far as to say that there was no point in expecting Crane's work to be remembered or written about.

Ambivalence of this kind is the hallmark of the relationships between James and his neighbours, an ambivalence that might more honestly be called duplicity. James, exquisitely polite to Conrad on social occasions and in his tributes to his work, was cruelly patronizing behind his back. 'Poor dear Conrad' was not an acquaintance to boast about; when Ottoline Morrell expressed a wish to meet him, James was querulously discouraging. Conrad was so rough, so queer, not the sort of man she should meet. And Conrad himself, while always friendly and deferential to Ford's face in the early years of their collaboration, sneered at his literary pretensions behind his back in a letter which was, unhappily, published in Ford's lifetime. Wells, too British not to be embarrassed by Conrad's obtrusively foreign manner, laughed behind his back at his exotic accent and his solemn attitude to literature. One of the first to draw public attention to Conrad's work, he was privately derisive of the terrible seriousness with which both Conrad and Ford would pursue the perfect word 'with a singleness and intensity of purpose that made the kindred concentration of Henry James seem lax and large and pale'.[15] To Conrad's face, he was full of admiration for 'the wonderful oriental style' and full of anxious concern that Ford might be allowed to tamper with it. In his autobiography, he offered a very different view. Conrad's writing was 'oppressive, as overwrought as an Indian tracery, and it is only in chosen passages and some of his short stories that I would put his work on a level with the naked vigour of Stephen Crane.'[16]

There was no such duplicity, however, in the almost excessive reverence with which both Ford and Conrad looked up to James and his works. Wells, never a man who was much given to worshipping at the shrines of his fellow-writers, bided his time. In the early years of their friendship as literary neighbours, he was the most charming and deferential of correspondents, seemingly grateful for all the criticisms which James was ready to offer in the cause of improving his writing. Only very occasionally would he let a hint drop that he regarded James's own works as less than perfect. 'I do get this gleam of discontent,' he remarked after reading his richly ruminative account of his homeland, *The American Scene*. 'How much will they get out of what you have got in?'[17] But it was not until James read *Boon* and its cruel parody of himself and his work that he realized how duplicitous Wells had been in his professions of admiration.

Ambivalence of this kind causes problems when we are trying to evaluate the true nature of these friendships. Ford, reminiscing about Crane, would have us believe that he saw him from the first as a rare and extraordinary man. Nothing could have been further from the truth. When Ford first saw him addressing a gathering of Fabians, he thought that Crane was gauche and arrogant and flatly refused to be introduced to him until on a later occasion Edward Garnett forced him into making a reluctant show of politeness. The person who tells us about these first encounters is Ford himself. The later, warmer feeling caused him to forget the dislike which he had once expressed.

The notion of a group conspiracy against British letters proposed by Wells and enthusiastically taken up by Ford was fanciful. No such conspiracy existed, but it could be argued that there was an unacknowledged conspiracy against handing down a legacy of truth to posterity.

Crane's stories about the days when he was a familiar figure in the shadier parts of New York were an impenetrable patchwork of truth and fantasy. His first biographers, facing the almost impossible task of sifting the truth out of the popular fictions, compromised by printing what seemed reasonably plausible. Wells, when he wrote his autobiography in 1934, reshaped the past to accommodate his later, less tolerant views of his neighbours. James, discreet and cautious, did his best to render the past impenetrable by burning his letters and papers. Jessie Conrad, spurred on by her loathing of Ford, became freely inventive in her memoirs of the Pent Farm days. The felt injuries of Ford's patronizing manner and his excessive claims as a moulder and inspirer of her husband's works were vigorously repaid by anecdotes which, while unintentionally often very funny, cannot be regarded as unvarnished truth. Conrad himself was a far from reliable recorder of the past, but the chief and most notorious culprit was Ford Madox Ford.

It is to Ford that we owe some of the most detailed and evocative descriptions of 'that quarter of the world which I know and love best', by which he meant the Romney Marshes. His portraits of local characters are richly humorous and vivid, of Ragged Ass Wilson, gardener and handyman, Ned Post the mole-catcher, of poachers and tramps, sharp-tongued matriarchs, easy-going drunken sons. His poems, little read today, convey the beauty of a rippling field of wheat, the lovely desolation of the marshes, the rustle of high hedges at dusk. It is Ford who finds just the turn of phrase to conjure up Rye, the words which will make us see Winchelsea sleeping on its small walled hill. It is Ford who takes us into Pent Farm and shows us the great kitchen with its floor of wave-shaped bricks and, above it, the room where he and Conrad used to work, with its windows of leaded diamond glass, frosted green with age. We see the fat sleepy cats curled by the window while Conrad, leaning back in his rush-bottomed armchair, nods and listens. Beyond the windows, we see the long flat lines of the country sliding away.

As an impressionist, Ford succeeds magnificently. It is the details and dates which suffer under scrutiny. An argument can be made that Ford's fictions display the characters of his friends and neighbours more clearly than many more scrupulously accurate accounts, but they are always to be digested with a large pinch of scepticism. It may be that Henry James went four or five times in a winter to tea with Ford after the windy two-mile walk from Rye to Winchelsea. It is inconceivable that he took tea every second day with a young man for whom his regard was never high. It is unlikely that it would have been to Ford that James unburdened himself of anxiety about poor Stephen Crane. It is less likely still that James would have hurried over to Winchelsea to consult Ford's housemaid when he was plunged into a domestic crisis. But Ford would have it so.

Conrad and Crane provided splendid material for some of Ford's most lavish imaginings. Crane, ambling along the English lanes in outlandish clothes, presented himself as a raffish Quixote with

Hengist or Horsa for his raw-boned Rosinante. Carried away by his imaginative powers, Ford went on to picture him hunched over his desk, painfully covering huge pages with tiny spiderlike writing. The image becomes a little less moving when we discover that Crane wrote in a round clear hand on paper of normal size. Wells could look down the road with a shudder of embarrassment at the sight of a small, gesticulating figure urging his little Kentish pony forward with loud foreign cries. To Ford, Conrad had the air of a prince riding past his subjects in his carriage. To see him approach in his pony-cart was immediately to be convinced that Nancy was 'the horse of the Cid'. One would dearly like to believe the story of Conrad, jolted out of sleep in a railway-carriage, springing at Ford like a tiger under the impression that he was an assassin and grovelling over his revisions on the floor of the same carriage. Belief is suspended by the fact that Ford is the teller of the tale.

A brilliant fabulist who could reduce himself to tears with the pathos of his own inventions, Ford distorted the truth with fictitious detail or dovetailed one story with another, quite different occasion, in order to make the scene more vivid and convincing. He was not in the least ashamed of doing so. He was, on the contrary, quite blatant about it. 'Where it has seemed expedient to me,' he explains in *Return to Yesterday*, 'I have altered episodes that I have witnessed but I have been careful never to distort the character of these episodes. The accuracies I deal in are the accuracies of my impressions.' And, lifting his defence to a grander scale: 'A lie is a figurative truth, and it is the poet who is the master of these illusions.'

I may be doing Ford an injustice in attaching his name to that second statement. It comes from *Romance*, one of the works in which he collaborated with Conrad, and Conrad's attitude to the truth was as complex as Ford's. A masterly teller of stories drawn from his youth in Poland or his experiences at sea, he would unblushingly alter and elaborate on his tales. Like Ford, he played with the past as a mathematician will play with fractals, endlessly forming new patterns which can, with patience, be resolved back into the original design. Less good-humoured than Ford, he grew extremely annoyed at any attempt to correct the new pictures he had made. Jessie Conrad, no mistress of tact, once interrupted him to tell him that he had made a mistake in his story. Conrad was not amused.

> On one of his naughty days he said that *The Black Mate* was his first work, and when I said, 'No, *Almayer's Folly* was the first thing you did,' he burst out, 'If I like to say that *The Black Mate* was my first work, I shall say so.'[18]

The Black Mate was not his first work, but Conrad shared with his collaborator a cheerful readiness to carry the high ideal of his craft into his life. The novelist's business, as they understood it, was to make fiction convince by its air of reality. 'My task which I am trying to achieve is . . . to make you hear, to make you feel – it is above all, to make you see,' Conrad wrote in his foreword to *The Nigger of the 'Narcissus'*.

As with fiction, so with life. We will never know whether or not Henry James told Ford about the gratifying collapse of Mr Kipling's expensive new motor-car in which Kipling had boastfully promised to transport James to his home; what Ford gives us is a wonderfully accurate representation of James at his malicious best, relating the story. The reader's delighted reaction is that if it didn't happen, it should have. To borrow from Ford a phrase he used to express his affection for the Rye area, his tales are of the infectious and holding kind. Imaginative truths are often the most seductively plausible.

2

A PROVINCIAL GENTLEMAN: JAMES AT RYE

One summer we took a house at Rye, that wonderful inland island, crowned with a town as with a citadel, like a hill in a medieval picture. It happened that the house next to us was the old oak-panelled mansion which had attracted, one might almost say across the Atlantic, the fine aquiline eye of Henry James. For Henry James, of course, was an American boy who had reacted against America; and steeped his sensitive psychology in everything that seemed most antiquatedly and aristocratically English. In his search for the finest shades among the shadows of the past, one might have guessed that he would pick out that town of all towns and that house from all houses.

G. K. Chesterton,
Autobiography, 1936

At any rate, it is an infectious and holding neighbourhood. Once you go there you are apt to stay. Or you will see in memory, the old walled towns, the red roofs, the grey stones, the country sweeping back in steps from the Channel to the North Downs, the great stretch of the Romney Marsh running out to Dungeness.

Ford Madox Ford,
Return to Yesterday

My choice is the old world – my choice, my need, my life.

Henry James,
Notebooks, 1881

45

1897	Henry James rents Lamb House.
1899	A fire at Lamb House.
1899– 1900	James working mostly on short stories.
1900/1	Miss Weld starts working as his secretary. Work includes 'The Beast in the Jungle', 'The Birthplace' and *The Ambassadors*.
1902	The London flat, De Vere Gardens, is sold and the furniture transported to Lamb House.
1903	James begins to diet and starts *The Golden Bowl*.
1904/5	The American visit.
1907	William James resigns from his professorship at Harvard. Henry James employs Miss Theodora Bosanquet as his secretary, tours France with Edith Wharton and publishes *The American Scene*.

2

A PROVINCIAL GENTLEMAN:

JAMES AT RYE

By 1895 Henry James had been living in the smoke and grime of London for close on twenty years. His London homes, Bolton Street, Piccadilly and De Vere Gardens, Kensington, had been less than a stone's throw from two of the city's prettiest parks, Green Park and Kensington Gardens, but a London park offers no substitute for a country walk and James was beginning to feel a longing for the real thing, not the urban imitation. He had already developed a taste for the more tranquil charms of the English South Coast but so, unfortunately in James's view, had the urban working class. A view of the Channel was not an adequate compensation for the holiday racket of Ramsgate's 'sordid sands'; the pleasure of Robert Louis Stevenson's company at Bournemouth could not mitigate his irritated sense that the town had become 'cocknified to death'. Dover was more agreeable. The Lord Warden Hotel, where Stephen Crane would spend his last night in England, provided comfortable accommodation, and James liked to stay in places where Europe was almost visible. It was pleasant to command a view of 'the summer-smooth channel, with the gleaming French coast, from my windows, looking on some clear days only five miles distant, and the guns of old England pointed seaward, from the rumbling, historic castle perched above me on the downs . . .'[1] A view of the French coast, which he had known since childhood when the young Jameses were being given their 'sensuous education' in Europe, was an enticing invitation to bite on the sweet madeleine of memory.

Further along the coast, travelling west, he had also found a congenial new friend in W. E. Norris, a reclusive novelist who lived with his daughter in a hilltop house in Torquay. En route to visit Leslie Stephen in Cornwall in 1894, James stayed with Norris for three days and was enchanted by the 'peerless beauty' of Torquay. A second and longer visit in 1895 increased his enthusiasm. He had started to hanker seriously after a different form of life. 'I would give a great deal not to be going back to London for the winter,' he wrote

47

to his brother William in America. 'I yearn to spend it in the so simplified country.' The idea of buying a country house of his own had not yet occurred to him; he wanted to rent a retreat where he could concentrate on his work. Distance was against Torquay; he was looking for somewhere in easy reach of the city, where he could enjoy rather than endure his main form of exercise, bicycling. Torquay was no place for a corpulent amateur cyclist. 'I can't manage the steep hills,' James confessed. 'It's all steep hills.'

Word was put around and an architect friend, Edward Warren, came up with a solution. His associate, Sir Reginald Blomfield, owned a small house at Point Hill, Playden, on the edge of Rye. If James wished, he could rent it for the summer of 1896. James did wish. He accepted, went, and was instantly enslaved.

Extensions and alterations have done little to alter the character of Point Hill. Tucked away above a winding lane and behind high walls, the brief and diverse row of handsome houses present their backs to the visitor and their faces to the broad terraces and shady well-kept gardens ranged high above the town. Point Hill is Rye's miniature version of Virginia Water. It exudes a quiet but unmistakable air of superiority. It is the estate agent's dream. Here, more than at Lamb House, James could relate to his pleasant sojourns at Bellosguardo overlooking Florence as he surveyed the town from the umbrageous cool of a trained and arching ash-tree which conveniently shadowed Blomfield's terrace.

Rye was only a five-minute stroll down the hill, the marsh roads called for no terrible exertions on his daily bicycle rides, and the summer was glorious, hot enough to allow him to dine out on the terrace every evening. When the period of his tenancy came to an end James decided that, rather than returning to the stifling heat of a London August, he would stay on for another two months at Rye. The Vicarage was available and, despite being 'shabby' and 'fusty', it was roomy, pleasantly situated and possessed of a pretty old brick-walled garden. Guests provided him with an occasional diversion from work on *The Spoils of Poynton* and his novelization of an unrealized play, *The Other House*, but for the last month James was contentedly solitary with 'not a creature to converse with, in general, but my sleepy dog and Crusoe-like, a charming, sociable canary-bird . . .'

Among the few visitors at the Vicarage was young Ford, who was spending the last of the summer with his wife's parents at Winchelsea, having recently completed a biography of his grandfather, Ford Madox Brown. It is not beyond belief that Ford hoped for a friendly appreciation of his book from the more famous writer; an excellent excuse for introducing himself came in the form of an anxious telegram (three in one day, by Ford's account) from a mutual friend, Mrs Clifford, begging him to let her know the state of James's health. 'She urged me to go and see him,' Ford explained, 'but I remained too shy.' It was not for his shyness that Ford was ever known. He wrote to ask himself over and received a polite but cautiously phrased invitation to lunch.

The visit was not a success. A paunchy red-nosed butler in a cutaway jacket seemed to be hell-bent on despatching the lunch into the diners' laps despite James's angry rebukes, and the conversation was designed to make the young guest squirm with discomfort:

> The whole meal was one long questionnaire. He demanded particulars as to my age, means of support, establishment, occupations, tastes in books, food, music, painting, scenery, politics. He sat sideways to me across the corner of the dining table, letting drop question after question. The answers he received with no show at all of either satisfaction or reproof.[2]

James's letter had conveyed that the visit would be more warmly appreciated for being brief. Unwisely outstaying his welcome, Ford was punished by being made to listen to a robust attack on the members and friends of his family, the Pre-Raphaelites of whom he had just finished writing a fairly glowing account in his biography. James glowed, too, but only with indignation. Dante Gabriel Rossetti was dismissed as a man of ungovernable lechery whose personal appearance was squalid and whose famous partiality to greasy ham and eggs was frankly nauseating. Swinburne's poetry was declared to be as obnoxious as the cheap alcohol which no Watts Dunton could have prevented him from imbibing – Ford's assurances that Mr Swinburne now only drank a pint of beer a day were swept aside. And as for Ford's uncle, William Rossetti, whose only talent appeared to be for turning a potentially funny story (Herbert Spencer's absent-minded proposal to George Eliot) into an intolerably dull one – sighing over Mr Rossetti's inadequacy, James led his guest to the door. It was a cruel blow to poor Ford's self-esteem to find that instead of being received as a scion of 'the governing classes of the literary and artistic worlds', he was perceived only as the pitiable product of an uncouth tribe of bohemians. He did not cross James's threshold again for five years.

The account of this ill-starred lunch is Ford's own and, as with all his lively recollections, it requires a certain amount of reading between the lines. James was not in the habit of being uncivil to young writers who sought him out, although he was sometimes brutally frank about the quality of their work. To be so gratuitously rude about Ford's family, he must have been considerably provoked. We must assume either that he did not intend his slights to be taken too seriously or that Ford had been judged sufficiently bumptious to require taking down a peg or two. We can be very sure that Ford was speaking the truth when he said that James had little regard for him as a serious writer.

Some time before he came to Rye, James had been greatly struck by a watercolour in the house of his friend Edward Warren. It was of an attractive Georgian red-brick building which had the embellishment of a handsome bay-windowed pavilion perched on a wall to the east side. This was Lamb House, built in 1720 by James Lamb, a gentleman who had the delicate job of being the Controller of Customs at a time when Rye was a favourite haunt of smugglers. The Lambs' new house was discreetly elegant, appropriate to the standing of the leading family of Rye who could boast that George I had been their house-guest (the king's ship had been driven ashore in a violent storm, obliging him to take the best available accommodation) and that he had stood godfather to Mr Lamb's son, born during his brief visit. The Lambs' cup of happiness was filled when the royal christening present arrived, a magnificent silver engraved bowl, and was only slightly tarnished by the discovery that it was silver plate.

Both the house and its history charmed James. 'I marked it for my own . . . the first instant I beheld it,' he wrote to his sister-in-law Alice James, 'so perfectly did it* . . . offer the solution of my long-unassuaged desire for a calm retreat between May and November. It is the very calmest and cheerfullest that I could have dreamed – *in* the little old cobble-stoned, grass-grown, red-roofed town, on the summit of its mildly pyramidal hill and close to its noble old church.'[3] Discreet enquiries of the local ironmonger revealed, disappointingly, that the house was currently inhabited by a former mayor, Mr Francis Bellingham, together with his wife and son, and that there was scant chance of its coming onto the market, certainly not at a low price. There was nothing to be done but to look, sigh and renounce; James returned to London. The following summer found him back at cocknified Bournemouth and visiting long-lost American cousins at Dunwich in Suffolk, but Rye was not

* This and the preceding clause have been transposed here to clarify the reading of the sentence.

forgotten and he was full of regret that neither the Blomfields' home nor the Vicarage had been available for a second visit.

Bicycling in Suffolk one September day in 1897 with Edward Warren, James returned to the subject of country houses and of Lamb House in particular, so exactly suited to his needs if it could only have been available. Two days later, with the eeriness of pure coincidence, a letter arrived from the ironmonger in Rye. He had thought Mr James would wish to know of a dramatic change in the situation. Old Mr Bellingham had died. His wife did not wish to remain in the house and his son was preparing to follow the Gold Rush to the Klondike. The house might very well be available, if he was still interested.

James was most interested, although the sudden translation of his dream into reality was so unexpected as to be almost unnerving. He persuaded Warren to go down to Rye with him that week as an *ex officio* surveyor and was given a very reassuring report. The house had been well maintained and would need only a certain amount of replumbing and furnishing to be immediately habitable. James seems to have made up his mind on the spot. Ten days later, he had signed a lease which gave him the house for £70 per annum for twenty-one years. 'And *they* do all the outer repairs!' the new tenant gleefully noted. Two years later, when the house passed into the possession of Mrs Bellingham – 'a South African theatrical person' – on the death of the unlucky young gold-rusher, James decided, against the cautious advice of his brother, to increase his commitment and to purchase the freehold for £2,000, £1,200 of which would be covered by taking over the existing mortgage. Eight hundred pounds was not a great price to pay when it could purchase security and release him from his gnawing envy of the handsome properties in which his closest literary friends were comfortably established. 'My whole being cries out for something that I can call my own,' James wrote to William, justifying a decision he had already made.

Early in November 1897, two months after signing the lease, James made a second visit to the house with the ever-obliging Warren and Alfred Parsons who had designed the sets for James's recent and ill-starred theatrical venture, *Guy Domville*, and who was, under his other hat, an expert landscape gardener. Parsons was full of enthusiasm for the Lamb House garden, a pretty rectory affair with espaliered fruit trees climbing up the high red walls and a handsome mulberry tree shading the lawn. With Warren, James made a closer inspection of the interior, the hall with its gracefully proportioned oak staircase and a small panelled room leading off to the right (this became a convenient extra writing-room for guests), while the study and dining-room to the left opened onto the garden. Features from an older Elizabethan house had been incorporated into the large kitchen to the rear. Upstairs, they found four bedrooms, of which James promptly selected 'The King's Room' for his own future use while setting another, 'The Green Room', aside as a winter writing-room. The four bedrooms on the pokier third floor would house his servants when he brought them down from London. The panelled walls of the best rooms were, in Warren's opinion, far too good to be hidden behind paper; it was agreed that they should be stripped and that a bathroom with running water should be installed. Warren's wife, Margaret, would oversee the measuring and making of curtains; James needed only to apply himself to hunting down 'a handful of feeble relics' with which to furnish his new home.

House-renovation is seldom a quick business and it was not until June 1898 that James was able to move into his new home, bringing with him the feeble relics (prints, maps and some rather good Georgian mahogany) and all that could be spared from the London flat. Impatience or economy may have caused him to skimp on necessary precautions in an old house; a near major disaster occurred within six months when a beam under the Green Room floor over-heated and caught fire one night, spreading the conflagration down behind the walls of the dining-room below before the smoke was detected. Nobody was hurt but floors had to be torn up and walls broken down before the last smouldering embers could be ex-tinguished by the fire brigade. The house was left 'befouled and topsy-turvy' and the indispensable Warren was recalled to repair, restore and generally improve.

Impractical people are often uncommonly clever at finding others to compensate for their deficiencies. James was no exception to this rule. His frank confession of ineptitude in all horticultural matters was wisely made to a Miss Muir Mackenzie of neighbouring Winchelsea, a lady whose expertise was matched by her enthusiasm for gardens. 'I am densely ignorant,' James admitted to her, '– only just barely know dahlias from mignonette – and shall never be able to work it in any way. So I shan't try – but remain gardenless – only go in for the lawn; which requires mere brute force – no intellect.' Miss Muir Mackenzie rose to the bait and promptly took over the running of the garden and of George Gammon, the 22/– a week gardener James had inherited from the Bellinghams and who was still in charge when E. F. Benson came to live at Lamb House in the 1930s. Directions were issued, plants bestowed and the 'Hereditary Grand Governess', as James ceremoniously named her, was rewarded with letters in his finest grand-fantastic style. Advice was solicited – were her splendid tobacco-plants to be left alone, pruned or helped to propagate? could fuchsias be safely transplanted from the drawing-room pots to garden beds? – and thanks given.

> Dear Grand Governess,
>   You are grand indeed, and no mistake, and we are bathed in gratitude for what you have done for us, and, in general, for all your comfort, support and illumination. We cling to you; we will walk but by your wisdom and live in your light; we cherish and inscribe on our precious records every word that drops from you, and we have begun by taking up your delightful tobacco-leaves with pious and reverent hands and consigning them to the lap of earth (in the big vague blank unimaginative border with the lupins, etc.) exactly in the manner you prescribe; where they have already done wonders towards peopling its desolation . . . while my reason abides I shall not cease to thank you for your truly generous and ministering visit and for everything that is yours, which *I* am, very faithfully and gratefully,
>   HENRY JAMES[4]

Miss Muir Mackenzie made practical improvements in the garden; in *The Awkward Age*, James immortalized the results. This was the first novel to be written at Lamb House and James only had to glance out of the window to find inspiration for the garden of Mr Longdon, a quiet middle-aged man who visits London from the Suffolk home whose privacy he cherishes. In earlier novels and stories, James had based his descriptions on the gardens and parks of the grand country houses where he had been a guest, but none was so harmonious and evocative of sleepy summer afternoons as this one of his own home.

> Mr Longdon's garden took in three acres and, full of charming features, had for its greatest wonder the extent and colour of its old brick wall, of which the pink and purple surface was the fruit of the mild ages, and the protective function, for a visitor strolling, sitting, talking, reading, that of a sort of nurse of reverie. The air of the place, in the August time, thrilled all the while with the bliss of birds, the hum of little lives unseen and the flicker of white butterflies . . . There were sitting places, just there, out of the full light, cushioned benches in the thick wide spread of old mulberry boughs . . .
>   Beyond the lawn the house was before him, old, square, red-roofed, well-assured of its right to the place it took up in the world . . . Suggestive of panelled rooms, of precious mahogany, of portraits of women dead, of coloured china glimmering through glass doors, and delicate silver reflected on bared tables, the thing was one of those impressions of a particular period that it takes two centuries to produce. 'Fancy,' the young man incoherently exclaimed, 'his caring to leave anything so lovable as all this to come up and live with *us*!'[5]

James's friends hardly needed to be detectives to recognize the source of the description, but for his public he provided a helpful clue in the form of a frontispiece photograph of Lamb House. His friends might have been amused by one liberty which James took in fiction, one which might have caused Miss Muir Mackenzie to raise her eyebrows. Mr Longdon is hailed not just as a great gardener but as 'one of the greatest'.

The domestic aspects of James's life at Rye were initially in the care of Mr and Mrs Smith, the couple who had looked after him in De Vere Gardens. Ford, on his visit to James at the Vicarage, had correctly deduced a drinking problem from the shade of the butler's nose – the Blomfields christened him 'Bardolph' for much the same reasons. The Smiths' fondness for the bottle was not unknown to James, but he had long since resigned himself to tolerating it for so long as they could carry out their work with a modicum of respectability. He could comfort himself that he was not so badly off as his neighbour, Stephen Crane, who had to ply his cook with drink before she would consent to prepare a meal. If the Smiths chose to spend their wages on alcohol, that was their affair. There had, it was true, been a disagreeable scene in De Vere Gardens just before the move to Lamb House, but James could find no other servants who were prepared to move to the country at short notice. Perhaps a change of scene would bring a welcome change of habits.

It did not. In the autumn of 1901, matters came to a sudden head when James was entertaining four guests over a weekend. Smith, who had apparently been drinking himself to oblivion for several days, passed out cold after Saturday lunch. The visiting ladies were despatched to London in blissful ignorance; the men, T. Bailey Saunders, a childhood American friend, and Hendrik Andersen, a young Norwegian sculptor, stayed to help and see what could be done. Nothing much could. Dr Skinner was called in to help, but Smith was beyond recall. 'I could not really communicate with him to the extent of a word,' James wrote to his sister-in-law, 'any more than with his wife, whom I have made over wholly to her own sister.' The sister, Mrs Ticknor, a thoroughly businesslike woman whose sympathies were all with James, did the only thing possible, namely, to pack up the Smiths' clothes and goods and remove them and their owners, leaving their employer to ponder mournfully on their folly:

. . . The revelations are sad – quite dreadful. The S.'s have had, all the years they've lived with me, excellent wages and *no* expenses . . . not even for clothes, for she has, it appears, bought none, for years (it was one reason she never left the house), and he has had all his from *me*. But it appears that they've not saved a single penny, and as they've done nothing else whatever with the money, they've simply, while in my service, spent hundreds and hundreds of pounds in drink – and left me still in debt for it . . . They were, at the end, simply two saturated and demoralized victims, with not a word to say for themselves and going in silence to their doom; but great is the miracle of their having been, all the while, the admirable servants they were and whom I shall ever unutterably mourn and miss.[6]

James was luckier in his next venture. Mrs Paddington, the cook-housekeeper whose arrival in awesomely respectable clothes from Gorringes was anticipated with lively mock-terror, turned out to be 'a pearl of price; being an extremely good cook, an absolutely brilliant economist, a person of the greatest order, method and respectability, and a very nice woman generally.'[7] Not everyone shared James's enthusiasm for her cooking. The American novelist, Edith Wharton, shuddered at the memory of the dreary rechauffée nursery food she had politely choked down; other guests tended to praise the hearty breakfasts and to overlook the rest of the day. Since James was on a rigid diet for most of Mrs Paddington's regime, he was unlikely to have been the best judge of her culinary skills.

The rest of the household comprised a very pretty housemaid, a respectable and competent parlourmaid, and a diminutive house-boy called Burgess Noakes who 'isn't very pretty, but is on the other hand very gentle, punctual and desirous to please'. Noakes was only fourteen when he started working for James; he was still there in the elevated role of butler-valet when his master died in 1916. When Harford Montgomery Hyde interviewed him for his account of James's domestic life, *Henry James at Home*, Noakes was able to provide him with a wealth of small but revealing details for his study, now sadly out of print.

'The old toff' was what Noakes and Gammon the gardener called James behind his back. The nickname was an affectionate one for an employer who was unfailingly generous, never giving less than half a crown for small services like taking the dog for a walk and always offering financial help to any needy person who came to his door. (Ford was probably telling the truth when he recalled how James had once begged him to draw on his purse if he was short of funds. Ford refused, but not without being touched by the generous impulse.) It is from Noakes that we have one of our clearest portraits of James's daily life at Rye:

I used to call him every morning regular at eight o'clock. After that he'd have his breakfast. He'd come down about nine o'clock, and about ten o'clock would start and work with his secretary. He was very regular in his habits, and he'd work on till about one o'clock; in the summer, of course, he'd work in the Garden Room. He'd have his lunch, and after lunch, he'd take his walk. He was a stout, heavily built man, but he was very active, right to the last, too. Off he'd go with his little dog, and many a time I watched him out of the door. Before he got half way up the street towards the church, you'd see him stop, the stick would go down – there he'd stand, with his head slightly bent and his finger in his watch-chain, like that, and all of a sudden off he'd go again. But he had a habit – if he wanted to remember anything or remind himself of anything – he had a habit of tying a knot in his watch-chain, sometimes two.[8]

A secretary had become indispensable to James since a savage attack of rheumatism in 1896 had made manual writing into a painful ordeal. He had been sending his manuscripts away to be typed since typewriters came into use in the 1880s; in 1897, having prematurely relegated his hand 'to permanent, bandaged, baffled, rheumatic, incompetent obscurity', he decided to employ a shorthand typist. William Macalpine, a quiet, dry young Scot, was persuaded to accompany James to Rye, where he was lodged in a hotel in nearby Watchbell Street. In the mornings, he took dictation; in the afternoons, he was a reliable but uncommunicative companion on his employer's cycling trips. Irreproachably sensible, Macalpine maintained a scrupulous detachment which could be mildly disconcerting. Later, James remembered how nervous he himself had been when dictating his first full-length work, *The Turn of the Screw*, in 1897. It was intended to terrify but Macalpine 'never from the first to last betrayed the slightest emotion, nor did he ever make any comment. I might have been dictating statistics. I would dictate some phrase that I thought was blood-curdling; he would quietly take this down, look up at me and in a dry voice say "What next?"'[9]

Regret was not unmixed with relief, we may surmise, when Macalpine left for a better-paid job in 1901. The next step was, for a confirmed bachelor, a courageous one. With the forceful encouragement of his sister-in-law, Alice, who was staying at the time, James sent off a request to Miss Petherbridge's secretarial bureau in London for a lady secretary who would type directly from dictation. Miss Weld, a product of Cheltenham Ladies' College and the daughter of a judge, was deemed entirely suitable both by Miss Petherbridge and, after an initial interview in the Garden Room of Lamb House, by James. It was agreed that she should commence as soon as possible, that she should adopt the uniform of a dark suit and a sailor hat, that she might crochet or knit during pauses in dictation and that she should lodge in Mermaid Street. Miss Weld confided to her diary that Mr James seemed a delightful man, although she had no great knowledge of his work – the only book by him she had read was *What Maisie Knew*, and that only with considerable perplexity. What, after all, was it, she wondered, that Maisie had known? It was into her uncritical ears that James poured the miraculous flood of his late novels, *The Ambassadors, The Golden Bowl, The Wings of the Dove* and *The Sacred Fount*. Uncomprehending, Miss Weld tapped diligently away, thinking to herself that it was 'exactly like accompanying a singer on the piano', a singer who always instinctively knew when she was falling behind and when she had caught up.

The ladies of the town paid a visit to assure themselves that Mr James's secretary was respectable and, to their mild chagrin, found nothing amiss. Fault could not be found with a young lady who dressed plainly, loved bicycling and walking and who spent her spare hours practising bookbinding in the Watchbell Street studio which James had acquired along with the house. In her four years at Rye, Miss Weld's most daring act was to purchase a more decorative piece of millinery than her sailor hat after being enjoined by James to 'glory in her femininity'.

The last and most intelligent of the secretaries arrived in 1907, two years after Miss Weld departed to get married. Theodora Bosanquet was shrewd, literate and discreetly observant. She was astute enough to keep a low profile – James did not like his secretaries to display too much of a mind of their own – and scholarly enough to be quietly amused that James should feel it necessary to tell her that *The Newcomes* was one word and that it had been written by Thackeray. Her observations, which were often acute, were restricted to the diary which she kept until James's death; her employer knew her only as an excellent and entirely reliable amanuensis who was prepared to take dictation in the evenings as well as the mornings so long as she was kept well supplied with chocolate bars and pots of tea, and whose work required a good deal less in the way of correction than that of her predecessor.

As soon as Miss Bosanquet had settled into her lodgings in Marigold Cottage, Mermaid Street, work began (not without some hesitations, faults and apologies from the nervous typist, who had only had two weeks' practice in taking dictation directly on to the machine) on James's largest and most unrewarding project, the revision of his entire *œuvre* for the new American edition to be published by Macmillan. Each novel was to be prefaced by a lengthy introduction in which James would assess and re-evaluate the book's merits and failings in the light of his own literary tenets. Invaluable though these have proved to be for all Jamesians, they brought their creator almost to his knees with exhaustion and all, as it seemed, for nothing. The edition for which he had entertained such high hopes did not sell well; meagre royalties were compensation for what he later perceived as 'the most expensive job of my life'. For Miss Bosanquet, however, the typing of the *Prefaces* and revising of the novels was a unique and absorbing way of getting to know James's novels.

Summer dictation took place in the Garden Room, an octagonal book-lined chamber which the typist found oppressively stuffy but which James liked for its commanding view. Pausing in the middle of unravelling one of those famously interminable sentences, he would stroll across to the bow-fronted window to contemplate a row of amateur sketchers perched on their stools outside his front-door, to deride the grunting ascent of a motor-car or to salute a passing friend. Theodora was happier when the winter brought a shift to the snugly panelled, green painted room known, not surprisingly, as the Green Room.

> It had many advantages as a winter work-room, for it was small enough to be easily warmed and a wide south window caught all the morning sunshine. The window overhung the smooth green lawn, shaded in summer by a mulberry tree, surrounded by roses and enclosed behind a tall brick wall. It never failed to give the owner pleasure to look out of this convenient window at his English garden where he could watch his English gardener digging the flower-beds or mowing the lawn or sweeping up fallen leaves. There was another window for the afternoon sun, looking towards Winchelsea and doubly glazed against the force of the westerly gales. Three high bookcases, two big writing desks and an easy chair filled most of the space in the green room, but left enough clear floor for a restricted amount of the pacing exercise that was indispensable to literary composition.[10]

Miss Bosanquet's diary, the main source for the brief but fascinating account of James at work which she published after his death, provides us with one of the sharpest images of the novelist's appearance during his years at Rye. The things which struck her most at their first meeting were his nervousness – she had expected him to be very self-possessed – and his clothes, a startlingly brash combination of green trousers, black coat and blue-and-yellow check waistcoat. There was a good deal more of him than she had supposed; he was strong, stout, even massive; his presence filled the room. The much-remarked-on resemblance to a sea-captain must, she decided, have been due to his beard; the expressive sensitive mouth which was now exposed could never conceivably have been ascribed to a naval officer. The face was too fat, but she was much struck by the eyes which were keen, grey and very penetrating.

Miss Bosanquet thought he looked like a Roman nobleman posing as a country gentleman; others discerned a clement Caesar, a kindly Napoleon. Edmund Gosse saw him as a jeune premier, past his prime; Arthur Benson saw something Elizabethan in the winter spectacle of James 'in a kind of Holbein square cap of velvet and black velvet coat, scattering bread on the frozen lawn to the birds'. Everyone was fascinated by his eyes – 'penetrating' and 'piercing' are the words which recur most frequently in contemporary descriptions – and by the slow deliberation with which he would hunt for the perfect word or phrase, the sometimes agonizing (for the listener) construction of sentences as elaborate in design as miniature cathedrals of thought.

Hypnotized by the ponderous style of delivery, visitors could hardly be blamed for failing to perceive in James 'the ever-bubbling fountain of fun which was the delight of his intimates', according to Edith Wharton. The visitor who was outside the circle of intimates would be more likely to form an impression of heavy, anxious courtesy and a tangible barrier of awkwardness which could be ascribed to a shyness or unease in their host. Lewis Hind, the young editor who was staying at Brede with the Cranes for the 1900 Christmas revels, clearly illustrates this aspect in *Authors and I*, where he draws his portrait of James from several visits to Lamb House:

> I see again the stocky, impressive figure, with large head and the observant eyes, advancing with outstretched hand into the cool hall, from the garden study, a book under his arm, usually French. This would be followed by a stroll round the trim garden, a disquisition, uneasily accurate, on the flowers and the views, followed by a set tea at a table perfectly arranged. Our host, if the company was sympathetic, would talk slowly, laboriously, delicately, with swift, ponderable efforts at humour, embracing all in the conversation and startling the timid when he directed towards them a question or a comment. Sometimes there was a pause in the conversation. When this happened, the pause could be felt. On such occasions, I would try to save the situation. Once, during a pause longer than usual, in despair, I praised the canary. For some seconds Henry James gave the bird his undivided attention, then he said – Yes, yes, and the little creature sings his songs with – er – the slightest modicum of encouragement from – er – me.[11]

To the amusement and a little to the surprise of his friends, James gave every appearance of being entirely at home in a social group which consisted primarily of retired sailors and soldiers, gossipy old ladies and the usual provincial smattering of the professional classes. Impeccable manners and a lively interest in local gossip ensured him of a welcome at the tea-tables; local tradesmen liked him for his easy informality of manner. 'He was on terms with the postman and the butcher's boy,' one visiting friend recalled. 'There was nothing austere or remote in his bearing. On the contrary he had the air of a curate making the rounds of his village.' The air, as time went on, became, through no fault of his, more like that of a royal visitor. Edmund Gosse remembered how the walk up from the station to Lamb House became a miniature triumphal progress with bows from ladies and salutations from shopkeepers and further pauses so that small girls could be greeted and patted on the head when they dropped him curtseys.

E. F. Benson made fun of the elderly ladies of Rye in his stories of Lucia and her rival, Miss Mapp, and, not surprisingly, drew the wrath of the inhabitants down on his head. James's *The Third Person* (1900) offers a kinder portrait with shrewder wit. Susan and Amy Frush are spinster cousins living in Marr, 'a little old huddled red-roofed, historic south-coast town' where they employ themselves in researching the history of the Frush family portraits.

Their desire was to discover something, and emboldened by the broader sweep of her companion, Miss Susan herself was not afraid of discovering something bad. Miss Amy it was who had first remarked, as a warning, that this was what it might all lead to. It was she, moreover, to whom they owed the formula that, had anything *very* bad ever happened at Marr, they should be sorry if a Frush hadn't been in it. This was the moment at which Miss Susan's spirit had reached its highest point: she had declared, with her odd, breathless laugh, a prolonged, an alarmed or alarming gasp, that she should really be quite ashamed. And so they rested a while; not saying quite how far they were prepared to go in crime – nor giving the matter a name. But there would have been little doubt for an observer that each supposed the other to mean that she not only didn't draw the line at murder, but stretched it so as to take in – well, gay deception. If Miss Susan could conceivably have asked whether Don Juan had ever touched at that port, Miss Amy would, to a certainty, have wanted to know by way of answer at what port he had *not* touched. It was only unfortunately true that no one of the portraits of gentlemen looked at all like him, and no one of those ladies suggested one of his victims.

A Don Juan of their own is more than either of the ladies dares to hope for, but that is what they get when the ghost of Cuthbert Frush starts to haunt their bedrooms at night. Poor Miss Amy, who has moved in theatrical circles and even published a novel, is mortified by Cuthbert's preference for seeing the older and frumpier Miss Susan in a semi-undressed state — neither lady would dream of allowing him to see her in a nightdress or less. Her small comfort is the thought that she knows more about men, but it seems cruel that Miss Susan should not only be sitting up all night with a dashing spectre but refusing to talk about it, and 'she proceeded rapidly to hug the opinion that Susan was selfish and even something of a sneak. Politeness, between them, still reigned, but confidence had flown, and its place was taken by open ceremonies and confessed precautions.' Equality is finally restored by Miss Amy's courageous exorcism of the ghost, leaving the cousins to wistful recollections of a spectral romance.

The Third Person is a funny, charming, oddly overlooked story which, in its portrait of a Cranford-like society, owed a good deal to James's new circle of acquaintances and which, in the lightness and gaiety of the narration and the absolute confidence of the comic touches, suggests a new easiness of mood, a new spirit of relaxation which had come with the move to Rye.

The children of the town adored him. There is, it is true, Hugh Walpole's tale of the two little vagrants who fled from the kindly gentleman who interminably ruminated on what and where they might best spend the coins he had bestowed on them, agonizing until they dropped the coins and fled with howls of terror, leaving James to wonder how he had alarmed them. But the majority of accounts tally with Arthur Benson's memory of 'a little maid of seven or eight, who threw herself upon H.J. with cooing noises of delight and kissed him repeatedly and effusively'. Miss Veronica Powles, who grew up in the house next to the Blomfields at Point Hill, remembers how pleased she used to be as a child when Mr James came to call on her father in the late afternoons. She thought him the most comfortable of grown-ups who always listened to the stories she told him with flattering gravity. Trying to pin down the secret of James's charm for children, she thought it lay in his naturalness. He never talked down – and he never made up – to them.

Old houses have a habit of exerting an insidious influence over new owners. Singing stars and actors seek privacy in medieval manors only to find themselves being inexorably transformed into country squires by the traditions which they have inherited from the past owners, the garden fêtes, the vicar's tea, the shooting parties, the sprightly gatherings in the name of charity. Lamb House had always been the home of Rye's mayors and Edmund Gosse's jokes about James being the mayor-elect of Rye were not too far from the truth of his newly acquired position. He had even become the owner of a family pew in Rye church. Respectability could go no further. Writing to Grace Norton, an American friend, James described the sense 'of being "looked-to" from so many "humble" quarters that one feels, with one's brass knocker and one's garden-patch, quite like a country gentleman, with his "people" and his church monuments'.[12] References in his letters to 'peasants' and 'yokels' and 'The Squire! – One's people!', while obviously facetious, convey a demure relish for his new role. He had started to take a lively interest in the history to which he had become an heir. When the former owner's mother invited him to inspect the famous bowl given to the Lambs by George I, James was delighted – 'for anything and everything associated with this dear old house has an interest for me, so deeply have I in these five years attached myself here. I have a feeling for every ascertainable fact of its history and am only sorry such facts are not more numerous.'[13] (This bowl, by then the colour of old gold, is generally agreed to have provided the title for the novel on which James had already embarked.) He delved into the history of the Lambs and of Rye's past with a zeal which makes one wonder why he never wrote about it as Ford did in *The Cinque Ports*.

Nor was James reticent about participating in local life. He attended the flower-shows at which his Mr Gammon was a regular winner of prizes. He subscribed to the Rye cricket club of which he was offered (and refused) the vice-presidency and attended their matches, although less for the pleasure of watching than for the pleasure of conversing with the ladies in the tent. He even, astonishingly, joined the Golf Glub, to which he made his main contribution in the tea-room. It amused him to say that he had chosen to live at Rye because he so liked seeing golfers in plus-fours; in truth, he despised the game of landing a ball in 'some beflagged jampots' as an expensive waste of time. It was for the air, the view and the teas that he occasionally visited the course.

'Ryers' have always been understandably fierce about protecting the appearance of the town and James's first real commitment in that direction was made when, to his outraged disbelief, he learned that Lamb House itself was under threat. He was working on *The Golden Bowl* in London in the winter of 1903 when news came that a particularly detestable tradesman called Gasson ('Gasson the dreadful') had bought a house and a large plot of ground just beyond the west end of the Lamb House garden and was proposing to turn it into a building plot, depriving James both of privacy and his only good view at one stroke. Gasson was, however, prepared to sell out for £200, a considerable price in those days. Grudgingly, James accepted the offer. 'I have had to buy the ground from him at an extortionate price and now have got to spend money on enclosing it all, all of which makes me sick,' he wrote to Miss Weld. But three months later, he had decided that the renewed sense of security in his refuge seemed 'almost worth the imposition'.

No sooner was Gasson despatched than Whiteman reared his head. Whiteman was a neighbour of James's who owned the freehold on two pretty little old cottages bordering on the Lamb House garden, one of which was inhabited by George Gammon, the gardener. These Whiteman proposed to pull down after evicting the tenants and to replace with functional modern buildings. James was horrified. Struggling to enlist support against his neighbour's proposals, he appealed for advice to Edward Warren, whose aesthetic and common sense had proved so reliable in the past.

I am trying, with feeblest resources, and another person or two is trying, to avert it if possible; but, so far as I myself am concerned, I should derive no end of moral support, by such brief communion with you on the spot (and face to face with the threatened treasure) as would morally (I speak only of *moral* aid) back me up.

You remember well of course the small quaint structures I mean – to the right of the little eternally-sketched vista stretching from my front doorstep towards the church: of which the one nearest me has the pretty little small-paned, square-cornered bay window resting its short pedestal on the cobble-stones. Both have their little old gables, colour, character, almost silvery surface, and have always been the making – the very *making* of the hundred or so water-colour sketches of the Vista annually perpetrated from in front of my door. It would *go*, without them – vista, character, colour, subject, composition, everything: above all the very tradition of the little old bit of street itself, and the long-descended pleasant legend of its sketchability.

What Whiteman proposes is to put up two raw, cheap, sordid workingmen's cottages and let them at eight shillings a week apiece. My gardener has for the last year occupied the hither one (the position is of course perfect for him, and for me). I have tried to intervene and supplicate, and with the effect of the *possibility* either of purchase (not by *me* – his terms are of course colossal) or of a lease, on conditions scarcely less exorbitant, in which I *should* have, rageingly, to play my part. The latter would be a 'repairing' lease – and it is on *that* matter that I pine for some kindly light from you: as to what it would cost me, currently, to meet the repairing obligation. The only thing is that time rather sickeningly presses. Whiteman is shakey, and his devilish little builder, Ellis, who has completed the horrible new plans for him, is, I fear, unremittingly and intensely poisoning his mind. I am trying to get him to give me (and the other person) to the end of the week to turn round. If you can't come for a night could you, possibly, for a few hours of the day?[14]

We have no record of Warren's response but, since the cottages were preserved, we can assume that, with or without his encouragement, James decided to undertake the additional expense of a repairing lease and to preserve the 'sketchability' of one of Rye's prettiest streets.

'I think a position in society is a legitimate object of ambition,' James had once observed. Having, by entirely legitimate means, obtained it, his ambition in regard to local Sussex society was to keep it at a distance. Eminence was against him. James's only hope would have lain in establishing himself, from the start, as a recluse; but the steady stream of friends from London would, in any event, have betrayed him for a man of sociable inclinations.

Too polite to refuse the well-intentioned invitations from his new neighbours, James solaced himself by abusing them behind their backs. An afternoon of amateur theatricals at the house of 'certain well-meaning, golf-playing, gardening, blundering Fuller-Maitlands' left him 'flabbergasted and terrorized' by his own account to Jessie Allen, a cherished London confidante, but he was nevertheless bound by courtesy to issue a return invitation both to them and to a dull couple from Winchelsea. The Harrisons, he grumbled to Grace Norton in a Christmas letter, 'are very ugly, very destitute of enchantments to sense, very supposedly delightful and very new to our neighbourhood, having but lately bought rather a pleasant old house there. Also I am deeply and incurably sated with them (as I know *you* are) in advance! All the same there come on Christmas to dinner the Edward Fuller-Maitlands (a childless, sketching and golfing couple lately established here), and with *them* I am likewise gorged, already, to such repletion that I am heavy even as with *their* heaviness.'[15]

Far more congenial were the occupants of Dial Cottage in Rye. George Prothero was an historian and editor of the prestigious *Quarterly Review*; his wife Fanny was a lively, busy little woman who kept an unofficious eye on the running of the Lamb household and kept its owner up to date on all the most interesting local gossip. Prothero was one of James's four chosen sponsors for his naturalization in 1915, but it was Fanny, unceremonious, companionable and shrewd, with whom he was on almost brotherly terms. When he was uneasy about his servants, it was Fanny who would wander into the kitchen, put her feet up on a chair and chat until she got to the heart of the problem. When James was ill, Fanny was ready to relieve Miss Bosanquet of the post of sick-nurse, sitting by the invalid's bed and keeping him amused in her 'Irishly amiable' way.

A welcome addition to the Rye circle were the Waterlows. James had known young Mrs Waterlow since she was a child. Her husband, Sidney, was a brilliant classical scholar whose ill-health had forced him to resign from the Diplomatic Service and who now amused himself by translating Greek plays. Waterlow, like James, enjoyed the combination of walking and talking and the two of them would frequently set off for long, leisurely afternoon strolls during which they discussed – among other things – the conflict between personal and social responsibility for the poor, the novels of Edith Wharton and George Meredith (although not in conjunction), the vulgarity of modern French literature, the narrow vision of G. M. Trevelyan, the historian, and the oddity of Ibsen's café life, sitting, as James disapprovingly understood it, 'day after day on the red plush benches, buttoned up in his black frock coat, glowering at everyone and drinking – champagne of all things, and more of it than was good for him'.[16] Not, James concluded, the best of ways to establish contact with life.

Fond though James was of drawing comparisons between the upper strata of English society and that of Rome in its decline, he showed no marked aversion to the company of the aristocracy. Work took second place on the day in 1903 when a telegram arrived from Lady Maud Warrender announcing her imminent arrival for the purpose of inspecting Leasam House at Playden. The Earl of Shaftesbury's daughter was a tall, dark, strikingly good-looking young woman with a majestic manner, a generous nature and a beautiful, deep contralto voice. Just the sort of person, James felt, who ought to be living at Leasam, a splendid Georgian house with grandly Italianate gardens spreading out above the picturesque huddle of Rye. The purchase was made and Leasam added to the list of agreeable homes where James could always be sure of a welcome. And hospitality was returned; only Lady Maud and her guests were forgiven for an unannounced visit which broke into his sacred morning hours of composition.

Towards the literary neighbours whose relationships with each other and with the Master are discussed later in this book, James maintained a cautious friendship. Ford's belief in their intimacy was not shared by James. Courtesy was the keynote of his acquaintanceship with Conrad, tender bafflement of his brief friendship with Crane. Only with Wells, sour though their relations became towards the end of James's life, was there a real sense of mutual curiosity, admiration, and even affection, incompatible though the two men were in their attitudes both to literature and to life.

Geographically close although their connection was never more than cordial, were the Kiplings, first at Rottingdean and then at Burwash. The friendship had been fuelled by Kipling's marriage to Caroline Balestier whose brother, Wolcott, had been James's first great male love before his tragically premature death in Dresden of typhoid. It was James who gave away the bride, but Mrs Kipling lacked her brother's brilliance and his beauty. Kipling always seemed to him 'a dear little chap', faintly risible in his nouveau riche role as the owner of 'a magnificent two hundred guinea car', chauffeurdriven. (Less mockery was made of Mrs Wharton's equally magnificent car, but then, that was rather more at James's disposal and not, consequently, to be derided.) For Kipling's work, he had lost enthusiasm long before he came to Rye. 'My view of his prose future has much shrunk in the light of one's increasingly observing how little of life he can make use of,' he wrote to Grace Norton. The violence disgusted him, and he frankly loathed the patriotic verses which Kipling penned at the time of the Boer War. And yet, strangely, he had once thought that Kipling 'contained the seeds of an English Balzac'.

It was not simply for his own ease of communication that James had chosen to live in Rye rather than Torquay. He had never intended that country life should deprive him of the company of his old friends. The telegram service, to which he was addicted and which, somewhere in the course of pushing his countless cables under the wire grille of Rye post-office, inspired him to write 'In the Cage', kept him in comforting contact. A great charm of Rye was the excellence of its daily train service to and from London. Any friends wishing to visit him could do so, he happily pointed out, 'in rather exceptionally easy conditions. That is, the 11 A.M. from Charing Cross to Rye is a super-excellent train in spite of your having to change at *Ashford* at about 12.30, and have a wait there of twenty-five minutes. But the run, after that, down here, is of the briefest, and places you almost at my door at about 1.30 – excellent time for luncheon. I meet you at the station of course, and we are but five minutes from my house. The 4.53 back restores you to Charing Cross at 7.39.'[17] There was a good deal to be said for living somewhere close enough to London to enable him to extend hospitality while escaping the burden of overnight guests: Bradshaw's railway guide proved a friendly accomplice in this respect.

Visitors, as young Ford had discovered, were not encouraged to outstay their prescribed hours of welcome, but James's frequent lamentations about the invasion of his privacy need to be taken with a large pinch of salt. Solitary though he was in his work, his was an essentially gregarious nature, thriving on the exchange of gossip, badinage and literary views. For these, James depended on his guests. Isabella Gardner, founder of Boston's Gardner Museum and queen of a magnificent Venetian palazzo, paused on her way from Italy to America, Lord and Lady Wolseley came over from Ireland, young Hendrik Andersen from Rome, Jonathan Sturges from New York. The less exotic London route brought down a steady stream of friends, and James became a familiar figure to the station-master at Rye. Edmund Gosse remembered seeing 'the large pale face, anxiously scanning the carriage-windows and breaking into smiles of sunshine when the newcomer was discovered. Welcome was signified by both hands waved aloft, lifting the skirts of the customary cloak, like wings. Then, luggage attended to, and the arm of the guest securely seized, as though even now there might be an attempt at escape, a slow ascent on foot would begin up the steep streets, the last and steepest of all leading to a discreet door which admitted directly to the broad hall of Lamb House.'[18]

For the above description we are indebted to one of James's closest friends and chroniclers. An affectionate but more detached account of what it was like to stay with James comes from the American novelist and historian, Hamlin Garland, visiting Lamb House in 1906. It was to Garland, shortly after his arrival, that James made the surprising admission that, if he could have his life over again, he would be an American. 'The mixture of Europe and America which you see in me has proved disastrous,' he said. 'It has made of me a man who is neither American nor European. I have lost touch with my own people, and I live here alone . . . I shall never return to the United States, but I wish I could.'* After adding his own and most properly patriotic sentiments to this confession, Garland continues with a more general but nonetheless interesting account of his visit.

---

* James could not have foreseen at this time that he would be returning to America in 1910 for a year, a visit which began tragically with the death of William James.

After our tea, which was served on a little table out under the trees, he took me to see the town, pointing out the most ancient of the buildings, well knowing that as a man from the plains of Iowa I would be interested in age-worn walls and door sills. He took me to the old Mermaid Tavern, in which there was a marvellous fireplace, as wide as the end of the room itself, with benches at the corners. Everybody we met seemed to know and like him; whether they recognized in him a famous author or not I cannot tell, but they certainly regarded him as a good neighbour . . .

At seven o'clock we dined in his exquisite little dining-room, and the dinner, which came on quite formally, was delicious. He had no other guest, but he presided at the service end of the table with quiet formality. The mahogany glistened with the care which had been lavished upon it, the silver was interesting and beautiful, and the walls of the room tasteful and cheerful – and yet I could not keep out of my mind a picture of him sitting here alone, as he confessed he did, on many, many nights. To grow old even with your children all about you is a sorrowful business, but to grow old in a land filled with strangers is sadder still.

It was late when I went to bed that night, my mind filled with literary and artistic problems called up by his profound comment. The questions of National art, of Realism and Idealism, of New World garishness and crudeness, of its growing power and complexity – these were among the matters we had discussed. That James lived on the highest plane of life and thought was evident. He had no distractions, no indulgences. He permitted himself no loafing, no relaxation. He had not the comfort of a comic spirit such as Clemens had.* He was in earnest all the time – a genial earnestness, but an earnestness which could not be diverted . . .

We breakfasted in such comfort, so simple but so perfect as to form the most delightful luxury . . . At the close of our meal I said, 'It is your habit to work in the morning – that I know, and I want you to keep to your routine. Don't permit me to interrupt your morning task.'

'Very well,' he said. 'I will take you at your word, but first I want you to see my workshop.'

His 'shop' was a small detached building standing in the corner of the garden, and in the large room littered with books and manuscripts I found a smart young woman stenographer at work. James showed me the changes he was making in his earlier books – work which I did not approve, for he was rewriting these stories. In my judgement he was not bettering them; on the contrary it seemed to me he was transforming them into something which was neither of the past nor of the present. I think he was now aware of my disapproval, for he went on to explain that he found in the early versions many crudities

---

* Samuel Clemens, whose pseudonym was Mark Twain.

which he could not think of allowing the future to observe 'if people ever take the trouble to look into my books', he added with a note of melancholy in his voice.[19]

James's expressed regret at having deprived himself of his American heritage was taken at face-value by the ingenuous Garland, to whom it does not seem to have occurred that his host might be saying what he felt would please a home-grown Iowa man.

Suiting his sentiments to his audience was a fault to which James was uncommonly prone. Nowhere is this more in evidence than in his early despatches to London from Rye. The festivities at Brede in 1899–1900 had been firmly turned down in favour of a quiet Christmas at Lamb House; to his London friends James presented himself as lonely and cruelly neglected. 'I've felt remote and unfriended,' he wrote to the novelist Rhoda Broughton in Richmond on the first day of the 'dreadful gruesome New Year'. To Lucy Clifford, another intractably urban acquaintance, he confessed to a longing 'to be sitting by your fire and tasting your charity – and your Benedictine. This second winter here has made me really homesick for town. Next year I shall, D.V. drink deep again.'[20]

It comes as rather a surprise after this declaration to find James spending his next Christmas at Rye and grumbling in just the same way to another London friend, Miss Jessie Allen. 'I find myself quite yearning again, even after but four or five days here, for the electric metropolis and the fringe of "South Belgravia",' he wrote to her. 'The country is dire in the short days.' But in December 1901 he was comfortably ensconced for his fourth successive Christmas at Rye while assuring Lucy Clifford of his 'yearning' to be in London.

Was he, or was he simply saying what he knew must please? Two days after writing of his lonely and wretched state to Mrs Clifford, James took up his pen to write in quite another vein to the sharp and witty Henrietta Reubell in Paris.

> The difficulty is that *au village* we have so little to tell – and I am positively *au village*. It more and more meets my bill, and I find myself reducing my time in London to three or four months a year . . . It's deadly dull *au village* at this season, but that is just one of my reasons for liking it. The autumn and winter charm of the country is the evenings – selfish and anti-social, with the firelight, the lamplight and the book – and always the same. It's rapture, a still unexhausted one (after long years of London), never to dine out.[21]

If we make a brief leap forward over ten years, we find James devastated by ill-health, depression and by the loss of his brother,

William, the thorn in his side he had never wanted to pluck out. The prospect of continuing to live in Lamb House, full of memories of William's last visit, became intolerable. The summer months at Rye could still beguile him; his winters from then on would be more cheerfully spent in a rented flat in Carlyle Mansions, with his writing rooms overlooking the Thames and with the loyal Miss Bosanquet on hand to type out the remarkable autobiography on which he had embarked after William's death. His feeling of 'horror and loathing' at the prospect of a winter in Rye was at this time fervent and unquestionably sincere, but what view should we take of the earlier letters? On the one hand, we hear James describing his absolute contentment at being snugly shored up in his study with the dog and the fire for company and with the comfortable sense that 'even a white December seafog is a cosy and convenient thing'. On the other, we have the picture presented to Miss Allen and Mrs Clifford of a wistful prisoner, dragging out the weary days before a longed-for release, and a return to London. Which are we to believe?

Leon Edel's theory might lead us to opt for the second self-portrait as the more honest one. Edel has argued that James learnt as a child to adopt a feminine role. William, the older and more boisterous brother, appropriated the masculine and active part; Henry protected himself in a disguise of girlish passivity. To assert himself was to risk punishment. The taking on of Lamb House, in the context of this interpretation, can be seen as an assertive act – one of which William disapproved – and for which a price would have to be paid. James's subconscious apprehensions came to the surface in *The Turn of the Screw*, written at the time he was in the process of acquiring the leasehold of his new home. Here, in little Miles's repressed masculinity, James returned to his own deepest fears and, by turning Rye into Bly, he seemed to his biographer to have acknowledged that Lamb House was 'on the remote levels of his buried life . . . a threat to his inner peace'.

If we accept this Freudian interpretation, James's woeful wails to his London friends can be heard as the cries of the captive begging for release from a house which Edel sees as haunted by 'all the ghosts of his boyhood – pushing, demanding governesses, Aunt Kate, his mother in her moods of severity'.

But there is a second and simpler explanation. We do not have to read any dire significance into James's talk of being 'doomed' to sign the lease on Lamb House, as Edel does; the mock-lugubrious note was one of which he frequently made humorous use.

I have tried in this chapter to convey the impression of James as a man who valued privacy while wishing to maintain his many friendships. The early letters in which he disparaged Rye and proclaimed his longing for the metropolis were addressed only to his London friends, the links to a social world on which he depended. He had retreated, but he had never intended to renounce London. To have written to Miss Allen or to Mrs Clifford as frankly as he did to Miss Reubell in Paris of his relish for his new-found tranquillity would have been to risk causing offence and to weaken the connecting threads which distance had rendered both more fragile and more precious.

3

THE MASTER AND THE PROPHET: JAMES AND WELLS

He was the most consciously and elaborately artistic and refined human being I ever encountered.

H. G. Wells,
Experiment in Autobiography

He is a great, but a rude talent, and I fear that rudeness isn't as convertible into the something or other that one prefers as one originally hoped. However, he has force and wit – precious possibilities.

Henry James to Mrs W. D. Howells, 1907

All this talk that I had with Conrad and Hueffer and James about the just word, the perfect expression, about this or that being 'written' or not written, bothered me, set me interrogating myself, threw me into a heart-searching defensive attitude . . . in the end I revolted altogether and refused to play their game.

H. G. Wells,
Experiment in Autobiography

For a chapter concerned with books rather than events, it seems more helpful to list the two authors' main publications between 1900 and 1913, adding only that *The Time Machine* was published in 1895, although James did not read it until 1900. The decline of the friendship between the two writers after 1913 is discussed in Chapter 9.

H. G. Wells

1900 *Love and Mr Lewisham*
1901 *The First Men in the Moon*
       Anticipations of the Reaction of Mechanical and Scientific Progress upon Human Life and Thought
1902 *The Discovery of the Future*
       The Sea Lady: A Tissue of Moonshine
1903 *Mankind in the Making*
       Twelve Stories and a Dream
1904 *The Food of the Gods, and How It came to Earth*
1905 *A Modern Utopia*
       Kipps: The Story of a Simple Soul
1906 *In the Days of the Comet*
       The Future in America: A Search after Realities
1907 *This Misery of Boots*
1908 *New Worlds for Old*
       The War in the Air, and Particularly How Mr Bert Smallways Fared While It Lasted
       First and Last Things: A Confession of Faith and Rule of Life
1909 *Tono-Bungay*
       Ann Veronica
1910 *The History of Mr Polly*
       The New Machiavelli
       The Country of the Blind and Other Stories
       Floor Games
1912 *Marriage*
1913 *Little Wars: A Game for Boys from Twelve Years of Age to One Hundred and Fifty and for That More Intelligent Sort of Girls Who Like Boys' Games*
       The Passionate Friends

James

1900 *Short Stories:* 'The Great Good Place', 'Maud Evelyn', 'Miss Gunton of Poughkeepsie', 'The Tree of Knowledge', 'The Abasement of the Northmores', 'The Third Person', 'The Special Type', 'The Tone of Time', 'Broken Wings', 'The Two Faces'
1901 *The Sacred Fount*
       Short Stories: 'The Beldonald Holbein', 'Mrs Medwin'
1902 *The Wings of the Dove*
       Short Stories: 'The Story In It', 'Flickerbridge'
1903 *The Ambassadors*
       Short Stories: 'The Beast in the Jungle', 'The Birthplace', 'The Papers'
1904 *The Golden Bowl*
       Short Story: 'Fordham Castle'
1907 *The American Scene*
(1907– Preparation of revised works
   9) for the New York edition)
1908 *Short Stories:* 'Julia Bride', 'The Jolly Corner'
1909 *Short Stories:* 'The Velvet Glove', 'The Bench of Desolation', 'Crapy Cornelia', 'Mora Montravers'
1910 *Short Story:* 'A Round of Visits'
1913 *Autobiographies: A Small Boy and Others*

THE MASTER AND THE
PROPHET: JAMES AND WELLS

Telegram to Alice James   Southport
                                                      4 January, 1891

'Unqualified triumphant magnificent success universal congratulations great ovation for author great future for play Comptons
radiant and his acting admirable writing Henry'

James's love-affair with the theatre began in the days of his New
York childhood when his savings were spent on attending matinées
at Barnum's 'Lecture Room', a place where red-faced ladies with
impressively large bosoms could be seen ranting, weeping and caper-
ing about in various and memorable travesties of the dramatic art.
Visits to the theatre in London and Paris were a part of the European
experience to which Henry James, Senior, exposed his children and,
in young Harry's case, these became the foundation for a lifetime's
enthusiasm. As a young man, and as a middle-aged one, he was an
attentive, astute and constant play-goer whose predilection, always,
was for the neat form and elegant wit of the Théâtre Française
productions, the brittle comedies of Sardou, Scribe and Dumas *fils*.

In his forties, James had toyed with the idea of writing plays. He
had no doubt of his ability. To his journal he confided that he had
the art of French comedy in his pocket and to his brother William he
boasted that he had not only mastered but surpassed Dumas and
Sardou in his knowledge of their craft. In his fifties, lured by the
prospect of handsome profits, he took the plunge. 'My books don't
sell, and it looks as if my plays might,' he wrote to Robert Louis
Stevenson in 1891. 'Therefore I am going with a brazen front to write
half a dozen.' Two or three years of coining in the money, enough
on which to retire and carry on 'the unmolested business of a little
supreme writing'. That was the plan.

James's five-year siege of the theatre makes for dispiriting reading.
The American's glorious reception in Southport was not matched in

London. The critics slated it, theatregoers avoided it, and friends did their best to escape mentioning it. James, disconsolate, blamed the débâcle on the emptiness of London in October and on the presence of four bad actors in the cast – 'too terrible a number for any play to carry'. William James, previously treated to accounts of the 'nuggets for investment' which would be shipped over from his brother's vast theatrical profits, now heard only of the terrible '*revanche*' which was being planned.

If determination alone was the recipe for success, James's revenge would have been magnificent. He had never before worked with such furious intensity of purpose. 'He wrote,' Leon Edel has aptly said, 'as if he were a soldier engaged in battle and his life depended on the outcome.' Script after script went out to the London managers; leading actresses were pursued and cajoled with all the considerable charm at James's disposal. 'I saw you at every turn and in every phrase which seemed to be, indeed, intensely and exclusively *you*,' he wrote of the unproduced *Disengaged* to Miss Ada Rehan, the Irish actress for whom Augustin Daly built his London theatre. He begged, he schemed, he revised and, in the face of continuous disappointment and rejections, he persisted. But an opportunity for revenge eluded him until, in 1894, George Alexander, a shrewd, calculating and far from intellectual actor-manager much admired for his dashing looks and style, thought he discerned the smell of success in a play which James had submitted to him the previous year. Its subject was a young man's vocation for the priesthood. Its title was, at his insist-ence, changed from 'The Hero' to *Guy Domville*. Doomville might, subsequently, have seemed more appropriate.

Alexander proved a demanding task-master with little or no regard for James's aesthetic sensibility. He commanded revisions, alterations to his own part – that of Guy – and the excision of several scenes. Raging over the mutilation of his work, James nevertheless did as he was told. The cast, at least, were good and the theatre, the St James's, a prestigious one; he could comfort himself with that.

The first performance of *Guy Domville* took place on 5 January, 1895. James, who had been in a state of agonized terror all day, sensibly decided not to give himself the additional torment of watch-ing it with the critics, but to arrive just in time for the final curtain. Oscar Wilde's *An Ideal Husband* had just opened at the Haymarket. James, who had never felt much enthusiasm for Wilde's glossily superficial wit, the smart epigrammatic exchanges which often crumble to dust under close analysis, went to deride – and stayed, glumly, to wonder at the audience's uproarious delight. His sense of the philistine nature of British playgoers was confirmed; his nervous apprehension as to their reception of his own and graver work was increased.

Among the illustrious audience down the road at the St James's was a very raw recruit to the ranks of dramatic criticism. H. G. Wells had been told that he could have whichever post came up first on the *Pall Mall Gazette*, then under the editorship of Harry Cust:

> 'Here,' said Cust and thrust two small pieces of coloured paper into my hand.
>
> 'What are these?' I asked.
>
> 'Theatres. Go and do 'em.'
>
> 'Yes,' I said and reflected. 'I'm willing to have a shot at it, but I ought to warn you that so far, not counting the Crystal Palace Pantomime and Gilbert and Sullivan, I've been only twice to a theatre.'
>
> 'Exactly what I want,' said Cust. 'You won't be in the gang. You'll make a break.'
>
> 'One wears evening dress?'
>
> It was not in Cust's code of manners to betray astonishment. 'Oh yes. Tomorrow night especially. The Haymarket.'[1]

An Ideal Husband, the first assignment, went well enough with Harry Cust on hand to do the review if his new critic felt unable to cope. (Wells coped, as always, with commendable professionalism.) Two days later, smartly arrayed in his brand-new evening suit, he was in the stalls of the St James's, alongside his eminent colleagues – William Archer from the *World*, Clement Scott from the *Telegraph* and A. B. Walkley from the *Star*. Loudly incongruous in a brown suit and flaming beard was the *Saturday Review*'s new drama critic, George Bernard Shaw; less conspicuous was young Arnold Bennett, reviewing for *Woman* under the pseudonym of Cécile.

It was not a night for brown suits. James was a man of formidable social and artistic connections; malice, curiosity, friendship, perhaps a mixture of all three, had brought out his friends and acquaintances in droves to witness his triumph – or his downfall. John Singer Sargent, Sir Edward Burne-Jones, Sir Frederick Leighton, George du Maurier, Lady Airlie, Mrs Humphry Ward, Edmund Gosse – the list continues, impressively.

The evening was, for every one, a memorable one.

The play, briefly, deals with (Act I) Guy's temptation away from his monastic vocation, (Act II) Guy's short and unconvincing career as a man about town before remorse seizes him and (Act III) Guy's embracing of the monastic life after a final burst of disillusionment. It was, Wells wrote in his review, '(a) fine conception, but altogether too weakly developed . . . finely conceived and beautifully written.

But the entire workmanship was too delicate for acting; and whether that is the fault of player or playwright is a very pretty question.'[2] The fault can, with hindsight, be attributed to both.

The first act went well enough. Ellen Terry's sister, Marion, was charmingly demure in grey silk, Mr Alexander was pleasingly earnest as her son's young tutor. William Elliott, playing the wicked Lord Devenish who lures Guy away from the virtuous life, had not succeeded in obeying James's injunction to look 'as much of a gentleman as is feasible – possible – to you' and managed only to look like a mustachioed villain from a burlesque comedy. But the audience were in agreement with William Archer that the first act was 'a masterly and exquisite piece of comedy'.

The disaster of the second act was due in part to James's switch from the earlier romantic mood to the wooden world of artificial comedy. The audience, led to expect the unfolding of a moving love-story, watched with perplexity and increasing restiveness a succession of stilted scenes in which burlesque, in the person of the 'obnoxiously played' Lord Devenish, was unpleasingly to the fore and in which Alexander, aware of losing his audience and his potential profits, developed a powerful facial twitch.

James's friends were puzzled and silent. The gallery was bored, and in the mood to show it. All they needed was the appearance of Mrs Edward Saker as Guy's elderly cousin. The play was set in the 1790s, and the luckless Mrs Saker had been given a properly authentic costume, a vastly crinolined black satin dress and, rising from a small frilled cap, a towering velvet hat crowned with unwieldy feather plumes. Duse or Bernhardt would have carried it off; Mrs Saker could not. She struggled, hopelessly in such clothes, to be inconspicuous – and was promptly singled out from the back of the pit by a horribly audible chorus line from the song, 'Where Did You Get That Hat?' The titters grew louder. The absurd plumed hat appeared to nod appreciation as Mrs Saker shrank with dismay. The audience was lost.

Neither ravishing scenery – a gracefully furnished room with latticed glimpses of a sunlit garden beyond – nor the reappearance of Marion Terry could save the third act from the audience's derision. The play now seemed not only tedious but incomprehensible. What business had Domville with rejecting the generous and unfailing love of the splendid Mrs Peverel (Miss Terry)? And what was their handsome, romantic 'Alick' doing playing this sanctimonious prig who seemed to change his mind every ten minutes? When, giving the line all he'd got, Alexander announced that he was the last of the Domvilles, his answer came promptly from the gallery: 'It's a bloody good thing y'are.' 'The play,' Wells decorously noted in his review, 'was received with marked disapproval by a considerable section of the audience.'

It was not the reviewers' job to record the finale but later, in his autobiography, Wells described what seemed to many of those present to be a piece of diabolical cruelty on the part of Alexander. James had returned from the Haymarket, nervous but hopeful as, standing in the wings, he heard a roar of sound, a burst of applause . . .

> There were some minutes of uneasy apprehension. 'Author' cried voices. 'Au-thor!' The stalls, not understanding. redoubled their clapping.
>
> Disaster was too much for Alexander that night. A spasm of hate for the writer of those fatal lines must surely have seized him. With incredible cruelty he led the doomed James, still not clearly understanding how things were with him, to the middle of the stage, and there the pit and gallery had him. James bowed; he knew it was the proper thing to bow. Perhaps he had selected a few words to say, but if so they went unsaid. I have never heard any sound more devastating than the crescendo of booing that ensued. The gentle applause of the stalls was altogether overwhelmed. For a moment or so James faced the storm, his round face white, his mouth opening and shutting and then Alexander, I hope in a contrite mood, snatched him back into the wings.[3]

The accuracy of Wells's account is confirmed by that of another sympathetic witness, Violet Hunt. 'He was,' she wrote later, 'so surprised, so pained, so brave. His large white handkerchief covered his face and, from behind it, appeared to issue chunks and gobbets – the maimed fragments of a clever speech [before his] retiring sadly and patiently, rather like an elephant who has had a stone put into his trunk instead of a bun.'[4]

Chaos broke out as Alexander and James left the stage. The author's friends and supporters continued loyally, but faintly, to applaud; the gallery responded with a new burst of catcalls and hissing which turned to clapping as Alexander returned, alone now, to the stage. 'T'ain't your fault, gov'nor, it's a rotten play,' bawled one sympathizer before the manager raised his hand for silence and began gently to reproach them. '. . . these discordant notes tonight have hurt me very much. I can only say that we have done our very best . . .' The mollified gallery applauded. The houselights went on and the subdued audience began to ebb away. It was left to the critics the next day to praise James for a sensitive if weakly motivated play, and to berate the gallery for a deplorable response to it. One critic, A. B. Walkley, went so far as to claim James's superiority as a playwright to Wilde.

It has often been suggested that the play's uncouth reception was part of a vendetta directed not at James, but at Alexander. An anonymous telegram had arrived before the first night, offering him 'heartiest wishes for a complete failure', and some reports intimated that there had been organized claques in the gallery and that drinks had been circulated with unusual freedom among the 'veriest roughs'. But it is not easy to see why, if this was the case, Alexander should have been given such an enthusiastic reception in the first act. Conspiracy theories are always seductive, but the right answer, in this case, would seem to be the drabber one. The audience was only in part an educated one; the philistine element, bored observers of James's supersensitive characters, got out of hand. Only, happily, on the first night: *Guy Domville* played for four weeks in London and one week on tour to respectful and sympathetic audiences.

To James, however, it had become apparent that his siege had run its course and could not be justified by persistence. It had not been wasted experience. Loss was converted into gain as he began to make use of the 'divine principle of the Scenario' to work out his novels and to realize, in his last and richest works, the integration of picture and scene which he had long pursued and which the writing of plays had taught him how to perfect. (The dramatic aspect of James's late novels does not immediately reveal itself to the reader who, to discover it, should look not for the drama of consciousness, the mental ordeal which James had learnt to dramatize many years before, but the arrangement of each novel into a series of carefully orchestrated and symmetrically balanced scenes of confrontation.)

It would have taken an uncommonly prophetic eye that night to foresee the friendship which would develop between the pallid bewildered playwright who had been dragged so mercilessly into the lions' den and the observant young journalist who sat scribbling his theatre notes in the stalls. Wells was twenty-six years younger than James and, although frantically busy, he had not yet made his name. His divorce from Isobel, his first wife, had just come through; he had for the past year been living in lodgings with Amy Catherine Robbins. (Jane to Wells, who disliked her given names.) Miss Robbins, a consumptive like Wells, had no money; Wells had only a hundred pounds left after he had provided for Isobel. For income, they were dependent on the number of brief, entertaining and topical articles which Wells could churn out each week.

The market for this kind of work was then almost limitless. London at the turn of the century had close to thirty daily newspapers, while the number of weekly and monthly magazines catering for the newly literate British public ran into hundreds. His scientific training provided Wells with a basis for a good many of his pieces and stories, but he was ready and willing to write on any topic under the sun with his inimitable brand of cocky confidence. So, among the seventy-five articles, five stories and a serial which he succeeded in selling in 1894, we find such odd sequences of subject as 'My Abominable Cold' and 'The Extinction of Man', 'A Stray Thought in an Omnibus' and 'The Rate of Change in Species'. He was earning £1,000 a year from his writing, but it was hard work, and it was hack work, and it was not the kind of life into which Wells wanted to be trapped.

He had two goals in sight; to be well-known and to make money as quickly as possible. By the end of 1898, he had achieved both. He had written the majority of his short stories and had already published a fair number of them; he had arrived among the bestselling authors of his time with a succession of hurriedly written but original and immensely readable novels. *The Time Machine, The Wonderful Visit, The Wheels of Chance, The Island of Doctor Moreau, The Invisible Man* and *The War of the Worlds* had brought him fame, money and an escape from London lodgings into, first, a rather dismal semi-detached villa in Woking and then, with the help of his new literary agent, J. B. Pinker, 'Heatherley', 'a picturesque but insanitary house in the early Victorian style' near Pinker's own home in Worcester Park.

Dorothy Richardson, a schoolfriend of Jane's and an early recruit to the legendary ranks of H.G.'s admirers, was a frequent visitor to Worcester Park and a shrewd, if prejudiced, observer of the Wellses in their early married life. Thinly disguised as Hypo and Alma Wilson, they appear in what Wells thought an astonishingly accurate account given in Chapter IV of Richardson's *The Tunnel*, from the *Pilgrimage* cycle of novels. He, apart from references to such intimate peculiarities as his habit of snuffling and snorting between sentences, came out of it rather well as a man of 'overwhelming charm', clever, competitive and magnetic. Jane, as Alma, was less kindly treated. She 'went on and on, sometimes uncomfortably failing, her thin voice sounding like a corkscrew in a cork without any bottle behind it, now and again provoking a response which made things worse because it brought to the table the shamed sense of trying to keep something going . . . Everything she said was an attempt to keep things up. Every time she spoke, Miriam was conscious of something in the room that would be there with them all if only Alma would leave off being funny.'[5]

Richardson's account was as ungenerously deprecating as Beatrice Webb's of 'a pretty little person with a strong will, mediocre intelligence and somewhat small nature', but it contained a germ of truth. As a social hostess, Jane was nervous, shy and uneasy. Luncheons and dinner-parties were ordeals to be endured without pleasure. 'She would look anxious, almost frightened,' Frank Swinnerton remembered. 'But let the company once be dispersed without mishap, and she would escape from constraint and become as loquacious as a child. She was then really happy.'[6]

A lack of social assurance is not the most heinous of failings, and a lack of libido did not make Jane the worst of wives for a man who had a superabundance of it. Tolerance was her weapon and while she exercised it – but at what cost to herself? – Wells would remain, after his fashion, faithful. His pleasure was taken elsewhere, but Jane, finally, held the strongest position as his confidante, his ally, and his friend. Her chosen role was that of the Victorian angel of the house, soothing, ministering, arranging, placating. She interviewed servants, dealt with business matters, typed manuscripts and checked proofs. A ready participant in the charades and games which Wells adored – so long as he could win – Jane had a light and carefree side which responded to and complemented, the whimsical and childish streak in her husband.

Fair weather and a fancy for a cycling holiday brought the Wellses down on their tandem to James's part of the world in the summer of 1898; ill-health was a major reason for their decision to remain there.

Three years of writing like a human machine had taken their toll of Wells's fragile constitution, and cycling was not what any doctor would have ordered for a man with a feverish cold and an abscess on his kidney. They had cycled no farther than Seaford when Wells collapsed. Part of the planned itinerary had been a visit to Dr Henry Hick, who Wells had met through a new friend, the novelist George Gissing. Telegrams were exchanged and after a series of 'malignantly uncomfortable' local trains had jolted the invalid to New Romney, he and Jane were installed under the kindly Hick's supervision and told to abandon any idea of going back to 'Heatherley' – except in a bath chair. 'And then,' Wells remembered, 'there began the serious business of finding a new home. According to the best advice available, a long period of invalidism was before me. I had to reconcile myself to complete exile from London, and contrive to live in dry air with no damp in the subsoil and in as much sunshine as possible.'[7]

Not being much given to tragic attitudes, Wells promptly set about turning his near-demise into comic material for his 'picshua-diary', annotating the pictorial record with appropriately frivolous comments ('After the Great Illness'; 'His First Galumph after his illness').

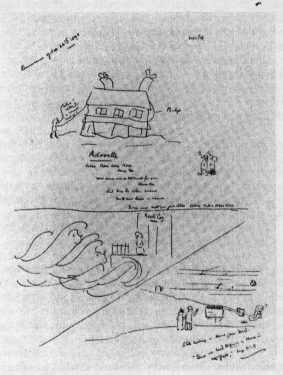

Early days at Sandgate – 'the serious business of finding a new home'.

Wells contemplated Rye, and decided in favour of living a few miles to the east at Sandgate, as pleasantly unfashionable then as it is today. Sandgate was not picturesque, but it was pretty without being pretentious, and peaceful without being too remote. The steep cliffs and the straggling promenade below offered splendid views of the Channel, and the air was bracingly suitable for an invalid. The only drawback, to a modern mind, was the depressingly antiquated nature of the houses. 'Servant-murdering basements, sanitary insanities, and not a decent bathroom anywhere,' Wells grumbled before he sent Artie and Ann Kipps off to experience the discomfort of inhabiting one of them. Through Kipps, we hear Wells's own disgust at the prospect of living in a house with 'a basement, no service lift, blackleading to do everywhere, no water upstairs, no bathroom, vast sash windows to be cleaned from the sill, stone steps with a twist and open to the rain, into the coal–cellar, insufficient cupboards, unpaved path to the dustbin, no fireplace to the servants' bedroom, no end of splintery wood to scrub – in fact, a very typical English middle-class house.'[8] It was not the sort of house in which Wells, any more than his haberdasher hero, intended to end his days.

The first six months were spent, not very satisfactorily, in a small rented cottage so close to the sea that the salt spray lashed the roof in winter, but Wells's health improved and they decided to persist with Sandgate while moving to Arnold House, a semi-detached villa more in the style of 'Heatherley' and standing in a more protected position than 2, Beach Cottages. It was not ideal but Wells, like Kipps, 'settled down for a time and turned himself with considerable resolution to the project of building a home.'

James called it a treasure house by the seashore, a praising but misleading description for a brightly modern, plainly furnished building on top of a cliff. The architect was a friend of Dr Hick's, C.F.A. Voysey, 'that pioneer in the escape from the small snobbish villa residence to the bright and comfortable pseudo–cottage'. Unlike the easily intimidated Kipps, Wells refused to be browbeaten into accepting Voysey's more grandiose schemes; the architect was responsible for Spade House's rough-cast exterior and overhanging eaves, but Wells was adamant when it came to the interior. He had had his fill of underheated houses with damp cellars and old-fashioned kitchens; Spade House was going to be easy to run and luxurious to inhabit. (It was reportedly the first small English house which could boast of having a private lavatory attached to each bedroom.)

Wells had to pay close on £3,000 to get what he wanted. The locals, fascinated by such lavish expenditure, decided that he must be the Wells of newspaper reports who had outwitted the croupiers at Monte Carlo. The house's name was clearly a reference to the card suit which had brought him luck. (The odd name stemmed, more mundanely, from Wells's refusal to have his home vulgarly emblazoned with the decorative hearts which were Voysey's trademark; he inverted them – and named the house accordingly.) Spade House may have lacked the baronial splendour of Brede Place or the gentlemanly elegance of Lamb House, but it was airy and light and gloriously functional. It had a croquet lawn, a tennis court and a handsome tiered garden in which the newly tubby Wells exercised himself by pushing a lawn-roller while Jane supervised the planting of flowers. It was not a treasure house, but it was a handsome symbol of success.

The links with the neighbourhood of writers were quickly established. Crane's prankish side made for an agreeable friendship of a light-hearted kind in which both families could romp unselfconsciously through games of animal grab, and the Wellses readily entered into the cheerfully bohemian spirit of the Brede Place household. On a more serious level, Wells found it hard to understand Crane's unwillingness to use his powerful narrative gift for political ends, or his good-tempered refusal to be drawn into the kind of literary discussion which Wells relished.

Ford and Conrad were too far to the opposite extreme to be a constant pleasure. They had, Wells later conceded, compelled him to take the art of writing a little more seriously, but their ardent pursuit of a single perfect word or phrase when any of six might do the job was foreign to his nature. Initially, he was sufficiently enthralled by the 'fine, fresh, careful, slightly exotic quality' of Conrad's prose to be horrified at the prospect of its being tampered with by his elected collaborator, Ford; in time, he came to regard Ford as the greater of the two and too little appreciated, both for his anglicizing of Conrad and for his own independent contribution to literature.

Ford, for all his high seriousness about the writer's vocation, was an easy and congenial companion, and as ready a charmer of women as Wells himself. A fascinating, if not entirely veracious raconteur, he was an amenable guest, looking, the Wellses' governess remembered, like a handsome German student with his long blond hair and braided velvet jacket. Less politically motivated than Wells, he became for a time a fellow-conspirator and abetter in the latter's plan to break up the 'Old Gang' of the Webbs, G. B. Shaw and Hubert Bland (the urbane and promiscuous husband of Edith Nesbit, the children's authoress), who ruled the Fabian Society. Wells's dream of a new socialist movement led by the reformed Fabians had little to do with Ford's dislike of 'the profession of free love going hand in hand with an intense sexual continence that to all intents and purposes ended in emasculation' – but differences of opinion were obscured by the pleasure of plotting. The scheme failed, ignominiously, but a strong enough bond had been formed for Wells to propose himself as co-editor and fund-finder when, in 1908, Ford decided to launch the *English Review*. It was also agreed that Wells's new novel, *Tono-*

Bungay, should be serialized in the *Review* prior to its publication in book form.

The *Review* survived, for fifteen months, under Ford's editorship: the friendship did not. Ford's editorial wishes directly conflicted with Wells's commercial expectations. Ford believed, or chose to believe, that he was doing his friend a favour in giving space to an unmarketable novel; more reasonably, he was infuriated by the speed with which Wells found excuses to withdraw his early offers of editorial and financial assistance. Wells, horrified by Ford's cheerful profligacy as an editor and sceptical of his unrealistic estimates of the *Review*'s likely profits (from which he was to be paid for the serialization), gave forceful expression to his anxiety. By January 1909, it had become clear that, far from getting the £600 per serial appearance which he had been led to expect, he would be lucky to get anything. There were no profits. The first four issues of the *Review* had in fact produced a deficit of approximately £1,600. Wells was furious, especially when he heard that Ford was proposing to remainder copies of the *Review* before *Tono-Bungay* had even appeared in book form. The only course open to him was to refuse to allow the serialization to continue. Ford, rather grandly, made it apparent that he was deeply saddened by such squalidly commercial behaviour and that he was not inclined to condone it: Wells, whose distress over the fate of one of his finest works is readily understandable, continued to back the *Review* and in later years to contribute to the financial support of Ford. But the friendship was wrecked beyond repair.

Wells did, however, make one significant contribution to Ford's life. He introduced him to Violet Hunt. It was two years since Wells himself had embarked on a brief but enjoyable affair with this lively, witty and, from some angles, beautiful woman* who had grown up in the same Pre-Raphaelite circles as Ford. Discretion was not Violet Hunt's strongest suit, but she had successfully complied with the unspoken rules of Wells's extramarital affairs – passion without monogamy, intelligent debate without quarrelsomeness, desire without expectation. They had remained on affectionate terms and Wells had a sufficiently high opinion of her writing to suggest that she should show some of her stories to Ford and see if he couldn't publish them. And so, armed with three of her tales, Violet went off to 84, Holland Park Avenue where Ford ran the *Review* from a maisonette placed unfortunately – from the point of view of smell – above a fishmonger's and poulterer's shop. Ford gave her tea, selected, with

---

* A beauty which is not easily divined from the profile photographs favoured by Violet, which cruelly emphasize her worst feature, a long and beaky nose.

his usual flair, the best of the three stories, and decided that he would like to see more of 'the immodest Violet', as she was dubbed by her friends.

Ford's reputation was not unblemished, but Wells would hardly have thought he was sending a lamb into the wolf's lair. Violet Hunt had already earned herself a reputation for being fast and modern, a writer of daring novels whose affairs, with Wells, with Somerset Maugham and with Oswald Crawfurd (a dilettante novelist who gave her syphilis), had lent her the image of an English Colette. She was almost ten years older than Ford, but she was glamorous, funny and, if not intelligent, very well-informed. A history of married lovers was probably in her favour; Ford may well have assumed that here was the kind of woman to let sleeping wives lie. He offered her the job of manuscript reader; in a short space of time she became his mistress. Their relationship as common-law man and wife lasted, uneasily, until 1918 when Ford met and fell in love with Stella Bowen.

'My dear Mr Wells,' Conrad wrote in October 1898 from Essex. 'I am writing in a state of jubilation at the thought we are going to be nearer neighbours than I dared to hope a fortnight ago. We are coming to live in Pent Farm . . .'[9] Proximity reduced jubilation to a state of cordial, and mutual, bafflement. The relationship between Conrad and Wells was polite but never comfortable. There was no ease of talk, and little understanding. It was not the Polish writer's neurotic, depressive side which irked Wells so much as his intellectually alert but utterly un-English mind. Conrad's exaggerated mannerisms embarrassed him, his harping on truth and inner meanings seemed too critical, too pryingly analytical, and grimly void of humour. 'We never really "got on" together,' Wells wrote later. 'I was perhaps more unsympathetic and incomprehensible to Conrad than he was to me. I think he found me Philistine, stupid and intensely English; he was incredulous that I could take social and political issues seriously; he was always trying to penetrate below my foundations, discover my imaginative obsessions and see what I was really up to. The frequent carelessness of my writing, my scientific qualifications of statement and provisional inconclusiveness, and my indifference to intensity of effect, perplexed and irritated him. Why didn't I *write*? Why had I no care for my reputation?

'"My dear Wells, what is this *Love and Mr Lewisham about*?" he would ask. But then he would ask also, wringing his hands and wrinkling his forehead, "What is all this about Jane Austen? What is there *in* her? What is it all *about*?"'[10] It is, we may be sure, a mildly cruel caricature of Conrad's interrogative manner, but it clearly conveys Wells's impatience with his exotic, too earnest neighbour.

And yet, curiously, with the serious and mannered James, Wells achieved both friendship and mutual literary respect, although an innocent reader would never guess it from Wells's own account, written eighteen years after James's death.

> I bothered him and he bothered me. We were at cross purposes . . . From his point of view there were not so much 'novels' as The Novel, and it was a very high and important achievement. He thought of it as an Art Form and of novelists as artists of a very special and exalted type. He was concerned about their greatness and repute. He saw us all as Masters or would-be Masters, little Masters and great Masters, and he was plainly sorry that 'Cher Maître' was not an English expression. One could not be in a room with him for ten minutes without realizing the importance he attached to the dignity of this art of his. I was by nature and education unsympathetic with this mental disposition. But I was disposed to regard a novel as about as much an art form as a market place or a boulevard . . . You went by it on your various occasions.[11]

Significant though that difference in attitudes was eventually to become, it was initially a stimulus rather than a barrier to an affectionately quarrelsome friendship which lasted for nearly fifteen years.

On the literary plane, it was a good-humoured war between the worlds of aesthetics and ideas. The Jamesian novel was reaching its most refined level as an elaborate and highly wrought construction, rich in implication, vivid in its economically bestowed scenes of intense effect which glow at us like precious stones from an intricately chased setting. It may be that for some readers these late novels seem to drag their slow length along an unbearably tortuous course, but it is during that serpentine route that they gather their power, the menacing sense of unseen evil, the intimation of unspeakable corruption. To make the reader feel and interpret without resort to the novelist's usual ragbag of emotional trickery was James's singular achievement.

Wells, on the other hand, rattled his novels off with speed and verve, but with precious little regard for subtle effect or elaborate construction. Imagination, humour and vitality were his strengths; his stories burn with his own abundant curiosity. There is no exquisite gemlike flame here but a furnace stoked with ideas, inventions, scientific prophecies. Wells was an educationalist and a reformer by nature, not an aesthete. He wrote to make money, but he also wrote out of a wish to make people think, to provoke them into a sharper sense of their own changing society. The later novels, in which the characters are reduced almost to the level of placard-carriers for Wells's ideas, have not survived well, but the modern reader of the early scientific romances and the inimitable narratives of 'ordinary' lives like those of Kipps and Mr Polly, can readily understand James's excitement – and his wish to offer Wells the benefit of his critical supervision.

Ford liked to hint that James envied Wells his popularity and influence; Anthony West has gone further and stated that his father was made to bear the full weight of the older writer's intolerable patronage. The letters – infuriatingly one-sided due to James's decision to burn the greater part of his private correspondence – make it clear that the final rupture stemmed neither from commercial nor from social disparities too deeply felt, but from the pupil-master relationship. Wells was not the man to spend a lifetime in gracefully submitting to unsolicited criticism. Initially, he was flattered by James's interest and happy to have one of the lords of the literary establishment as a supporter, but unlike the other young writers who offered their backs to James's critical whip, he had no inclination to sycophancy and no wish to alter his writing style. He admired the tenacity with which James ploughed his lonely furrow, steadily producing treasures too obscurely magnificent for the average reader to discern; *he* had no intention of abandoning his own profitable little garden patch for such impecunious and unrecognized glory. To be widely read and well-paid was ambition enough for the time being. He was still young; glory could wait. 'We must plant the pathway of the years with nice little bushy bargains to flower in due season,' he wrote to his agent. 'When we've got ten years ahead we'll come back & fill in between.' At the back of his mind, too, there must always have been the memory of that humiliating evening at the St James's Theatre. It was all very well for James to lecture and criticize him, but he, Wells, had witnessed his lack of the common touch, his failure to excite an audience's interest or to appeal to their understanding.

It was while Wells was still under the care of Dr Hick that James first met him. Using the guise of neighbourliness, he and his house-guest, Edmund Gosse, bicycled over to New Romney to wish the invalid well and, discreetly, to ascertain whether he needed help from the Royal Literary Fund. 'They took tea with Dr Hick and us and were very charming and friendly,' Wells remembered, 'and Jane and I were greatly flattered by their visit.' Wells made the next overture, inviting James to visit him at Beach Cottage and regretting that no houses had been available in Rye. He had been reading *The Turn of the Screw* and offered a sufficiently probing criticism of the ambiguous presentation of the governess to provoke her creator into a courteous defence:

> Of course I had, about my young woman, to take a very sharp line. The grotesque business I had to make her picture and the childish psychology I had to make her trace and present, were for me at least, a very difficult job, in which absolute lucidity and logic, a singleness of effect, were imperative. Therefore I had to rule out subjective complications of her own – play of tone etc.; and keep her impersonal save for the most obvious and indispensable little note of neatness, firmness and courage – without which she wouldn't have had her data. But the thing is essentially a pot-boiler and a *jeu d'esprit*.[12]

Work, he added, was the only reason he had still failed to visit Sandgate; he was working on *The Awkward Age* and 'parting with a day has been like parting with a pound of flesh'.

It was Wells's first taste of the artful deference James employed to undercut criticism without insulting the critic; none knew better how to kill with graciousness. The young author of *The Time Machine*, made aware of his presumptuousness, decided to back off. 'The story is not wrong – I was . . .' he offered. 'It isn't at all a lovely story but I treated it with a singularly vulgar lack of respect, and if you were not a novelist I should doubt of your forgiveness.'[13]

Forgiveness was granted. In the next extant letter, nine months later, James was disposed to be ponderously playful about his new friend's proposal that they should conduct their next conversation while reclining, in imperial style. 'You have a bed of laurels – and eke of banknotes, to recline on; but go to; – I also, *without* the mattress, will be Olympian; I will lie at *my* length – or breadth – beside you.' He did not, however, make any reference to *When the Sleeper Wakes*, which Wells had sent him four months previously, and it was only the arrival of a second offering, *Tales of Space and Time,* which shamed him into apologies and lavish – but carefully general – laudations. 'You fill me with wonder and admiration,' he wrote, but with reference to Wells's energy rather than to his writings of 1899.

The Time Machine, which James read in January 1900, marked the moment at which he became self-appointed judge and mentor. Yes, Wells was magnificent, even wonderful, but how much more wonderful would he be if he could allow himself to be guided. 'I am beastly critical . . .' he wrote. 'I re-write you, much, as I read – which is the highest tribute my damned impertinence can pay an author.' Wells's reply was spirited enough to encourage him to persist in his role; he urged a speedy visit to Lamb House. 'You would find me alone, but the pleasure for me would be less divided and defeated. *Then* we could talk! Think of it, dissolute man! . . . Name your day – almost any one would suit *me*; and do come.'

Six months later, James was perusing *Love and Mr Lewisham* and feeling secure enough as an approved mentor to let his disappointment show; 'a bloody little chunk of life' was all he would allow it to be, a description which was not much modified by the 'great charm' which he claimed to have found in it. Charm was not what Wells had striven for, nor can he have been greatly pleased by James's sly congratulations on the completion of Spade House, which contain more than a hint of condescension towards 'an organic full-blown British home!' The spanking newness of Spade House held no charms for James who consistently produced an overload of work as his excuse for not availing himself of Wells's hospitality. In any case, he offered on one occasion, he could not dream of staying except as a paying guest, and he knew that Wells would not allow him to pay. The prophet, perforce, must come to the mountain, bringing with him George Gissing, who was gratifyingly impressed by 'the lovely old Georgian house, superbly furnished' and who James in his turn found 'highly sympathetic', although disturbingly fragile, 'worn almost to the bone (of sadness).'

By 1901, confident that he had pin-pointed the weaknesses in Wells's work, James began to aim at them. His objections were carefully sweetened with praises for *Anticipations* ('your brilliant book . . . extraordinarily and unceasingly interesting'), but it is unlikely that Wells was deceived. He was told that he had simplified 'to excess' and that he had failed to represent life. 'Subject of your speculations as it is,' James wrote, 'it is nevertheless too much left out. That comes partly from your fortunate youth – it's a more limited mystery for you than for the Methuselah who now addresses you. There's less of it with you to provide for, and it's less of a perturber for your reckoning. There are for instance more kinds of people, I think, in the world – more irreducible kinds – than your categories meet.' Unwisely, one feels, James went on to point to the different worlds which he and Wells occupied and to intimate that his was the superior one.

If Wells was offended, he gave no sign of it. His novels continued to arrive at Lamb House for James's 'fond and fascinated perusal'; their author continued to resist offers of improvement. If only, James wrote in January 1902, he could be permitted to collaborate, 'to intervene in the interest of – well, I scarce know what to call it . . .' High-class literature, Wells must have silently added with a grin, but he did not pick up the gauntlet and James was obliged, after a fruitless pause, to pick it up and try again on a more playful note.

> It is only that my sole and single way of perusing the fiction of Another is to *write it over* – even when most immortal – as I go. Write it over, I mean, *re*-compose it, in the light of my own high sense of propriety and with immense refinements and embellishments. I am so good in these cases as to accept the subject *tel quel* – to take it over whole and make the best of it. I took over so, for instance, in my locked breast, the subject of Two Men⋆ etc. and the superstructure I reared upon it had almost no resemblance to, or nothing in common (but the subject!) with, yours. Unfortunately yours had been made public first – which seemed hardly fair. To obviate this injustice I think (and to secure an ideal collaboration) I should be put in possession of your work in its occult and pre-Pinkerite state.

Wells would only have had to compare notes with Conrad or Ford – Crane was already dead – to discover that he was the only one of James's neighbours who was being singled out for this curious compliment of abstract editing. He makes no comment on it in his autobiography, although it can hardly have slipped his memory. We have no way of knowing whether he was amused, flattered, irritated, or, which seems the most likely, a little of all three. James's next letter to him suggests that Wells had continued to skirt the topic, or to parry it by querying James about his own writing methods.

Behind the pleasantries, the literary badinage, there lay a wealth of disappointment of which Wells could hardly have been unaware. His own books were being discussed, read, translated, whereas James was paying for the luxury of 'working on one's own scale, one's own line of continuity and in one's own absolutely independent *tone*'. *The Ambassadors*, published in 1903, represented a personal triumph for James's method. Dramatic, richly pictorial, marvellously suggestive, it was a novel in which tragedy and comedy were perfectly integrated, but in which the prevailing mood was of laughter and light. To James, conscious of the weaknesses in his recently published *The Wings of the Dove*, this was unquestionably the finer book, and the best 'all round' of his novels. It deserved honour. It deserved to sell. How bitter then it must have been for James, thanking Wells for his 'generous and beautiful' letter of praise, to report that he had found no market for it. 'My book has been out upwards of a month,' he wrote, 'and, not emulating your 4,000, has sold, I believe, to the extent of 4 copies. In America it is doing better – promises to reach

⋆ *The First Men in the Moon.*

400.' It is not a self-pitying letter, but the obvious affection and the reiterated expressions of gratitude suggest that James was more than usually appreciative of encouragement and admiration, even from a recalcitrant pupil.

Wells's enthusiastic responses to James's own writings continued to be received with a florid show of gratitude and self-deprecation – *so* generous, *so* undeserved – while James benignly maintained the position of literary guru, gently marvelling at his friend's prolific output and at the variety of his enterprises, advising him to get acquainted with his American readers, putting him in touch with his old friend W. D. Howells as a useful authority on American publishing houses. (It may well have been James's suggestion that sparked off the idea for Wells's whistle-stop American trip two years later in 1906.)

When James returned from his own more leisurely American tour in 1905, he was greeted by *A Modern Utopia* and *Kipps*. The time had come to lay criticisms aside and applaud. 'I don't see . . . how I can "write" you about these things,' he wrote, '– they make me want so infernally to talk with you, to see you at length. Let me tell you, however, simply, that they have left me prostrate with admiration, and that you are, for me, more than ever, the most interesting "literary man" of your generation – in fact, the only interesting one. These things do you, to my sense, the highest honour, and I am lost in amazement at the diversity of your genius.' He could not resist a little mockery at the 'cheek' of a young man in Sandgate offering a scheme for the Life of Man, and he used the word six times to make the impertinence of it felt, but all was in a spirit of genuine elation. Wells had fulfilled, and exceeded, all of his expectations. He had, in *A Modern Utopia*, produced a vigorous satiric novel, unflawed by an intrusive sentimentality, 'the interference of which Thackeray is full'. And he had described the English lower middle classes in a novel which was a masterpiece of observation, knowledge and life, written with 'such a brilliancy of *true* truth'. It was that, the air of absolute truth, for which James reserved the highest praise. The great Victorian novelists' representations of the shopkeeping classes struck him as marred by an excess of the picturesque and romantic elements; authorial intrusions robbed their creations of conviction. But in *Kipps*, Wells had 'seen the whole thing in its *own* strong light'.

It was an achievement which James could appreciate all the better for having attempted it himself twenty years before in *The Princess Casamassima*, when he wanted to give a true and unsentimental picture of the life of a young man from the London slums. James had been determined to avoid the creaking Victorian mechanism of rhetoric and mawkishness; he had researched his background as zealously if not as meticulously as Zola; he had walked about the less salubrious London streets, sat in pubs, visited Millbank prison, taken notes on the English vernacular speech. The result was in part an impressively lifelike portrait of working-class life in London, of frugal gentility and revolutionary plans. Millicent Henning, overblown, forceful and irrepressibly vulgar, is the novel's most memorable character and one of the most jollily likeable of James's heroines. But the princess, resurrected from one of James's earliest works, *Roderick Hudson*, as a world-weary beauty who sees anarchy as the remedy for society's ills, fails to exert the mysterious fascination of her younger self. Hyacinth Robinson, the sensitive young bookbinder torn between the desire to join and the urge to destroy the glamorous world and the glorious artistic heritage which the Princess represents and scorns, is too weak, too Domville-like in his cerebral vacillations to retain the reader's sympathy and interest. His love of the beautiful has an unpleasant whiff of snobbery for which his romantic background – he is the bastard son of a peer and a French dressmaker – fails to offer sufficient excuse. He is, in modern terminology, a bit of a wimp.

A novel about anarchy was not what the fearful reader of the 1880s wanted to turn to for reassurance in a period of social turbulence and unrest; if James had hopes of winning a larger audience by offering them a less rarefied milieu than he habitually depicted, they were speedily dashed. One wonders how large a pang of envy he suppressed when he sat down to praise and celebrate the more marketable struggles of Artie Kipps, 'a mere born gem', as it seemed, as effortlessly produced as if Wells had simply plunged into a pool and brought him up, ready and complete, 'this rounded pearl of the diver'. But pleasure had the upper hand. Wells was obeying one of James's cardinal rules and writing about what he knew, a world he could handle with absolute assurance.*

Conrad, too, had been full of praise for *Kipps*, although concerned that the critics might undervalue its strengths, but it was James's letter which pleased the author more. Anxious that Macmillan should give the book maximum publicity – they had loftily rejected his suggestion of sandwich-boards to be displayed outside London theatres – he sent them James's tribute by way of an endorsement of his own faith in the book.

---

* When Conrad penetrated the same world two years later in *The Secret Agent*, there was no similar burst of responsive enthusiasm from Lamb House. People should write of what they knew; what could a Polish exile know of the London underworld? As much, one might think, as the American who had anticipated him.

Speculation about the conversations between James and Wells has always been free, since we have no way of knowing what they talked about. But James's response to *Kipps* makes it clear that their talks did not significantly touch on personal literary struggles and ambitions. He would never have described *Kipps* as 'a mere born gem' if Wells had let him know that the novel was the result of eight years of spasmodic planning and re-drafting.

In 1898, when the invalid's bath-chair had threatened Wells's dreams of prosperity, he had devised and partly written a much larger novel in which Mr Waddy (Kipps's invisible benefactor in the later book) was cruelly confined to a bath-chair just before becoming enormously rich. And, in the eighth chapter of *The Wealth of Mr Waddy*, the story of Kipps began. It was to have been a vast novel on the Dickensian scale, teeming with sub-plots and additional characters, and Wells was firmly convinced that it was the best thing he had yet done. But bits and pieces of a gigantic project by a young author who had only just begun to make his mark were not tempting bait for the London publishers. Wells was forced to abandon the manuscript for more lucrative work.

In 1904, he took it up again, to be ruthlessly pared, pruned and reshaped. The misanthropic Waddy was banished to the wings along with Chitterlow's wife, Muriel; Chitterlow himself was changed from a ruthless schemer into a good-hearted rogue; Kipps's parents vanished and Ann Pornick was brought forward as the female counterpart for kindly incorruptible Artie. Artie himself stood in the way of Wells's plan to turn the last section of *Kipps* into overt socialist propaganda. Impatient though Wells was to move into his new role of prophet, Artie Kipps was too fully developed a character to be successfully converted into a puppet for his creator's ideological purposes. The manuscript schemes were scrapped in favour of artistic integrity. Complexity had been the undoing of *The Wealth of Mr Waddy*: simplicity was the saving of *Kipps*.

James could hardly have been expected to divine the bulky shadow of Mr Waddy looming behind the slimmer form of Kipps: he was more at fault in seeing *Kipps* as a signpost to Wells's literary future. Of the two books which he had just read, *Kipps* was the one which symbolized a closing door. Later, Wells would admit that he had 'scamped' it, hurrying it to an end so that he could get on with the more important business of using fiction to influence politics. *A Modern Utopia*, not *Kipps*, pointed to the road Wells had decided to take.

Nothing could have been further from the homely sweetness of *Kipps* than James's own most recent publication. *The Golden Bowl* was the last and most fascinatingly elaborate of the three novels (*The Ambassadors, The Wings of the Dove, The Golden Bowl*) which represent the technical summit of his art. Lacking the relevant letter, we know that Wells pursued James for a copy and, having got one, wrote to him about it. Certainly, he would have been familiar enough with the novel to pick up the warning allusion to a symbolic golden vessel in the next critical epistle of 10 November, 1906, written in response to *In the Days of the Comet*. The words were up on the signpost now, and James did not find them reassuring.

Written at a time when Wells's sexual activities were becoming club-room gossip, *In the Days of the Comet* cheerfully fanned the flames of scandal by its bold recommendation of sexual freedom. What had been tentatively hinted at in *A Modern Utopia* now became explicit; in the new world created by the passage of the comet, jealousy and frustration are magically resolved by group marriages in which 'unstinted' love is accessible to all parties and welcomed as a social panacea. The novel was designed to cause maximum embarrassment to Wells's associates in the Fabian Society who were understandably reluctant to have their policies linked to a creed of sexual anarchy; the book had already caused uproar both in Fabian circles and in the press. What, Wells must have wondered, would be the reaction of the fastidious, discreet James, he who had horrifiedly pointed to the picture of his mother when a female guest (Violet Hunt) introduced the subject of passion to the breakfast-table at Lamb House? Would there be a tirade of disapproval, or merely a grieving murmur of distaste?

There were to be neither. Little though James relished the combination of sex with bacon and eggs – who does? – he would go so far as to say that he had been beguiled by the 'wild charm' of his friend's fantasy of sexual liberation: the reviewers who had expressed outrage were dismissed as 'ignobly stupid'. He could not honourably claim to have enjoyed the book, but his concern was less with the content than with the style and the direction. Gently, firmly, and quite consistently, he sought to remind Wells of the novelist's high duty to his art. The golden bowl of art is to be contemplated, hallowed, polished, brought to perfection with infinite pains. If, like Wells, you have 'a golden vessel which you flourish about with a hand of inimitable freedom', you run the risk of dropping it.

Wells ignored the warning and James continued to swallow down the uninhibited frankness of Wells's novels in 'deep rich draughts' and to gape at the daring originality and energy with which Wells spun and juggled the sacred golden vessel for which he showed an increasingly blatant disrespect. James could keep his position as the philosopher-king of pure literature; Wells's pen was a sword to slice through barriers, wield over new republics.

James was fascinated, absorbed – and repelled. His letters reflect a continuing battle between admiration and dismay, never more so than in his response to *Ann Veronica*, Wells's remarkable study of a New Woman. He saw again – had never doubted – that Wells was unique and diabolically powerful. He could say that 'you are to me so much the most interesting representational and ironic genius and faculty, of our Anglo-Saxon world and life, in these bemuddled days, that you stand out intensely vivid and alone, making nobody else signify at all. And this has never been more the case than in A.V., where your force and life and ferocious sensibility and heroic cheek all take effect in an extraordinary wealth and truth and beauty and fury of impressionism.'

So far, so good; too high, if anything, a tribute to a flawed and careless novel remarkable only for its brash support of youthful rebellion against 'old-fashioned' moral standards. But James was more shocked than he would directly admit. In his novels, he had always relied on the metaphor to convey the nightmare world lying just below the gilded surface; here, he reserves until the last a terrifyingly vivid image to express the revulsion he would not openly acknowledge. He represents *Ann Veronica* as a choking body in the moment before death, a monster who 'lives and kicks and throbs and flushes and glares – I mean hangs there in the very air we breathe'.

The New Machiavelli, which he read two months after its publication in 1911, inspired James to still more lurid imagery, and franker reproof, in the endeavour to lash Wells back into line. He pointed first to the broken golden bowl of art, reduced now to 'splendid golden splotches . . . innumerable morsels of a huge smashed mirror', and then to the vandal, a gluttonous undiscriminating giant; in other words, Wells. 'Your big feeling for life,' he wrote, 'your capacity for chewing up the thickness of the world in such enormous mouthfuls, while you fairly slobber, so to speak, with the multitudinous taste – this constitutes for me a rare and wonderful and admirable exhibition, on your part, in itself . . .' That, one would think, was blunt enough, but James went on to abuse Wells for having 'again' made use of that 'accurst autobiographic form . . . it has no authority, no persuasive or convincing force – no grasp of reality and truth isn't strong and disinterested.' This was certainly intended for a body blow. Wells might care nothing for art, but James could be sure of wounding him on the grounds of his failure to persuade or convince. What is a prophet worth if he can't do that? The love aspect, he added, for good measure, was insurmountably flat-footed, although he had suggestions as to how Wells might successfully have treated it.

Even the most impassioned Jamesian would agree that this was a gratuitously disagreeable letter, and that James had exceeded his role of tutor and mentor by a long way. Wells could have been excused for a sharp response, but his reply was a model of restraint. He thanked James for his ideas, agreed about the autobiographical form and declared himself quite ready to 'kiss the rod' of 'loving chastisement'. He would be the whipping-boy for his work, if that was what James wanted, but he would not be bullied into altering his view of the novel as 'the only medium through which we can discuss the great majority of the problems which are being raised in such bristling multitude by our contemporary social development.'[14] The novelist's duty was, in other words, to sacrifice art to life.

James's criticisms were heard but unheeded, but the vivid imagery of disgust lodged itself in Wells's mind, perhaps more deeply than he knew. When, in 1913, he gave an answer to James's observations on his novel, *The Passionate Friends*, his letter made striking use of those same images. James had, we remember, compared one of his novels to a choking, half-dead creature and had warned him not to smash the golden bowl of art. Now, years later, Wells was ready to offer a defiant riposte:

> My art is abortion – on the shelves of my study stand a little vain-gloriously – thirty-odd premature births. Many retain their gill slits. The most finished have still hare lips, cleft palates, open crania. These are my children! But it is when you write to me out of your secure and masterly *finish*, out of your golden globe of leisurely (yet not slow) and infinitely *easy* accomplishment that the sense of my unworthiness and rawness is most vivid. Then indeed I want to embrace your feet and bedew your knees with tears – of quite unfruitful penitence.

It is worth noticing one significant change in the imagery. James had consistently portrayed the golden object as a bowl or vessel which iconography associates with the image of a grail or chalice. The novelist in this image becomes the priest or holy man to whom the vessel of art is entrusted. He holds it up with care, fearful of spilling the sacred liquid or of letting the vessel fall. But Wells has altered the image to a golden globe in which he sees the novelist imprisoned, an ageing Buddha in the life-denying cage of his palace of art.

Nothing so clearly illustrates the chasm between James and Wells as their books on America. Have pen, will travel, was the motto they had both prudently adopted before crossing the Atlantic; a commissioned record of impressions would cover the cost of the enterprise. Wells's *The Future of America* came out in 1906; James followed a year later with *The American Scene* from the same publisher, Chapman & Hall.

James landed at New York on the 30 August, 1904. It was twenty years since he had stepped on American ground; had Hardy not already made famous use of the title, he had planned to call his book 'The Return of the Native'. William James, himself under the spell of 'the heaven-scaling audacity' of the new American city, had warned his brother that he would feel more of an alien than a native; James arrived in New York in a heightened state of anticipation and dread, to find hardly a trace left of the 'small, homogeneous, liquor-scented, heated-looking city' of his childhood. It had been his intention to write 'the best book (of social and pictorial and, as it were, human observation) ever devoted to this country', a grand literary gesture of conciliation to the land he had elected to abandon. The note which ended by dominating *The American Scene* was one of regret. The tribute became an elegy for the America of his boyhood. When, later, he evoked that era in *A Small Boy and Others*, he achieved a lyricism of description which was heightened by the knowledge that this was a past which had been eradicated, driven out of existence. Only prose could retrieve and preserve it.

James spent nine months struggling to come to terms with the foreignness of the new, and in exploring the America he had never seen. His unexpected success as a lecturer – 'The Lesson of Balzac' was sufficiently well-received to be frequently repeated – helped to pay the way as he travelled to Charleston, Miami, St Louis, Philadelphia, Los Angeles, San Francisco, Chicago, Washington, visiting friends, seeking out old acquaintances, attending lengthy literary conventions, preparing the material for his book. Neither gout, toothache, nor fatigue was permitted to curtail his exhausting schedule.

There were, mercifully, a multitude of friends on hand to offer their homes for periods of respite. At Philadelphia, he stayed at Butler Place with his old friends, the Wisters, the daughter and son-in-law of the English actress, Fanny Kemble, with whom James had formed a close attachment in her later years. The doors of Henry Adams's house on Lafayette Square were open to welcome him into Washington; at Cape Cod, he was able to relax into English social

gossip with another visitor, Howard Sturgis, the thoroughly anglicized son of an American banker who had become one of James's
dearest friends. And at Lenox, Massachusetts, Edith Wharton was
waiting to envelop him in the kind of luxury which James, rather
half-heartedly, claimed to despise. A million dollars a year was
apparently the average income in those parts. 'Everyone is oppressively rich and COSSU', James sighed, but he returned for a second
visit. The house was unkindly described as 'a delicate French château
mirrored in a Massachusetts pond . . . a monument to the almost
too impeccable taste of its so accomplished mistress', but James was
nevertheless grateful to a hostess who allowed him the freedom of
the mornings to write and who used her dashing motor-car to
introduce him to a New England which he had never before more
than partially seen. Less luxury but an abundance of comfort and
freedom to work was available at William's house below Chocorua
mountain in New Hampshire. Here, he had a suite of rooms to
himself and could wander at leisure through the russet autumn
woods above the house or towards the pretty linked lakes which it
overlooked.

In the red-brick streets surrounding Beacon Hill in Boston and in
the sunny peace of Cambridge, the past became tangible. At night,
in November, he walked alone to Cambridge Cemetery to find a
small group of graves huddled together on a moonlit ridge. His
father, his mother, his sister, Alice, and a little child of William's
were buried together here. Overwhelmed by the memories he had
struggled to recapture, confronted by the certainty that this was the
moment for which he had made the voyage, the moment which
justified the whole enterprise, James wept. For what? For the cheerful
extrovert child he had never been? For the settled life he had been
denied by his father's idea of a travelling education? For the parents
with whom he had never achieved any real ease and understanding?
For sharp, clever Alice who had embraced death as a release from
endless pain? Or did the whitened plain of Soldiers' Field, wanly
visible on the other side of the River Charles, prompt some more
universal grief? All we know from his own record of the night is that
his grief was mixed with 'a kind of anguish of gratitude' and that he
willingly surrendered to the overpowering sense of 'the infinite pity
and tragedy of the past'.

Where Cambridge offered the comfort of continuity, New York
gave him a feeling of severance and displacement. His past here had
gone, buried under the great grey edifices of a new city. It felt to him
as though one of his limbs had been brutally amputated and discarded
by an alien race, the new rulers of 'that altogether unspeakable city'

which reminded him of a broken-toothed comb jabbing uneven spikes at an almost invisible sky.

It was James's misfortune to have been given an acute sensibility to his urban surroundings. As an old man, he could still remember with piercing clarity the Paris he had visited as a small child, the dusky smell of peaches in his grandmother's Albany garden, the shuffling rustling heat of the dame's school to which he had been carried, crying and kicking, for his first hour of education, 'the queer empty dusty smelly New York of midsummer' through which he had loitered, gazing at theatre-bills, the delight of walking down Broadway, 'the joy and adventure of one's childhood'. The same keen responsiveness had made him flinch when he visited Paris in the 1870s and saw 'the deadly monotony that M. Haussmann [had] called into being . . . its huge, blank, pompous, featureless sameness', the machine-made arabesques on the vast white houses which now uniformly lined the Avenue de l'Opéra. Now, looking up to the jagged skyline of a city which had once dazzled and exhilarated him, he was bewildered and appalled.

Commerce, it seemed, had cheerfully cut history's throat. His first home in Washington Place had been usurped by 'a high, square, impersonal structure'. Trinity Church, once one of the city's land-marks, cowered in the shadow of a building with 'a south face as high and wide as the mountain-wall that drops the Alpine avalanche . . . upon the village'. Where William saw heaven-scaling audacity, James saw a hideous defiance of proportion. 'The great city is pro-jected into its future as, practically, a huge, continuous fifty-floored conspiracy against the very idea of the ancient graces, those that strike us as having flourished just in proportion as the parts of life and the signs of character have *not* been lumped together, not been indistinguishably sunk in the common fund of mere economic inconvenience.'[15] And yet, faint-heartedly, he comprehended William's excitement as he stared up the face of Trinity Church's neighbour and saw how 'the vast money making structure quite horribly, quite romantically, justified itself, looming through the weather with an insolent cliff-like sublimity'.

It was the brazen rule of business which most dismayed him, the 'colossal greed' so frankly and inescapably on show. When, later, James wrote 'The Jolly Corner', he sent Spencer Brydon back to New York to meet the man he would have become had he not left, a rich and elegant stranger, 'evil, odious, blatant, vulgar'. Through Brydon's eyes, we see New York with the revulsion James felt as he described 'the dreadful multiplied numberings which seemed to him to reduce the whole place to some vast ledger-page, overgrown, fantastic, of ruled and criss-crossed lines and figures . . . in the vast wilderness of the wholesale, breaking through the mere gross generalization of wealth and force and success.'

More repugnant and disturbing than the new architecture was the new American. The sheer mass of the urban population presented him with a spectacle of uniform depression and apathy. He looked with horror on 'the consummate monotonous commonness, of the pushing male crowd, moving in its dense mass – with the confusion carried to chaos for any intelligence, any perception; a welter of objects and sounds in which relief, detachment, dignity, perished utterly and lost all rights'. But more alarming and more unexpected was the absence of any sense of national consciousness in the vast and ever-swelling tide of immigrants from all corners of the world.

He could not see them as individuals. Visiting Ellis Island, he was a silent witness to 'a drama that goes on, without pause, day by day and year by year, this visible act of ingurgitation on the part of our body politic and social'. On the streets of New York and in the rural heart of New Hampshire, he found himself surrounded by these new Americans, a breed as strange to him as Martians and with whom he felt that he was expected to be on easy terms. 'Repeatedly, in the electric cars, one seemed invited to take them for granted – there being occasions, days and weeks together, when the electric cars offer you nothing else to think of. The carful, again and again, is a foreign carful; a row of faces, up and down, testifying, without exception, to alienism unmistakable, alienism undisguised and unashamed.' It was not so much their foreignness which daunted James as their lack of it. He looked for the picturesque and individual charm of the Italian, the Spaniard, the Armenian and saw only the mournful anonymity of the expatriate. It was as if, he thought, the process of becoming American had 'immediately glazed them over as with some mixture, of indescribable hue and consistency, the wholesale varnish of consecration, that might have been applied, out of a bottomless receptacle, by a huge white-washing brush'. They had lost what they had been; they had not yet become anything else.

An alien himself in all but legal standing, James failed to see the irony of his new role as a passionate supporter of the American identity. 'What meaning, in the presence of such impressions, can continue to attach to such a term as the "American" character?' he gravely asked. 'What type, as the result of such a prodigious amalgam, such a hotch-potch of racial ingredients, is to be conceived as shaping itself?'

Regret for the smaller, more discreetly cultured city of his youth made Henry James sound at times uncommonly like Henry Adams who in his most patrician frame of mind, was capable of sneering at 'a furtive Yacoob or Ysaac still reeking of the Ghetto, snarling a weird Yiddish at the officers of the customs'. But *The American Scene* is much more than a whining complaint against progress. It is also, as the title suggests, richly, mesmerizingly visual. Long before the cinema screen began to brand our minds with the harsh early images of New York with which we have all become unthinkingly familiar, James was composing the newly mechanized city into comparably vivid and striking scenes. An unerring eye and ear enabled him to present an unforgettable picture of the city from the Bay on a fine morning, to bring life 'to the motion and expression of every floating, hurrying, panting thing, to the throb of ferries and tugs, to the plash of waves and the play of winds and the glint of lights and the shrill of whistles and the quality and authority of breeze-born cries . . .' Across the water, he painted the city in black as a 'monstrous organism', its scattered members laced together 'as by the ceaseless play of an enormous system of steam-shuttles or electric bobbins . . .'

> One has the sense that the monster grows and grows, flinging abroad its loose limbs even as some unmannered young giant at his "larks", and that the binding stitches must for ever fly further and faster and draw harder; the future complexity of the web, all under the sky and over the sea, becoming thus that of some colossal set of clockworks, some steel-souled machine-room of brandished arms and hammering fists and opening and closing jaws.

Wells, newly arrived in New York from the *Carmania*, could also see the city's resemblance to a monster. He, too, was initially appalled by the spectacle of the population as 'the black torrent, rippled with unmeaning faces . . . the great crowds of cheap base-looking people hurrying uncivilly by'. It took only a few hours of city life to change his mind. He strolled into the glittering prosperity of Fifth Avenue, bathed in light on a sunny day, and 'became aware of effects that were not only vast and opulent, but fine.'[16] The newness, the energy and optimism, the feeling that all America was on the upward and forward move, that the skyscrapers were like vast packing cases waiting to be opened and put to new use – all this was immensely exciting to a man of Wells's temperament. He compared New York to Rome and found it 'not simply more interesting . . . but more significant, more stimulating, and far more beautiful'. Developments being carried out by the City Club in the slum areas of Chicago encouraged him to see the beginnings of a new socialism which would usher in 'a more orderly and more beautiful age'. Squalor, chaos and ugliness were all apparent and duly recorded, but Wells frankly expressed his preference for the cities which were noisily and sometimes hideously mutating as they emerged, to the genteelly conservative Boston where the citizens 'admire Botticelli, and have a feeling for the roof of the Sistine chapel', where Longfellow and Tennyson were revered and where the electrically lit dome of the State House seemed as shockingly modern an outrage as, say, a neon E.R. on the Round Tower at Windsor. Where James had found comfort and reassurance in the stalwart rows of red and brown houses, Wells saw an unhealthy devotion to the past and sensed 'an immense effect of finality'. Boston was kind, hospitable and unnervingly well-read, but it offered the spectacle of a society to whom the mere existence of the twentieth century was an affront.

Gracefully and lyrically, James lamented the passing of the mid-nineteenth-century America which only Boston was left to represent. Wells, disciple of the new and prophet of the future, used his pen as a surgeon's knife to operate on the ills of the present. His, William James prophesied after reading one instalment, would be hailed as '*the* medicinal book about America'. Chicago was, for all the City Club's endeavours, 'a Victorian nightmare', crying out for discipline and organization. New York could dazzle him with its lavish sense of 'spending from an inexhaustible supply', but the spenders were few, the society dismayingly ill-balanced with wealth accumulating in the vaults of a shrewd élite. For the rest, poverty remained the great equalizer with 'this efflorescence of wealth above and spreading degradation below'. He noted with horror that with no national minimum 1,700,000 children under fifteen were working in mines, factories and sweatshops, that the numbers were rising and that Italian immigrants imported young children expressly for this purpose. He wrote with outrage on 'The Tragedy of Colour' and, in particular, of those of mixed colour, excluded from white society by a law almost as inflexible and unpleasant as that of apartheid. Was their blood any worse, he wished to know, than that of the southern planters who prided themselves on their ancestry? 'It is the same blood flows in these mixed coloured people's veins. Just think of the sublime absurdity, therefore, of the ban. There are gentlemen of education and refinement, qualified lawyers and doctors whose ancestors assisted in the Norman Conquest, and they dare not enter a car marked "WHITE" and intrude upon the dignity of the rising loan-monger from Estonia. For them the "Jim Crow" car . . .' Admirable though the sentiments are, the racial chapter is one of the weakest in Wells's book, conveying more indignation than knowledge and reading like the professional rant of a demagogue.

Wells was on stronger ground when he berated the New Yorkers for their sanctimoniously moral treatment of Maxim Gorky, whose first American visit coincided with his own. It was Wells's first encounter with a man for whom he had an enduring admiration and respect, and he was immensely taken by him. So, initially, were the Americans – until, that is, they discovered that his companion and interpreter, Madame Andreieva, was not legally his wife. 'It was,' Wells wrote, 'like a summer thunderstorm. At one moment Gorky was in an immense sunshine, a plenipotentiary from oppression to liberty, at the next he was being almost literally pelted through the streets . . . The Gorkys were pursued with insult from hotel to hotel. Hotel after hotel turned them out. They found themselves at last after midnight in the streets of New York City with every door closed against them. Infected persons could not have been treated more abominably in a town smitten with a panic of plague . . . To me it was astounding – it was terrifying.' To so fervent an advocate of liberal morality as Wells, this display of sexual rectitude was peculiarly nauseating, and he attacked it with considerable force and feeling. It was this section of the book that prompted William James's enthusiastic response.

'And always I have been saying to myself, "Remember the immigrants; don't leave them out of your reckoning."'

Wells had been reading the serialized version of *The American Scene* while writing *The Future in America* and he was careful to pay tribute to the older writer as 'the chief master of one's craft' and 'my illustrious predecessor'. Disapproving though he was of a society which allowed money to remain in the hands of a privileged few, he was prepared to cite *The Ambassadors* and *The Golden Bowl*, 'most spacious and serene of novels', as being the finest literary representations of 'these irresponsible American rich . . . their refinement, their large wealthiness, their incredible unreality'. But when it came to the matter of the immigrant who James found distressingly ubiquitous and – for linguistic reasons – uncommunicative, Wells took issue with him. Visiting Ellis Island, he noted with more optimism than his predecessor that the majority of the newcomers were young, sturdy and hopeful. Where James had wrung his hands over the loss of national character, the extinction of 'antique refrains', Wells rubbed his at the wonderful efficiency of the system. 'In one record day this month 21,000 migrants came into the ports of New York alone; in one week over 50,000. This year the total will be 1,200,000 souls, pouring in, finding work at once, producing no fall in wages. They start digging and building and making. Just think of the dimensions of it.'

Enthusiasm was rapidly displaced by unease, however. Initially captivated by the efficiency of a country which could provide work for all, he was soon moved to ask if this was enough, whether the immigrant was not worse off than the 'artless, rather uncivilized, pious, good-hearted peasant' that he had been before. James had given the impression of America as a polyglot country in which English was in danger of becoming a lost tongue. Perfectly true, Wells concurred, but only if you penetrated the lowest social levels. 'The immigrant does not clamour for attention. He is, indeed, almost entirely inaudible, inarticulate, and underneath . . . Mr James has, as it were, to put his ear to earth to catch the murmuring of strange tongues.' The bare fact as he saw it when his first euphoria had worn off was that America, desperate to accelerate the process of industrial development, was 'importing a large portion of the peasantry of Central and Eastern Europe and converting it into a practically illiterate and industrial proletariat'. Only a narrowing of the gap between employer and worker, he harshly concluded, marked America's true emancipation from its early history of slave-trading.

James's response to *The Future in America* was unusually prompt, posted the day after reading it. Never had he better displayed his gift for disguising antipathy as admiration. It had made him 'squirm'. It was the performance of 'a "strong man" or a conjurer [juggler]'. How he envied Wells his ability to simplify! How regrettable that 'you tend always to simplify overmuch'. The needling continued. He himself had wondered what was to become of America and, with his greater knowledge and experience of living there, had realized that there was 'absolutely *no* profit in scanning or attempting to sound the future . . . and yet here you come and throw yourself *all* on the future, and leave out almost altogether the America of my old knowledge.' And, at last, he grew blunt. It was a vulgar book. 'I think you, frankly – or think the whole thing – too *loud*, as if the country shouted at you, hurrying past, every hint it had to give and you yelled back your comment on it . . . How glad you must be to have cast it from you!'[17] And how glad, one feels, James was to have cast Wells's book from him.

But Wells was ready to give as good as he got. 'I wish there was a Public worthy of you . . .' he wrote after praising *The American Scene* for its evocations and its temperate judgements. 'I do get this gleam of discontent. How much will they get out of what you have got in?'[18]

There was, on this occasion, no reply.

4

THE BROTHERS:
HENRY AND WILLIAM

I'm always sorry when I hear of your reading anything of mine, and always hope you won't – you seem to me so constitutionally unable to enjoy it.

Henry James to William James, 1905

Forgive! forgive! and don't reply, don't at any rate in the sense of defending yourself, but only in that of attacking *me*, if you are so minded.

William James to Henry James, 1907

He did surely shed light to man, and *gave*, of his own great spirit and beautiful genius, with splendid generosity. Of my personal loss – the extinction from so far back (really from dimmest childhood) I won't pretend to speak. He had an inexhaustible authority for me, and I feel abandoned and afraid, even as a lost child.

Henry James to H. G. Wells, 1910

I went once to Brown's Hotel to say goodbye to him before his departure for America with William James who was very ill. While I was with him a message came and he hurried away. I waited and waited but no one came, so at last I started downstairs. I passed an open bedroom door and saw William lying on the floor and Henry standing over him. As I hurried down I caught an expression of misery and despair on Henry's face that I shall never forget.

'Henry James: a Reminiscence' by Hugh Walpole,
Horizon, 1940

1842   William James born in New York.
1843   Henry James born in New York.
1878   William James marries Alice Howe Gibbens.
1879   Birth of Henry James (Harry).
1882   Death of Mr and Mrs Henry James, Senior.
        Birth of William (Billy) James.
1884   Birth of Herman James.
1885   William James made Professor of Philosophy at Harvard. His third son,
        Herman, dies.
1886   Purchase of summer home at Chocorua, New Hampshire.
        Henry publishes *The Bostonians* and *The Princess Casamassima*.
1887   Birth of Margaret Mary (Peggy) James.
1880   William builds a new home in Cambridge, Massachusetts.
1890   William publishes *The Principles of Psychology*.
        Henry publishes *The Tragic Muse*.
1892   Death of Henry and William's younger sister, Alice James, in England.
1897   William James publishes *The Will to Believe and Other Essays*. Henry rents
        Lamb House, and publishes *The Spoils of Poynton* and *What Maisie Knew*.
1898   William lectures on the West Coast, suffers from heart-strain and publishes
        Human Immortality.
        Henry publishes *The Turn of the Screw*.
1899   William publishes *Talks to Teachers on Psychology and to Students on some of
        Life's Ideals*. Henry publishes *The Awkward Age*.
1902   William delivers the Gifford Lectures at Edinburgh and publishes *Varieties
        of Religious Experience*. Henry publishes *The Wings of the Dove*.
1907   William publishes *Pragmatism* and resigns from his professorship.
1908   William delivers the Hibbert Lectures at Oxford.
1909   William publishes *A Pluralistic Universe* and *The Meaning of Truth*. Henry
        publishes *Italian Hours*.
1910   Death of William James and of their younger brother, Robertson James.
        Henry James lingers on in America after William's death.

I have not given the dates of all Henry James's publications in this period. These can
be found in the date-list for Chapter 3, and in the Bibliography.

THE BROTHERS:

HENRY AND WILLIAM

Wells must often have relished the irony of having two members of the James family keenly following his literary career and simultaneously urging him in opposite directions. While Henry* endeavoured to keep him bowling down English country lanes with Kipps and Mr Polly instead of marching up the stony hill of political idealism, William James was all for the harsh ascent.

William's literary heroes were Tolstoy, and Kipling – 'more of a Shakespeare than anyone yet in this generation of ours, as it strikes me.' He compared Wells to both, very favourably. The lectures published as *First and Last Things* in 1907 prompted him to describe Wells as 'the Tolstoy of the English world. A sunny and healthy-minded Tolstoy . . .' Earlier, after reading *A Modern Utopia, Anticipations* and *Mankind in the Making*, he had been still more fervent in his enthusiasm. 'You "have your faults, as who has not?"'† he wrote to Wells in 1905, 'but your virtues are unparalleled and transcendent, and I believe you will prove to have given a shove to the practical thought of the next generation that will be among the greatest of the influences for good . . . in fact you're a trump and a jewel, and for human perception you beat Kipling, and for hitting off a thing with the right word, you are unique. Heaven bless and preserve you!'[1]

As a political prophet with a genius for presenting difficult ideas lucidly and forcefully, Wells appealed immensely to William, whose own writings on psychology were so direct and readily understandable to the layman. And, when they met, William warmed more readily than his brother to the ebullient jollity and ease of Wells's manner, and to his insouciance about social niceties. Having been promised a meeting with another Rye visitor, G. K. Chesterton, one

---

* I have used the brothers' given names throughout this chapter for increased simplicity.

† Inaccurate quotations are an irritating and frequent feature of William's letters. (Mistress Quickly, quoting Horace, had said, 'but nobody but has his fault' in *Henry IV*.)

summer at Lamb House, and discouraged by Henry, who had not yet been formally introduced, William confessed to Wells that he had been told off for trying to arrange a meeting by way of a ladder against their adjoining garden walls. Henry had been horrified; Wells, hugely amused, carried William off to Spade House and effected the desired introduction en route. He liked William – it was almost impossible *not* to like that kind, neurotic, enthusiastic man – and, when he died in 1910, Wells wrote to Henry of 'a sense of enormous personal loss' and 'a very living affection for him'.[2]

The James children had always been encouraged to speak their minds freely. They were expected to relish argument and to conduct their intellectual battles with spirit and verve. Henry, reticent, passive and shy, was from an early age a little in awe of the elder brother who thrived on contentious discussion. 'I play with boys who curse and swear', he remembered William boasting as a schoolboy; William's own early letters have a distinctive note of kindly patronage towards young 'Harry'. Harry was noted to be disgustingly attached to wearing his oldest and grubbiest clothes. Harry spent too much time shut away in his room. Harry was feeble. 'We are going to put Harry through a splashing big walk daily.' And, by not fighting back, the younger brother condemned himself to a lifetime of William's well-meant bullying. In 1880, aged thirty-seven, he wrote of his beginnings as a writer 'when I was young and you bullied me', but the time had not come for William to relinquish his role. Just as Henry had appointed himself as the unsolicited mentor of Wells's literary undertakings, so did William elect himself as the frankest and most impenitent critic of his brother's work and, on several occasions, of his style of life. The previous chapter of this book suggests a priggish and didactic side to Henry's character, but his relationship to William reveals another aspect of patience, sweetness and good humour. He accepted his brother's admonitions and reproaches as amiably as Wells accepted his. Like Wells, he never allowed criticism to deflect him from his chosen course.

The decision to rent Lamb House was, unusually, taken without prior consultation with William but when, in the summer of 1899, the opportunity arose to buy the freehold for £2,000 – a larger sum than he had ever contemplated having to produce at one time, but for something which he was very sure he wanted – Henry looked to his brother for encouragement. William had not yet seen Lamb House, but he had heard all about it. He was reminded of its charm, its elegance, its merits as a good investment. It was, was it not, the right thing to do?

William was taking the baths at Bad-Nauheim after one of the nervous collapses to which he was debilitatingly prone. William, when forbidden to work, always became irascible. He was not in a mood or in a condition to look kindly on Henry's flirtations with the property market. With him at Bad-Nauheim (unfortunately for Henry), was a snobbish physician called Baldwin who had spent a night at Lamb House and, having a taste for statelier homes, had formed a poor impression of it. Baldwin did not think it at all a good investment. Taking his word for it, William sent off a sharply discouraging letter only partially modified by a second one offering financial help with the imprudent – as he saw it – purchase. The offer was briskly refused; Henry, usually adept at seeming impervious to criticism, was sufficiently hurt on this occasion to show it. He had not wanted cold cautions; he had wanted approval. 'It was the impulse to *fraternize* – put it that way – with you, over the pleasure of my purchase, and to see you glow with pride in *my* pride of possession, etc . . . I reckoned, alas, without Baldwin.'[3]

Visiting Rye for the first time that autumn, in the company of his wife Alice⋆ and their daughter Peggy, William felt as ill at ease as Gulliver in Lilliput as he walked about 'the little town, with its miniature brick walls and houses and nooks and coves and gardens . . . all exceedingly tiny (so that one wonders how *families* ever could have been reared in most of the houses) . . .'[4] Henry was hospitable, but William's descriptions of Lamb House convey more impatience than pleasure in its doll's-house charms. It was, he owned, exquisite in its way, full of 'quaint little stage properties . . . little brick courts and out-houses, old-time kitchen and offices, panelled chambers and tiled fire-places, but all very simple and on a small scale.'[5] To William, used to the expansive landscape and the airy uncluttered rooms of his New Hampshire home, Rye was uncomfortably enclosing and claustrophobic. For Henry, too, the invalid's visit was more of a trial than a joy. 'The dark month he spent here was a tension of the keenest – a strain of the sorest,' he confided to his old friend Lucy Clifford, after the Jameses had gone.[6]

A family link remained in the form of Peggy, William's fourteen-year-old daughter who was, none too happily, upholding the James tradition of a European education by attending a school in Harrow on the outskirts of London.

Readers of *What Maisie Knew* and *The Awkward Age* are sometimes understandably mystified by Henry James's compassionate under-

---

⋆ Not to be confused with Henry and William's sister, Alice James, who died in 1892.

standing of the mind of a young girl. How could a middle-aged and childless bachelor have acquired such a tender and thorough knowledge of the griefs and longings of Maisie Beale and Nanda Brookenham? Part of the answer lies in his relationship with Peggy to whom, in William's absence, he played the role of a father. If he was often lonely, so was his little American niece – and Henry was touchingly assiduous in his efforts to see that she was not neglected. It became a ritual part of his London visits that Peggy and her favourite schoolmates should be taken out and escorted to suitable entertainments at the theatre and the music halls, or to the primitive films which offered all the excitement of novelty. When Queen Victoria was mourned with all the pomp and ceremonious display at which the British excel, Peggy's uncle went off to buy her a suitable black hat before taking her to spend the day with friends whose windows would provide the best possible view of the procession.

Peggy's English Christmas, the first of the century, was to have been spent in Harrow with a Mr and Mrs Thatcher Clarke, friends of her parents, and their brood of noisily uncongenial sons. Henry, remembering that he had in August suggested she should spend it with him, issued a kindly summons and filled the Lamb House larder with all the delicacies Fortnum & Mason could offer to comfort a homesick teenager.

The visit was a great success. Peggy ate with relish and required little more entertainment than to be sat by the fire with her nose in *Redgauntlet*. 'She doesn't read her uncle; and perhaps it's as well,' Henry reported to Miss Allen in London. When the weather was tolerable, the two of them would set off on long windy walks with Nick, the lively little fox-terrier who had recently joined the household. 'Nothing much happened,' reported Peggy, whose epistolary style was plainer than Henry's. But 'it was very nice' and she was full of affection for the devoted uncle who treated her ideas and endeavours with such flattering gravity. Nobody, he wrote to assure her, had photographed him so successfully as she on her last visit, and nothing would please him more than that she should send him some more copies. 'I greatly miss you, dearest Peggot,' he wrote, 'and my small dashes down into High Street are solitary and sad . . . Give my love, my blessing to my three young music-hall friends; and recall me very kindly to their father and mother. I embrace you, dearest Peg, on both cheeks, and am your always-affectionate uncle . . .'[7]

A bookish and quiet young niece was a very easy guest to entertain; it was with mixed feelings that Henry prepared himself for another noisy family descent on Rye for the Easter of 1901. Struggling towards completion of the first part of *The Ambassadors*, one of his most elaborately plotted books, he longed for peace to get on with it, although William's habitually xenophobic diatribes provided him with some useful fodder for the secondary character of Waymark, a middle-aged New Englander convinced that all is rotten in the state of Europe.

Hospitality had to come first. He had not only William, Alice and Peggy on his hands, but Harry, his oldest nephew. William, still in indifferent health, was mostly occupied with work on the Gifford lectures he was to give at Edinburgh, but the other members of the family had to be entertained. Henry took them to see Brede, abandoned and ghostly since Crane's death the previous summer, and on long afternoon walks. 'That is to say when Nick allowed us to go,' Peggy wrote to her second brother, Billy, 'by not chasing sheep or chickens, and having to be brought home again. It is too funny for words sometimes when it happens and it nearly drives Uncle Henry to distraction and he yells in a terribly loud voice "Oh! oh! oh! oh! oh! you little brute! you little brute! you beast! oh! oh! oh!" Then he hurries home with the unfortunate wretch and leaves Mamma and me to follow on at our own sweet pace.'[8]

Alice, a handsome strong-faced woman who had become very fond of her effusive and ineffectual – from the domestic point of view – brother-in-law, made herself thoroughly at home. It was with her encouragement that Henry took the bold step of employing a female secretary; when Miss Weld arrived, Alice was ready to look her over and suggest suitable working clothes. A dark plain suit, she thought.

The Jameses departed to Edinburgh, which William liked well enough to compare it to Boston, and then to Europe, for Nauheim, Strasbourg, the Vosges and Paris, while Peggy remained at Rye, exploring the coast by a wonderfully blue summer sea and meeting her uncle's literary visitors; Edmund Gosse, her compatriot Wendell Homes, the Conrads, the Fords, Wells and, briefly, Gissing when he came over from Spade House to spend a night. Miss Muir Mackenzie, the Grand Governess, arrived from Winchelsea to offer ideas about the garden and Peggy was set to work helping Mr Gammon to dig over the borders and to transplant fuchsias and geraniums. She was, her uncle gratefully wrote, 'a most soothing and satisfactory maid' with whom he had enjoyed an 'idyllic intimacy and tranquillity'. Her English schooling ended that summer, and Henry found himself missing her almost as he might have done a daughter.

The next year brought a new family ambassador to Rye. Billy, William's second son, was just the sort of carefree, loquacious young man on whom Henry doted in later life. At the age of twenty, he was slim and pleasant-looking (his Emmett cousins thought him devastatingly handsome) with an endearing spontaneity and readiness to enjoy whatever turned up which won him an immediate and high place in his uncle's affections. Billy's only worry, that he would be thought shallow or boring, was soon dismissed; it was inconceivable, he wrote to his father, that Uncle Henry would ever become a bore to him! Reading that, one wonders what William had said about his brother.

A fortnight flew past. Billy, like his father before him, was an enthusiastic sketcher; Henry found a local artist to teach him how to use colour and, perhaps, to sow the seeds for Billy's later decision to study art rather than medicine. He flirted with the Emmett girls, invited over to provide him with youthful company. He went off to explore the marshes on a bicycle while Henry was dictating to Miss Weld. When Kipling came over to lunch in his spanking new £200 car, Billy helped to entertain him. The guest was charmed; a visit to his own home in the expensive but capricious 'Amelia' was promptly arranged.

The three most important things in life, Billy remembered his uncle telling him, were to be kind, and then to be kind, and then to be kind – an echo of Guy Domville's vale, 'Be kind to him. Be good to her. Be good to her,' which he was too young to recognize. He had known nothing but kindness in his uncle's house. When he left for Paris and then Geneva – the English visit was part of a year in Europe – a firm friendship had been established. Harry, William's eldest son, was appointed as his uncle's literary executor, but Billy and Peggy were his darlings who could do no wrong.

1903 was the year in which Henry began tentatively to plan a return to America and, as was his habit, to solicit William's advice. And as was also his habit, to wish that he had not. William, dreading the prospect of entertaining an anglicized Henry who, he felt sure, would grumble about everything, did his best to deter him. Modern America would only inspire him to 'physical loathing', he wrote; their eating habits would disgust him, their speech would appal him. Lecture-giving was the most dreadful ordeal – he should certainly give up that idea. The only way he could conceivably profit from a visit was by travelling 'far and wide, to the South, the Colorado, over the Canadian Pacific to that coast, possibly to the Hawaiian Islands'. But this was far too expensive to be contemplated. Really, it would be much better not to come. 'This is rather a throwing of cold water,' William added, 'but it is as well to realize both sides, and I think I can realize certain things for you better than the sanguine and hospitable Alice does.'[9] It was almost as crushing as the response to the letter about purchasing Lamb House and Henry was again stung into defending himself. He had not wanted advice. He had wanted – and again been denied – fraternal support.

William's dread was real. He himself had been airily dismissive of his brother's 'little bijou of a house and garden'; he was sure that Henry's revenge would be one of merciless disdain for his Chocorua home. Three days after his broadside at Rye, he wrote in an uncharacteristically defensive vein to Peggy. 'Poverty-stricken this New Hampshire country may be – weak, in a certain sense, shabby, thin, pathetic – say all that, yet, like "Jenny", it *kissed* me; and it is not *vulgar* – even H.J. can't accuse it of that – or of "stodginess", especially at this emaciated season.'[10] It was as though he could already hear his brother's gibes ringing in his ears.

William's fears were groundless. Henry came to Chocorua in the autumn of 1904 and was frankly charmed by its rural simplicity and peace. 'He seemed to enjoy nature here intensely,' William wrote afterwards, and 'found so much *sentiment* and feminine delicacy in it all. It is a pleasure to be with anyone who takes in things through the eyes. Most people don't.'[11] The enjoyment conveyed was sincere and profound. Five years later, Henry was still remembering the enchantment to which he had succumbed and regretting the brevity of his stay in one of his most loving letters to William (one for which, sadly, Professor Edel found no room in his edition of the letters). 'The very smell and sentiment of summer's end there,' he wrote, 'and of Alice's beautiful "rustic" hospitality of overflowing milk and honey, to say nothing of squash pie and ice-cream in heroic proportions, all mingle for me with the assault of forest and lake and of those delicious orchardy, yet rocky vaguenesses and Arcadian "nowheres", which are the note of what is sweetest and most attaching in the dear old American, or particularly New England, scenery. It comes back to me with such a magnificent beckoning looseness – in relieving contrast to the consummate tightness (a part, too, oddly, of the very wealth of effect) *du pays d'ici*.'[12]

To Henry, evidently, the American visit signified a renewal of emotional family ties. In his private notebook, he recorded that one of his happiest experiences that year had been an evening walk with William through the shady suburbs of Cambridge and of how everything had seemed to gain in 'life and light' when touched by 'his extraordinary play of mind'. He was ready again to be charmed and beguiled. But simply by making the journey to America, he had opened a new vein of rivalry. He had shown his ailing brother that he was not too old or staid to go adventuring. He had, it was true, been quite happy to sink back into the comforts offered at the Whartons' luxurious home, but he had also been unexpectedly intrepid in his ventures into the unknown terrain of St Louis, Chicago and Los Angeles. He was in California when William, announcing that he had always wanted to see Greece, went. The unconscious urge, one can't help but feel, was to show that anything Henry could do, his elder brother could do better. Ignoring the fact that he had a serious heart condition, he visited Naples, Capri, Sorrento and Amalfi, travelled extensively among the Greek islands, addressed a congress in Rome (in French), set off again for a second tour through Italy and then France before returning to Boston in time to confound Henry with his exploits.

There is another indication that William's attitude to his brother was not one of unmixed affection at this time. Greeting him on his return home was the news that he had been elected a member of the newly formed Academy of Arts and Letters, to which Henry had been elected three months previously. Both brothers were members of the Institute of which the Academy was an offshoot, but the Academy was a much smaller body in which, William felt, two Jameses would be one too many. 1905 was a year in which he was endeavouring to disencumber himself of the onus of honorary positions, but the oddity of the refusal which he despatched on June 17, 1905, while Henry was still in America, was in the language. 'I am the more encouraged to this course,' he wrote, 'by the fact that my younger and shallower and vainer brother is already in the Academy . . .' William's notorious fondness for stinging raillery cannot be used to explain away the sharpness of this attack. The letters provide no clue to its cause, unless we turn back to the year 1900 when William had been feeling ill enough to send Henry an account of his 'fever and bleeding' which had broken out shortly after his arrival in Bad-Nauheim. Henry's disconcerting response to this was a letter telling William how wonderful he felt – and looked – after shaving off his beard. 'It had suddenly begun these three months since, to come out quite white and made me *feel* as well as look, so old. Now I feel *forty* and clean and light . . .'[13] This was to take frivolity to the point of callousness and to merit entirely the accusation of being vain and shallow. It is not impossible that this bit of ill-timed self-preening lodged itself in William's mind and that, in a period of his life when illness and depression were his familiar demons, it rankled more deeply than he could openly acknowledge.

The American visit did not herald a new period of sweetness and light.

William had always been an outspoken critic of his brother's work.

He entreated him from the earliest days to use a simple and lucid vocabulary. (To say a thing once, clearly, and then drop it for good was William's own aim and often his achievement in prose.) He warned Henry against affectations after reading his French travel-pieces: 'It will be a good thing for you to resolve never to use the word "supreme", and to take great care not to use "delicate" in the French sense of a "cultured and fastidious" person.'[14] He deplored the thinness and emptiness of *The Europeans*, although *Daisy Miller* pleased him. He had seen the 'bright, short, sparkling thing of a hundred pages' which should have been *The Bostonians* instead of five hundred pages of 'descriptions and psychologic commentaries . . . charmingly done for those who have the leisure and the peculiar mood to enjoy that amount of miniature work . . .'[15] With *The Reverberator* and *The Tragic Muse*, William had felt more at home; the first, one of the lightest works, was judged to be 'masterly and exquisite . . . simply delicious', while the second was 'a most original, wonderful, delightful and admirable production . . . although the final winding up is, as is usual with you, rather a losing of the story in the sand . . .'[16] To this loftily corrective form of literary criticism, Henry responded with what an occasionally penitent William saw as 'angelic humility' while quietly defending his literary intentions.

What William wanted, and had found in Wells's work, was direct-ness of style. He had never ceased the struggle to impress the import-ance of this on his brother. When he detected a move in the direction of greater simplicity and clarity, he went out of his way to applaud it. Confronted with the veiled obscurity of Henry's later work and with the evidence that his advice had been discounted, he was puzzled and annoyed.

William was not alone. Arthur Benson, one of the coterie of clever, literary-minded younger men whose company the ageing novelist relished, found himself incapable of sharing the enthusiasm of Percy Lubbock and Howard Sturgis for the later novels. 'H and P both maintain that his books give them a deep sense of mental power and spoil them for other books,' he wrote in his diary for 1905. 'I am baffled. I suppose I am not subtle in mind. I hate H.J.'s obscurity and finesse of thought – I hate his involved style. I feel I am near beautiful things and cannot see them. I am in a mist, and I don't think that a mist which conceals beautiful things is better than a mist which conceals ugly things. It is the mist I see.'[17] The difference – an important one – was that Benson kept his reservations for the privacy of his diaries while William addressed them to Henry with a bluntness which bordered on cruelty. To *The Wings of the Dove*, he had merely responded that it was a very 'rum' way of writing but that '"in its way" the book is most beautiful'. This, from William, was praise. But as Henry showed every sign of continuing in this new 'rum' way of writing, William grew harsher. He had, some years before, conceded that he and Henry were too different to be good judges of each other's work. Now, forgetful of that sensible concession, he launched a full-scale attack in the attempt to bring Henry back from his 'method of narration by interminable elaboration of suggestive reference' to the world of simple story-tellers.

He embarked on *The Golden Bowl* in the autumn of 1905, shortly after Henry's departure. Reading it, he was bewildered, and then irritated, while ready to admit that it was, after a fashion, successful. 'But why won't you, just to please Brother, sit down and write a new book,' he pleaded, 'with no twilight or mustiness in the plot, with great vigor and decisiveness in the action, no fencing in the dialogue, no psychological commentaries, and absolute straightness in the style. Publish it in my name, I will acknowledge it, and give you half the proceeds. Seriously, I wish you *would*, for you *can*; and I should think it would tempt you, to embark on a "fourth manner". You of course know these feelings of mine without my writing them down, but I'm "nothing if not" outspoken.'[18]

Henry was prepared to put up with an astonishing amount of criticism from his brother, but this was more than even he was prepared to receive with a show of humble gratitude. William's literary tastes were, in his view, atrocious, and he was angry enough to say so. His response was as blunt as William's. The gloves, for once, were off.

> I mean (in response to what you write me of your having read the *Golden B.*) to try to produce some uncanny form of thing, in fiction, that will gratify you, as Brother – but let me say, dear William, that I shall be greatly humiliated if you *do* like it, and thereby lump it, in your affection, with things, of the current age, that I have heard you express admiration for and that I would sooner descend to a dishonoured grave than have written . . . I'm always sorry when I hear of your reading anything of mine, and always hope you won't – you seem to me so constitutionally unable to 'enjoy' it, and so condemned to look at it from a point of view remotely alien to mine in writing it, and to the conditions out of which, *as* mine, it has inevitably sprung . . .

And yet, he added bitterly, 'I can read you with rapture . . . Philosophically, in short, I am "with" you, almost completely, and you ought to take account of this and get me over altogether.'[19]

The hint was clear enough, but William failed to take it. A dishonour to write anything which would please him? 'Well! only write *for* me, and leave the question of pleasing open! I have to admit that in "The Golden Bowl" and "The Wings of the Dove", you have succeeded *in getting there* after a fashion, in spite of the perversity of the method and its *longness*, which I am not the only one to deplore.'[20]

Any irritation which Henry may have felt at this persistent and uncalled for needling was forgotten two months later. Billy was again visiting him at Lamb House when news came of a catastrophic earthquake in San Francisco where William had just delivered the finest lecture he ever gave on 'The Moral Equivalent of War'. His brother and son were appalled; frantic cables were sent, begging for reassurance. Work was out of the question; neither of them could sleep for worrying as the days passed and no message came to tell them whether William and Alice were alive or dead. The earthquake occurred on April 18, 1906; not until two weeks later did William write to say that they had escaped unharmed. He hadn't, he said airily, 'reckoned on this extremity of anxiety on your part . . . and so never thought of cabling you direct'. The tone of the letter suggested that he found Henry's concern absurd. How could he, he asked, have foreseen 'the thought of our mangled forms, hollow eyes, starving bodies, minds insane with fear, haunting you so . . .? In general, you may be sure that when any disaster befalls our country it will be *you* only who are wringing of [sic] hands, and we who are smiling "with interest or laughing with gleeful excitement."'[21] It was almost a rebuke.

William read *The American Scene* the following year. He could neglect to send news of his welfare; he could never resist an opportunity to express his dislike of Henry's defiant obscurity and to beg him to abandon it in favour of plain, clear prose. He could not accept what by now would have been glaringly apparent to a less stubborn man, that his criticisms, however hurtful, were not being, never had been, heeded. The temptation to register a last protest was too strong. Determination inspired him to new eloquence on a familiar theme; the letter became a favourite source of quotation for anti-Jacobites.

The whole purpose of Henry's writing method, as William now saw it, was to promote bafflement, to avoid anything so vulgar as the statement of a fact, 'but by dint of breathing and sighing all round and round it, to arouse in the reader who may have had a similar perception already (Heaven help him if he hasn't!) the illusion of a solid object, made . . . wholly out of impalpable materials, air, and the prismatic interferences of light, ingeniously focused by mirrors upon empty space.' It was an illusionist's trick, by which the 'little initial perception' was made to seem vastly bigger and more substantial by being 'swathed in this gigantic envelopment of suggestive atmosphere'. Couldn't Henry understand that nineteen out of every twenty readers were being driven mad? '"Say it *out*, for God's sake, they cry,"' William went on, '"and have done with it." And so I say now, give us *one* thing in your older directer manner . . . Give us that interlude; and then continue like the "curiosity of literature" which you have become. For gleams and innuendoes and felicitous verbal insinuations you are unapproachable, but the *core* of literature is solid. Give it to us *once* again! The bare perfume of things will not support existence, and the effect of solidity you reach is but perfume and simulacrum.' From the general, he turned to the particular, to give reports of the readers who had found *The American Scene* 'totally incomprehensible', and to explain how much better it would have been if he had provided a fuller contrasting portrait of Europe. Finally, to cap it all, to Henry who had unstintingly praised his brother's books, he prophesied that 'even' he might enjoy his study of pragmatism, as though he, too, had been a martyr to fraternal criticism![22]

Poor sales seemed to confirm William's report that most of his friends had found *The American Scene* impossible to read; there were pundits and readers in plenty to declare that Henry James's style would, as one correspondent of *The Times* put it, 'drive a grammarian mad'. It did not lessen the pain caused by William's dreadful frankness. The normally discreet Henry read the letter aloud to Morton Fullerton, one of his closest friends and one of the few to have written in praise of the book; to his nephew, Billy, he simply observed that William's letter had been 'admirable . . . a series of very interesting restrictions, reserves and happy *damnations*, or almost, in respect to my American book' which he would prefer him not to see.[23] The only record we have of his response to William is an unusually cryptic note dated 31 May, 1907: 'You shall have, after a little more patience, a reply to your so rich and luminous reflections on my book – a reply almost as interesting as, and far more illuminating than, your letter itself.' But the promised letter, if ever written, was lost or destroyed.

The hurt was felt, but no grudge was born. When, two years later, Henry read *The Meaning of Truth*, he was quick and generous with his praises. The contrast to William's didactic attitude to his own work is striking. 'I find it,' he wrote, 'of thrilling interest, triumphant and brilliant, and am lost in admiration of your wealth and power. I palpitate as you make out your case (since it seems to me you so utterly do,) as I under no romantic spell ever palpitate now; and into that case I enter intensely, unreservedly, and think you would allow almost intelligently . . . Clearly you are winning a great battle and great will be your fame.'[24]

Illness had sealed an unwelcome but lasting bond between the brothers. It was more than forty years since William had fallen victim to 'that delightful disease in my back, which has so long made Harry so interesting'. Both had had more than their share of nervous depression of the kind which raises phantoms of fear and makes the most trivial work seem an intolerable burden. Both, to their credit, had used work as a sword to fight off the demons of despair.

A bad heart had diminished and constricted the freedom which William joyfully anticipated would be his after resigning his Harvard professorship in 1907; Freud, meeting him in 1909, was immensely struck by the cheerful courage he showed in dealing with the angina attacks which had by then become cruelly frequent. 'I have always wished that I might be as fearless as he was in the face of approaching death,' he wrote in *An Autobiographical Study*.

As a young man, William had studied medicine; throughout his life, he had taken a keen interest in following its scientific progress. He was too well-informed to suffer any delusions about the seriousness of his condition; he was too much of a workaholic to allow illness to interrupt his work plans. Visits to Europe were still undertaken and new friendships in England were consolidated with, among others, the Bertrand Russells and Lady Ottoline Morrell who found him 'intensely lovable, simple and human, with immense sensitive kindness and understanding of life and other human beings' when he and Alice stayed with her at Newington in the pre-Garsington days. At the same time, William was writing hard, to produce the lectures which became *A Pluralistic Universe* and *The Meaning of Truth* as well as the more ambitious but modestly titled *Some Problems of Philosophy* which was published after his death.

William was at work on this his last book in the New Year of 1910 when alarming news came from England of Henry. He had been in uncertain health for some time. In the winter of the previous year, convinced that he, too, was suffering from angina, he had taken advice and been examined by Sir James Mackenzie, a celebrated heart specialist. Mackenzie had found no evidence of a heart condition and had suggested that the real problem was psychological. Apprehension of illness had produced a condition which, when combined with obesity and an unbalanced diet, had the appearance of a cardiac problem. A change of regime had produced an improvement, but now there had been another and more serious collapse.

Miss Bosanquet's account was the first to arrive. It was followed by a letter from Henry, explaining that he had not wanted to alarm them but had waited 'till I could write you *firmly* and emphatically that I am on my way to real valour, or at least, validity, again'.[25]

The shakiness of his writing – he was still in bed, writing his letters with a pencil – offered a sad contradiction to the heroic declaration. Reading of sudden weight loss, black depression and fatigue, William and Alice decided to despatch Harry, the most practical of the family, to see what could be done and to advise whether they themselves should come to the rescue.

Harry arrived at Lamb House on 27 February, and rapidly took charge of the situation. Dr Skinner – the same Dr Skinner who had been so rashly optimistic in his diagnosis of Stephen Crane's last illness – had been kindness itself to his uncle, even taking him out on his rounds so that he could enjoy the country air (an act of questionable prudence in a wretched winter), but he was a country practitioner, not an expert on nervous diseases. Harry, anxiously observing the invalid's daily swings from elation to sobbing despair, was not convinced by Henry's own belief that it resulted from a digestive disorder brought on by his passion for Fletcherizing.* Taking Dr Skinner with them, Harry carried his uncle off to London to be examined by Sir William Osler. Osler's diagnoses confirmed Mackenzie's of the year before. There was no physical disorder: on the contrary, Henry was unusually fit and strong for a man in his late sixties. He had nothing to fear.

The comfort Henry drew from this report was short-lived; the illness he was suffering from was a mental one and it was to last until late in the summer.

Many causes have been given for Henry's breakdown and it is likely that it was brought on by several factors, to which long periods of solitude and an excessively rigorous diet undoubtedly contributed. His age had been painfully highlighted by his new and intensely passionate relationship with young Hugh Walpole, then at the beginning of his rise to successful mediocrity. Hugh was all cockiness and ambition. He was young, full of vitality and unusually handsome; he had no doubt whatsoever that he was going to be a celebrity and a great writer. His confidence may have amused Henry. It may also have made him reflect more painfully than usual on his vanished youth and, at twice Walpole's age, his own lack of public recognition. His greatest works had been written; he had gone to extraordinary lengths to revise them to his own standards of perfection for the monumental New York Edition of twenty-three volumes. We can only guess at what dreams he had; we know that Sir Edmund Gosse was not the only one of his friends who judged the revised edition

---

* Henry had, since 1904, been following the faddish diet of Dr Horace Fletcher, which required all food to be reduced to liquid by chewing before it was swallowed.

to be execrable. Sales had been slow and small; the venture on which he had spent four years of his life could only be seen as a failure. Further attempts to break into the charmed circle of the theatre had, while producing no such débâcles as the first night of *Guy Domville*, been depressingly ineffectual. He may also – although this is pure conjecture – have begun to grieve over the loss of the mass of private papers which he had impulsively destroyed in the previous year. But it was, above all, the terrible sense of failure represented by the unsaleability of the New York Edition which haunted him and preyed on his mind and which, sadly, had now reduced him to a sobbing and hysterical invalid, dolefully recording a state of continuing misery in his pocket diaries. Edith Wharton, visiting him at Lamb House in March, was horrified by the change in his appearance and manner and by the tearful entreaties that she should not go away and leave him. Writing to their mutual friend, Morton Fullerton, on 19 March, 1910, she described how, 'for a terrible hour', she had been forced to look into 'the black depths over which he is hanging – the superimposed abysses of all his fiction'.

> I, who have always seen him so serene, so completely the master of his wonderful emotional instrument – who thought of him when I described the man in 'The Legend'* as so sensitive to human contacts & yet so *secure* from them; I could hardly believe it was the same James who cried out to me his fear, his despair, his craving for the 'cessation of consciousness', & all his unspeakable loneliness & need of comfort, & inability to be comforted!

Out of the invalid's hearing, she talked quietly with Harry James about the importance of seeing that his uncle was treated by a neurologist rather than a specialist like Osler, and of providing him with the constant companionship he craved until William James arrived.

William's own ill-health had already turned his thoughts towards another visit to Bad-Nauheim. The pathos of Henry's letters now determined him to accelerate his departure and to stay with Alice at Lamb House until Henry should feel more able to cope with his morbid horror of solitude. 'Letter from H.J. very pathetic – decides me to go over immediately,' he noted on 13 March.

The Jameses arrived at Liverpool on 6 April after an easy crossing and travelled from London to Rye the next day, to be greeted with tears of joy by the bedridden Henry. He was, as is apparent from his

---

* In 'The Legend' Edith Wharton had told the story of a man who suffers from profound depression because of the scant attention given to his writings.

daily pocket-book notes, in no state of mind to take in the gravity of William's condition; his own sickness blinded him to it and William, who talked lightly of getting his heart 'tuned up' again, chose to ignore it. Instead, with great good sense, he persuaded Henry to stop feeling guilty about his loss of appetite and to eat only when he felt like it. 'Better day and enormous relief from cessation of *disciplinary* food and beginning of free attitude,' Henry gratefully noted on 17 April. Two days later, he was well enough to go out in the car, but the next week brought a relapse. 'Bad nervous day,' he noted, '– very bad, after bad night. W. and A. alone in car to Pennsey. Sad day – bad day.'

The beginning of May heralded what seemed to be a real improvement and a relieved William decided to set off for Bad-Nauheim, alone, since Henry's need for company was still being plaintively expressed.* His need, if not the greater, was the more loudly proclaimed, so Alice, sick with worry about William, stayed behind to be 'an unspeakable blessing' to her brother-in-law. Happily, Henry's dislike of Germany was rapidly overtaken by his loathing of 'flat and stale and illness-haunted Rye'. Assured of companionship, he was prepared to leave home. On 6 June they departed for Calais, arriving at Bad-Nauheim four days later.

A month later, Alice would be ready to remember the patience and consideration which 'these two good men' had shown, but the venture was not a success and neither patience nor consideration had been apparent at the time. William, tormented with pain, was irritable; Henry, clinging to company because he could not bear his own, was fretful and morose. Alice, the nurse and peacemaker, was put under an intolerable strain. 'A difficult day. Every word I spoke proved the wrong one,' she noted two days after their arrival. A few days later, she wistfully recorded that William had been 'very *kind as of old*'. 'William cannot walk and Henry cannot smile' was perhaps the saddest entry. Henry, now determined to retain their company at all costs, told Mrs Wharton that he had decided to accompany them to America for the winter. 'I must break with everything – utterly – of the last couple of years in England,' he wrote. 'I feel that the completeness of the change là-bas will help me more than anything else can . . .'[26]

Professor Edel dates Henry's recovery from 21 July, when he recorded having woken up 'in great relief', but the pocket diary

* An act of typical selfishness on William's part, in the view of Edith Wharton, who did not like him and was ready to see both Henry and his nephew as the victims of the 'neurotic, unreliable . . . other brother – William o' the wisp James.' She spoke, of course, in ignorance of the seriousness of William James's own condition.

suggests that the change of scenery had already worked the improvement. They arrived in London on 12 July and only one more 'bad day' was entered in the book. William, on the other hand, had deteriorated. The doctors at Bad-Nauheim had been unable to pretend that they thought the baths had done him any good and he himself was feeling weaker every day. Released from the introspectiveness of his own ailment, Henry was suddenly alive to the gravity of his brother's illness. 'William sadly down and weak' (20 July). 'Poor – very bad, days and nights for William. Alice, as always, wonderful and heroic' (24 July). Mackenzie was called in to do what he could and poor Alice took hope from his reassuring comments. Back at Lamb House again, Dr Skinner called daily, without charge, and was full of encouragement. 'Papa is really better,' Alice wrote to Harry. 'Skinner says his heart is *much* better. So we have a right to expect an improvement now all along the line.' William himself was less sanguine. All he wanted now was to achieve the journey home and to get back to the peace of his beloved Chocorua.

The reversal since the Jameses' arrival in England in April had been tragically extreme. William was now almost bedridden, capable of only the mildest forms of exertion, while Henry, although he described himself as still being in a '*struggling* upward state', had made an extraordinary recovery of health and spirits. In London, he had felt well enough to entertain his young favourites, Hugh Walpole and Jocelyn Persse; at Lamb House, the urge to socialize began to work again. Hearing that Edith Wharton was coming to England, he sent off an eager account of his availability, and wishes. 'I think I should be able to get in the course of the [of next] week a couple of nights in town and could come out to a tea or lunch, or even dinner with Howard [Sturgis] – especially if *She*★ should be with you and open her arms and wings to, and for, me. I might manage it for Tuesday or Wednesday – or for Wednesday and Thursday – especially [again] if you should motor over from Folkestone and pick me *up* here and take me. Don't fail of this.'[27] Two days later, he wrote to Sturgis, presenting their visit as one of Edith's impetuous plans in which he was only 'a limp field-flower' about to be plucked from Rye and 'hurled on your hospitality'. Henry was himself again.

Edith Wharton was on her way to France; Henry saw her off on the Folkestone boat on 9 August before returning to Lamb House to make his last-minute preparations for the American voyage. Two days later, he, Alice and William left Liverpool with Burgess the

★ Mrs Wharton's car.

house-boy and valet, on the *Empress of Britain*, a Canadian steamship. The crossing to Quebec was miraculously serene – 'no flaw or cloud on it but William's aggravated weakness and suffering,' Henry noted, 'to see which and not be able to help or relieve is anguish unutterable; now more and more.'[28] Even an attempt to walk along the deck was too much now for William's fragile strength; he was confined to his bed or the wicker chair which Alice had purchased for him for the rest of the journey.

Everything about their arrival seemed cruelly designed to worsen William's condition. The weather was savage and they were obliged to walk for a considerable distance before spending a miserable night at the Frontenac Hotel (Alice thought it 'horrid' and Henry 'horrible and vulgar') and rising at four in the morning in order to catch the train. William, suffering acutely now, was sick at the station. The officials at the Customs House seemed dedicated to the art of delay. The train journey was uncomfortable and interminably slow. Billy was there to meet them at Intervale and drive them the last two-hour lap to Chocorua, but the damage had already been done. Billy, whose expectations had been based on his mother's last cheerful letter from England, was appalled.

A doctor was called in, and milk was prescribed every half-hour to activate the digestive system while the morphia which William now craved to kill the pain was at first withheld. 'Cruel *cruel*,' he whispered to Alice, who dared do nothing without the doctor's approval. The weather was glorious, but the house was darkened by the evidence of William's sufferings and the impossibility of alleviating them. A Boston heart specialist arrived to offer promises of a good recovery, but neither Alice nor Henry could share his optimism. Writing to Grace Norton, one of the oldest remaining friends of the James family, Henry confessed that his own fears were 'of the blackest' and that he was in a state of abject terror at the prospect of losing 'my wonderful beloved brother out of the world in which, from as far back as in dimmest childhood, I have so yearningly always counted on him'.[29] As a brother, he was desolate and afraid; as a creator, he raged at the arrest of a brilliant mind. 'His noble intellectual vitality was still but at its climax – he had two or three ardent purposes and plans,' he wrote to another friend.

They were not to be realized. Alice was cradling William's head as he slipped from a drugged sleep into death just before daybreak on 27 August. Death, the ultimate cosmetician, smoothed away all signs of suffering. 'Wonderful beauty of the dear face!' Alice wrote two days later when Billy had photographed it for the plaster mask he wanted to make. The autopsy was carried out, showing an acute enlargement of the heart. 'He had worn himself out,' Alice noted. 'They have laid him in the coffin and I can see him no more.' William James was given his funeral service in the Appleton Chapel at Harvard Yard in the presence of his family and former colleagues before being cremated at Mount Auburn Cemetery. Professor Edel declares his ashes to have been buried in the family plot at Cambridge, but William James's biographer, Gay Wilson Allen, holds that they were taken home to be scattered over the philosopher's favourite river at Chocorua.

Years before, visiting Henry in London, William had been struck by what he called his 'powerlessness' in all respects but his dedication to his work. The perception was correct, but it extended only to the times when the brothers were together. In William's company, Henry reverted to the passive role which had been his childhood defence against the older boy's more exuberant nature. The mask had become so much a part of him that he was hardly aware of putting it on; deprived of the need for it by William's death and the authority which it bestowed on him as the oldest male of the family, he felt doubly bereft. 'I sit heavily stricken and in darkness,' he wrote to Thomas Perry, who had known both brothers since their early schooldays, 'for from far back in dimmest childhood he had been my ideal Elder Brother, and I still, through all the years, saw in him, even as a small timorous boy yet, my protector, my backer, my authority and my pride. His extinction changes the face of life for me – besides the mere missing of his inexhaustible company and personality, originality, the whole unspeakably vivid and beautiful presence of him.'[30] His happiest days with William had been during their brief autumn together at Chocorua; the memory of them was very close as he sat answering the letters of condolence in the painfully quiet house. 'I feel abandoned and afraid,' he confessed to H. G. Wells, 'even as a lost child.'

With William gone, he could be a child, or feel a child, no more. Alice had sustained him when he needed her; now, in her grief, she turned to him for support.

The specific support required was in providing an additional link to the spirit world. William had been an enthusiastic dabbler in and spokesman for psychical research. In 1892, he had infuriated his dying sister Alice by discussing her symptoms with a Boston medium whose spirit messages he had eagerly relayed. 'It is taken for granted apparently that I shall be spiritualized into a "district messenger",' Alice acidly commented in her diary after hearing the tidings she was expected to convey to her parents in Summerland, as the spirit world was then called. Her greatest dread was that William's favourite medium, 'the dreadful Mrs Piper', would be asked to raise her own spirit after her death; she asked only that her 'defenceless soul' might be left in peace. That wish had been granted, but William and his wife remained firm believers in the ability of mediums to establish contact with the dead. Before his death, William had told Alice that he would be continuing his research into the subject when he reached Summerland and that she should hold séances through which he could communicate his new findings. Henry, as his brother, would be an invaluable contributor to these sessions.

Henry was as little enamoured of the spirit world as his sister had been but, to comfort Alice, he agreed. They spent September together at Irving Street, the handsome house in Cambridge which had been built twenty years previously to contain William's expanding family. Young Somerset Maugham called on them there and was intrigued to hear of the efforts which were being made to summon William's spirit. He had, it seemed, made no discoveries for his spirit refused to be conjured into speech, but Henry was given cause to speculate on the whole business of an afterlife.* In his essay, *Is There a Life after Death?* written that year, he expressed his own conviction that there was none. Immortality was, he thought, dependent on what man made through his creative endeavours. If William was to have an afterlife, it would be through his works, not through the jabbering tongues of mediums.

Henry made his own contribution to the earthly immortalizing of William.

Back in England after spending a full year in America, he surrendered to the pull of London where he had wisely retained a permanent pied-à-terre, his room at the Reform. The resourceful Miss Bosanquet, whose sex prohibited her from working for him on the club's premises, found him two very satisfactory rooms backing onto her Chelsea flat, and to these James came each day to dictate the first part of his autobiography, *A Small Boy and Others*. (Billy, who had just married yet another Alice, was presented with Lamb House as a honeymoon home of which he would be a trusted caretaker in its owner's absence.)

A Small Boy and Others and its sequels, *Notes of a Son and Brother* and the unfinished *The Middle Years* were conceived, as was the case

---

* Messages were received, later, but of a nature so trivial and platitudinous that even the credulous Alice could hardly have believed in them. Henry, who was sent a transcript, found them disgusting, 'the hollowest, vulgarest and basest rubbish'.

with so many of the novelist's works, on quite a modest scale, from which, inexorably, they burgeoned and swelled. The family had wanted him only to publish some of William's early letters with a brief memoir. But, as Miss Bosanquet later noted, 'An entire volume of memoirs was finished before bringing William to an age for writing letters.' To remember was to be drawn back, and Henry, whose memory was prodigious, had forgotten almost nothing. Strong in the sense that he was the last of the Jameses who could recall and evoke that remarkable family, he broadened his theme and defended his need to do so. 'We were,' he began, 'to my sense, that blest group of us, such a company of characters and such a picture of differences, and withal so fused and united and interlocked, that each of us, to that fond fancy, pleads for preservation, and that in respect to what I speak of myself as possessing I think that I shall be ashamed, as with a cold impiety, to find any element altogether negligible.'[31] It was impossible, in short, to extract William from the family portrait which presented itself. The tributes to William which Alice quite forgivably craved to see in print were given, and generously, but not in the expected form. The husband she saw through Henry's eyes was not the great philosopher and humanist but the gregarious, witty, overbearing boy against whom the younger brother had wistfully measured himself – and found himself wanting. Here, she and everybody else could learn of the struggle it had taken Henry to break himself of the humble habit of believing that William, who always claimed to know best, was necessarily always right.

William, in one of his most forthright letters (quoted here on page 118) had proposed that Henry should give up his obscurities and learn to write in his brother's style, in return for which, he jokingly added, he would be ready to lend his name as the new book's author. The clear implication was that his style was greatly superior to Henry's. Now, after his death, Henry was ready to return the insult. He had been given William's letters on the understanding that he would present them as they stood. Instead, he revised them almost out of recognition, reshaping them to his own more mannered style. When the family protested that this was not at all what they had wanted or asked for, Henry was ready with his defence. It would have been no kindness to his brother to publish, untouched, 'those rough and rather illiterate copies I had from you . . .' He needed no séances to hear William pleading with him to improve their ragged style. For himself, he could not doubt that William would have wished his letters to be converted into a form 'more engagingly readable and thereby more tasted and liked'.[32]

The autobiographical books had begun as a labour of love. Hidden away in them, in this rewriting of William's prose, is a quiet revenge on the brother who had rashly suggested that in literature as in every other field, his was the greater talent from which Henry might benefit by imitation. It was left to the excellent Harry to edit his father's letters and present his life in the tenderly respectful form to which Henry had refused to descend.

5

THE COLLABORATORS:
FORD AND CONRAD

Art lives upon discussion, upon experiment, upon curiosity, upon variety of attempt, upon the exchange of views and the comparison of standpoints . . .

Henry James,
The Art of Fiction, 1884

We would write for whole days, for half nights, for half the day, or all the night. We would jot down passages on scraps of paper or on the margins of books, handing them one to the other or exchanging them . . . if I know anything of how to write almost the whole of that knowledge was acquired then. It was acquired at the cost of an infinite mental patience, for digging out words in the same room with Conrad was exhausting. On the other hand, the pleasure derived from his society was inexhaustible; his love, his passion for his art did not, I believe, exceed mine, but his power of expressing that passion was delicious, winning, sweet, incredible.

Ford Madox Ford,
Return to Yesterday

These interrupted relations must be taken up again. The cause of my silence is as usual the worry about stuff that won't get itself written. *Vous connaissez cela.*

I miss collaboration in a most ridiculous manner. I hope you don't intend dropping me altogether.

Conrad to Ford, 1902

1857   Jozef Teodor Konrad Korzeniowski born in the Ukraine.

1873   Ford Hermann Hueffer, born in Surrey, England.

1886   Conrad Korzeniowski becomes a British subject and continues working as a seaman (1878–1894).

1894   Ford elopes with Elsie Martindale and goes to live in Bonnington.

1895   Conrad publishes *Almayer's Folly* and takes the anglicized name for his own.

1896   Ford publishes *Ford Madox Brown*.
          Conrad publishes *An Outcast of the Islands* and marries Jessie George.

1897   Conrad publishes *The Nigger of the 'Narcissus'*.

1898   Conrad and Ford meet. Conrad moves to Pent Farm and collaboration begins.

1900   Conrad publishes *Lord Jim*.

1901   Conrad and Ford publish *The Inheritors – An Extravagant Story*.

1902/3 Conrad publishes *Youth and Two Other Stories*, and *Typhoon and Other Stories*.

1903   Conrad and Ford publish *Romance*.

1904   Conrad publishes *Nostromo*.

1905   Conrad publishes *The Mirror of the Sea – Memories and Impressions*.

1907   Conrad publishes *The Secret Agent* and leaves Pent Farm.

1908   Ford involved with Violet Hunt and with editing the *English Review*.

1909   Ford rents rooms for the Conrads in Aldington, near his own home.

1910   Conrads move to Capel House.

THE COLLABORATORS:

FORD AND CONRAD

Ford Madox Ford* died in a Deauville hospital in 1939. Time has not dealt generously with him. He is known to most of us only as a sentimental fantasist who produced two remarkable works, *The Good Soldier* and *Parade's End*. Even on these opinion is sharply divided. Graham Greene has done the former the paradoxical disservice of overpraise; Anthony Powell is among those who have dismissed it as thin and imitative. *Last Post*, the fourth book of *Parade's End*, has displeased many readers, among them Ford himself who, in 1930, requested it to be omitted from a projected one-volume reprint on the grounds that he had never liked it. But Ford, like Conrad, was notoriously volatile in judging his own work; in 1926, he had taken an exuberantly affirmative view of the book.

There's no disputing that Ford was an incorrigible romancer whose faith in his own stories was seldom shared by his listeners or by the readers of his imaginative reminiscences. Nor is there anything to be gained by arguing against his womanizing reputation. To Ford, as to many of his fictional surrogates, loneliness and fear were the mainsprings of passion; he depended on women to solace and reassure him, and an astonishing number were ready to do so. The combination of a brilliant mind with an appearance of helpless vulnerability was, it seems, devastating in its effect. It's true, too, that Ford overwrote – of his eighty-one books, only a dozen deserve to be kept in print. But a dozen would be enough to rebuild his flagging

---

* Here and elsewhere in this book, I have used for Ford the name which he adopted in 1919. His German father began the process of anglicizing the family by changing his name from Hüffer to Hueffer when he became an English resident. Ford Hermann Hueffer, the name under which Ford lived in Kent and Sussex from 1894 to 1910, is here preserved in quotations from correspondence.

Konrad Korzeniowski had already adopted the name of Joseph Conrad when he arrived in the area in 1898, and used his Polish patronym only for family letters. The obvious convenience of substituting a given name for a surname may have appealed to, and have subsequently been borrowed by, Ford.

reputation, among them a selection of his poems, his magnificent Tudor trilogy, *The Fifth Queen*, written at a time when most historical fiction was quite as trashy – if not as indelicate – as the sixties 'bodice rippers', his enchanting portrait of the Kent and Sussex coast, *The Cinque Ports*, and the autobiographical books, *Return to Yesterday, Ancient Lights, It was the Nightingale* and *Portraits from Life*. And, flawed though it is, I would add *Provence*, a blatantly personal travel book in which Ford returned to his favourite image of himself as the simple country squire, man of the soil. ('I am a Small Holder again. I am at home again beside my plot of ground.') The 'plot' at the time of writing was a mustard-and-cress pot on a New York windowsill, but such niceties of truth rarely troubled Ford.

In the modernist movement of literature, for which James had broken down the barriers and prepared the way, Ford is grudgingly acknowledged to have played a part. It was a significant and influential one. As the editor of the *English Review* and the *transatlantic review*, he consistently distinguished himself by his unerring flair for attracting and encouraging the brightest and the best of young novelists and poets, including D. H. Lawrence, Ezra Pound, Ernest Hemingway, James Joyce and Wyndham Lewis. He also, sadly, distinguished himself as a most incompetent businessman – both magazines had to be rescued from the trough of Ford's financial miscalculations – and as a figure of fun to the writers whose talents he husbanded. At the best he seemed to them a pinkly wheezing walrus, obese and adenoidal; at the worst, he resembled a literary Falstaff, verbosely boastful, bulging with fantastic stories to which they were expected to listen with respectful admiration. The young are notoriously callous. Hemingway was not the only protégé who pilloried Ford as an absurd charlatan and posturer, but the publication of *A Moveable Feast* made him the most famous of his indictors. Only Pound was loyal.

Flawed by an excess of sentiment and self-indulgence though much of Ford's writing is, the best of his work as exemplified in *The Good Soldier* brings together matchless technique and a profound understanding of the social revolution which was already, by 1915, tearing at the roots of traditional British attitudes and values. In the terrible dance of death enacted by the Ashburnhams and the Dowells, a last minuet which culminates in suicide and madness, Ford created a precise and unforgettable image of that change. Elsewhere, in his poems and in several memorable passages from his novels, he gave us some of the most glorious descriptions of pre-war rural England to emerge after Thomas Hardy. He was, had set out to be, a fine writer. Occasionally, he was a great one.

It is necessary to remind ourselves of what Ford was to achieve before embarking on a chapter which deals only with his formative years. He was forty when he wrote *The Good Soldier*. He was barely twenty when he settled in the south of England, less than twenty-five when he began collaborating with Conrad. The theory, then, was far ahead of the practice. Fascinating though the collaboration remains as a piece of literary history, the results, *The Inheritors* and *Romance*, can only be enjoyed today by old-fashioned adolescents. A fifteen-year-old might still be swept along by the stories: adult readers will only be intrigued by the mystery of who contributed what.

Ford was twenty in 1894 when he eloped with Elsie Martindale, a doctor's daughter, and went to live at Bloomfield Villa in Bonnington, a pretty little Kentish village above Romney Marsh. Elsie, who knew the area well after many years of summer holidays at the family's Winchelsea home, was then a tall striking-looking girl, dark-haired, luscious-skinned and with a taste for the rich, vibrant-coloured clothes which accentuated her gypsyish looks. But Elsie was only bohemian in appearance; staunchly Catholic, she was a model housekeeper and a stickler for correct behaviour. (Her husband would later observe that Elsie could have become a splendid hospital matron.) Ford, most often remembered as a lumbering figure of elephantine proportions, was at that time tall and slender with the slightly hooked nose of his maternal grandfather, Ford Madox Brown. His blue eyes and clear pink cheeks, combined with the startling head of straight, canary-coloured hair he had inherited from both sides of the family, gave him the look of a gangling young farm-hand, a resemblance which was heightened by the donning of rustic smocks and gaiters. (The hempen homespun look was much favoured by the Fabian circles in which the Fords then moved.) Only the voice let him down. Long before Bedford Square arrived on the literary map, Ford was talking in a Bloomsbury drawl, a lugubrious and resonant tenor bizarrely unsuited to the summoning of hens and geese. Ford never wearied of presenting himself as a simple man of the land, but he never succeeded in sounding like one.

A love-affair had brought him to this south-eastern corner of England; a new love-affair began with the endlessly surprising landscape he now delighted in exploring, and in which he was prepared to settle for a lifetime. The Fords occupied at least five homes in the next decade, but all of them were within a thirty-mile radius of Bonnington. Ford was an enthusiastic walker, and he came to know that thirty-mile radius almost as well as the back of his hand. What his early poems lack in the penetrating detail of the born countryman, they make up for in fluent evocation and atmosphere. 'Up here, where the air's very clear,/And the hills slope away nigh down to the bay,/It is very like Heaven,' he wrote in *The Great View,* and in *Night Piece*: 'When one's abroad, in a field – the night very deep, very holy,/The turf very sodden a-foot, walking heavy – the small ring of light/O'the lanthorn one carries, a-swinging to left and to right,/Revealing a flicker of hedgerow, a flicker of rushes – and Night/Ev'rywhere.'

Ford was to write better poems than these, but none which carried more evidence of feeling for the land. The villagers, once they had understood that there was no sinister motive in his curiosity, were ready enough to tell him the sort of tales Ford loved and which he stored up for later use in *Thus to Revisit*. There we learn of old Meary Spratt, picking mushrooms on the marshes in a somewhat unorthodox fashion ('"He! He! He!" she would scream, "here is a nice little one, a little pinky one! Now I'm going to pick you! Up you come, my little darling! Ah, doesn't it hurt!"') and of Meary Walker, fending off cancer by wearing a hot brick tied under her breast, and of the way Poacher Rangsley outwitted Keeper Finn and the local policeman when they burst into his house.

> Powerful keen eyes they has Keeper Finn and Peeler Hogbin. Sees a pheasant's feather on the floor by Mistress Rangsley's foot and a hare's foot on the gun-rack. They pounces on the pot and what does they find boiling? Tater-peelings! You see? Tater-peelings for the peeler . . . How did Rangsley contrive that? – Picked up the feathers and the foot in game-dealer Vidler's shop up to Ashford Market when he'd bin to sell his mistress' duck eggs. Heard the Quality had it in mind to git him out of his cottage.

Ford was entranced. His mind was swirling with romantic stories of the vengeful ghosts of marauding Danes lurking in Aldington Woods, village murders, daredevil smugglers. He was still finishing his uncharacteristically sedate biography of Ford Madox Brown, but the smuggling tales gave him an idea for a very different kind of book, a full-blooded adventure story with a Sussex setting. This was 'Seraphina', later to become *Romance*, a novel which proved a severe test to the enthusiasm of both Ford and Conrad for their collaborative enterprise.

Bloomfield Villa was a damp and unsatisfactory purgatory; in the autumn of 1896, Ford and Elsie moved three or four miles to their first real home, The Pent, which they were to sublet to the Conrads two years later.

The attraction today is hard to see. The Pent is a featureless red-brick farmhouse stranded between nondescript Postling and the main road to Folkestone. At the back, it is shadowed by towering trees which shut out any glimpse of the North Downs: the front looks out onto the farm stockyard. The only view of the countryside is of a drably dropping plain of fields. But the Fords were charmed by it, charmed even by the fact that 'it smells like a *real* farm', as Elsie happily wrote to Olivia Garnett. 'Our furniture and everything show to so much more advantage than they did at B.,' she went on, 'and we have just room for it all, not any too much. In fact, we certainly could not have done better.' Elsie, the more practical of the two, was pleased by the absence of damp and the generous proportions of the rooms. ('A huge kitchen, quite twenty feet I should think and a large pantry. Five good sized bedrooms.') Ford was delighted to have found somewhere approximately close to 'the old country gentleman style up to wh. we are trying to live'. Years later he was still wistfully remembering the pretty leaded diamonds of the window-panes, the big homely kitchen with its brick floor laid in waving patterns and its low oak-beamed ceiling, the long quiet parlour with roses bobbing on the windowsills and cats curled on the chairs. (It was just as well that the Fords were fond of cats: The Pent was a rats' playground.) It was not so very inconvenient to have to go out to a separate wash-house at the back, unless it rained. It was pleasant to boast of owning the finest tithe-barn in southern England, even if it had no practical use. Ford, in short, was delighted with his find. And, like the eighteenth-century landowners with whom he felt most spiritually at home, he promptly started improving his property. Assisted by Ragged Ass Wilson (so named locally for his threadbare trousers), he set to work, 'restoring it on the most approved lines to its original antique condition of great rafters and huge ingles with rackets and crocks'.[1]

Wilson was a man after Ford's own heart, interested in everything he did and everything he saw, ready to spend a whole night unblocking one of The Pent's ingle-nooks before going out to a full day's work of hedge-cutting or tree-pruning. Ford had the ideas, Wilson the practical experience needed to execute them. 'He could lay bricks, cut out rafters, plaster, hang paper, paint, make chairs, corner-cupboards, fish, poach, snare, brew, gather simples, care for poultry, stop fox's earths . . . His capacity for work was amazing . . . I think,' Ford added as an afterthought, 'he was happy. In fact I think all those people were as happy as they were wise and unlettered . . . I do not believe that any one of them ever betrayed either me or even each other.'[2] It was a splendidly naïve judgement, typical of Ford's romantic side, the side which chose to turn The Pent into an unlikely museum of Pre-Raphaelite treasures, a William Morris table, Christina Rossetti's writing-desk, Madox Brown's picture cupboard, a death-mask of Dante Gabriel Rossetti. Ford had had a Pre-Raphaelite childhood (Madox Brown's house was his home after his father's premature death, the wild band of Rossetti cousins were his next-door neighbours), and his attitude to The Pent and to the country locals suggests the influence of that movement's belief in the ennobling of manual work and the embracing of primitive simplicity.

Ford's first uncomfortable meeting with Henry James at the Vicarage in Rye had been inspired by curiosity and by the hope that James might perhaps give a favourable notice to his forthcoming biography of his grandfather. There was no notice, but Ford did not despair of establishing a friendly relationship. By his own account, he succeeded to a remarkable degree. By the accounts of others, James resigned himself with as much grace as he could muster to the fact that a Ford on the scent was as inescapable as a starving tiger in pursuit of his prey.

Professor Edel, whose opinion of Ford is low enough to allow him only to 'have borrowed a high seriousness about the art of fiction' from James and Conrad, subscribes to the latter view. James was, he suggests, forearmed. He saw in Ford the living prototype of his own fictitious Colonel Capadose, described in a short story of 1888, 'The Liar'. Capadose, like Ford, was a man unable to resist the pleasant art of fabrication; unlike Ford, Edel primly points out, he stayed with his wife. Edel's reading of the relationship is that James was prepared to be cautiously friendly, even to offer a few words of encouragement, but that he judged it prudent to keep his distance. The friendship was one of Ford's myths, a piece of wishful thinking. Miss Bosanquet's recollections of her employer's undignified attempts to jump ditches or hide behind trees rather than meet Ford on a walk, are confirmation enough.

It would be easier to share Professor Edel's view if Ford had presented a picture of uniform sweetness and light. He did not. He was willing to admit that he often irritated James and to cite the occasions, but the portrait which he paints of their acquaintanceship convincingly suggests that a friendship did exist and for a period of years rather than months. He was ready to confess that he played no part in the Lamb House summer season when 'Mr James's garden overflowed with the titled, the distinguished, the eminent in the diplomatic world . . .'[3] (One of Ford's rash exaggerations: James seldom had more than four guests.) The friendship, as he describes it, centred on their shared affection for the Rye to Winchelsea walk, a walk which could most agreeably be undertaken in congenial company. Many were the occasions, if we believe Ford, when James would walk over to have tea with him at Winchelsea and share the walk back – and vice-versa. Nothing, if we believe Professor Edel, could have been more distasteful to James than to walk anywhere in Ford's company. Cordial communications between James and Ford are conspicuously absent from his final volume of James's letters. Limited space may have necessitated their exclusion. Douglas Goldring, in *The Last Pre-Raphaelite* (1948), includes a handsome selection of letters from James to Ford which leave the reader in no doubt that Ford was telling the truth. He was one of the first neighbours to be told in December 1897 of the dates when James planned to be at Lamb House and hoped to see him there. In December 1903, James wrote, proposing to 'beleaguer the Bungalow' (Ford's Winchelsea home) with a party of six American ladies and a young priest who might count as an extra female by the length of his skirts. In 1904 he was happily accepting invitations and apologizing for using the typewriter while making jokes about his plans to crib from Ford's latest work (*The Soul of London*). In January 1906, he was inviting the Fords 'to come over some day next week to tea? *Any* day – if you will but give me a hint.' Arthur Mizener, Ford's biographer, came nearer to the truth than Edel in saying that, during those early years, James 'clearly enjoyed Ford's company and often . . . sought him out'.[4]

Professor Edel rests most of his case on the evidence of Theodora Bosanquet, and Miss Bosanquet did not start working for James until 1907. There is no reason to doubt her account of James's eagerness to avoid Ford: the question is, what had happened to make him wish to do so? One possibility is that he had heard some distasteful gossip about Ford and his sister-in-law.

Mary Martindale, a striking girl with fiery hair and a spirit to match it, had been obsessed by Ford ever since he had begun courting her sister. Ford, initially, was too entranced by his wife to pay much attention to Mary's predatory glances. In 1901, Dr Martindale persuaded the Fords to leave Stocks Hill, their pretty but primitive home at Aldington, and move to the two-storeyed clapboard cottage owned by him at Winchelsea and known, obscurely, as The Bungalow. (It was later renamed The Little House.) Mary, living almost next-door at her parents' handsome Tudor house, Glebe Cottage, became, as one of Ford's biographers delicately puts it, 'almost one of the household'. Their affair began in 1901 and continued, intermittently, until Ford fell under the spell of Violet Hunt in 1908. (Here, too, it is interesting to note, Mary Martindale managed to prove, by making friends with Violet, that she was an indispensable part of the household. Where Ford and Violet went, Mary, as often as not, went too.) The liaison between Ford and his sister-in-law was not one which James, if he knew of it, would have easily condoned. Scandal of such an interesting nature would not have been confined for long by the ancient walls of Winchelsea.

There are other indications that Ford had begun to get on James's nerves by the time Miss Bosanquet came to live at Rye. In 1906, very full of his recent visit to America and forgetful of James's own pilgrimage of 1904, Ford rashly began to expound on American politics and civilization, about which he knew little or nothing at that time. The result was a disagreeable surprise. 'He stopped as if I had hit him and, with the coldly infuriated tone of a country squire whose patriotism had been outraged, exclaimed: "Don't talk such *damnable* nonsense!" He really shouted these words with a male fury. And when, slightly outraged myself, I returned to the charge . . . he exclaimed: "I should not have thought you wanted to display such damnable ignorance," and hurried off along the road.'[5] The reader does not need a vast amount of insight to perceive that James had had enough of Ford; the narrator, ever the optimist, rationalized the outburst. Certainly, James could be brutally direct on occasion, but that was his way. 'I will not say that loveableness was the predominating feature of the Old Man; he was too intent on his particular aims to be lavishly sentimental over surrounding humanity.'[6]

Assuming that relations were cordial for four or five years, we have an ample time-span into which to place Ford's treasurehouse of undated anecdotes, but much of his reminiscing still has to be discarded as, at the least, forgetful, at the most, unblushingly inventive. His knowledge of James's domestic arrangements was shaky enough for him to provide seven servants where there were never more than five; he recalled 'grey-stone' garden walls, a 'majestic' house and an 'immense' lawn (for those imaginary crowds of summer visitors?) where Lamb House had red-brick garden walls, a modest aspect and a lawn rather less than the size of a tennis court. He transformed the drunken downfall of the Smiths (the cook and butler who had accompanied James to Rye) into a mass departure of the household culminating in a dramatic entry by the constabulary. He descended occasionally into such wild absurdities as the announcement that 'it was held in Rye that he [James] practised black magic behind the high walls of Lamb House'.

A reasonable knowledge of the personalities involved is all the amateur detective needs to discover the fabulist also at work on sundry other occasions. We have, for instance, the remarkable tale, allegedly from the horse's mouth, of James being welcomed into Maupassant's home and introduced, as though it was the most normal of events, to a recumbent female, masked but otherwise naked as Eve, and being readily persuaded that she was a *femme du monde*. Or James's confession to having used Ford as a model for Merton Densher in *The Wings of a Dove*. There are resemblances to Ford in that 'longish, leanish, fairish young Englishman . . . visibly absent-minded, irregularly clever', but James, who never acknowledged his use of living persons for his fictions, would not have admitted it. We can also dismiss the charming fantasy that James consulted Ford on business matters, something which no man in his right mind would have dreamed of doing. The announcement that 'I was for him the strong, silent man of affairs' is nearer the truth when read for its unfortunate double-entendre. And then there is the story already referred to in Chapter 1 which depicts James covertly creeping into Ford's home to solicit his housemaid's advice on the wisdom of employing a 'Lady Help' at Lamb House. Here, Ford runs into trouble on two counts. James was not the kind of man to skulk in back passages, discussing his problems with domestics: it was emphatically not his style. And the servant so grandly described as 'one of the housemaids' was non-existent. There were no housemaids in Ford's Winchelsea home. Well, his first published work was a volume of fairy stories . . .

The inventions are the icing on the cake. Scrape them off and you can still find plenty of cherries in the sponge. Ford gives us an evening at Lamb House in the glow of candlelight, himself, silent and entranced as James exchanged beguiling and extraordinary stories with Jonathan Sturges, 'a queer tiny being who lay crumpled up on the stately sofa'. He recalls the fantastic, elaborate acts of kindness of which James was always capable and over which he would take endless pains. 'His practical benevolences,' Ford notes, 'were innumerable, astonishing – and indefatigable.' He illustrates the point with the story of a concerned and embarrassed James working up the courage to offer him money on a day when he had admitted to feeling depressed.

> One day, going, as we seemed eternally in those days to be doing, down Winchelsea Hill under the Strand Gate, he said:
> 'H . . . you seem worried!' I said that I was worried. I don't know how he knew. But he knew everything . . .
> 'If it's money, H . . .' he brought out. '*Mon sac n'est pas grand . . . Mais puisez dans mon sac!*'

I explained that it was not about money that I was worried, but about the 'form' of a book I was writing. His mute agony was a painful thing to see. He became much more appalled, but much less nervous. At last he made the great sacrifice:

'Well, then,' he said. 'I'm supposed to be . . . Um, um . . . There's Mary . . . Mrs Ward . . . Does me the great honour . . . I'm supposed to know . . . In short, why not let me look at the manuscript!'

I had the decency not to take up his time with it . . . *Les beaux jours quand on était bien modeste!*[7]

Ford was to regret not having taken up the offer, but he did not pretend that it had been made out of any great interest in his work. 'Curious and interesting' was James's cautious response to one of his books of poems; *The Cinque Ports* was accorded the even more ambiguous compliment of being a 'brave book'. Of *Romance*, according to Ford, James said that 'it was an immense English plum-cake which he kept at his bedside for a fortnight and of which he ate a nightly slice'. It was not the warmest of tributes. When, in 1914, *The Times Literary Supplement* published James's essay on the younger generation of novelists, Ford's name was conspicuously absent; he let it be known that he had not bothered to read Ford's brief book about him published three months previously.

It would not have pleased him. Ford's *Henry James*, while not much worse than Conrad's over-rated monograph – its reputation has survived on the strength of one shrewd phrase, 'the historian of fine consciences' – is slapdash and embarrassingly adulatory for the wrong reasons. Ford's personal problems are transparently addressed under the guise of objective criticism. *What Maisie Knew*, cited to demonstrate James's detachment from social problems, becomes a vehicle for Ford's view on marriage and on divorce procedure. His main objection to James as 'an observer, passionless and pitiless' is offered without qualification or substantiation; his praise for 'the greatest man now living' is based on the odd assumption that James was a dedicated realist, intent on precise and accurate representation. 'He, more than anybody,' Ford asserts, 'has observed human society as it now is, and more than anybody has faithfully rendered his observations of it.' It is hard to imagine a tribute more calculated to infuriate James, who had himself written that 'life has no direct sense whatever for the subject and is capable, luckily, for us, of nothing but splendid waste.'[8]

Communications between James and Ford had become infrequent by 1904 or 1905. They were brusquely terminated in the autumn of 1909. It is possible that Ford wrote his tribute in the hope of retrieving the friendship; it is likely that it succeeded only in hardening James's determination to bury it. Ford had, by that time, made himself an embarrassment as well as an irritatingly persistent neighbour. The embarrassment arose from his affair with Violet Hunt.

The Fords' marriage had been seriously undermined by Elsie's discovery in July 1905 that her husband had been sleeping with her sister four years previously, was doing so still and disinclined to promise that he would cease to do so in future. It would, for any wife, have been a painful and mortifying experience; it hastened Elsie's transformation from a glowingly rosy girl into a sombre and lonely woman, hiding her pathetic sense of insecurity under a fiercely implacable exterior. She and the little girls, Christina and Katharine, remained in the country, moving only from Winchelsea to Aldington, while Ford began to spend most of his weekdays in London. There were casual affairs. The relationship with Mary Martindale, his sister-in-law, continued. Elsie, neurotic and suffering increasingly from ill-health, clung to the hope that life would one day return to normal. Her first and pitiful question to the doctor after an operation in 1908 was about the resumption of sexual relations with her husband.

Ford met Violet Hunt at a dinner-party of the Galsworthys in March 1907. A month later, she approached him at another party to ask if he would review her novel, *White Rose of Weary Leaf*. She was already attracted to him; it seemed a promising sign when he appeared at one of her garden-parties that summer without his wife. Her chance to meet him on his own came in October when Wells, her former lover, sent her along to Ford to show him her work, a meeting described here in Chapter 3. Ford was as available and as interested by her as she had hoped; a month later they were meeting each other three times a week.

Violet was witty, attractive and, at the age of forty-five, eager for marriage. Ford, always in search of the perfect woman, thought he had found her. Violet was not perfect, but she was a much more satisfactory partner than Elsie for the romantic dramas in which he liked to indulge. If he talked darkly of suicide and then nudged her hand into discovering a bottle marked POISON in his pocket, Violet could be relied on to thrill to the thought of rescuing a great writer from a tragic end. The more sceptical Elsie might have suggested he drink it, placing him in a difficult situation.

By Christmas 1908, London's literary society had accepted them as a couple; the news did not take long to reach Sussex. Elsie appears to have resorted to the time-honoured ruse of provoking jealousy, or seeking to do so. She wrote to her husband to tell him that his friend and partner in the *English Review*, Arthur Marwood, had been trying to seduce her.*

Jealousy can only be provoked where desire still exists. Ford was fond of Elsie but she was no longer, to him, desirable. He sent a sympathetic note, saying that he was 'rather astonished' by the idea of Marwood behaving in such a way, but that he supposed he would have to end the friendship, if she insisted. It was made clear that he hoped she would not. He signed off on a jocular note – 'Well goodbye old thing – Preserve Yr tranquillity' – cruelly void of any sense of affront. Elsie's fears were confirmed soon afterwards by a proposal – the first of many – that she should accept £400 a year in exchange for seeking a divorce. Separation, Ford explained, would enable him to love her more. Elsie refused. Ford's aunts and uncles, staunch Catholics all, were on her side; her father was terrified of the scandal if, divorced by one daughter, Ford took it into his head to marry the other. (Mary Martindale was still in hot pursuit.)

It is hard not to sympathize with Elsie. It was bad enough that she should have had to endure being supplanted by a sister without having to face the prospect of being left for a middle-aged and singularly ugly woman (Elsie could only have seen photographs and Violet, from most angles, was strikingly unphotogenic) who was flaunting herself before their friends as Ford's future wife. Elsie would not give him up, but she could not imagine how she was going to go on.

She kept her distance for a summer. In October 1909, her control snapped. She took a train to London with the children's governess and, with the reassuring backing of her lawyer, marched into Ford's London flat for a confrontation – only to learn that he was holidaying in France, with Violet. It was too much. When the holidaymakers stepped off the train at Charing Cross late that evening, they were greeted by a white-faced Elsie, together with the lawyer and the governess. 'A vestal virgin suddenly confronted with the irate goddess whose shrine she would seem to have profaned',[9] was how Violet chose to remember herself that night. She remembered, too, how the runaway husband had taken one look at Elsie and murmured to his travelling companion: 'It's all up, old girl. You will see. There'll be no divorce.'

---

* The more probable truth was that Elsie had confided in him as a friend of the family and that Marwood's efforts to console her were misconstrued by a naïve and overwrought woman.

'Conscious and cruel' was Henry James's impression of Brede Place when he revisited it shortly after Crane's death.

Stephen Crane: Ford described him as 'the most beautiful spirit I have ever known'.

'. . . a clean shave had revealed in all its beauty the noble Roman mask and the big dramatic mouth.' (Edith Wharton) Henry James in 1912, as drawn by John Singer Sargent.

Henry James with his father in 1854. 'So many young impressions come back to me as gathered at his side and in his personal haunts.' (Henry James)

Henry and William James. 'From far back in dimmest childhood he had been my ideal elder brother. . .'

'I greatly miss you, dearest Peggot.' Henry James's niece, Peggy (Mary Margaret), sitting on the knee of her father, William James.

Konrad Korzeniowski in 1874, on the brink of his naval career. 'The Conrad of those days was Romance . . . he was the most marvellous raconteur in the world.' (Ford)

Wells and Conrad. 'He was always trying to penetrate below my foundations, discover my imaginative obsessions and see what I was really up to'. (Wells)

Conrad. 'His black torpedo beard pointed at the horizon. He placed a monocle in his eye.' (Ford)

Violet Hunt, genially known to James as 'the Improper Person of Babylon', shows off her profile. He called himself her 'country cousin'.

Ford the family man photographed in the late 1890s, with Elsie and the two children, Christina (right) and Katherine.

Hugh Walpole photographed in London, 1909.

Ford in 1909. 'What he is really or if he is really, nobody knows now and he least of all; he has become a great system of assumed personas and dramatized selves.' (Wells)

Miss Edith Jones against a studio backdrop.

Edith Wharton indulging her private vice in the garden at The Mount.

Henry James and Howard Sturgis photographed by Edith Wharton at The Mount. 'I think I may safely say that Henry James was never so good as with this little party at The Mount.'

Henry James playing croquet in the garden at Qu'Acre. Left to right: Henry James, Clare Sheridan, Howard Sturgis, Wilfred Sheridan.

Cora Crane and Henry James at the Brede Garden Fête. 'And I tried to look so beautiful,' James ruefully observed when he saw the photographs.

Howard Sturgis, William Haynes-Smith (The Babe) with Misery and her misbegotten son, at Qu'Acre.

'...the little old, cobble-stoned, grass-grown, red-roofed town, on the summit of its mildly pyramidal hill.' (James) An engraving by Hollar after van Dyck. The original is at the Pierpont Morgan Library in New York.

Henry James at Lamb House. 'I wish indeed you could only see Lamb House *now* – at the prettiest moment of the summer.' (James)

Nor was there, although Elsie later bitterly regretted not having abandoned the struggle and avoided the humiliation of being dragged into the newspapers when Ford elected to serve a ten-day prison sentence rather than return to her. When Elsie still showed no sign of changing her mind, he rashly let himself be persuaded that he could legally marry Violet by adopting German citizenship. A reporter from the *Daily Mirror* got his scoop from the happy couple.

AUTHOR WEDS
Mr Ford Madox Hueffer married abroad
to Well-Known Lady Novelist

> The Daily Mirror is able to announce that Mr Ford Madox Hueffer, the famous novelist, has been married on the Continent to Miss Violet Hunt, the well-known authoress . . .
>
> Mr Hueffer was seen at the Red House, Spa, Belgium, yesterday, before starting for his daily motor-car ride with the second Mrs Hueffer.
>
> 'I don't want to advertise myself,' he told the Daily Mirror, 'but it happens that both my wife and myself have books appearing today . . . I married her in Germany after divorcing my former wife on a technical ground, desertion, as I had a perfect right to do, being domiciled in Germany.
>
> 'I am heir to large entailed estates in Prussia and have therefore retained my German nationality.'[10]

Fantasies, fantasies. There had been a 'marriage' ceremony, but Ford had never obtained his naturalization papers and Violet was still Miss Hunt. And yet, curiously, they seem to have persuaded themselves that all was well. They visited Ford's relations at Münster as man and wife, and Ford wrote to Conrad that he was 'at peace at last'.

His serenity was short-lived. They had barely set foot in England as Mr and Mrs Hueffer when the *Daily Mirror*, under threat of a court-case from Elsie, renounced its report and published an apology to the injured wife. When a second reference to Violet as 'Mrs Hueffer' appeared in a little magazine called the *Throne*, Elsie again threatened to sue if she did not receive a public apology. The *Throne*'s owners would have done well to profit from the *Daily Mirror*'s example; instead, most rashly, they allowed Ford and Violet to persuade them that the marriage was a valid one and that there was no cause for alarm. Elsie would never dare to bring the case to court; if she did, they would be there to testify on the *Throne*'s behalf.

The case, one of lively interest to the newspapers, was brought before Mr Justice Avory in the Court of King's Bench on 7 and 8

MRS. HUEFFER WINS HER LIBEL SUIT

Verdict for Wife of Novelist with
£300 Damages.

BOOKS SHE NEVER READS.

Judge Declines to Hear Statement Concerning
Miss Violet Hunt.

A wife's claim to her name was vindicated
yesterday when £300 damages were awarded
in Mr. Justice Avory's court to Mrs. Elsie
Hueffer, the wife of the novelist, Mr. Ford

February, 1913, and lost almost before it began by the conspicuous
absence of the two vital witnesses, Ford and Violet. They had
discreetly departed for France a few days before the trial, Violet
returning in time to learn that Elsie had been awarded £300 and costs
(a £1,000 pay-out spelt the end of the ill-fated *Throne*) while she
herself had been publicly and humiliatingly deprived of the right to
be called Ford's wife. Elsie had not succeeded in getting Ford back,
but she had obtained the grimmer satisfaction of driving her rival
into social purdah.★

★ Traditionalists of the older generation remained unforgiving, and many of
them did not hesitate to give Violet their reasons for refusing her invitations. The
young were less particular and many of them recorded lively memories of the
afternoon gatherings at South Lodge, where Pound tyrannized the tennis players,
Ford flirted with the prettiest guests and Violet presided over the plum-cake and
crumpets. Few of the guests saw in their host and hostess the stuff of which romance
is made. Ford had become gross, a flabby pink-faced giant whose yellow moustache
dribbled down the sides of a perpetually gaping mouth – always gaping a little more,
Wyndham Lewis maliciously observed, when there was a pretty girl in sight. Violet
had grown witchlike and old, although she still clung to the coquettish ways of her
girlhood. 'She looked old, yet she was gay,' D. H. Lawrence noted in 1912. '. . . She
coquetted and played beautifully with Hueffer: she loves him distractedly – she was
charming, and I loved her. But my God, she looked old.'
Ford's last years with Violet were some of the most important in his life. He
wrote *The Good Soldier*, published in 1915, and, as part of the third battalion of the
9th Welch Regiment, he went into the war and gained the experiences on which he
was to base his most ambitious work, *Parade's End*. In 1918, he met a young
Australian girl, Stella Bowen, and the Ford–Hunt liaison came to an end. Violet,
surrounded by Ford memorabilia, lived on at South Lodge, giving and going to
parties, hoping when there was no hope left that she might still become Mrs Hueffer
or, perhaps, be created a Dame. The stigma of her unmarried name never ceased to
haunt her.

Henry James had known and liked Violet Hunt for several years before she met Ford.* She was a tolerable novelist, an amusing companion, and full of literary gossip. Lamb House had been invaded by her on several occasions and the experience, while exhausting, had been an enjoyable one for her host. So when, in October 1909, a letter arrived from the voluble 'Purple Patch' – James's affectionate nickname for her – he wrote to suggest a visit.

> My dear Violet,
>   Yes, indeed I am at Rye – where else should I be? For I am here pretty well always and ever, and less and less anywhere else. There are advantages preponderant in that; but there are also drawbacks; one of which is that I am liable to go so long without seeing you. But to this, on the other hand, there are possible remedies – as, for instance, that of your conceivably (I hope) coming down here for a couple of nights before very long . . . We can have a long jaw (with lots of arrears to make up), and weather permitting, eke a short walk . . .
>   Yours ever,
>   HENRY JAMES[11]

I quote the letter at some length to correct the picture which is often presented of Violet thrusting herself on James. It is clear that she did not and that James had heard little, if anything, of her liaison with Ford. It was only after she had secured an invitation to stay that Violet made a terrible error of judgement. She was eager to see divorce proceedings begin and to put an end to the scandal which had already begun to spread. It occurred to her that Henry James would be a powerful ally; she may even have taken it into her head that he could use his influence on Ford's wife as a respected neighbour and friend. Ford, too, was confident that James would support them, confident enough to write him a letter explaining that – as he then believed – he would soon be able to make an honest woman of Violet as Elsie was about to divorce him. The letter went off by the same post as Violet's note of glad acceptance.

James was appalled. He was not a prude: he had been a sympathetic witness and go-between in Edith Wharton's affair with their mutual friend, Morton Fullerton. But Edith in love was tactful and discreet, while Violet had always been the very soul of indiscretion. He was, besides, very fond of Fullerton, while it was over two years since he had eschewed Ford's friendship. To welcome Violet into his house would not only lay him open to hearing a good many embarrassing details, but would invite the risk of his name being involved in some

---

* An account of their friendship is given in Chapter 6.

highly unsavoury publicity. Mrs Hueffer was his neighbour; how would it look to her and everyone else if he was reported to be entertaining Violet Hunt? Furious at having been trapped in an intolerably awkward situation, he decided to extricate himself as quickly and completely as possible.

> Dear Violet Hunt,
>   I should be writing to you tonight to say that it would give me great pleasure to see you on Saturday next had I not received by the same post which brought me your letter one from Ford Madox Hueffer which your mention of the fact that you have known of his writing enables me thus to allude to as depriving, by its contents, our projected occasion of indispensable elements of frankness and pleasantness. I deeply regret and deplore the lamentable position in which I gather you have put yourself in respect to divorce proceedings about to be taken by Mrs Hueffer; it affects me as painfully unedifying, and that compels me to regard all agreeable and unembarrassed communication between us as impossible. I can neither suffer you to come down to hear me utter those homely truths, nor pretend at such a time to free and natural discourse of other things, on a basis of avoidance of what must now be most to the front in your own consciousness and what in a very unwelcome fashion disconcerts mine. Otherwise, 'Es wäre so schön gewesen!'* But I think you will understand on a moment's further reflection that I can't write you otherwise than I do, and that I am very sorry indeed to have so to do it. Believe me then in very imperfect sympathy
>
> Yours
HENRY JAMES[12]

It was useless for Violet to beg him, as she now humiliatingly did, not to judge her too harshly. Her second letter only made James feel how right he had been to take a strong line. He could only regret that Ford had put her into such a wretched position, 'lamentable – oh lamentable! What sort of a friend is it would say less'. He did not care to be told that he knew Ford had been separated from his wife 'for years. I neither knew, nor know, anything whatever of the matter; and it was exactly because I didn't wish to that I found conversing with you at all to be in prospect impossible.'[13] To Ford, who had rashly rushed in to take up the cudgels on Violet's behalf against any judgement of her behaviour, he sent a stiff little note pointing out that he had deplored not her behaviour but 'the situation of her being exposed to figure in public proceedings. I don't see how any old friend of hers can be indifferent to that misfortune.'[14]

---

* It would have been delightful.

The folly was Violet's, but the fault, in James's eyes, was Ford's.

Violet's final letter in this exchange, in which she claimed the right as a friend to speak freely and frankly about her position, went unanswered. By the time she came to write her memoirs in 1926, she had succeeded in persuading herself that she had behaved rather well. '. . . I had written and warned him that there might be a slight atmosphere of mess about me. There were several counts on which my presence in court might have been required. Supposing I had "called" him! 'Enery would have died. America would have squirmed. No, I would not bring whatever it was into the house, as one says of scarlet fever or measles.'[15]

James's letter contains no clue to his feelings towards Violet after this unfortunate episode, but there were no further invitations to Lamb House, and only a flicker of the old warmth can be detected in his responses to her letters. The friendship was cautiously resumed when he moved to London in 1913.

Ford had been living in the country for four years before the momentous meeting with Conrad in the autumn of 1898. He and Elsie, in one of their many phases of house-moving, had established themselves at Gracie's Cottage, Limpsfield, known as 'Dostoevsky Corner' on account of the stream of Russian visitors passing through the home of their neighbours, Edward and Constance Garnett. It was Garnett, Conrad's literary mentor, who brought about the introduction.

> Conrad came round the corner of the house. I was doing something at the open fireplace in the house-end. He was in advance of Mr Garnett who had gone inside, I suppose, to find me. Conrad stood looking at the view. His hands were in the pockets of his reefer-coat, the thumbs sticking out. His black torpedo beard pointed at the horizon. He placed a monocle in his eye. Then he caught sight of me.
>
> I was very untidy, in my working clothes. He started back a little. I said, 'I'm Hueffer.' He had taken me for the gardener.
>
> His whole being melted together in enormous politeness. His spine inclined forward; he extended both hands to take mine. He said: 'My dear faller . . . Delighted . . . Enchanté!'[16]

Garnett had a knack for finding homes for his friends – it was he who suggested Brede Place to the Cranes – and Conrad was now anxious to escape from a dreary temporary home in Essex. Ford was eager to sub-let The Pent to congenial tenants who would not mind putting him and his wife up from time to time. 'Nothing could suit me better,' Conrad wrote to him shortly after their meeting. 'I only hope you won't find me too objectionable . . . I could not look upon you as an invading enemy.'

Plans for a literary collaboration were afoot within a month of their first encounter, founded on a mutual passion for technique and form and, according to Ford, on Conrad's eagerness to profit from the teachings of 'an acknowledged master of English'. In Ford's version of events, Conrad had acted on the advice of William Henley, poet, editor and, allegedly, the model for Long John Silver in *Treasure Island*.

> He stated succinctly and carefully that he had said to Henley . . . 'Look here, I write with such difficulty: my intimate, automatic, less expressed thoughts are in Polish; when I express myself with care I do it in French. When I write I think in French and then translate the words of my thoughts into English. This is an impossible process for one desiring to make a living by writing in the English language . . .' And Henley, according to Conrad on that evening had said: 'Why don't you ask H. to collaborate with you? He is the finest stylist in the English language of today . . .' The writer, it should be remembered, though by ten or fifteen years the junior of Conrad was by some years his senior at any rate as a published author, and was rather the more successful of the two as far as sales went.[17]

There is no reason to quarrel with the first part of this account. Conrad's second language was French and the syntax of his early works is often that of a rather cumbersome translation. To think in one foreign language and write in another was a harsh discipline for a man to whom writing was always a harrowing and arduous process. The second part is less acceptable. It was this kind of egotistical distortion of the truth which infuriated Jessie Conrad who, if she carried her vindictiveness to excess, had some cause to detest Ford. It was true that his first slim work, *The Brown Owl*, was published three years before *Almayer's Folly*, Conrad's literary début. It was absurd, however, for a man who had written one unremarkable novel to claim superiority in 1898 to Conrad, who had written *An Outcast of the Islands*, *The Nigger of the 'Narcissus'*, *Youth*, *Karain*, a part of *The Rescue* and a substantial section of *Lord Jim*.

Conrad had indeed discussed the possibility of a collaboration with Henley, but his letter of 18 October, 1898 is a defensive one which suggests that Henley, far from recommending it, had questioned the prudence of such a venture.

> When talking with Hueffer my first thought was that the man there who couldn't find a publisher had some good stuff to use and that if we worked it up together my name, probably, would get a publisher

for it. On the other hand I thought that working with him would keep under the particular devil that spoils my work for me as quick as I can turn it out (that's why I write so slow and break my word to publishers), and that the material being of the kind that appeals to my imagination and the man being an honest workman we could turn out something tolerable – perhaps; and if not he would be no worse off than before . . . The affair had a material rather than an artistic aspect for me . . .[18]*

In plain words, Conrad regarded Ford not as a master of English prose, but as a very professional craftsman.

Money was certainly an important factor. Critical esteem had not made the Conrads rich; ingredients for the recipes in Jessie's home cookery book are painfully plain, showing the need for careful budgeting. They lived above the bread-line, but the margin was a narrow one. Both *The Inheritors* and *Romance*, the two books of Ford's on which Conrad was ready to collaborate and share the profits, were potential money-spinners. The first was a venture into the lucrative vein of science-fiction which Wells had already begun to mine with such success; the second, an adventurous narrative rich in local colour and incident, was aimed at the mass-market, despite all the talk of its being a new form of novel. The speed with which Ford wrote was an added incentive; it is unlikely that Conrad foresaw how much of the workload would fall on his own shoulders.

The main impulse was a warmer one. Conrad had found in Ford a man who adored talking about books and who could provide the stimulant of daily companionship on an equal intellectual footing. Conrad was the superior artist; in knowledge, Ford was more than a match for him. The English have never been known for their delight in literary conversation for the sheer fun of it; Ford prided himself on being foreign in this respect. It was this side of him which attracted Conrad and enabled the friendship to endure for so long. He was often viciously disparaging of Ford's writing, but he never lost his love of Ford's rambling, discursive, acquisitive mind. To a man who liked talking of books and hearing stories about writers, the gift of Ford's friendship was as irresistible as the key to Ali Baba's cave. 'I miss you more and more,' Conrad wrote to him after one of their estrangements. 'I am certain that with no other man could I share my rapture.'[19] He had more respect for Wells and James and more love for Stephen Crane. Mentally, his strongest rapport remained with Ford.

---

* Ford's version of the discussion between Henley and Conrad presents it in the context of a personal encounter but when Henley died in 1904, Conrad expressed a regret that he had never had the opportunity to meet him.

Stephen Crane, with whom Conrad had already made friends, had disappeared to Havana on a mysterious mission at the time Conrad moved to The Pent, but Wells was within easy visiting distance. He had singled out Conrad's first novels for review. Conrad wrote to announce his arrival and to say that he was in 'a state of jubilation' at the prospect of having such a distinguished neighbour. Wells managed to suppress his own elation. He was out when the Conrads paid their first call, and he was out again on their second visit when the doorbell stuck and refused to stop ringing until the discomforted visitors retreated. 'We would have waited but we'd left the baby in the gutter (there was a fly* under him),'[20] Conrad wrote to Wells with his regrets at having again missed a chance to meet him.

Conrad must have related the incident to Ford since it features in his recollections. The characters, however, have undergone a signal change and a sequel has been added. Jessie Conrad and the baby have been replaced by Ford. It had all, as he misremembered it, been Conrad's idea. For himself, he had shuddered at the prospect of making a state visit to announce their collaboration, but Conrad had insisted and all embarrassment had been dissolved by mirth when the doorbell began to ring of its own accord. What a delightful visit had followed, he suavely continued. How well he remembered sitting in the garden of Spade House with Mr and Mrs Wells and their house-guests, listening to Conrad's tales of storms at sea. Ford had forgotten that the Wellses were still living at Beach Cottage at that date, gardenless. Unluckily for his memoirs, Wells left his own account of the first meeting. It took place at Pent Farm, where Conrad received his esteemed visitor with an almost oriental courtesy for which Wells did not greatly care. 'He spoke English strangely,' he noted, and added that he looked very like Captain Kettle.

The man did not appeal to him, but Wells had enough faith in Conrad's writing to be appalled by the idea of a collaboration. He said nothing at the time, but at some point after Ford's move to Stocks Hill in Aldington in March 1899, Wells bicycled over there to see if he could not be dissuaded. 'Mr Wells came to persuade me not to collaborate with Conrad. With an extreme earnestness he pleaded with me not to spoil Conrad's style. "The wonderful oriental style . . . It's as delicate as clockwork and you'll only ruin it by sticking your fingers in it." I answered that Conrad wanted a collaboration and as far as I was concerned Conrad was going to get what he wanted. I can still see the dispirited action of Mr Wells as he mounted his bicycle by the rear step and rode away along that ridge of little

* Horse and open cart.

hills . . .'[21] (Ford, incidentally, shifted this occasion back to the day after the doorbell incident.) Years later, Wells was to change his view and write that Conrad 'owed a very great deal to their early association; Hueffer helped greatly to "English" him and his idiom . . . and conversed interminably with him about the precise word and about perfection in writing.'[22]*

Henry James had been more reticent but no less dismayed than Wells. Greatly though he under-valued the quality of Conrad's writing, seeing him as an evocative writer of picturesque sea-stories, he thought enough of him to express his anxiety to Edward Garnett, Conrad's literary guardian. 'To me this is like a bad dream which one relates at breakfast!' he wrote. 'Their traditions and their gifts are so dissimilar. Collaboration between them is to me inconceivable.'[23]

Dissimilarity was in fact no barrier when the goal was identically perceived. 'We had the same aims and we had all the time the same aims,' Ford wrote. 'Our attributes were no doubt different. The writer probably knew more about words, but Conrad had certainly an infinitely greater hold over the architectonics of the novel, over the way a story should be built up so that its interest progresses and grows up to the last word.'[24]

Conrad was hard at work on *The Heart of Darkness* and *Lord Jim* in his first year at The Pent; Ford, left to hammer away at *The Inheritors* by himself, grew peevish and had to be reassured. 'What you have written now is infinitely nearer to actuality, to life to reality than anything (in prose) you've written before . . .' Conrad told him. 'Whether I am worth anything to you or not it is for you to determine . . . Heinemann (and McClure too I fancy) are waiting for our joint book and I am not going to draw back if You will only consent to sweat long enough.'[25] Fed with the promise of eager publishers, Ford consented to sweat and to accept the revisions which Conrad insisted must be made. The revising and the securing of the publishers' interest was his part of the collaboration; the book, in all but name, was Ford's. 'There is not a chapter I haven't made him write twice – most of them three times over,' Conrad boasted to Edward Garnett, who was urging Heinemann to take on the book.

---

* Conrad, regarding Wells as 'the one honest thinker of the day', took a lively interest in his work, while recognizing that they were irreconcilably opposed in their attitudes to humanity. Wells's error, in his view, was to pay insufficient attention to the perfidious nature of human imbecility and to adopt a tone of 'cold jocular ferocity' when addressing social problems. Their differences, he was forced to conclude, were 'fundamental', but their divergences, he made haste to add, were not great. He remained enduringly grateful, whatever their differences of opinion, for Wells's discreet endeavours to promote his name.

To Ford, Conrad maintained an enthusiastic front and, while contributing little on paper, gave willingly of his time. 'Would it do you good to come and talk over the last chap: again? I am ready for that now.'[26] Ford came with Elsie, and stayed two weeks, an experience which Jessie found most trying. 'No doubt our guests suffered quite as much as I did,' she wrote without conviction. 'I had often to hold myself in strict restraint.'[27]

By March 1900, *The Inheritors* was in the publishers' hands. 'Splendid reports of novel original popular great hopes society hit . . .' Conrad cabled Ford on 26 March.[28] To Garnett, on the same day, he wrote in a very different vein, mocking Ford for taking the project seriously and explaining that he himself had regarded it as nothing more than 'a sort of skit . . . This is collaboration if you like!' he went on. '. . . There were moments when I cursed the day I was born and dared not look up at the light of day I had to live through with this thing on my mind. H. has been patient as no angel had ever been. I've been fiendish. I've been rude to him; if I've not called him names I've *implied* in my remarks and in the course of our discussions the most opprobrious epithets. He wouldn't recognize them. 'Pon my word it was touching. And there's no doubt that in the course of that agony I have been ready to weep more than once. Yet not for him. Not for him.'[29]

It cannot be said that the letter shows Conrad in an attractive light; the impulse to represent himself to Garnett as Ford's superior was one that might honourably have been resisted. To Ford, who knew nothing of the betrayal until Garnett published the letter twenty-eight years later, Conrad continued to present a smiling face. He invited his esteemed '*collaborateur*' to lunch and told him that the novel's readers had been quite 'distracted with admiration'.

The readers may have been. The reviewers were not. Most of them took *The Inheritors* to be Conrad's work; few of them thought it did him credit. With such a flat reception, Conrad had to struggle to raise Ford's morale by describing as excellent a tepid review in the *Daily Telegraph* ('Not food for everyone, but . . . a work to be read and well weighed by the thoughtful'),[30] and exclaiming 'This indeed is fame', which it was not. More substantial praise came from America in the *New York Times Saturday Review*, but it was offered to Conrad while Ford was passed over in silence. For the first and last time in his life, Conrad responded to a review; he did so on Ford's behalf. 'The book,' he wrote, 'is emphatically an experiment in collaboration . . . it seems as if Mr Conrad alone were credited with the qualities of style and conception detected by the friendly glance of the critic . . . The elder of the authors is well aware how much of these generously estimated qualities the book owes to the younger collaborator.' As for the 'flashes of that "private vision"' which the critic had singled out for praise, he added, they were all Ford's and, had it not been for his deference to Conrad's scruples, there might have been many more of them.[31] The reader is tempted to detect a twinge of remorse for that earlier betrayal to Garnett. Whatever the motive, it was a generous letter and, in view of his desire for the collaboration to continue, a wise one. It helped to blunt Ford's growing sense that Conrad was reaping all the benefits of his labours and with no one the wiser for it.

With *The Inheritors* out of the way, the collaborators were ready to return to their earlier project of 'Seraphina', later to be retitled *Romance*. An historical adventure story loosely based on fact, 'Seraphina' was intended to be a modern treatment of familiar material, in which they would present 'the scenes and events and people strictly realistically in a glamour of Romance . . . it is a serious attempt at *interesting, animated* Romance, with no more psychology than comes naturally into the action.'[32] The revision, as with *The Inheritors*, was monopolized by Conrad; the creative work was much more equally divided. Part I was by Ford, heavily revised by Conrad, Part II by Ford with light revision and nautical additions by Conrad; Part III was a joint effort, Part IV (thought by both to be the best) entirely by Conrad with a few of Ford's interpolations, Part V almost entirely by Ford. The result, a curious mosaic of both men's styles, ranks low among the works of either. The characterization is weak, the plot poorly motivated, the dialogue often absurd. Even the fourth and best part is full of writing which is not even half good, but woefully bad: 'He gulped, blinked the whites of his eyes, then, in a whisper full of rage – "Horror shame, misery and malediction; I have betrayed you."' What might be tolerable when exalted by the music of a Verdi aria is painfully flat in prose. And yet there are moments when the greatness that was to follow in *Nostromo* is thrillingly apparent. Just when the reader's lip has begun to curl at the fiftieth description of the pure and womanly charm of Seraphina, he comes up against that other, unmistakable voice: 'How often the activity of our life is the least real part of it!'

Ford's plan was that they and their families should go to Belgium for the summer of 1900 and combine work on 'Seraphina' with an agreeable holiday; Conrad was all for the idea. Ford went on ahead while Conrad stayed to finish *Lord Jim* in a twenty-one-hour marathon stint and collect a cheque for it which would help to subsidize the trip.

It was not a happy one. Bruges was unbearably stuffy in July; they moved out to Knocke-sur-Mer where the Conrads' baby, Borys, caught dysentery and almost died. 'It was a nightmarish time, that terrible August we spent in Knocke,' Jessie remembered and added, for once, a kind word for Ford who 'was always at hand to shift my small invalid, fetch the doctor or help with the nursing'.[33] 'Well, it's over. We shall try to be home by the 20th,' Conrad reported to Galsworthy in August, but the book had not progressed a jot.

Back in England, they settled down to a protracted spell of collaborative endeavour at The Pent. 'Working at Seraphina. Bosh! Horrors!'[34] Conrad grumbled to Galsworthy, but to Pinker, his new literary agent, he wrote more cheerfully that the book was ready to be looked at and would be finished by Christmas. This, as Pinker would discover during his long association with Conrad, was a wish, not a certainty; works in progress and works which were never to be realized would always be reported on with a confidence which plunged into depression as the writing started to lag behind the predicted finishing date. Gloom descended in the winter of 1901 as 'Seraphina' increasingly presented itself as an obstacle to his own work. He had finished *Typhoon* and had *Falk* to complete before he dared to commit himself to his share of the collaboration. Money was short and Ford was pressing; Conrad, as always in times of despair, grew ill. Gout and toothache became a recurring refrain in his letters. Jessie had been suffering from neuralgia ever since the disastrous holiday and now, to cap it all, her mother descended on them and fell ill on the first day of her visit. Not until the end of April did Conrad feel up to making another attack on 'Seraphina', at the Fords' new home in Winchelsea, The Bungalow.

Work continued at The Bungalow and The Pent, broken only by Conrad's finding an anecdote about a shipwrecked sailor in Ford's *The Cinque Ports*; it begged to be turned into a short story. 'Seraphina' was laid aside for the writing of *Amy Foster*. Years later, Ford would be happy to claim *Amy Foster* as 'a short story originally by the writer which Conrad took over and entirely re-wrote'. a claim which led to a furious repudiation by Conrad's widow. At the time, Ford was far from pleased at being left to work alone; he needed mollifying. 'Dearest Ford, don't think evil of me,' Conrad pleaded. 'I am doing my damnedest . . . Anyhow I've worked as hard as I know how. I think I'll finish my castaway* tomorrow; and at any rate I intend if at all possible and you will have me to come up to you for a couple of days on Monday and work there at Seraphina . . . Or are you

* *Amy Foster.*

going to London just then? *Do not let me interfere with your plans*. I can work here too; and *shall* work – never fear.'[35]

Blackwood's unexpected rejection of the unfinished novel triggered off a new burst of energy, and Conrad kept his word. The co-authors shuttled to and fro between Winchelsea and The Pent along the dusty roads of late summer, writing, arguing, theorizing, absorbed as two children in their private world of the imagination. To Jessie, alone and cross in her hot bedroom, they seemed peculiarly tiresome children of a thoughtless kind. 'For hours after I had gone to bed the voices would reach me through the floor . . . sounds of wordy strife and disagreement penetrated to my ears, and raised voices came distinctly into my room.'[36] Ford, oblivious of Jessie's resentment, remembered it as a period of fabulous engrossment.

> We would write for whole days, for half nights, for half the day, or all the night. We would jot down passages on scraps of paper or on the margins of books, handing them one to the other or exchanging them. We would roar with laughter over passages that would have struck no other soul as humorous; Conrad would howl with rage and I would almost sigh over others that no other soul perhaps would have found as bad as we considered them. We would recoil one from the other and go each to our own cottage – our cottages at that period never being further the one from the other than an old mare could take us in an afternoon. In those cottages we would prepare other drafts and so drive backwards and forwards with packages of manuscript under the dog-cart seats.[37]

Small wonder that Jessie felt excluded; Ford could almost be describing the intimacy of a marriage.

By November the end was again in sight, with Conrad writing triumphantly to Pinker that 'I've at last finished S. I've put remarkable guts into that story . . . the thing is greatly improved, made more interesting and exciting.'[38] His optimism was premature. They were still hard at it in December with Ford working on the conclusion while Conrad honed the fourth – and best – part; the finishing date had to be put back again when Ford had his misadventure with the chickenbone in the New Year. 'Seraphina seems to hang about me like a curse,' Conrad wrote savagely. In March, they could do no more to it. 'Seraphina is finished and gone out of the house she has haunted for this year past,' Conrad told Galsworthy. 'I do really hope it will hit the taste of the street – unless the devil's in it.'[39]

The devil was up to the challenge. The spring of 1902 was, in every sense, a cruel one. Winter fog clung grimly to the land. The advance on *Romance* (as it would now be retitled) shrank to almost half the anticipated £400 and there were strong hints from Pinker that the book would have to be taken in hand once more and drastically pruned if he was to sell the serial rights. The Fords' older daughter, Christina, developed an alarming inflammation of the lungs. Blackwood rejected *Falk*. Ford warned Conrad that he would have to start looking for a new home as he could not afford to keep up the lease on The Pent while Conrad was always behind with his share. Conrad fell into one of his black despairs. He would not leave. 'I am afraid we can't afford to move from here. Simply can not. Il ne faut pas y penser.'[40] He was 'deadly weary of writing'; neither cheering letters from the Wellses nor a £300 grant from the Royal Literary Fund (largely based on the recommendation supplied by Henry James) could raise the pall of gloom from his shoulders. The frustration he had felt when 'Seraphina' got in the way of his own work was forgotten in a glow of nostalgia for the happy days of collaboration. 'These interrupted relations must be taken up again,' he wrote to Ford in mid-April. 'I miss collaboration in a most ridiculous manner.'[41]

Ford did what he could to help. He dropped his notion of giving up the lease on The Pent and set about encouraging Conrad to get on with his next project, *The End of the Tether*,* a title which aptly reflected its author's state of mind. 'My mind is becoming base,' Conrad told Garnett, 'my hand heavy, my tongue thick – as though I had drunk some subtle poison that will make me die, die as it were without an echo.'[42]

Ford's encouragement was the more generous in that he was also going through a very difficult period. Christina was ill again; Elsie had fallen into a state of nervous depression in which her obsessive self-reproaches for imaginary crimes against her family and friends made for a strained and unhappy household. It is possible that she had already begun to suspect that Ford was having an affair with her sister; the letters, unfortunately, provide no clues. The condition was, however, serious, serious enough for Conrad to send a pre-paid telegram simply asking 'How is Elsie?'

Concern for Ford's wife was swept away by the disaster which struck The Pent on the night of the telegram's despatch.† Conrad had been working round the clock to get *The End of the Tether*

---

* There is no doubt that Ford was behind this. In a letter to Elsie Hueffer on 17 March, 1902, Conrad said that he was just starting *The End of the Tether* 'as Ford has suggested and advised'.

† The telegram is stamped 24 June by the post-office, the day after the disaster, but it seems likely that it was handed in on the previous day, given that Conrad wrote Ford two letters on 24 June.

completed and off to Blackwoods by 24 June. On the night of 23
June, the glass shade of an oil lamp on the writing table exploded
and the lamp caught fire. The manuscript and the typescript of the
second half of the story went up in flames before the fire could be
put out. 'O but the heart break!' Conrad cried out in one of two
distraught letters to Ford on the following day.

Implicit in the letters was an appeal to which Ford rose – would
he come to the rescue? He did. It was in his interest to do so; there
was no possibility of getting Conrad to help cut *Romance* to Pinker's
requirements until *The End of the Tether* was finished. What is not
clear is the extent of Ford's assistance. Conrad's own letters provide
no clue. Jessie tells us only that they took a little cottage near to the
Fords in Winchelsea and that the writing went on through the night
with Ford providing moral support and sandwiches. Ford's own
account suggests a synthesis of two separate events, the rewriting of
the burnt manuscript and the final revision of *Romance* which was
carried out that autumn.

> Conrad wrote; I corrected the manuscript behind him or wrote in a
> sentence – I in my study on the street, Conrad in a two-roomed cottage
> that we had hired immediately opposite. The household sat up all night
> keeping soups warm. In the middle of the night Conrad would open
> his window and shout, 'For heaven's sake give me something for *sale
> pochard*; it's been holding me up for an hour.' I called back, 'Confounded
> swilling pig!' across the dead-still, grass-grown street . . .
>
> Our telegrams would ask what was the latest day, the latest hour,
> the latest half minute that would do if *The End of the Tether* was to
> catch the presses. *Blackwood's* answered, at first Wednesday morning,
> then Thursday. Then Friday night would be just possible . . . At two
> in the morning the mare – another mare by then – was saddled by the
> writer and the stable-boy. The stable-boy was to ride to the junction
> with the manuscript and catch the six-in-the-morning mail-train. The
> soup kept hot; the writers wrote.[43]

Ford, with his wonderful flair for creating a drama, makes it sound
like the ride of Paul Revere; Conrad, more staidly, confirms that it
was finished at dawn.

The curse of 'Seraphina' was still hanging over them in September
of the following year when proof-reading interrupted Conrad's work
on *Nostromo*, which Ford, again, had encouraged him to start writing
and to which he had contributed a couple of reasonably Conradian
paragraphs. (It was one of Ford's most valuable functions as a
collaborator that he could always produce the few lines necessary to

get Conrad going again.) Conrad was heartily sick of the whole project – 'We really cannot give any more of our time to *Romance*,' he wrote irritably to Pinker – and was only concerned that Ford should stop telling people that it had taken six years to write. Three, he thought, would sound a good deal better. Ford ought to consider the unfavourable comparisons reviewers would draw with Stevenson, who could write a romance, single-handed, in a year. It wasn't, he added, as though they had written *Madame Bovary*. *Romance* was not an epoch-making volume.

Conrad, evidently, was apprehensive and the reviews which greeted *Romance*'s appearance in October suggested that his fears were well-founded. His sufferings were easier to bear than those of Ford, who was again blamed for all the faults while Conrad was given the credit for the virtues, but there was no doubt that the enterprise had, financially, been a failure. *Romance* did not 'hit the taste of the street' as they had hoped; the serial rights remained unsold. In material terms, it was a terrible disappointment. But it would be wrong to infer that the two writers had laboured fruitlessly. Conrad's command of English prose was unquestionably broadened; Ford learnt to orchestrate his material and to aim for a greater precision than had been apparent in his earlier work. Both *Nostromo* and *The Good Soldier* were finer books as a result of that early collaboration and exchange of knowledge.

The collaboration did not begin to reach the same kind of intensity until 1908 and the beginnings of the *English Review*, but the links remained close. In 1904, when they were by choice living almost next door to each other in London, Ford proved an invaluable ally, encouraging Conrad to continue with *Nostromo*, helping him to dramatize his short story 'To-morrow' as a one-act play, giving him a story out of which was to grow *The Secret Agent*. He also played an important part in the evolution and realization of Conrad's two autobiographical books, *The Mirror of the Sea* and *A Personal Record*, in both of which the style is much closer to Ford's than Conrad's. Unquestionably, he urged Conrad to write them and worked from Conrad's dictation; he also rewrote much of the earlier section of *The Mirror of the Sea*, freely interpreting the stories which Conrad told him. Jessie's role as amanuensis, the only one through which she could hope to enter the world of Conrad the writer rather than Conrad the family man, was thus supplanted.

There was a reason. Jessie's health, seldom good, declined sharply after a heavy fall in 1904 which badly damaged the cartilage in her knees.* It seemed at the time as though she might never walk

* Jessie had been having problems with her legs since April 1903, when Conrad had been much concerned about her lameness.

again; operations, convalescent holidays and time still left her with a perpetual limp. Heart trouble and neuralgia compounded the problem; in 1905 she had a nervous breakdown while bearing her second child. For moral support at this time, Conrad had to look elsewhere.

Illness is not known to be a sweetener of the temper and it is worth bearing Jessie's physical ailments in mind when we see that her dislike of Ford reached a level of near pathological hate the following year. It was this black mood which coloured the notorious diatribes against Ford which she would publish in 1926 and 1935 as *Conrad as I Knew Him* and *Joseph Conrad and his Circle*.

The germ of dislike was already strongly implanted. Ford was the vociferous cuckoo in the nest who had usurped her place. His passion for the role of the English country gentleman struck her as absurd and his genial references to her as a fisherman's daughter were peculiarly galling to a woman who was intensely conscious of her precarious social standing. She was ready to take umbrage. In the summer of 1906 and from then on, umbrage was taken with a vengeance.

Ford suggested that the Conrads should come down from London that summer to stay at his Winchelsea home for a fortnight; he would join them for weekends. It was, in Jessie's view, a cunning plot to lure Conrad back to the south and provide Ford with a comfortable alternative to his own home at weekends. The Ford household had become rather too hot for him since the disclosure of his affair with Elsie's sister; the Conrads would help to relieve the strain. There may well have been some truth in Jessie's suspicions; Conrad's most recent biographer, Zdzislaw Najder, points to the fact that Ford would do his level best three years later to involve Conrad and Jessie in his liaison with Violet Hunt. But there were also more honourable reasons for the invitation, and for Conrad to take it up with enthusiasm. Ford wanted his collaboration on a pot-boiling enterprise called *The Nature of a Crime* – of which Conrad was later eager to forget that he had written a few pages – while Conrad himself was in need of advice and encouragement on *The Secret Agent*.

They arrived in Winchelsea on 11 May and stayed for just under a fortnight, during which Ford came over for weekends which seemed to Jessie interminably long, 'the longest I have ever known, and a fit punishment for any sins I might have committed, or even contemplated'. The recitation of her sufferings should be tediously petty but is, to a heartless reader, perversely enjoyable if regarded as material for the Grossmiths' chronicles of Mr Pooter's misfortunes, *The Diary of a Nobody*. Jessie has much in common with Mr Pooter.

There was, first of all, the incident of the greasy Panama hat which

Ford dared to put in the oven to dry over Jessie's Sunday joint. 'I removed it to a chair as close to the fire as possible, and resolutely closed the oven, voicing my displeasure in as few words as possible.' The few words did not discourage Ford from making the 'fantastic request' that she should sew a new ribbon into the hat, since she had been kind enough to point out the greasiness of the old one. Jessie did so, 'dutifully'. Next morning, accused by Ford of making a hole in Elsie's tablecloth, Jessie took her revenge. She did not think that mattered, she sweetly said, since Elsie would not be seeing the tablecloth. To which Ford responded, why not? 'I rose quickly to my feet and hastily turned another corner of the cloth towards him, saying slowly and distinctly: "I said she most probably would not see it. You see my name on the corner. I brought my own linen, and I shall take it home with me. Are you satisfied?"' Forgivably, Ford walked out without answering. She simmered with rage when Henry James – 'so essentially a gentleman' – came to tea and Ford shut her in the kitchen. Her temper reached boiling point when she found that Ford had hung his bedcovers up as a curtain and wrapped himself up for the night in Conrad's 'carefully pressed and ironed' morning coat and striped grey trousers.[44] Driven beyond what she regarded as her heroic restraint, Jessie saw no reason to continue even to pretend to be friendly to a guest who was clearly determined to humiliate and enrage her. The more likely but equally enraging truth was that Ford was blithely unaware of causing any offence to a woman he only tolerated for her husband's sake.*

Ford was enjoying his first real taste of success in 1906 with the publication of the opening volume of his Tudor trilogy, *The Fifth Queen*. Conrad was unfeignedly delighted for him. With regard to his own career, he was trapped between pleasure and irritation. He had, in the past year, become fascinated by the darker side of city life of which he had gained some first-hand knowledge in 1905, when he was briefly living in the notoriously scruffy Kennington area. 'Verloc', later *The Secret Agent*, had been the result, completed in November 1906. Having, as he thought, put the high seas behind him, Conrad was only moderately pleased to find himself being hailed by the reviewers as a master mariner for *The Mirror of the Sea*,

---

* Time hardened Jessie's conviction that she had always detested Ford. Her husband's letters suggest that it was not always so. In 1906, Conrad wrote to Ford that Jessie wished him to know that she 'has for you far more affection than she knows how to express'; in 1907, he told Ford that Jessie was 'very grateful to you the "Onlie begetter" of this work of art like the late lamented Mr H. of Shakespeare's sonnets.' The work in question was the cookery book which Ford had suggested she should write.

just published. Kipling, Galsworthy and Wells united in praising it and Henry James sent an unusually warm letter of appreciation for an 'adorable book . . . I find you in it all, *writing* wonderfully, whatever you may say of your difficult medium and your *plume rebelle*. You knock about in the wide waters of expression like the raciest and boldest of privateers – you have made the whole place your own *en même temps que les droits les plus acquis et vous y avez les plus rares bonheurs*. Nothing you have done has more in it.'[45] But Conrad was glum: 'Behind the concert of flattery, I can hear something like a whisper: "Keep to the open sea! Don't land!" They want to banish me to the middle of the ocean.'[46]

Still owing Ford rent, the Conrads left The Pent in 1907. The doctors had urged Wells to stay on the south coast for his health; in Conrad's case, it was thought that higher land would benefit him and also Borys, whose medical history had recently featured a catalogue of disasters, with scarlet fever, whooping cough, pleurisy and the threat of tuberculosis. Someries was a large farmhouse on Sir Julius Wernher's estate in Bedfordshire which had the advantage of being on higher ground than The Pent, and to Someries the Conrads removed themselves. Conrad, rudely observing that 'a flavour of South Africa and Palestine hangs about our old walled garden', detested his new home and referred to it in his letters as 'that damned Luton place'. He longed to be back in the South and in closer touch with his old friend over the inauguration of the *English Review* which he had readily involved himself in helping to organize. The *English Review* was seen by both men as a way of promoting the kind of writing they admired and their aims were, on this occasion, synonymous. A secondary reason for wanting to see Ford was that he had begun work on *A Personal Record* in the summer of 1908; Ford had declared his readiness to undertake again the role of secretary and memory-prompter, as he had so successfully done with *The Mirror of the Sea*.

In August 1908, Conrad took his family off to Aldington where Ford and Elsie were living in uneasy conjugality. The Fords' home, as Jessie was quick to note, was spacious, comfortable and well-furnished; their own rented lodgings in a local farmhouse were unpleasingly inferior.

Ford's claims to have taken down *A Personal Record* from Conrad's dictation are convincingly reduced but not entirely dismissed by Professor Najder; it remains clear that Conrad's approach to this book about his early life sharpened and grew more confident during his three weeks of discussing it with Ford in Aldington.[47] The book was of particular interest to Ford since Conrad was prepared to let him publish these 'intimate personal autobiographical things' as a series for the *English Review*; they struck the magazine's editor as being excellent copy.

Jessie's grumbles went unheard. The authors were back in harness, brothers-in-arms again, united in the cause of the *English Review*, ready to fight for all they thought best in English literature.

Elated by this return to what were now remembered as the halcyon days of their partnership and full of excitement about the *English Review*, Conrad invited the magazine's editorial staff to come to Someries in November to complete the first number, to be published in December. Jessie, excluded again, retained wrathful memories of being kept up all night by 'the sounds of footsteps and voices conversing between the ground floor and the banisters. The consumption of lamp oil and candles was prodigious.' Ford had treated her like a servant and, as usual, had outstayed his welcome.[48]

March 1909 found the Conrads back at Aldington again in quarters which were even less to Jessie's liking than those of the previous year. Ford, whose London flat was above a poultry and fish shop, saw no harm in installing his friend in four tiny rooms over the Aldington butcher and beer-shop. On killing days, when the butcher started curing bacon for Hythe market, closed windows could not keep out the squeals from the slaughter yard or the sickly stench of the curing shed. Sanitary arrangements were virtually non-existent and the only water to be got came from an open ditch by the roadside; Jessie could hardly be blamed for complaining.

Conrad, too, soon began to regret this second return to the south. They had barely installed themselves in their uncomfortable rooms before the ugly complications of Ford's private life threatened to engulf them, with Elsie trying as hard as her husband to suck them into the maelstrom of bad-feeling. Disgusted by Elsie's hurrying over to drop hints that their friend, Marwood, had been trying to seduce her, Conrad made no secret of his distaste and disbelief. When, undeterred, she went on to propose that Ford should spend his country weekends with them over the butcher's shop, he bluntly spoke his mind – and wrote to tell Ford that he had done so. 'What is the point of such a proposal; what object, what purpose can be served by re-creating such an equivocal situation? . . . I can't breathe in situations that are not clear. I abhor them. They are neither in my nature nor in my tradition, nor in my experience.' To Ford himself, he issued a sharp warning to keep his domestic troubles to himself if he did not wish to find himself 'with only the wrecks of friendship at your feet'.[49]

The situation worsened a few weeks later when Ford issued a

peremptory reprimand to his old friend for having failed to give a properly obsequious welcome to Willa Cather, whose employers, *McClure's Magazine*, were backing the *English Review*. 'Stop this nonsense with me Ford,' Conrad wrote back fiercely. 'It's ugly. I won't have it.'[50] A savage altercation which then ensued over the occasion of his postponing his instalments of *A Personal Record* for the *English Review* decided Conrad to sever all connections with Ford. He used the thin excuse of his dislike for David Soskice, Ford's brother-in-law who was now involved in negotiations for the financing of the magazine, to refuse to write any more for it. His letter of explanation was, for the first time in eleven years, addressed to 'Dear Hueffer' and signed 'Yours, J. Conrad'. To Pinker, who represented both of them, he wrote more frankly of the impossibility of continuing to have dealings with such an impossible man. 'He's a megalomaniac who imagines that he is managing the Universe and that everybody treats him with the blackest ingratitude . . . I do not hesitate to say that there are cases, not quite as bad, under medical treatment.'[51] Fourteen years later, when Ford tried to persuade him to write something for the *transatlantic review*, of which he had just become the editor, the memory was still disagreeable enough for Conrad to refuse. He had, he said unconvincingly, 'dried up'.

Two years after their estrangement, Ford published a rather feeble skit called *The Simple Life Limited* under the pseudonym of Daniel Chaucer. In it, he satirized Conrad as a writer of Lithuanian or Polish extraction called Simeon Brandeiski, a man whose intolerable laziness prompts him to hire a secretary to turn his inspirations into books. She becomes her master's mistress and, eventually, his wife. It may have been, as Professor Najder suggests, that Ford was slyly alluding to Conrad's marriage to a typist; at the back of his mind, there must also have been the memory of his own role as Conrad's devoted drudge. If Conrad read the book, he made no reference to it; he left us his own portrait of Ford in *Chance* as de Barral, the crooked financier.

Old friendships die hard and Ford would continue to cling to the hope of resurrecting some flicker of warmth from the ashes. Conrad remained polite but withdrawn, both to Ford and to Elsie, who suggested in 1920 that they should pick up the old threads. Kindly but implacably, Conrad wrote to her to say that he could see no point in their doing so.

There were two final meetings in 1924, the year before Conrad's death. Ford was planning to publish *The Nature of a Crime* under both of their names; he wanted Conrad to write a preface to it.

Without enthusiasm, Conrad gave his consent and when Ford wrote back proposing a brief visit to Oswalds, their home near Canterbury, he felt unable to refuse. (Jessie, however, was quick to send her old enemy the times of the most inconvenient trains in the hope of putting him off.) Ford came and, deceived by Conrad's calm courtesy, began to hope that friendly relations could be re-established. He 'wants to be friendly in personal relations with me,' Conrad wrote to Pinker. 'In fact, *entre nous*, too friendly.'[52] His fears were borne out two months later when Ford suddenly burst through the door on an impromptu visit. Conrad was displeased; Jessie was furious. 'That odious Hueffer has just turned up. J.C. wanted to bring him up here for tea but I declined as what is the use of letting him get very friendly again. I dislike him profoundly.'[53]

A renewal of the old friendship was a hopeless fantasy of Ford's, but there had, in the intervening years, been a brief moment of *rapprochement*. In the December 1911 issue of the *English Review*, Ford wrote a perceptive and warmly appreciative tribute to Conrad. Touched as much as anything else by the generosity of spirit which the article displayed, Conrad wrote to him to express his gratitude – and to confirm Ford's memory of their happier times. 'What touches me most is to see that you do not discard our common past,' he wrote. 'These old days may not have been such very "good old days" as they should have been – but to me my dear Ford they are a very precious possession.'[54]

6

LIVING PRUDENTLY: JAMES'S FRIENDSHIPS

It is really good enough to be a kind of little, becoming, high-door'd, brass-knocker'd *façade* to one's life.
> Henry James on Lamb House to Arthur Benson, 1897

Think only of my love and that I am yours always and ever.
> Henry James to Hendrik Andersen, 1902

We must know, as much as possible, in your beautiful art, yours and mine, what we are talking about – and the only way to know it is to have lived and loved and cursed and floundered and enjoyed and suffered.
> Henry James to Hugh Walpole, 1913

1898	In Italy, James visits Mrs Humphry Ward and meets Hendrik Andersen in Rome.
1898	James had known Violet Hunt since she was a child but it was now that the friendship began to develop.
1903	James meets Jocelyn Persse in London. He is also involved in the embarrassing affair of Miss Grigsby, who wished it to be known that he was in love with her.
1909	Henry James breaks off his association with Violet Hunt and Ford Madox Ford. He begins a new relationship with Hugh Walpole, and is entranced by the beauty of Rupert Brooke.

6

LIVING PRUDENTLY:
JAMES'S FRIENDSHIPS

In 1925, when Violet Hunt was at work on her autobiography, *The Flurried Years* – a work more striking for its generosity of feeling than for its elegance of style – she found herself remembering a curious episode at Lamb House when Henry James had unlocked a secret drawer and taken out the photograph of a young woman, carefully wrapped in silver paper. He had touched it reverently, almost like a talisman. Violet, usually very forward with her questions, had felt that it was indelicate to ask who the woman was; years later, she could only suggest a sister, or, perhaps, a cousin.

It is possible that the treasured photograph was of Alice James; it is more likely that it was the one of Minnie Temple which he had begged his mother to send him in 1870, the year Minnie died of tuberculosis, aged only twenty-five. 'I should very much like to have it,' he had written then, 'for the day when to think of her will be nothing but pure blessedness.'[1]

Insofar as James was ever in love with a woman, he was in love with his witty charming cousin Minnie, his childhood companion during the idyllic Newport summers, the high-spirited girl to whom he and his friends were drawn like moths to the flame as she reached marriageable age. 'Most of those who knew and loved, I was going to say adored her,' he wrote as an old man still in love with the memory of her 'long light and almost sliding steps' and her pretty way of tossing her head. Minnie seemed a little barbarous to Mrs James, who thought a European education would have made the world of difference; her charm for Henry lay in her lack of sophistication. She was for him the embodiment of innocence, 'with all that wonderful ethereal brightness of presence which was so peculiarly her own'.[2]

He had been content to worship Minnie from a distance as 'the very heroine of our common scene'; death allowed him to take possession of her, to acknowledge and feed on his devotion to 'a steady unfaltering luminary in the mind' rather than 'a flickering wasting earth-stifled lamp'.[3] For a man who never betrayed any sign of physical desire for a woman or any taste for married life, it was better so. Minnie would never grow old now, would never do anything to disappoint him, would never threaten him: '. . . this on the whole surpasses anything I had conceived,' he told William less than a week after hearing of Minnie's death. 'She has gone where there is neither marrying nor giving in marriage! no illusions and no disillusions – no sleepless nights and no ebbing strength. The more I think of her the more perfectly satisfied I am to have her translated from this changing realm of fact to the steady realm of thought.'[4] These were curious sentiments for a young man of twenty-seven to express; they strangely foreshadow the thoughts of George Stransom fifteen years later as he creates a shrine of candles for his dead friends in 'The Altar of the Dead'.

> There were hours at which he almost caught himself wishing that certain of his friends would now die, that he might establish with them in this manner a connection more charming than, as it happened, it was possible to enjoy with them in life. In regard to those from whom one was separated by the long curves of the globe such a connection could only be an improvement; it brought them instantly within reach.[5]

Profoundly moving though the story of Stransom and the woman who unknowingly erects a shrine to his greatest enemy is, it contains a morbid element which many readers have found hard to take. There was something a little unhealthy, too, in James's satisfaction at having Minnie translated to a purely cerebral plane, and worshipping at her discreetly hidden shrine in Lamb House.

His photograph preserved her at the height of her youthful beauty. It was that image which would inspire him to immortalize her in his stories and novels as the quintessential young American girl, inexperienced and impulsive, leaning forward with outstretched arms to embrace whatever life should offer. Pandora Day, Daisy Miller and Isabel Archer all have in them something of the bright spirit of Minnie Temple. Through Isabel in *The Portrait of a Lady*, Minnie's life was extended. Isabel, as her surrogate, travels to Europe where she is courted and pursued before she enters the living death of marriage to Gilbert Osmond – a worse fate, in James's view, than the youthful extinction of Minnie. In his more piercingly tragic portrait of her as Milly Theale in *The Wings of the Dove*, doomed to die when 'she would have given anything to live', he seems at last to have faced the fact that, whatever his own feelings may have been, death had been the most terrible of prospects to Minnie herself. In the closing sentences of that novel, it is likely that he was reflecting on his own strange love for a dead girl as he made Kate Croy confront her lover with his loyalty to the dead Milly.

> 'Your word of honour that you're not in love with her memory.'
> 'Oh – her memory.'
> 'Ah' – she made a high gesture – 'don't speak of it as if you couldn't be. *I* could in your place; and you're one for whom it will do. Her memory's your love. You *want* no other.'
> He heard her out in stillness, watching her face but not moving. Then he only said: 'I'll marry you, mind you, in an hour.'
> 'As we were?'
> 'As we were.'
> But she turned to the door, and her headshake was now the end. 'We shall never be again as we were!'[6]

When a man fails to show any inclination to marry, it is customary to look harder than usual at his relationship with his mother. Mary James can be slotted into the category of the domineering mother, but her domination was of that subtle kind which poses as selfless devotion and proclaims self-sacrifice in order to obtain emotional control. Henry, the adored 'angel' of her four children, would call her one ('no more of an angel today than she had always been') in his notebook entry for 9 February, 1882, eleven days after her death. 'She was our life, she was the house, she was the keystone of the arch,' he wrote in a passion of regret. 'She was patience, she was wisdom, she was exquisite maternity . . . It was a perfect mother's life – the life of a perfect wife.'[7]

We cannot doubt the sincerity of the feelings expressed here, and yet, as both Leon Edel and Jean Strouse, Alice James's biographer, have pointed out, the mothers of James's novels suggest that he recognized more complex elements in Mary James's attitude to her children than could decently be discussed outside the realms of fiction. The mothers of his creating mind are almost daemonic. Mrs Brookenham and the Duchess in *The Awkward Age* prey on their children; the first and second Mrs Farange are heartless manipulators of a young girl's feelings in *What Maisie Knew*; Madame de Bellegarde destroys Claire de Cintré's life by refusing to let her marry a foreign commoner in *The American*; Juliana de Bordereau, a mother-figure to her niece Tina in *The Aspern Papers*, reduces her to the role of a captive slave. Looking at that list, it is hard to believe that James was unaware of his mother's manipulative side.

Ironically, most of Mrs James's manipulations were directed to the end of making sure that her son found himself a wife. In 1874, when he was travelling in Europe, she went so far as to write and urge him to contemplate the joys of matrimony. He was thirty years old. It was time for him to settle down. 'You would make, dear Harry, according to my estimate, the most loving and loveable and happiest of husbands. I wish I could see you in a favourable attitude of heart towards the divine institution of marriage.'[8]

James, passing an agreeable year in Rome and Florence, was ready to offer the comforting news that he had been 'within an ace of falling wholesomely in love', but the marital ball was returned smartly to her court. 'If you will provide the wife, the fortune, and the "inclination" I will take them all.'[9] Mrs James did not take up this invitation, resigning herself instead to the sad fact that two of her offspring, Henry and Alice, were not of the marrying kind.

Confirmed bachelors are, of necessity, deft side-steppers of temptations and proposals. James only missed his step on two occasions.

The first was the absurd incident of Miss Emilie Grigsby, a rich and plumply pretty young redhead from Kentucky who was eager to make her mark in English literary society. She was twenty-three when, spotting James at a London tea-party, she approached him and simperingly inquired whether he did not share all her friends' view that she looked just like Milly Theale. Perhaps James murmured a polite affirmative; it was enough for Miss Grigsby, who would spend the rest of her life announcing that she had been the model for a book which James had written before he ever met her. Invitations were issued and declined until, feeling that he had been unnecessarily churlish, James decided to offer the sop of a ten-minute call on the young lady at the Savoy, her London residence.

It was hardly a courtship, but Miss Grigsby was not averse to spreading a few hints. In the spring of the following year, 1904, James was outraged by the arrival of a jocular letter from William, asking about his forthcoming marriage to Miss Grigsby. If William had heard about it, James could gloomily suppose that it was the talk of Cambridge. He was furious. The idea of his being engaged to anyone, he angrily wrote back, was quite 'fantastic . . . *She* must have put about the "rumour" which, though I thought her silly, I didn't suppose her silly *enough* for. But who – of her sex and species – isn't silly enough for *anything*, in this nightmare-world of insane *bavardage*? It's appalling that such winds may be started to blow, about one, by not so much as the ghost of an exhalation of one's own . . .' And, in case William should have missed the point, he signed himself with careful emphasis as 'your hopelessly celibate even though sexagenarian Henry'.[10]

William was satisfied, but the press had not yet supped their full on the story. On 4 January, 1906, the *New York Evening Journal* printed an article which, while carefully stating that nothing had been confirmed and that Miss Grigsby's friends treated her story with considerable scepticism, brought vulgarly to the fore the image of the elderly novelist making a fool of himself over a young girl. With a qualifying 'It may or not be true', the article stated that James had been 'deeply in love with Miss Grigsby – that at sixty-five he sneered at conventionalities and in full knowledge of her past he laid his great fame at her feet and asked her to marry him'. The piece was accompanied by a caricature depicting a lascivious Henry James eyeing a portrait of the delectable Miss Grigsby. James's wrath may easily be imagined; prudently, he refrained from comment.

The second incident took place the following year and concerned another daughter of Kentucky, Miss Elizabeth Robins, an actress renowned for her dramatic interpretations of Ibsen's controversial women. Meeting her in 1891, when she was appearing in *A Doll's House*, James was much struck by the combination of a strong and very determined character with a pretty, touchingly vulnerable appearance; she, in turn, was greatly taken by him, confiding to her diary that he was 'delightfully grave' and that she liked him better than any male American she had met abroad. In her public role, Miss Robins was at the centre of a furore over her appearance in plays which were considered shockingly frank both in their exposure of adulterous relationships and in their broaching of such unmentionable subjects as syphilis. In her private life, Miss Robins maintained considerable discretion. Her long affair with the drama critic, William Archer, was conducted in secret; her later career as a novelist-cum-investigative journalist was cloaked by a pseudonym until another Ibsenite, Mrs Pat Campbell, spotted a bundle of proofs and decided to tell all.

Discretion veiled Miss Robins's past as efficiently as her present. James, admiring her iron will, was probably unaware of the lengths to which her steely determination to make her name had driven her former husband. Mr Parkes, an actor whose odd habit it was to keep a suit of stage armour in his room, had tried in vain to persuade her to give up acting and stay at home. Foiled in his attempt, he had donned his armour and drowned himself in the Charles river after leaving a note of explanation for his wife to read on her return home. The publicity had been disagreeable; Miss Robins came to England determined to leave her past behind.

In 1891, when they first met, James was looking for an actress to play the part of Claire de Cintré in his adaptation of *The American*;

Miss Robins seemed ideal. It was bad casting – she lacked the lightness required for the part – but the friendship with James continued to ripen, based as soundly as it was on their mutual interest in Miss Robins. She was eager for parts that would test and extend her range; James was confident that he could write just such a part with her in mind.

James's extant letters to his compatriot are affectionate, but by no stretch of the imagination could they be described as amorous. There is, however, evidence that the relationship did develop into something more than a cordial friendship. It comes from one of the entries which Percy Lubbock, a close friend of James's, chose not to publish from Arthur Benson's diary for 1905: the 'again' suggests that Benson knew about the embarrassing affair of (but not with) Miss Grigsby in 1904.

> 12 Nov. – 16 Dec. 1905
> Two other things I forgot to put down which Gosse told me. One is that Henry James has fallen again under the fascination of an American actress and authoress, a hysterical and demented widow, known as Miss Robbins [sic]. Gosse says that he daily expects to hear their marriage announced. She, he says, is 30, fanciful, neurotic, selfish and not in love with him. He is over 60. Gosse says deliberately that he thinks it a failure of mind and will-power in H.J. And he augurs the worst miseries if it takes place.[11]

The marriage did not, of course, take place. The question is only, did anything at all take place? Did the famously lustrous blue eyes and appealing ways of Elizabeth Robins make this unlikely conquest?

We only have Gosse's word for it, and Gosse was a malicious scandal-monger, and yet there is the name and a description which fits well enough. It is true that Miss Robins was nearer forty-five than thirty in 1905, but that is not enough to discredit the evidence; it has always been the business of an actress to look younger than her years, and her prerogative to adjust the calendar accordingly. It is possible that Gosse was telling the truth. There is clearly no confusion with Emilie Grigsby – the 'again' rules that out. Nor can we argue a case against it from the knowledge of Miss Robins's affair with William Archer since there is no suggestion that she responded to James in kind.

No love letters are extant, but we know from James's earlier relationship with Constance Fenimore Woolson that he was capable of going to extraordinary lengths to destroy personal correspondence which he feared might incriminate him. (He gained entrance to Miss Woolson's Venetian apartment after her death, and there destroyed his letters to her.) It is entirely possible that he persuaded Miss Robins to get rid of any personal letters he had penned to her.

Existing letters offer meagre clues. Elizabeth Robins was one of his two companions – the other was Edith Wharton's friend, Walter Berry – on his journey home from America in July 1905. His correspondence tells us that he found her agreeable. A later letter to Mrs Clifford written on 17 February 1907 suggests that Miss Robins was deliberately keeping James at a distance. If Gosse's report was true, she might well have been anxious to avoid any personal conversation with her pursuer. The letter certainly conveys an unusual degree of frustration in the correspondent.

> There popped in Elizabeth Robins – but on such a footing of universal engagement and entanglement and with not a minute to be able to arrange for, not a single solitary *one*, for a whole fortnight, that after subsequent vain reachings out and telephonings and strugglings and yearnings, I had to come away with no other glimpse of her but that poor frustrated instant (she arriving after I had risen to go). The fury of social submersion in which she elects to live and 'work' staggers my intelligence . . .[12]

James may well have been enamoured of Miss Robins. She was an intelligent woman and a pretty one, and she was possessed of considerable charm. So, was the fury of social submersion increased to avoid an awkward encounter with a man whom she had no wish to offend? It is not impossible.

No hint of romance can be detected in James's long-standing friendship with Violet Hunt, who allowed James to indulge himself in playing one of his favourite roles, that of the shy and infirm old bachelor who looks on wonderingly at the tireless energy displayed by his younger friends. He called her 'the woman-about-town' and gave himself the persona of 'the country cousin'.

Violet first met James when, not yet old enough to know better, she had stared with unabashed interest at the stout and anxious-looking gentleman who was endeavouring to purchase indigestion pills in a London pharmacy. She had, since then, grown up into a forceful and striking-looking young woman with a reputation for intelligence which was only matched by her name for being a woman much given to passionate affairs. She would not have been reluctant to have had one with James if he had showed any interest. She gave him a hint by drifting 'as I know how' into the drawing-room at Lamb House on a chilly November evening in 1907, dressed only in a skimpy white Chinese dressing-gown. She could offer the excuse of

being unwell; James was most solicitous and admiring, but not willing
to be seduced. Violet, thwarted, had to make do with discussing the
highly respectable novels of their mutual friend, Mrs Humphry
Ward.

Violet made several visits to Lamb House, where she readily
supplied its owner with the latest news about Lucy Clifford, to whom
they were both devoted. James, in turn, looked forward to his
London tête-à-têtes with 'the Improper Person of Babylon', as he
irreverently rechristened her, either at her little house in Adelphi
Terrace or at one of the several clubs to which she belonged. He
balked at Violet's endeavours to coax him into meeting her smart
circle of London friends. 'Let me crudely tell you that it's death to
me to meet new women, & make new acquaintances. Notes, dinners,
complications of every sort are sown by it even as dragons' teeth,'
he wrote after one such invitation in 1906.[13] She should not wonder
if he had not seen her for some time. It was on account of her
'furiously (I won't say curiously) social character. You are Society,
and I am more and more contemplative detachment – hanging on to
the world after the fashion of a very obese spider.'[14] But the rejections
were good-humouredly made and the preference James showed for
having Violet all to himself did not displease her.

The charm of the friendship for James was, in Violet's eyes, in
gathering the newest nuggets of scandal and gossip which she could
be relied on to produce (her 'little mice' as she coyly called them).
As an audience, however, he was not ideal. She learnt, with difficulty,
to suppress her irritation when he checked her in mid-stream. 'He
would hold up a story as soon as he had got all he needed out of it;
extend a finger – "Thank you so much – all I want" – and leave you
with the point of your anecdote on your hands.'[15] It was an infuriating
habit, but one to which she understood that it was necessary to
submit with grace.

James would seem, until the unfortunate publication of her liaison
with Ford, to have been greatly entertained by this loquacious romancer and to have enjoyed her company enough to relish entertaining her alone at his country home. He was a sympathetic audience
to her family problems (Violet had been given the arduous responsibility of caring for her invalid mother by her married sisters, aptly
nicknamed Goneril and Regan in her memoirs for their harsh indifference). Violet, in turn, felt that she did James good. She livened him
up. 'I do not think that permanent solitude and everlasting dictation
was the best life for Henry James,' she told American readers of her
memoirs. 'Dictating made him slightly prosy; solitude made him
sad. He seemed to sigh continually for the fresh welling of founts of

A graphologist's interpretation of Henry James's character, made from samples of his handwriting. This is probably the first time that an analysis of his handwriting has been published.

The writer is an emotional man who is distressed if people do not share his views. He prepares letters – and probably conversations – well ahead in order to avoid unpleasantness or misunderstanding Although he seems to write effortlessly, it is likely that rough notes have been made in preparation for the letter.

Unlike most men, he shows his feelings freely to his friends and is eager to discuss any slights he feels he has suffered He likes to receive attention and kindness but the loyalty which he expects from others is not always returned The temptation to be maliciously amusing at other people's expense is quite strong. Nervousness and insecurity underlie his seemingly relaxed and effortless manner. He is subject to unpredictable emotional swings, from happiness to deep depression. He worries a good deal about his health. Socially, he is tenacious and eager to please.

His large and unusually ornate capital letters suggest that he is not an original thinker. He is not religious. As a guest, he can be exhausting, since he likes conversation to be orchestrated for his benefit. As a host, he feels under no pressure to return hospitality. He can, however, be relied on to 'sing well for his supper'.

The depressive tendency is unusually marked in his writing.

scandal . . .'* He reminded her of a wicked priest, saying, '"Go, my daughter, go in peace and sin some more."'[16] Her readers learned that Violet 'was the weak prop by whose help he made his little descents into reality, the Purple Patch, the violet ray in his spectrum.'[17]

Violet enjoyed playing the woman of the world for his benefit – and James enjoyed the performance, except on the occasions when indiscretion got the better of his guest and she launched into accounts of her past affairs. With the polite brutality of which he was always capable when cornered, James would cut her short, rising to his feet abruptly to leave her 'like a dog who has had his bone'. He had no wish to hear about her liaison with Wells or of the agonies she had endured at the hands of their mutual friend, Oswald Crawfurd. Stories almost always pleased James; revelations disquieted and discomforted him.

Violet shared Ford's ability to reshape her stories according to whim. In the American edition of *The Flurried Years* she attributed her nickname of 'The Purple Patch' to her fondness for the colour which was immensely fashionable at that time. (Even typewriter-ribbons printed in purple, hence, perhaps, the expression 'purple prose'.) She had seen a letter from one of the gossiping ladies of Rye which stated that '"Mr James was seen driving about the marsh yesterday in a victoria with a lady in a purple veil." That was, indeed, I. I wore this ridiculous encumbrance to keep my hair tidy and a purple coat to match, and pillow for my back. That was why he called me the Purple Patch.'[18] But to her English readers, Violet offered the information that James had given her the nickname by way of an apologetic reference to her behaviour and his attitude at the time when he forbade her to visit Lamb House because of her connection with Ford. (It was not, incidentally, an ethical decision on James's part. He was one of the first to urge Edith Wharton to consider leaving her husband and he was very happy to meet his friend Sidney Waterlow when he was divorcing Alice Pollock to marry a Miss Eckhardt. It was the fear of publicity which decided him to keep Violet at a distance.)

By 1926, when her autobiography was published, Violet was eager to make light of that humiliating time when she had been told she would not be welcome at James's home. 'For that little *rixe* of last year was all 'Enery's old-maidishness of spirits . . . He was like the ladies of Cranford, providing themselves with umbrellas and goloshes [sic] for fear of possible downpour . . . He always, from that time,

---

* Violet cut down on her confiding asides in the English edition of her memoirs.

called me the "Purple Patch" and in 1913 he told me to "go on being one" and giving him teas at my club."[19]

This, like many of Violet's recollections, is an airy blending of fact and fantasy. The friendship was cautiously renewed, but never on the old easy terms. There were no more invitations to Lamb House and, although letters were exchanged, there is no evidence that James returned to his old custom of 'teas at the club' with Violet. We have her word for it that she visited him in 1915 to talk about a fund-raising article that he had written, but James's diary shows no record of the occasion. Nor, in 1913, does he make any note of having seen Violet to effect a reconciliation. On 19 April, 1912, he tersely notes that he has seen Ford and Violet and gone home with them for half-an-hour. It is the only entry for that year to which he appends a careful note of the length of time spent on the visit, and half an hour is not a long visit. This, we must assume, was the occasion which Violet, in her autobiography, transformed into a blissful afternoon which James seemed reluctant ever to bring to an end. The half-hour, in her version, is merely the length of one of the delightful, interminable sentences which he bestowed on them.

Quite as forceful and better placed than Violet to keep James under her thumb was Lady Maud Warrender, the smartest of his neighbours at Rye, and one he was most ready to cultivate. She first descended on him one day in 1903, announcing herself with a peremptory telegram inviting herself to lunch. She had come to inspect Leasam, a charming Georgian country house overlooking the town, and had promptly fallen in love with it. Sir Reginald Blomfield, the architect whose house James had once rented at Point Hill, could make the necessary improvements and extensions; the gardens would have to be redesigned – what did James think?

James was all in favour of the idea. Lady Maud was a daughter of the Earl of Shaftesbury. She and her husband were close friends of Edward VII and their circle comprised an intriguing blend of aristocrats and intellectuals. (Not that the two are necessarily mutually exclusive.) Their presence would lend a pleasing elegance to Rye.

Lady Maud, who remained devoted to Leasam, fulfilled all the expectations to which James was led by their first meeting. A gifted singer of commanding appearance – she was almost six foot and fond of wearing unusually high-crowned hats – she loved filling her pretty new home with amusing friends. Here, on a summer evening at the end of one of his favourite walks up shady Point Hill, James was welcomed into the kind of English setting he excelled in describing

– the leisurely Edwardian world of Fawns and Mertle in *The Golden Bowl* and *The Awkward Age* – and in which he was effortlessly at ease. Strolling along the Italianate terraces with a sympathetic glance for the Warrenders' garden cemetery of Leasam dogs, or sitting in one of the airy, well-proportioned drawing-rooms, he could always be sure of agreeable company and civilized conversation. Sir Edward Elgar might be there, Arthur Balfour, a Duchess or two, Ellen Terry, the Kiplings, and always a pianist ready to accompany Lady Maud if she chose to sing to them in her mellow and remarkably deep contralto.

Sometimes, impelled to entertain her friends with an excursion, Lady Maud would turn the tables and invade Lamb House, sweeping down the hill with a party of house-guests to demand hospitality in her cheerfully autocratic way. And, while most uninvited visitors were brusquely shown the door, she was always welcomed in. 'Lady Maud is such a handsome good-natured creature,' James would apologetically murmur to his secretary as the morning's work was hurriedly put away, 'one has to forgive her everything.'[20]

Ignorance is, on occasion, bliss. James might not have been so ready to forgive Lady Maud's intrusions had he known of the entertainment he was providing for her guests. Pretty witty Mary Crawshay, hearing that he had joined the followers of Horace Fletcher who dutifully chewed all food into liquid before swallowing it, caused much mirth at Leasam by asking when he had felt the call of the Salivation Army, while another unnamed guest, noting that Mr James's secretary was decorously housed in Watchbell Street, recited this little rhyme:

> Henry has a little Lamb
> House – and not a sheep.
> When ladies come to stay with him
> He puts them out to sleep.[21]

With these exceptions and, of course, the most important one, Edith Wharton,* Henry James remained most at ease with older women or with those like Mrs Humphry Ward whose gravity was such that they could never have seemed young. Fanny Kemble was the oldest of them all and the one he had loved best for her age-defying wit and for her fund of extraordinary recollections of Regency England when she had been the darling of the London stage before

---

* The relationship with Edith Wharton and with their mutual circle of friends which centred on Howard Sturgis's home in Windsor at Queen's Acre, is discussed in Chapter 8.

she married a rich Philadelphian and became a passionate abolitionist – but Fanny had died in 1893, long before James came to Rye. So too, in 1894, had Constance Fenimore Woolson, the ironic and independent American writer to whom James had been an affectionate companion but not, on the evidence, a lover, for some fourteen years.

In the summer of 1887, James had written *The Aspern Papers* while staying alone with Miss Woolson at the Villa Brichieri, a dark but handsome building situated on the steep hillside of Bellosguardo overlooking Florence. It had been a halcyon period and one in which James found himself enjoying domestic life, the nearest he ever came to the experience of marriage. True, he and Miss Woolson occupied separate apartments in the villa in which they wrote and, we must assume, slept, but the separation was no greater than in most marriages where both parties work at home. They only had one visitor, Rhoda Broughton, and, after Miss Woolson's tragic death (she threw herself out of a window in Venice) Miss Broughton remained to James as the only witness to their intimate friendship. With her and with her alone, he could talk about that perfect summer. That, perhaps, is the main reason for the frequency with which Miss Broughton's name features in James's engagement-books. Old men do not forget, they only grow more selective in their memories, and more eager to dwell on them.

Sumptuously dressed in brilliant colours, she had a lively determined manner, a no-nonsense attitude to intellectual matters and a fondness for keeping her friends in order. Short and energetic, she had a small face with a sharply tilted nose and very bright eyes. Rhoda Broughton was the same age as Miss Woolson, three years older than James. He had not expected to make a friend of her. He had written a disparaging review of one of her novels in the *Nation*, reviling her for 'coarseness of sentiment and vacuity of thought' before comparing her efforts at sublety to 'the gambols of an elephant'. Many a Victorian three-decker novelist was more deserving of such accusations than Rhoda and few were more modest about their talent. Meeting her at a London dinner-party and relishing her ebullient pugnacity, James decided that it didn't matter what her books were like. She delighted him. Then and always, she was 'the gallant Rhoda' to whom, in lonely moments, he would wistfully write of 'our old and so valid friendship' and to whom, face to face, he could speak with the absolute frankness which Rhoda expected of her friends. She hated falseness, and she wanted no favours: if James invited her to go to a play with him, as he often did, she would accept with pleasure – on the condition that she might pay for her own seat. Percy Lubbock, who knew them both well, made a digression in his short study of another mutual friend, Mary Chol-mondley, to describe their relationship. The secret of its success lay, he thought, in Miss Broughton's refusal to be intimidated. 'Rhoda loved him greatly, but feared him not at all; she welcomed him with delight, but she didn't cherish or spoil him; and she could disconcert him at times, what with her boldness of attack and her insensibility to the shades and the semi-tones and the fine degrees of civilized thought. It was beautiful to see them together, complicated cosmo-politanized America and barbarous old Britain.' Britain, in his recollection, usually emerged victorious from their good-tempered arguments.

Rhoda was not to be persuaded into visiting Rye. In his letters to her, as in the letters he sent to his other old London friends, Miss Allen and Mrs Clifford, James tried to convince her that he was wretched in his exile, pining for the moment when he might cross 'the blessed Kensington fields' again to visit her. Rhoda's imaginable response would have been a bark of laughter, and disbelief.

Jessie Allen and Lucy Clifford complete the trio of James's urban admirers and confidantes in whom the eager passions of youth had given way to the forceful character of independent middle-age.

Jessie Allen was a sprightly spinster, well born and reasonably well-off, a gregarious gossip whose generosity with her letters – she seldom sent one of less than thirty pages – was matched by her lavishness in the giving of presents. Her Christmas gift in 1901 of two magnificent bearskins for Lamb House earned her the nickname of Goody Two Shoes, a reference to Oliver Goldsmith's Margery Two Shoes who could never resist a generous impulse.

Miss Allen, who inhabited a small and prettily cluttered house in Eaton Terrace, was clever enough to choose friends who had larger houses and enjoyed having her to stay. Edel points out her resem-blance to the lively Maria Gostrey in *The Ambassadors*, but Miss Allen was also an older version of Edith Wharton's Lily Bart in *The House of Mirth*, a woman who for her own convenience had culti-vated the art of being a perfect guest, so sought after that she could be sure of a welcome at any number of grand houses. Lily, who did it from financial necessity, relied on her remarkable beauty to get her invitations; Miss Allen, who was no beauty and who did it for pleasure, relied on her sharp wit. When James first met her, she was a fellow-guest at the Palazzo Barbaro in Venice; in the mass of correspondence which ensued over the next seventeen years, references to the palazzo and its owners, the Daniel Curtises, were frequent and not always kind. Miss Allen was quite as much a mistress of malice as James was a master; they understood each other perfectly.

'Dear pampering Goody', James called her, full of gratitude to a friend who would hunt for tenants when he needed them, sympathize with his fury over the carryings-on of Miss Grigsby, warn him about the subscriptions his friends were soliciting for his seventieth birthday present, and, above all, listen to his grumblings, about dull neighbours, aches and pains or the awful experience of trying to keep up with the Whartons on a vastly expensive holiday in France.

The move to Rye had inevitably meant a reduction of James's social activities. Far more precious to him than a couple of bearskins was 'Goody's' present to him of her own life. James was grateful for Violet Hunt's 'little mice'; he was ecstatically so for Miss Allen's long letters which allowed him to observe a world in which he no longer had the desire to mingle. There was no need; 'Goody' did it for him. 'I sit blinking, gasping, clapping my hands,' he told her, and wondered that he had 'presence of mind left for an articulate "Thank you"'.

> How you keep it up, and how exactly you lead the life that, long years ago, when I was young, I used to believe a very, very few fantastically happy mortals on earth *could* lead, and could survive the bliss of leading – the waltz-like, rhythmic rotation from great country-house to great country-house, to the sound of perpetual music and the acclamation of the 'houseparties' that gather to await you. You are the dream come true – you really do it, and I get the side-wind of the fairy-tale . . .[22]

It was Lucy Clifford's bustling, kindly nature that had inflicted young Ford Madox Ford on James for that uncomfortable lunch at the Vicarage in Rye. She had heard that her old friend was having trouble with his eyes and, unable to make a visit herself, she commissioned Ford to find out if anything was seriously wrong.

James forgave her on this and on every occasion when Lucy intruded too forcefully or spoke her mind with ringing sincerity. When he threw a tantrum over the well-meant plan to raise money by subscription for his seventieth birthday present, it was Lucy who told him that he was being 'cold, callous and ungracious' and shamed him into submission. And when the great birthday arrived and James was presented with a golden bowl and the news that Sargent was to paint him, it was Lucy who snatched him away from the celebrations to give him lunch at her club. When James died, Lucy was the only woman-friend who was remembered in his will, with a legacy of £100. (About £2,000 today.)

Lucy Clifford was only twenty-four when her husband, a brilliant mathematician, died. Faced with the prospect of bringing up two little daughters, she decided to live by her prolific pen, writing novels, plays and articles. Her literary talent was considerably smaller than her commercial success, but she became quite a figure in the London literary world, a favourite with the young writers who attended her Sunday parties and whose names she was always eager to promote. Rudyard Kipling was among those who owed her a considerable debt from helping to draw attention to his work.

James was already in his thirties when they first met in 1880. Already well-established as the author of *The American, The Europeans* and *Washington Square* and possessed of all the necessary literary connections for a successful career, he had no need of Lucy's benevolent patronage. He simply liked her and fell most contentedly into the role of a clever protégé, since that was how she clearly liked to think of him. She called him her 'nevvy' and he, when he remembered, called her 'Aunt Lucy'.

She was a very comfortable kind of an aunt, always delighted to see him and to bring out the Benedictine bottle if he dropped in on her after going to a play, full of sympathy and practical advice when he wrote to her of domestic crises at Lamb House. Lucy could be relied on. She was amusing without being malicious, forceful without being autocratic. She never took offence, not even when James, whose *Guy Domville* débâcle she had witnessed with dismay on the opening night, told her off for writing plays which were insufficiently dramatic. The trouble with her hero, he thoughtfully explained to her in 1909, was that he was too passive. This, from a man whose heroes could be accused of positively wallowing in passivity, was rich, but Lucy forbore to make the obvious riposte. She, simply, adored him, and he thought her 'one of the finest bravest creatures possible'.

Last but by no means the least important of James's women friends in later life was Mary Augusta Ward, whose fame and commercial success were assured after her monumental study of the mid-Victorian crisis of faith in *Robert Elsmere*. Mrs Ward, mildly parodied as Mrs Foxe in Aldous Huxley's *Eyeless in Gaza* and as Pearl Bellars in the same author's *Limbo*,* was the archetypal blue-stocking, industrious, scholarly and of the highest moral tone. A passionate advocate of higher education for women, she was paradoxically opposed to

---

* Huxley could write with authority: Mrs Ward had been a second mother to him in his young and impressionable years.

the suffragette movement (as was James), holding that a woman's influence is most strongly exerted from the home.

James viewed her with a mixture of affection and exasperation. He was irritated by her well-meant praises for the happy ending of *The Sacred Fount* when he had made the conclusion of that most difficult of his novels as bleak as a closed coffin lid, and by the moral objections she gravely raised to the relationship of Merton Densher and Kate Croy in *The Wings of the Dove*. He was not terribly pleased, either, when she published his letters to her about *Robert Elsmere*, making them look, to his eyes, like a quack's testimonials for a patent medicine. Her novels showed no sign of having benefited from his lengthy criticisms; irony, an art of which he was a master, was wasted on Mrs Ward. She was an admirable woman, but not a humorous one. He couldn't, he ruefully told Edmund Gosse, 'communicate with her worth a damn'. And yet there was a goodness and kindness in her nature which he found utterly endearing. His teasing was of the gentlest kind. Could she imagine *him* living in a vicarage? Didn't he seem to see a little bit of H.J. in her portrait of Mr Bellasis?

There was one subject on which he was able to communicate with her most successfully, that of diet. Mrs Ward was a latecomer to the wonders of Fletcherism, the science of slow mastication; James was delighted to advise her and to applaud her wisdom in having taken it up. Nothing, he assured her, would ever be the same once 'the divine light' of Fletcherism had shown itself to her. He himself had been practising it hard for two years (he took it up in 1904) and was convinced that 'it's the greatest thing that ever was. Grapple it to your soul with hoops of steel . . . I munch unsociably and in passionate silence, and . . . it is making me both unsociable and inhospitable (without at the same time making me in the least ashamed of so being. I brazenly glory in it).'[23]

James's letters to Mrs Ward are of particular interest to us for the light they shed on his literary techniques and theories as he set about the rewriting of her novels. In July 1899, he returned the proofs of *Eleanor* with some valuable criticisms – her American girl from New England would be curious, but certainly not shocked, as she had suggested, by the papist rituals she would see in Rome; an American reader would not find her a credible compatriot – before presenting her with the *Eleanor* he would have written.

Make that consciousness full, rich, universally prehensile and *stick* to it – don't shift – and don't shift *arbitrarily* – how, otherwise, do you get your unity of subject or keep up your reader's sense of it? To which, if you say: 'How then do I get *Lucy*'s consciousness,' I impudently retort: 'By that magnificent and masterly *indirectness* which means the *only* dramatic straightness and intensity. You get it, in other words, by Eleanor.' 'And how does Eleanor get it?' 'By *Everything*! By Lucy, By Manisty, by every pulse of the action in which she is engaged of which she is the fullest – and exquisite – register. Go behind *her* – miles and miles; don't go behind the others, or the subject – i.e. the unity of impression – goes to smash.' But I am going too far . . .[24]

Too far for Mrs Ward, whose *Eleanor*, when published, showed not a trace of James's influence. But not too far for the detached reader, who can see James thinking aloud, using the letter as an extension of his notebooks, trying out the ideas he would put to full and magnificent use in *The Ambassadors*, written the following year. We only need to substitute the name of Lambert Strether for Eleanor to find the connection.

Mrs Ward's English home was Stocks, one of the country houses which James had visited and envied before deciding to become a freeholder himself rather than a wandering tenant. But his fondest memories of her were linked to the Villa Barberini, the Italian home which Mrs Ward, with her usual thoroughness, rented for the summer of 1899 in order to get the proper Italian flavour for her latest novel. Here, driven out of Rome by the stifling heat, James gratefully agreed to spend a couple of nights. Charmed by the singular beauty of its situation, he stayed a week.

The villa itself was stark and underfurnished, but glorious gardens and magnificent views provided ample compensation. The house was at Castel Gandolfo, perched high above the swooping plains of the Campagna James had always loved; through the villa windows, far below, he could look down on the blue Alban lake and the ruins of an imperial villa built for Domitian.

For Mrs Ward, the visit offered a new view of James. She was astonished by his fluency in Italian and by the breadth of his knowledge of Roman history and art; she was much taken by his easy informality as she watched him drawing the local people into conversation and wandering at his leisure through the shadowed ruins of Domitian's villa. She kept one other memory, a significant one. They went, one afternoon, on an excursion to Lake Nemi and the temple of Diana where excavation works were in progress. Loitering among the unearthed pillars and artefacts, they found a boy, 'straight and lithe and handsome as a young Bacchus', in Mrs Ward's memory. James was unabashedly entranced. He walked beside the boy, gazing at him, listening abstractedly as the young Italian chattered about the head of a marble statue he had discovered during the excavating. He asked the boy's name and, learning that it was Aristodemo, repeated it with dreamy satisfaction, almost, Mrs Ward observed, as if he was caressing the name's owner.

Thirty years later, a woman of such high moral tone as Mrs Ward might have viewed the encounter between the ageing novelist and the handsome boy with unease and disapproval. In the pre-war years, society saw nothing particularly shocking in the looks and language of homo-eroticism unless, as in Wilde's case, it was incontrovertibly linked to homosexual activity. The Victorians and Edwardians were more sophisticated than we are today in understanding and accepting that a man can love and physically worship one of his own sex without seeking any closer contact than an embrace or, at most, a kiss. Homosexuality was rife and, if discovered, was treated as a criminal act to be punished with imprisonment and social ostracism, but it is important to remember that there was an immense chasm between the voracious sexual appetites of men like Wilde and the near non-existent ones of men in James's mould whose loves were of a romantic nature, with the yearning more passionately expressed in words and looks than in actions. This was the era of lad-love when the schoolmasters, clergymen and scholars of the Uranian group were circulating pamphlets and poems which, at their most idealistic, proposed adoration of the young male body without sex as the noblest form of love, along the lines of Walter Pater's magnificent essay on Winckelmann in which he argues that Winckelmann's pure love of beautiful young men 'perfected his reconciliation to the spirit of Greek sculpture'. (Not all Uranian works, it should be said, aspired to this elevated plane.)

Male love, in the 1890s and the early part of this century, was frequently experienced in the spirit of Winckelmann. Looking at James's circle of friends, it is apparent that, while a few were actively homo- or bisexual (Edith Wharton's lover, Morton Fullerton, was of the second kind) the majority were, like James himself, lovers in the Pater mould. Edmund Gosse, a devoted husband and father, was deeply in love for four years with Hamo Thornycroft, Siegfried Sassoon's uncle. He was in a state of 'melting ravishment', 'oddly bewitched'. When Thornycroft married, Gosse wrote to him of the past four years as 'the summer of my life, which I have spent in a sort of morning-glory walking by your side'.[25] Arthur Benson, the prolific author and diarist who was a friend to both Gosse and James, thought of all sexual relations as 'rather detestable in their nature; a thing per se to be ashamed of', and yet he went through all the sufferings of a jealous lover when young Hugh Walpole transferred his affections to James, to whom Benson had introduced him. Howard Sturgis, the witty and ever-hospitable 'Howdie' whose strong and lively face betrays no hint of effeminacy, lived most companionably with Edward Ainger, his beloved Eton tutor and, subsequently, with his sturdy young friend, William Haynes-Smith. Nobody ever suggested that there was anything irregular about the relationship between their fastidious friend and Ainger or Haynes-Smith, known to them all as 'the Babe'.

They could, and did, discuss each other's grand passions with a frank and avid interest which had much to do with the possessive adulation of the older men for the younger members of their circle, but which it would be rash to interpret as the gossip of a group of promiscuous homosexuals. The concern was, rather, with the suitability of the chosen love. Benson, contemplating young Percy Lubbock's infatuation with 'a common perky calculating youth', disapproved and drew unfavourable comparisons: 'Howard Sturgis loved the Babe and H.J. loved Hugh Walpole – but neither H.S. nor H.J. were ever under any illusions as to the Babe's or H. Walpole's intellect or character or superiority.'[26]

There was, however, a degree of physical intimacy and this, within the circle, was of a fairly promiscuous kind. In this, James was a willing participant. Talking to Gaillard Lapsley in the spring of 1913 about James, Benson was surprised to learn quite how willing. The knowledge afforded him little pleasure. Lapsley had been describing an emotional scene he had had with James.

> Lapsley said, 'If I had caught him in my arms, kissed his cheeks, as I have often done, it would be all right' – this power of receiving caresses is a new light to me on H.J. – he lives in an atmosphere of hugging – that is probably the secret of Hugh Walpole's success, the kisses of youth – he is jaded by the slobbering osculations of elderly men with false teeth.[27]

Benson's masochistic observation (the toothless kisser is himself) was as true of James in 1899 when he was so enchanted by Aristodemo as it was in 1913. He was nearing sixty when he visited Mrs Ward, and he was feeling it. His beard had not yet been shaved off and, although his was an imposing face, it was not a youthful one. Time was slipping away and, as Leon Edel neatly puts it, Christopher Newman was about to become Lambert Strether. It was a time when, robbed of his own youth, he could only seize it again vicariously by embracing the company of those who possessed it. He would do so with the innocent hunger of an Isabel Archer or a Milly Theale, arms stretched wide to embrace all that was new.

Shortly before his arrival at the Villa Barberini, James had been captivated by a young sculptor he had met in Rome. Hendrik Anderson was a Bostonian of Norwegian birth. He was tall, serious, arrestingly blond. He dreamed of working on a monumental scale, of celebrating male beauty in statues as arrogantly naked as Michelangelo's David. In more ways than one, he bore an eerie resemblance to Roderick Hudson, the young American sculptor of James's early novel.

James, despite his passion for the vast canvases of Paul Veronese, was no great admirer of the monumental in sculpture. Looking for something in Andersen's Roman studio which would not look too absurd in the little rooms of Lamb House, his attention was caught by an attractive terracotta bust of Conte Alberto Bevilacqua. He bought it for the not inconsiderable sum of £50.

The bust arrived at Rye twelve days after his own return there in July and James arranged it in a place of honour on the dining-room chimneypiece before sending off the first and most restrained of many letters to his 'dear Hans Andersen'. (The great Danish writer, a friend of Gosse's, was a distant relation.) The time had not come for lavish endearments; James left Andersen to put his own interpretation on the excessively tender references to Bevilacqua, his representative. 'I've struck up a tremendous intimacy with dear little Conte Alberto,' James told him, 'and we literally can't live without each other.'[28]

Andersen, an ambitious young man who had known only a modest success, could not fail to be flattered. James had influential friends and was clearly inclined to be a benevolent patron. He had already decided to go to America that summer; he suggested making a visit to Lamb House on the way.

The visit took place in August 1899 when James, who had just agreed to buy the freehold of his house, was in euphoric mood. Andersen was as charming and companionable as he had remembered, very content to listen even though he did not have much understanding of James's finer intellectual points. Henry was wise and playful; Hendrik was callow and solemn; it mattered little since they had in common the hope that Hendrik would do great things. His artistic hopes played, we may be sure, a part in their talks and the more cultured James forbore from argument and felt no boredom. Nothing sounds banal to the lover, and he was in love. Alone again, he wistfully retraced the tracks where Andersen and he had bicycled through the twilight. He laid plans for him to come and live in the Watchbell Street studio, happily prophesying that 'we shall be good for each other; and the studio good for both of us'.[29]

The visit lasted a brief three days. Their correspondence spanned fourteen years but they only met again five times, and never for more than a few days. Separation fuelled rather than diminished James's love; he would, slowly and sadly, come to acknowledge the limitations of Andersen as an artist – the limitations of a man who didn't, in his sculptures, recognize that there were any limits – but distance saved him from seeing any other flaws in the loved object. His letters to Andersen were yearning, tender and written in the kind of language which, taken out of the context of their time, sounds like that of a consummated love. Writing in the winter of 1902, when Andersen's brother, Andreas, died, he described himself as wanting to take 'infinitely close and tender and affectionately healing *possession* of you . . . to put my arm round you and *make* you lean on me as on a brother and a lover, and keep you on and on . . .'[30] Seeking to comfort him, he offered his own source of solace, the sense of pure possession which the death of Minnie Temple had stirred in him: 'Well, he is *all* yours now: he lives in you and out of all pain. Wait, and you will see . . .'[31]

We have seen already that the critical instinct in James towards the works of his friends was never repressed, and even Andersen was sometimes given a lash where he might have hoped for a caress. Photographs of his latest works in 1904 provoked James to offer a warning. They were, he said, 'admirably interesting' but 'difficult to speak of to you – they terrify me so with their evidence as of *madness* (almost) in the scale on which you are working.'[32] He could not pretend to like Andersen's multitude of 'naked and intimately associated gentlemen and ladies, flaunting their bellies and bottoms and their other private affairs': the best response he could offer was an uneasy facetiousness. He was puzzled by the coldness of his friend's works; if he must work on creating huge naked figures, they should, he thought, at least seem to live. But the critical faculty swiftly gave way to the frustration he felt at not being able to be with his dear, dear Hendrik. 'When the Devil *shall* we meet,' he wondered. '. . . it's hideous that you're not here and that you won't be. How long and close, in imagination and affection, I hold you! Feel, Hendrik, the force and the benediction of it . . .'[33]

Not until 1912, by which time he had found a new object on which to lavish his affection, did James begin to question Andersen's sanity. The vast and orgiastic sculptures had troubled him; he was appalled to hear that the new idea was for 'a colossal ready-made City' with forty architects working on it from the sculptor's designs. His warnings of the dangers of megalomania went unheeded. Andersen, who might have done very well creating sets for Cecil B. de Mille, had already persuaded various eminent Europeans to consider his scheme for a world communication centre; he was intoxicated by his own vision – and he wanted James to support it. He sent a copy of his pamphlet on the 'World Conscience', along with a letter insisting that James should say what he thought.

James did not like to be pressurized. The time had gone for gentle remonstrances. He was, at last, brutally blunt. He warned Andersen again 'to dread as the hugest evil of all the forces of evil the dark danger of Megalomania' and, since he had been told to do so, he said what he thought of the new scheme.

> I don't so much *understand* your very terms of 'World' this and 'World' the other, and can neither think myself, nor *want* to think, in any such vain and false and presumptuous, any such idle and deplorable and delirious connections – *as they seem to me*, and as nothing will suit you, rash you, but that I should definitely let you *know* that they seem to me . . . I simply loathe such pretentious forms of words as 'World' anything – they are to me mere monstrous sound without sense.[34]

There was, for the first time, no mention in this letter of physical longing; the pressure he described in it was not the old affectionate pressure of his embrace but the pressure which Andersen had so unwisely put on him to approve.

Hugh Walpole was not of the intellectual calibre of James, but he was a more suitable object for adulation than Andersen who was, at the least, unbalanced. (References in the letters to recurrent attacks of depression and 'blind staggers' suggest a disturbed mind.) Hugh was far from mad. He was shrewd, cheerful, charming, talented – and immensely ambitious. He amazed Arthur Benson in 1909 (just after he had met James), by announcing that he was going to be one of the great names of the twentieth century. 'This he said to me not conceitedly or excitedly, but calmly and confidentially,' Benson noted with astonishment. 'Now I do not see any signs of intellectual power of perceptions or grasp of subtlety in his work or himself . . . he seems to me in no way likely to be great as an artist.'[35] Time would confer on Walpole the trappings of literary greatness, respectful reviews, a knighthood and an eminent biographer, but the quality of greatness eluded him in his work. Relentless creative energy, an impressive story-telling talent and a flair for self-promotion took him a very long way, but only within the second league.

A clergyman's son from New Zealand, Walpole was still struggling to find his way into the English literary coterie when he made his overture to James in 1908. At the age of twenty-four, he was just starting to be used as a reviewer; he had already hit on the idea of sending his notices to authors with friendly little letters of self-introduction. He had not yet had the chance to review James; instead, he sent his letter of homage in the company of glowing testimonials from Percy Lubbock and Arthur Benson. Only ignorance of James's friendship with Lucy Clifford can have prevented him from soliciting another from that kindest of patrons to hopeful young writers. James's response was affable, and was shortly followed by an invitation to dine with him at the Reform Club.

Walpole, already something of an authority on celebrities, was overwhelmed, and not merely by the grandly gloomy splendour of the Reform. James was 'perfectly wonderful. By far the greatest man I have ever met,' he reported to his family, 'and yet amazingly humble and affectionate – absolutely delightful.'[36] A weekend at Lamb House that spring was a still more entrancing experience. James, in a fever of apprehension, had warned him that it would be grim and dull, but the house which had offered such a benevolent welcome to Anderson was no less generous now and Walpole fell under the spell as James set out to captivate him. There were, doubtless, earnest discussions about literary style and form, but there was also a good deal of laughter. James had a wicked sense of humour and he treated Walpole to one of his finest flights of fantasy on the theme of their mutual friend Arthur Benson being seduced in a brothel by a prostitute posing as a devoted reader of the *Church Family News*. The intimate jokes, the urbanely flattering manner, the pleasure of being treated as an intellectual equal, all conspired to please. Walpole was enthralled. 'He is beyond equal,' he reported gravely. 'I cannot speak about him.'[37]

Others were more than ready to speak about them both as James began to take his protégé about in society, escorting him to house-parties, giving dinners for him, showing him off in the literary circles Walpole had so longed to penetrate. James could understand and sympathize with that wish; as a young man in Paris, he had known what it was to stand without a key on the wrong side of the gateway to society. Now, James was known everywhere and, as his constant companion, Walpole also began to taste the pleasure of celebrity. He liked being told (by Fanny Prothero) that nobody had such an influence as he on the 'très cher maître', as James had asked to be called. He liked being given presents, a splendid writing-desk, a handsome mirror. He liked being showered with adoring letters and boasted to Arthur Benson that he quite often received two in a day. Benson listened and smiled and kept his reflections for the diary in which, eight years before, he had decided that it was time for the ageing James to meet his maker.* In 1902, he had thought of James as fit only for the graveyard; now, nearing seventy, he seemed as frisky as a lamb again. Walpole, clearly, was good for James – but was James good for Walpole, Benson wondered as the young man recited his latest social exploits? It seemed to Benson that it had all gone to his head. 'But it must be very surprising to have Henry James fall in love with you, to go everywhere, to meet everybody, to be welcomed by all the best literary men of the day – Wells, Max Beerbohm, Gosse etc to have a dinner given you at the Reform etc – he must have a great deal of ballast!'[38]

Emotion rarely blunted James's critical faculties. He did everything in his power to facilitate his young friend's transition from occasional journalist into a writer of novels by establishing him in London's foremost literary circles and by drawing attention to his name, but he denied himself the easy pleasure of offering insincere praises. His strictures were, indeed, devastating in their frankness. After reading *Maradick at Forty*, Walpole's second novel, he reproached him for being 'irreflectively juvenile', for having failed to have any plan of composition and for having sunk instead into 'a vast formless featherbeddiness'. 'It isn't written at all, darling Hugh,' he added for good measure.[39] *Mr Perrin and Mr Traill* was more gently received, but he was still impelled to ask where the centre of the subject was meant to be and to suggest how improvements might have been made. Walpole, following in the steps of Mrs Ward and H. G. Wells, thanked his mentor for his kind suggestions – and continued to write in his own thoroughly unjamesian style, one with which his rapidly growing band of readers seemed perfectly content. The criticisms which were so wounding to gentler souls like Howard Sturgis, who was almost ready to give up writing after reading James's letter about *Belchamber*, were water off a duck's back to Walpole. The literary introductions and the ability to bask in the knowledge that he was the accepted literary protégé of Henry James outweighed any irritation he might have felt.

However, even Walpole was faintly embarrassed by the 1914 article

* 'Miss C[holmondeley] told me the dreadful game. A mentions 3 friends, real friends – having mentioned them he has to take them to the top of St Pauls – push one over leave one (for ever) on the top and bring one down – he is to say which. I pushed Henry James over, as fitted to die, left Gosse on top, and brought Howard Sturgis down.'[40]

in which James made excessive amends for having been too harsh about his work. This was 'The Younger Generation', published in two parts in *The Times Literary Supplement*. It was, for James, an astonishingly ill-judged piece and one which was read with surprise and displeasure by many of his friends, 'a mere vomit of thought' in the opinion of Arthur Benson. Conrad, whose age (51) should have preserved him from inclusion, was annoyed and hurt to be delicately dissected as the author of *Chance* while his other and greater books went unmentioned. (To James, they had seemed to be, of late, 'wastes of desolation'; he thought he was doing Conrad a favour.) Wells was castigated along with Arnold Bennett for 'mere squeezing of material, mere squeezing of the orange' and singled out for his airy unconcern for the effects James thought he should have striven to achieve. D. H. Lawrence, whose talent Ford had been one of the first to recognize and who, with the publication of *Sons and Lovers* in 1913, had become a name to be reckoned with, was simply mentioned and dropped 'to hang in the dusty rear' behind Compton Mackenzie's *Sinister Street*. Named before both of them and named as often as James dared was Hugh Walpole, as the bright young star of the literary firmament. He could not claim felicity of style or remarkable profundity for the author of *The Duchess of Wrexe*, a romantic drawing-room comedy liberally adorned with quotations from his own novels and from his own private letters to Walpole; he could, and did, lavish praises on its author's youthful exuberance as though exuberance was the most desirable quality in a novel. What, he asked, did style matter in the work of an author of such charming 'temperamental freshness . . . a juvenility reacting, in the presence of everything, "for all it is worth"'? 'He enjoys in a high degree the consciousness of saturation, and is on such serene and happy terms with it as almost make of critical interference, in so bright an air, an assault on personal felicity.'[41] Small wonder that James's friends raised their eyebrows.

'The Younger Generation' did James more harm than it did Walpole good; his knowledge of younger writers was shown to be as limited as the judgement which could devote some seven hundred laudatory words to a bad Walpole novel and dismiss *Sons and Lovers* in half a sentence. He was writing, admittedly, at a time when the brightest and best of the young (Huxley, Wyndham Lewis, Joyce and Woolf) had not yet produced their first novels, but, with such a title, it was extraordinary to make no mention of Galsworthy, Forster, Mansfield or Maugham, all of whom had been published and reviewed well before 1914. To extol *Sinister Street* and ignore *Howards End* was inexcusable on any other grounds than the bigotry of old age.

Hendrik Andersen had, like one of the charming princes in his famous relation's fairy-stories, worked a kind of magic on James's hitherto unawakened emotions. He had warmed the frozen surface; unpent, James's tender feelings gushed out in a flood of passionate words over the young Norwegian and his successors. 'I not only love him – I *love* to love him,' he once said to Walpole of Jocelyn Persse, a sunny young Irishman in whom he saw only merit where Walpole, Persse's rival, saw mediocrity. It was this feeling, not simply of being in love but of the delight of conveying and expressing it, which permeated his letters to Walpole. As a boy, so far as we know, he wrote no love-letters; his letters as an elderly man are the more touching for the freshness of their sentiments. Walpole was his 'dearest darlingest little Hugh'; he signed himself to him as 'yours, yours, yours, dearest Hugh, *yours*! H.J.' He told him he adored him and sulked at finding *Mr Perrin and Mr Traill* dedicated to another sympathetic friend – who could be more sympathetic to Walpole's interests than himself, he wished to know? He sent him verbal pats and embraces and begged him to try to love him more. When Walpole made the embarrassing gaffe of sending out duplicate invitations to the novelist's seventieth birthday with the recipients' names left glaringly blank as Dear ——, James insisted on bearing all the blame. He loved Walpole, even though the latter's lengthy sojourn in Russia caused the friendship to slide a little after 1914. (It was James who, horrified to learn that Walpole was suspected of going there to avoid being called up, sent him a tactful letter to that effect.*) But there is no reason to suppose, any more than with Andersen, that the passionate friendship ever developed into a full sexual relationship. Walpole himself would later say that he had offered his body to James and that James had simply said, 'I can't, I can't.' After some seven decades of cheerfully acknowledged and unregretted celibacy, it was an understandable response.

What James was prepared to do, and did with some brio, was to flirt. Smitten by the Apollonian good-looks of Rupert Brooke after a brief visit to Cambridge in 1909 when he was already infatuated by Walpole, he referred to him as 'the insidious Rupert – with whose name I take this liberty because I don't know whether one loves one's love with a (surname terminal) *e* or not.'[42] Young Gaillard Lapsley, a member of the Howard Sturgis circle, was told how delightful it was to let the imagination feast on him 'in the passive, the recumbent, the luxurious and ministered-to posture' and entreated to make Lamb

---

* Rumour was unkind. Walpole had tried to enlist and had been turned down on account of his poor eyesight. The decision to go to Russia was taken subsequently.

House his home and to believe that 'I miss you, in truth, at all times.'[43] Charm and youth earned Max Beerbohm laughter and forgiveness when that ingenious parodist made fun of his style and caricatured his obesity. Pats, caresses and wistful thoughts were bestowed on Hendrik Andersen at the same time that they were being still more amply lavished on Hugh Walpole. Jocelyn Persse's name was trailed before Walpole with what seems to have been a mischievous desire to rouse him to jealousy. ('Jocelyn P(ersse) continues to adorn a world that is apparently so easy for him. I lately dined and went to a play with him . . . and he was, as ever, sympathy and fidelity incarnate.')[44]

There were to be a good many such references to Persse in James's letters to Walpole, who found the relationship quite incomprehensible. What could Jocelyn Persse possibly have to say of interest? He was charming, of course, but a charming dunderhead who had never read a word James had written and who knew nothing except, perhaps, the art of living. Passing Persse on a London street one day, Walpole turned to his companion and shrilly asked him to imagine the extraordinary fact that there walked a man with whom James had been madly in love.

Extraordinary and infuriating though it must have been to Walpole to know it, James's relationship with Persse developed into the most tender and unaffected of his late-flowering relationships with young men. They had met at a party in London in 1907 when Persse was thirty, blond, elegant and extrovert. James watched him with the same intensity that had so struck Mrs Ward when she saw him observing Aristodemo. They spoke, and warmed to each other at once, not from any intellectual rapport but from an immediate liking of each other's natures. Persse was a nephew of Lady Gregory, the widowed benefactress of Yeats, but he had none of his aunt's sharp intelligence or her love of literature. What he possessed instead was an endearing straightforwardness and ease of manner, a love of travel and a fund of good stories. He enjoyed life, he loved people, and he liked nothing better than a good 'jaw' with an old friend. He was kind, loyal and sweet-natured; if James felt lonely, he could rely on Persse to come rushing down to London to cheer him up with a jolly evening at the theatre or the music-hall. Persse had that rare quality which we call 'life-enhancing', and it was for that quality that James so loved him. When Walpole, who had just met him, wrote to ask what on earth James found to talk to him about, he was answered with an airy shrug. 'I have no fear at all but that Jocelyn found his bright account in your kind company – though when you come to the question of "subjects in common", heaven save the mark! – or of the absence of them – I have nothing to say to you but that I know (none better) what you mean. One gets on with him in a way without them, however, and says to one's self, I think, that if *he* doesn't mind, well, why should one either? At any rate I am glad you were gentle with him.'⁴⁵ Walpole took the hint. He did not make a second attack.

Andersen, Walpole, Persse: no one of the three was ideally suited to match the complex and subtle mind of James, but each in his way served to defend him against an increasing awareness of the loneliness of old age and each in his way fed the love which was for James as great a delight to be able freely to bestow as to receive. Andersen allowed him unembarrassedly to release a torrent of feeling the more passionate for having been so long suppressed; Walpole provided him with the pleasure of a stimulating companion who was prodigal with the embraces which so comforted the old man; Persse gave him the best gift of all, an enduring affection given without self-interest and with a touching anxiety lest he should be getting in the way of James's work. As James said of Persse, so might Persse have said of his feeling for James. He simply loved to love him.

LIVING DANGEROUSLY: THE CRANES

There are few men that I have liked – nay, indeed, revered – more than Crane. He was so frail and so courageous, so preyed upon and so generous, so weighed upon by misfortunes and so erect in his carriage. And he was such a beautiful genius.

Ford Madox Ford,
Return to Yesterday

He was essentially the helpless artist . . . he wasn't the master of his home; his life was altogether out of control; he was being carried along.

H. G. Wells,
Experiment in Autobiography

. . . his passage on this earth was like that of a horseman riding swiftly in the dawn of a day fated to be short and without sunshine.
Joseph Conrad in his
Introduction to *Stephen Crane* by Thomas Beer

What a brutal, needless extinction – what an unmitigated unredeemed catastrophe! I think of him with such a sense of possibilities and powers.

Henry James to Cora Crane, 1900

1871   Stephen Crane born in New Jersey.

1893   Crane publishes *Maggie, A Child of the Streets*.

1895   Crane publishes *The Black Riders, and Other Lines* and *The Red Badge of Courage*.

1896   Crane publishes *George's Mother* and *The Little Regiment* and meets Cora Taylor on his way to Cuba.

1897   Crane and Cora work together as journalists covering the Greco-Turkish War and move to England. They meet Harold Frederic, Joseph Conrad and Ford Madox Ford. Crane publishes *The Third Violet* and *The Open Boat and other Tales of Adventure*.

1898   According to legend, Crane meets James at a London party and rescues him from the embarrassment of having his hat filled with champagne by an intoxicated lady. With Conrad's help, Crane raises the funds to go to Cuba. Cora takes in the Frederic children and decides to rent Brede Place.

1899   Crane returns to England and publishes *War is Kind*, *Active Service* and *The Monster and Other Stories*. James attends a garden fête at Brede but stays away from the celebrations to welcome in 1900.

1900   Crane publishes *Whilomville Stories* and *Wounds in the Rain*. He dies at the Villa Eberhardt in Badenweiler before completing his last novel, *The O'Ruddy*. Cora leaves Brede Place and returns to Jacksonville to run the Court, a brothel.

1905   Cora marries, aged forty-one, the twenty-five-year old Hammond McNeil, a railway conductor.

1907   McNeil is found guilty of wilfully murdering Harry Parker, a railroad worker of nineteen, for being involved with Cora. Cora flees unpleasant publicity and returns to England and, briefly, to Sussex. The Conrads give her lunch and the Wellses give her tea, but Henry James is 'not at home' to her.

1910   Cora, after resuming her place as the hostess of the Court in 1908, dies of a stroke.

LIVING DANGEROUSLY:

THE CRANES

American blood was the only inescapable link between the master of Lamb House and the baron of Brede Place. Their first meeting was in London at a party where James had put in a brief appearance, just long enough for an exuberant lady called Madame Zipango to decide it would be very amusing to fill his top-hat with champagne. James did not share her sense of humour and he made his displeasure felt. Crane, who privately thought James was making a good deal of fuss about nothing, good-naturedly came to the rescue by despatching the lady and restoring the hat.

Meeting Crane again after his arrival as a neighbour in Sussex, James was struck by his similarity to Robert Louis Stevenson, a close friend of his who had died two years before Crane's arrival in England. It was not the first time that Crane had heard about the resemblance and he was too blunt to pretend that it gave him any pleasure. He may have gone so far as to say, as he had on previous occasions, that only one thing nauseated him as much as the modern bathing suit and that was the prose of Robert Louis Stevenson. To James, who felt that his remark had been, if anything, excessively flattering to Crane, this was not a gratifying response. In future, while urbanely polite to his face, he would take no trouble to be polite behind his back. Officially, he was 'my young compatriot of genius'; privately, he was dismissed as the American equivalent to a costermonger from Whitechapel.

Appearances of friendship between neighbours had, however, to be maintained, and grimly correct, James did his best. He invited the Cranes to tea with Mrs Humphry Ward, ignorant of the fact that Crane considered her *Robert Elsmere* to be 'a lot of higgling rubbish'* and its author 'a feminine mule'.[1] When Cora expressed a wish to

---

* *Higgling*: a word employed by Crane as a schoolboy insult to his teachers. He liked the sound of it enough to go on using it as an expression of good-humoured contempt.

join the ladies' section of the Mermaid Club in Rye, James readily lent his name as one of her sponsors. He donated £50 to the fund organized by Cora to raise money for the illegitimate children of Harold Frederic and Kate Lyon and for the legal costs incurred by their mother when she was defending herself against the charge of having killed Frederic by refusing to allow him to be attended by a professional doctor. When the Cranes gave a garden fête at Brede, James dutifully attended, smiled at the camera for sixpence a shot, ate Cora's doughnuts and had his fortune told.

The fortune-teller was Kate Lyon's niece, 'Snubby' Ritchie Jones, a pretty dark-eyed girl whose nickname owed its origin to a very small nose. Miss Ritchie Jones spent much of 1899 at Brede and entered with great glee into the atmosphere of bohemian gaiety. It is from her recollections of many years later that we get much of the evidence for believing that James was on the warmest of terms with the Cranes.[2] Both Crane's biographer, R. S. Stallman, and Cora's, Lillian Gilkes, have taken her word for it that James was a frequent and welcome guest. He came over, we learn from their source, about once or twice a week on his bicycle and was on such easy terms that he could walk unembarrassedly into the room where Cora and her young guest sat drying their hair by the fire. Nothing, apparently, could have pleased him more than to sit listening to a canine aria accompanied by Miss Ritchie Jones at the piano, except to join in a late-night jam session of music produced by home-made harmonicas of tissue-covered combs.

There is no reason to call Miss Ritchie Jones a liar, but it is possible that, over a distance of many years, she came to believe that James had been a more frequent and enchanted visitor than was the case. It may have been that he *once* listened to the dogs' song, *once* walked into the wrong door by mistake, *once* was trapped into staying late by bad weather and put a good face on the Cranes' musical entertainment. It is unlikely that 'the great friendship' amounted to much more than that.

Correspondence between Cora and James gives no hint of such a joyously informal relationship. A note to Cora politely regrets that she was out when James called. A letter after the garden fête thanks her for sending a photograph and protests that he was enjoying his doughnut more than his startled stare suggests. 'But no, surely, it can't be any doughnut of *yours* that is making me make such a gruesome grimace. I look as if I had swallowed a wasp, or a penny toy. And I tried to look so beautiful.'[3] That, together with the cheque of £50 which he sent to help cover the costs of Dr Skinner's visits during Crane's last illness, is all the evidence we have of James's affection for the Cranes. The cheque betrays more anxiety about Skinner's losses than interest in Crane's getting the best possible treatment. James had the warmest of feelings for the Rye doctor who would show him such kindness during his own periods of illness. If his concern had been primarily for the Cranes, he would surely have sent it sooner (it arrived on the day Crane died). He was enraged later to learn that the cheque had not been used as he wished but had gone towards paying off the mass of debts accumulated by taking Crane for his cure at Dordracht. Now that Crane was dead, James felt no further need to be cordial to or about his widow. A letter from Pinker, whose patience and resources were being severely tried by Cora's financial demands, stimulated a less than chivalrous response from James. 'She is indeed, clearly, an unprofitable person,' he wrote to his agent, 'and I judge her whole course and career, so far as it appeared in this neighbourhood, very sternly and unforgivingly. I sent her a contribution which reached her at the moment of Crane's death . . . and yet I learn that the young local doctor here, who gave almost all his time to them, quite devotedly, during Crane's illness, and took them to the Black Forest, has never yet, in spite of the money gathered in by her at that time, received a penny, and doesn't in the least expect to. It's really a swindle.'[4] The judgement was unnecessarily harsh. Skinner's fare and lodging had been paid, if not his fees. He had never been reproached by Cora for the disastrous inaccuracy of his diagnosis – an excessively optimistic one – of Crane's illness.

We do not know what James thought of *The Red Badge of Courage*. Neither is it clear if he admired its author for taking the sentimentality out of a war which had become a favourite romantic background with American popular novelists and which James himself had only chosen to represent in his early tales of grieving girls and wounded soldiers. It is hard to imagine that he had any real respect for Crane's work; he never accorded him the dubious honour of rewriting his novels or stories. The two were legions apart, as dissimilar as, say, Flaubert and Jack London; their writings were the products of different aims, different areas of knowledge and interest and different backgrounds.

Henry James was the indulged son of a civilized American family of the Boston temperament. Stephen Crane's father was a respected Methodist minister, a severe and unworldly man; his mother, also of solid Methodist stock, was an enthusiastic member and supporter of the Temperance Movement. The Jameses' interests were broad, their minds were lively and inquiring. They wrote fluently, and they suffered no difficulties or inhibitions about expressing their ideas.

James was taught that experience enriched the mind; Crane was brought up to regard experience as a dangerous seduction. Stephen was the sickly fourteenth child to grow up in the prim New Jersey household in which dancing, drinking and smoking were held to be abominable vices and in which the reading of novels was discouraged as a dangerous means of promoting a morbid love of excitement. Crane wasted little time in rebelling against this dour discipline. Dr Crane died when his son was eight. A military school was selected by the widow as a means of instilling moral fibre into her wayward child. Unfortunately for Mrs Crane, the Hudson River Institute turned out to be a pleasantly relaxed boarding-school which allowed its pupils to do pretty much as they liked. Crane remembered it as a 'bully time' during which he smoked, drank, gambled and fell in love at least three times; his teachers remembered him as a friendly rebel who showed more promise on the baseball field than in his lessons.

A brief sojourn at Lafayette College and Syracuse University added more to Crane's reputation as a baseball player than as a scholar, but he had also started to write articles (on baseball, among other subjects) for the *New York Herald Tribune*. At night, he wandered around the slum districts of Syracuse, talking to the tramps and prostitutes. Before he left the university, he had written a first draft of *Maggie*, the story of a young streetwalker which would shock readers by its sympathetic portrayal of a girl in such a disreputable profession.

He had found his vocation and his mother could do nothing to dissuade him from following it. It was, he later told Willa Cather, a question of having 'the itch of the thing in your fingers, and if you haven't – well, you're damned lucky, and you'll live long and prosper, that's all'. It sounded like a romantically gloomy view of the writer's life, but it was founded on experience and would, in Crane's case, prove an accurate prediction of the future. His short and turbulent life was not a prosperous one, but the itch was always in his fingers. By the age of twenty, he was a fully-fledged garret writer, living as roughly as the characters of his stories and still enjoying the sense of being a social rebel as he took his friends down to the Bowery area of New York to meet the fighters, the drunks and the prostitutes to whom he had become a familiar companion of the nights.

Maggie (which he sometimes liked to boast had been scribbled in a couple of nights) did not make him rich. No publisher conscious of his firm's reputation wanted to be associated with it and Crane had to pay $869 to have it printed under a pseudonym, for the pleasure of seeing it reviled by the critics for the squalor of its subject and the depravity of its language. But *Maggie* found two important supporters, men of influence who would help to work a miraculous change in Crane's career and encourage him when he was almost ready to give up the whole enterprise. W. D. Howells, who had published Henry James's first novel, saw *Maggie* as an important new kind of social fiction; his friend Hamlin Garland was equally enthusiastic. 'They tell me I did a horrible thing [in *Maggie*],' Crane reported to a friend, 'but they say, "It's great." "And its style," said Garland to Howells, "Egad, it has no style! Absolutely transparent! Wonderful – wonderful!"'[5] With two influential literary godfathers, both ready to praise his novel and one to show a gratifying interest in his poems (Garland, a dabbler in spiritualism, was convinced that Crane was being sent them by an obliging and lyrical ghost), the future began to look bright.

Garland suffered from a disease which infected a good many of Crane's acquaintances, excessive credulity. When Crane brought *The Red Badge of Courage* into his office in 1894, Garland gravely noted that 'the coming of that story was just as mysterious as in the case of the verses, and I can believe it. It literally came of its own accord like sap flowing from a tree.'[6] Crane was pulling the wool over the editor's eyes; his great war-novel was the result of endless revision and methodical planning. It was true, as Conrad later noted with some envy, that Crane could write with extraordinary facility, producing a whole chapter at a time without a single alteration to the manuscript, but the echoes and correspondences of images in *The Red Badge* are finer for not being the product of such spontaneous writing. The slapdash and only occasionally brilliant spatter of defining colours which had marked his earlier work here became part of a carefully plotted design, underlining the theme and giving crucial emphasis to the deftly economical landscapes. The novel is as precise and logically conceived an imitation of naturalness as one of the Impressionist paintings to which Crane's work is frequently compared.

Times were still rough for Crane when he was writing *The Red Badge*. Only half the book could be put on Garland's desk; the shamefaced author had to admit that he had pawned the manuscript and had only been able to raise enough dollars to redeem half of it. Garland, relieved at such a simple answer to the mystery, gave him $15 to retrieve the second half and told him not to worry. 'You'll soon be able to pay it back and more. You're going to be on your feet mighty soon.'

Garland's prediction was borne out when the novel was hailed with glowing reviews on both sides of the Atlantic the following year. Howells had preferred *Maggie*, but most critics were ready to honour the war-novel as a work which invited comparisons to

Tolstoy and Zola. The *New Review* in London was prepared to say that 'Mr Crane's picture of war is more complete than Tolstoi's, more complete than Zola's.' It became a bone of contention whether England or America had been the first to recognize Crane's genius.

It was not the plaudits of the critics which beguiled Crane into deciding to make his home in England, but a concern for appearances. Like many a rebel before him, he ended by offering his wrists to the manacles of convention. In the autumn of 1896, his decision to defend the honour of Dora Clark, a prostitute who had been arrested for trying to solicit him, had led to widespread publicity of a damaging kind. He was praised for speaking the truth, which was that he had arranged to meet some 'chorus girls' that night as part of his research for a study of those favourite victims of the New York police. Praise did not save him from being represented as an opium addict – evidence of drug-taking had been found in his room – who consorted with prostitutes. He had already been accused by one American journalist of being a morphine addict and an intemperate drinker: the Dora Clark affair did not enhance his reputation.

Crane's name was already tarnished when he went to Jacksonville, a dreary town whose ugliness reminded him of 'soiled pasteboard that some lunatic babies have been playing with' to revise his new novel, *The Third Violet*, and to await instructions on his progress to Cuba, where he was to cover the war. The liveliest if not the most elegant place in Jacksonville was the Hotel de Dream, frequented by women of easy virtue and men with money to burn. It was run by Cora Taylor, a handsome blonde woman in her early thirties. Crane, always susceptible, was smitten.

He never reached Cuba. The *Commodore* struck a sandbank and went down a few miles out from Jacksonville, leading to colourful reports of Crane's death and scenes of noisy despair in the Hotel de Dream where Cora had been blissfully contemplating her escape to a new and better life. The obituary notices were premature. Crane and three others, including the captain, had made their escape from the boat in a ten-foot dinghy, having seen another seven men safely launched in the lifeboat and the rest (all except three, who refused to leave the ship, and died) insecurely afloat on rafts. The dinghy survived for some thirty hours in high seas before overturning, leaving Crane – who wisely jettisoned his money-belt of Spanish gold – and his comrades to struggle towards the Florida shore with only one loss to their number. A telegram went off that day to the Hotel de Dream – and was answered with Cora's usual extravagance by a suggestion that he should hire a special train to Jacksonville at once, for which she would pay. Crane, being marginally more prudent, wired her to come down to Daytona on the regular train the next day. The reunion was reportedly ecstatic.

The *Commodore* incident provided Crane with a splendid journalistic scoop and the material for one of his finest stories, 'The Open Boat', a work praised by both Wells and Conrad. To Cora, who had been convinced that she had lost her young lover to the sea, the drama set the seal on her passion. She could not bear the prospect of losing him again. She was ready, and eager, to travel with him wherever he wished to go. More specifically, she wanted to join him on his next journalistic skirmish to cover the Greco-Turkish war. She longed to be his wife – and Crane was ready to fall in with her desires. Cora's age was no deterrent (he had always preferred older women), her cooking was irresistible, and her role as a brothel-hostess added to her charm. Virtue had never intrigued him so much as a bad woman with a generous heart.

There was a problem. Cora was still married to Captain Donald Stewart when she met Crane and Stewart, while perfectly willing to let her lead as free and separate a life as he himself enjoyed, was not prepared to agree to a divorce. The scandal already attached to Crane's name, coupled with the scandal of living with a married woman, was not something to be lightly contemplated. Cora longed for respectability, and he could not hope to help her to acquire it if they stayed in America. The Dora Clark scandal had not reached England. At an ocean's distance from Jacksonville gossip, there was a fair chance of passing Cora off as a Mrs Crane of unblemished reputation.

Crane and Cora arrived in London from a tough two-month assignment in Greece in June 1897. With them came a dog, Velestino, two Greek servants, the Ptolemy brothers, and Cora's travelling companion from Jacksonville, Mrs Ruedy. The arrival was well-timed. *The Third Violet*, a brief romance of no great merits, had just come out and the London critics, eager to show that their appreciation of Crane's qualities was greater than that of his compatriots, had gone out of their way to praise the book. The Americans had dismissed it as a very third-rate violet – an opinion which its author was inclined to share – while the London *Athenaeum* saw it as a work which put Crane on equal footing with Henry James. The *Athenaeum*'s critic was not alone in the extravagant excess of his praises. Crane was London's literary darling of the month, the man everyone wanted to meet.

For his part, Crane was more interested in finding somewhere to live. Edward Garnett, who had praised his last work, *George's Mother*, as a masterpiece, was a man who would always go out of his way to help promising young writers. He invited the Cranes to come and visit him in the country and persuaded them to look at a house near to his own in Limpsfield Chart, on the Surrey–Kent borders. Either Garnett was irresistibly charming or the Cranes were desperate to make a choice. Ravensbrook was a singularly hideous brick villa of the kind H. G. Wells excelled at deriding; large, damp and expensive to maintain. The Cranes, to their speedy regret, decided to take it on. It was no worse than Bloomfield Villa, Ford's first country home, or Wells's detested Heatherlea, but it was a far cry from the romantic baronial home in which Cora had anticipated entertaining her new literary friends.

The Limpsfield–Oxted area was not short of literary figures, but most of them were a little too rarefied for the taste of Crane and Cora. By far the most congenial, and least representative, was the brilliant and versatile Harold Frederic whom they had already met in London and who had been munificent in his review of *The Red Badge*. Frederic, like Crane, was of American Methodist stock and, like him, had come to fiction from journalism. (His *The Damnation of Theron Ware* was competing for review space with *The Third Violet*.) Struggling to keep two households happy with a wife to be appeased at weekends and a mistress during the weekdays, Frederic was in a position to sympathize with the Cranes' problems of unwedded love.

Harold Frederic was a man who pushed himself as hard as Crane, always beyond reasonable limits: his early death the following August was the result of this as much as of his refusal to renounce cigars and whisky or his rash readiness to be attended by a practitioner of Christian Science rather than by a conventional doctor. Impulsive and generous and disconcertingly frank about his dislikes, Frederic shared Crane's mistrust of intellectual pretensions and his contempt for the dainty hypocrisies on which the sham of so many more orthodox households was based. Gentility disgusted him. James, sedately living out the fantasy of being an English country gentleman with his array of appropriate hats and gloves and walking-sticks for every occasion, was just the sort of person to arouse Frederic's loathing. He claimed to have initially been put off reading *The Red Badge* by the very fact that James had recommended it. James, he uncharitably observed, 'is an effeminate old donkey who lives with a herd of other donkeys around him and insists on being treated as if he were the Pope. He has licked dust from the floor of every third-rate hostess in England.'[7] Crane could be quite as vitriolic as this when he chose, calling Wilde 'a mildewed chump' and complaining that Robert Louis Stevenson 'has not passed away far enough', but on this occasion he rose to James's defence. According to Thomas Beer, who so delightfully described James as passing his last years 'in a series of recoils', Crane protested that he was a man of immense kindness, impossible to dislike. Without success. Frederic was prepared to stand up for Wilde, whom he disliked, at his trial – he hated to kick a man when he was down – but he remained obdurate in his scorn for James. Bullies are not fond of eating their words, and Frederic had the bully in him. To Crane, ill at ease in English literary society, Frederic was a refreshing companion and a good friend, a man who spoke his mind freely and shared his own professional attitude to their common craft. In Frederic's company, he could relax, untroubled by the fear that he would suddenly be invited to say what he thought of Flaubert or whether he considered his novels to carry a social message. This was the kind of conversation which Crane detested and, in Frederic's company, eschewed.

Garnett had brought Crane to Ravensbrook to enjoy the stimulation of more elevated company. A lunch with Edmund Gosse passed off quite comfortably and tea with Swinburne was not so much of a failure as might have been anticipated. But the Cranes were also expected to blend in with the Fabian group who had gathered around Garnett's home, The Cearne, making the area into a self-consciously homespun Arcadia in the approved William Morris mould. Crane refused to take them seriously. He amused himself by telling one of Garnett's friends that he had received his artistic education in The Bowery, eliciting grave interest in this unknown Fine Arts school. This sort of foolery would not do. The dourly kind Edward Pease, secretary to the Fabian Society, and his jolly, commanding wife, Marjorie, decided to take the newcomers in hand, to explain to them the Fabian way of life. Nobody minded in the least that they were not married (attempts to pass themselves off as man and wife had not been entirely successful) or that they kept an eccentric household of raffish dogs and quaintly foreign servants.

Edward and Marjorie Pease were prepared to be accommodating, but the Cranes must in return make some effort to fit in with the habits of the neighbourhood. Perhaps they hadn't tasted mead before? It was a most nourishing and excellent beverage, and so much better if one drank it in the authentic way, from a bullock's horn. They all did. And clothes. Mrs Pease was sure Cora would find it more comfortable to wear clothes she had made herself, and the medieval style was so flattering to the fuller figure. (Brisk exercise had kept Mrs Pease lithe, but Cora was indisputably plump.)

Cora was dubious. She had always rather fancied herself as a doyenne of fashion. She was not sure that she wanted to know how to set about making medieval clothes of the kind which the Fabian ladies wore. Mrs Pease was brisk. She must learn. Ford Madox Ford lived nearby. Who better than Madox Brown's grandson to teach her how to run up a William Morris-style robe?

Ford, who later remembered Mrs Pease as being a woman who only took yes for an answer, received his orders and made his visit, only to find Cora as uneasy about receiving instructions on dressmaking as he was about offering them. The enterprise was abandoned with mutual relief, but Cora was insistent that he should stay and meet Crane who was coming down from London later that evening. The dinner so hospitably offered was embarrassingly frugal and when Crane appeared bearing parcels of food from a London shop, the reason became apparent. Ravensbrook was proving an expensive house to run and neither Crane nor Cora had any notion of how to budget sensibly, with the unhappy result that they were no longer welcome as customers at the local shops. But this was a night of celebration. Crane had been to see his agent, J. B. Pinker, and Pinker had promised to get him £20 for every thousand words he wrote.* He was, as Ford remembered, in a state of wild elation, his huge eyes shining with delight as he talked of the poems he was going to write, the new home he was going to buy, the travels he and Cora were going to make. He paused only long enough to tell Ford that he was making a great mistake by cluttering his own poems up with so many words for the sake of the metre. Ford nodded obligingly, and fell quietly asleep on the drawing-room sofa.

Although Ford was ready here to submit that this was his first meeting with Crane, he later owned up to the fact that there had been earlier encounters of a less friendly nature. It was not until Crane moved to Brede that he fell under the spell of 'the most beautiful spirit I have ever known'. In 1897 only the determinedly neighbourly spirit of the Fabian neighbourhood in which they were both living forced Ford to make a grudging show of friendship.

He had read none of Crane's works at that time, but he had heard Crane spoken of as a genius. Neither Ford's first novel nor his biography of his grandfather had caused anyone to call him a genius. It might, he admitted, have been a case of secret envy. He was young and ambitious and it irked him to see Crane praised and admired for 'a best seller of fantastic proportions'. He had, he acknowledged, felt

---

* Either Ford or Crane was guilty of fantasizing. Pinker was far too canny to have promised anything of the kind to a writer he had only just taken on.

the same initial resentment of Conrad and James. 'That must have been because of the nature of adoration bestowed upon them by their respective groups. I was a young man with a little achievement of my own . . . So it may have been latent jealousy. But I think it was rather a form of dislike for being, as it were, taken by the elbow and thrust into the presence of personages before whom the thrusters orientally prostrated themselves.'[8]

His first sight of Crane was at a lecture which the young American had been asked to deliver at a Fabian meeting. Crane, who had never given a lecture before, decided to play safe by talking about something he knew well. He gave them a talk on the art of semaphore, having become a skilled 'flagwagger' during his two months in Greece. Ford, astonished that anyone should prefer talking about flags to theorizing on literary techniques – what an opportunity lost! – noted that the lecturer looked 'young, pained and dictatorial' and that his speech had been unmemorable. Offered an introduction, Ford coldly turned away and said he would prefer to do without one.

An introduction could not be avoided when Edward Garnett brought Crane over to visit him at Gracie's Cottage in June 1897. (This was the period during which the Fords had sublet Pent Farm to Walter Crane and were living at Limpsfield.) Ford was full of scorn for a brash foreigner who could mistake a farm cottage for 'a bully baronic ruin' and seek to ingratiate himself by asking if he could plant a souvenir rose-tree by the door. Folding his arms with a sardonic shrug of consent, Ford watched his visitor go to work with his spade. Crane, he was forced to admit, was no slouch when it came to digging.

After the Cranes had moved to Brede, Ford began to revise his judgement. He watched, fascinated, as Crane effortlessly swatted flies with a lightning movement of the bead sight of his gun. He found himself looking forward to the sight of that curious and most un-English spectacle of Crane riding down the lanes in cowboy costume. Amusement turned to affectionate concern as he saw the fury with which Crane kept at his work and the courageous way in which he dismissed the seriousness of his illness. Crane, in the last year of his life seemed to him the most heroic of his friends – 'honourable, physically brave, infinitely hopeful, generous, charitable to excess, observant beyond belief, morally courageous, of unswerving loyalty, a beautiful poet – and of untiring industry'.[9] When, in 1935, Ford published an article on techniques in the novel, he had no hesitation in placing Crane alongside James and Conrad as a pioneer in the revolution of literary style. It was a sea-change in attitude from that of 1897.

Ford was right to say that Crane was observant. He had been quick to take Ford's measure and to recognize the kindness and the intelligence behind the hectoring manner and the tone of drawling condescension. He was less irritated by Ford's ready assumption of his own superiority than was Cora, who decided on at least one occasion that she would not tolerate it. This was when Ford unexpectedly paid them a call at the same time as Sanford Bennett, a shy and unfortunate young friend of theirs recently married to a Frenchwoman after the suicide of his first wife. Mrs Bennett's family were old friends of the Pointilliste painter, Georges Seurat; Ford decided to dazzle on two fronts by educating her, in French, on the techniques used by the artist. That Mrs Bennett was rather better informed on the subject was a fact of which the Cranes and her husband were uncomfortably aware. The guests attempted to speak; Ford boomed on. Cora had had enough. Mrs Bennett, she brusquely said, spoke excellent English. They would all prefer a change of language, and a change of subject. Ford, for once, was silenced.

Crane was not so easily riled. When Bennett referred to Ford's schoolmasterish behaviour, he only laughed and said that, well, it was typical of the man. He meant no harm. 'He patronizes me, he patronizes Mr Conrad, he patronizes Mr James. When he goes to Heaven he will patronize God Almighty. But God Almighty will get used to it, for Hueffer is all right.'[10] Ford was quite pleased when this remark was reported back to him; he liked it enough to quote in one of his anecdotes about 'poor Steevie'.

Edward Garnett had been an industrious literary host to Crane, but the honour of his most important English introduction goes to a duller and less perspicacious man, Sidney Pawling of Heinemann's, who were currently publishing both Crane and Conrad. Crane had been following the serial publication of *The Nigger of the 'Narcissus'* with passionate interest. As soon as he arrived in England, he begged Pawling to introduce him to its author.

A lunch was set up for October 1897 and Conrad was as eager as Crane to attend it. *The Red Badge of Courage* had enthralled him and had been much in his mind when he was at work on *The Nigger of the 'Narcissus'*; it is very possible that he borrowed from Crane's famous description of the setting sun as a 'bloody wafer' for his lurid concluding image in *Lord Jim*. 'I *do* admire him,' he wrote to Garnett just before the lunch. 'I shan't have to pretend.'[11]

Nor did he. They eyed each other gravely across the restaurant table and shook hands 'under the encouraging gaze of Sidney Pawling, who, a much bigger man than either of us and possessed of a deep voice, looked like a grown-up person entertaining two strange small boys – protecting and slightly anxious as to the experiment.' They liked each other at once.

The small-boy image chosen here by Conrad exactly catches the nature of this first and most important encounter. Conrad, deeply gloomy at the prospect of becoming a father for the first time, a responsibility he anticipated without relish, was delighted to have had an excuse to escape to London. Crane was thrilled to see how impressed Conrad was by his tales of adventures in Greece. When Pawling left them in the late afternoon, they had scarcely begun to cover all the subjects they wanted to talk about. The afternoon, as Conrad remembered it, 'had a character of enchantment about it'. Wandering around London with no strong sense of which direction they were taking, they talked, and talked, so absorbed in conversation that Conrad almost walked under a carriage and had to be smartly pulled back by his companion. He was sure that Crane must have had some experience of war before writing *The Red Badge*. Crane said: '"No. But *The Red Badge* is all right." I assured him I had never doubted it; and since the title of the work had been pronounced for the first time, feeling that I must do something to show I had read it, I said shyly: "I like your General." He knew at once what I was alluding to, but said not a word. Nothing could have been more tramp-like than our silent pacing, elbow to elbow, till, after we had left Hyde Park behind us, Crane uttered with his quiet earnestness the words: "I like your young man – I can just see him." This was positively the only allusion we made that afternoon to our immortal works . . . A stranger would have expected more, but in a manner of speaking, Crane and I had never been strangers. We took each other's works for granted from the very first . . .'[12]

They discussed the nature of the universe over tea in an empty A.B.C. shop; by ten o'clock they had reached Piccadilly Circus and Balzac. Crane, with devastating simplicity, wished to be given a full account of the *Comédie Humaine*, contents, scope, plan, significance. Hoping he would forget about it, Conrad suggested supper – and found himself shouting descriptions of the novels 'over the rush of hundreds of waiters and the clatter of tons of crockery' while Crane listened with rapt attention. Looking at him with an affectionate, almost paternal eye, Conrad was struck by the thought that his was not the face of a lucky man. Sensitive, alert, intelligent, perhaps a little weak, and, somehow, ill-fated. Even as Crane smiled, he had the intimation, as Willa Cather had before him, that here was a man who was not destined for a long life. Perhaps because of that insight – or was it hindsight? – Conrad would always be a little protective of Crane, a little watchful of his own violent and hasty temperament when in his company.

They had forgotten to exchange addresses, but a month later Crane sent off a postcard via Heinemann, asking when they could meet again, and Conrad used the same route to send proofs of the finished *The Nigger of the 'Narcissus'* for Crane's opinion. Crane liked it, enough to write and ask Hamlin Garland if he could not get it published in America, and to tell Conrad that it was 'simply great', particularly the nigger's death, which was just 'too good, too terrible', and wouldn't he and his wife please come to Ravensbrook soon and 'Did not we have a good pow-wow in London?'[13] Conrad, who was plunged into his usual gloom over any work he had just completed, was cheered and touched. 'When I feel depressed about it I say to myself "Crane likes the damned thing" – and am greatly consoled. What your appreciation is to me I renounce to explain. The world looks different to me now, since our long pow-wow. It was good.' They couldn't manage a visit to Ravensbrook until Jessie's pregnancy was over, but they would be delighted to put him up in bachelor's quarters if he came to them.[14]* (Cora, it seems, had either been overlooked or unmentioned.)

A visit by Crane to Ivy Walls was set up for 28 November.

Jessie was charmed by her first American guest's gentle unaffected manner and by his solemnly affectionate descriptions of his new dogs, Sponge, Flannel and Ruby, who went everywhere in single file, as if engaged in some elaborate children's game. She liked his simplicity. She could leave her husband to talk to Crane without feeling that she had been excluded because of her stupidity, the impression she always gained from Ford.

The two men smoked and talked for half the night and Conrad was surprised and a little disconcerted by the hopelessness which Crane showed. Self-confidence was not a notable characteristic in his own personality, but it seemed that night to be entirely absent in his friend. He read the stories Crane had brought with him, 'The Open Boat' and 'A Man and Some Others', and endeavoured to lift his spirits by writing to him a few days later in an encouraging vein. His method was 'fascinating. You are a complete impressionist. The illusions of life come out of your hand without a flaw.'[15]

The compliment had more of an edge to it than Crane could have known. Impressionism to Conrad was only one of the many

---

* The contrast between Conrad's letters about his novel to Crane and to James is almost comically extreme. To the latter, he sent a copy with a courtly French note: 'On ne communique pas la réalité poignante des illusions! Le rêve finit, les mots s'envolent, le livre est oublié. C'est la grâce miséricordieuse du destin.'[16]

techniques the artist had to employ; he would later praise another friend, Robert Cunninghame Graham, for *not* using Crane's impressionistic style. To Edward Garnett, just after Crane's visit, he gave a harsher critical reaction. He knew that Garnett liked Crane's work and he was ready to agree that 'he has outline, he has colour, he has movement, with that he ought to go very far. But – will he? I sometimes think he won't. It is not an opinion – it is a feeling. I could not explain why he disappoints me – why my enthusiasm withers as soon as I close the book. While one reads, of course, he is not to be questioned. He is the master of his reader to the very last line – then – apparently for no reason at all – he seems to let go his hold. It is as if he had gripped you with greased fingers.'[17]

The self-despair which Crane had betrayed on the night of his visit was untypical: he may have been apprehensive of Conrad's reaction to his stories. Authors are seldom at their most cheerful and confident when awaiting the critical judgement of a respected fellow-writer. Conrad's letter must have been reassuring. A month later, Crane was feeling optimistic enough to suggest that they should collaborate on a play.

Crane, like James before him, had inhaled the dangerous scent of huge financial rewards for comparatively little work. Why should the two hard-up writers not get together and make a killing by writing a splendidly theatrical romance? He had worked up a plot already; he was certain it was a sure-fire success.*

The setting was to be the American West. The plot, as Conrad remembered it, was to consist 'in a man personating his "predecessor" (who had died) in the hope of winning a girl's heart . . . the action, I fear, would have been frankly melodramatic. Crane insisted that one of the situations should present the man and the girl on a boundless plain standing by their dead ponies after a furious ride (a truly Crane touch). I made some objections. A boundless plain in the light of a sunset could be got into a back-cloth, I admitted; but I doubted whether we could induce the management of any London theatre to deposit two stuffed horses on its stage . . .'[18]

It says much for Crane's enthusiasm and Conrad's fondness for him that they should ever have got as far as discussing technicalities.

---

* Nicholas Delbanco follows Conrad in dating this project to 1899, but a letter from Conrad of 3 February, 1898 ('Crane is worrying me to write a play with him') indicates that it was considerably earlier. Conrad's first and undated letter to Crane about the play refers to the imminent birth of the baby, which puts it back to January 1898. There is, of course, the possibility of their having discussed two plays: Garnett remembered one about a shipwreck which bears no relation to the play discussed above.

Conrad's initial response made without having seen the plot, was to flatter his friend out of any notion of collaboration. He would be delighted to advise, but 'I have no dramatic gift. *You* have the terseness, the clear eye[,] the easy imagination . . . I would be only a hindrance to you – I am afraid. And it seems presumptuous of me to think of helping You. You want no help. I have a perfect confidence in your power – and why should you share with me what then may be of profit and fame in the accomplished task?'[19]

Crane was not to be put off so easily. The plot, if we can trust Conrad's memory, was revealed to him during one of the London meetings in which they both revelled like small boys out of school, and this time he 'caught the infection at once. There and then we began to build up the masterpiece, interrupting each other eagerly, for I don't know how it was, the air around us had suddenly grown thick with felicitous suggestions.'[20] But the mood evaporated and the play was never written, although Conrad freely acknowledged that Crane's suggestion of a *doppelgänger* figure gave him the motif for 'The Planter of Malata' which he wrote thirteen years later. It may, too, have been this suggestion of a collaborative work that led Conrad to think it would be an ideal antidote to solitary endeavours. It was only a few months later that he suggested a working partnership to Ford.

The friendship gained a new dimension with the arrival of Borys Conrad on 15 January, 1898, making, his father wrote to Crane, 'a devil of a row. He yelled like an Apache and ever since this morning has been on the war path again. It's a ghastly nuisance.'[21] Fatherhood did not, in the early years, give Conrad much joy; he was too fond of his own role as Jessie's petted child to relinquish it easily. His first reaction on hearing the baby's wail was to shout to the maid to remove that screaming child before it upset his wife and he received the news that it was the cry of his first-born without any show of pleasure. Babies were a trial to a man of short temper, and Conrad's temper was very short. (His mother-in-law refused to visit them again after being ambushed in the outside lavatory by Conrad, armed with a rifle and shouting to her to 'Come out – damn you!' The explanation that he had taken her for a burglar did not lessen her wrath.) 'I hate babies,' he told Garnett – and meant it. When, on 19 February, 1898, the family made their first visit to the Cranes, Conrad insisted on keeping his distance from the vociferous infant. He would travel in the same carriage as Jessie and her young sister, Dolly (who had come to help look after Borys for six months), but he would not have it known that he was of their party. As good as his word, he hid behind a newspaper while Borys roared and sobbed. The other passengers, all female, directed sympathetic looks at the poor man who was being obliged to put up with this din until Dolly, a little maliciously, asked if he would get the baby's bottle out of his suitcase. Sympathy turned to stern reproach as Conrad sheepishly complied.

Conrad (initially) disliked Borys; Crane adored him. Strangely, none of the biographies points out that Crane and Cora must have longed for children of their own; dogs were only a substitute – as were the little Frederic children they took in – for the baby they never had. Crane was besotted with Borys from the start (as was Adoni, their young Greek servant, who alarmed Jessie Conrad by coming in to watch her in admiring silence as she bathed the baby in the Ravensbrook tub). His feeling for the baby, Conrad ruefully remembered, made their own friendship seem positively frigid by comparison. When had Crane ever lain stretched on the grass raptly gazing at *him* as he did at Master Borys? Puzzled and touched, Conrad watched the grown Crane playing intently with the small baby as if some secret rapport had been established. Later, as Borys grew strong enough to toddle across the grass at Brede, Conrad grew a little irritated by the way Crane always took the child's side. 'I could not see that the baby was being oppressed, hectored over, or in any way deprived of its rights, or even wounded in its feelings by me; but Crane seemed always to nurse some vague unexpressed grievance at my conduct. I was inconsiderate.'[22] A boy should have a dog, Crane announced and gave him one of Sponge's puppies, promptly rechristened Escamillo after the toreador in the opera which Conrad, when he was in a good mood, liked to whistle. A little later it was suggested that a boy should learn to ride and that Crane should teach him. Conrad agreed, saying '"If you give the boy your seat I will be perfectly satisfied." I knew this would please him; and indeed his face remained wreathed in smiles all the way to the front door.'[23] Crane was dead before the little boy was old enough to be taught.

The Ravensbrook visit was a great success. Garnett, who gave his blessing to this most suitable literary friendship, was probably drawing on his memory of those few days when he described the two writers in his introduction to Conrad's letters.

> Conrad's moods of gay tenderness could be quite seductive. On the few occasions I saw him with Stephen Crane he was delightfully sunny, and bantered 'poor Steve' in the gentlest, most affectionate style, while the latter sat silent, Indian-like, turning enquiring eyes under his chiselled brow, now and then jumping up suddenly and confiding

some new project with intensely electric feeling . . . I can still hear
the shades of Crane's poignant friendliness in his cry 'Joseph!' And
Conrad's delight in Crane's personality glowed in the shining warmth
of his brown eyes.[24]

The pleasant banter and idle plans for a joint holiday in Brittany
were put aside when Conrad and Crane were alone. Conrad was
feeling the pinch himself, but Crane was worryingly deep in debt.
Cora's generous extravagance was beginning to cost him handsomely. A lawsuit for alleged embezzlement had led to all his royalties
for the American edition of *The Red Badge* being frozen; his stories
were not being quickly placed and he had run up some $2,000 worth
of bills. 'I would like to hear all is well,' Conrad wrote to him in his
letter of thanks. 'It hurts me to think you are worried. It is bad for
You and it is bad for your art. All the time I was at the Garnetts we
have been talking of You. We conclude you must be kept quiet . . .'[25]
If Crane had only done that, kept quiet, his life-span might have been
extended by a few years. He did exactly the opposite. He went to
war. And Conrad helped him to go.

In April 1898, the United States decided to recognize Cuba's
independence from Spain: war between Spain and America was the
inevitable outcome. When Crane met Conrad one cloudy afternoon
in London during that month, he had already made up his mind to
leave for the States as soon as he could find the money for the fare.
He would enter the war as a reporter or a volunteer. He didn't mind
which. (His failure to meet the army's physical requirements settled
that issue; he eventually went to Cuba as a reporter for the *World*.)
He needed £60, and he was determined to lay hands on it that
afternoon. Conrad, despite the fact that his sympathies were with
Spain, was caught up in the wave of Crane's enthusiasm, and, after
they had made several unsuccessful attempts to raise a loan, he
suggested a visit to the offices of William Blackwood & Sons. Here,
with Conrad pledging his own work as security, they were given a
loan. He had only done as Crane had asked, 'yet now and then I feel
as though that afternoon I led him by the hand to his doom. But,
indeed, I was only the blind agent of the fate that had him in her
grip. Nothing could have held him back. He was ready to swim the
ocean.'[26]

To escape from his creditors, perhaps? Cora must have wondered
about that during the next nine months as she struggled to keep her
head above a flood of debts. Conrad's assurances that the return could
only be a matter of weeks began to sound thin; his letters to Cora
suggest that he was feeling more than a little guilty for the part he

had played in taking Crane away from her. His guilt must have increased when Cora received a newspaper cutting from Florida in September which stated that Crane had disappeared without trace in Havana.

Nobody knew what had become of him. Cora, already frantic, was almost hysterical with terror. Her pathetic misspelt letter to Paul Revere Reynolds, Crane's second literary agent, offers a testimony to her state of mind. 'I am in *great* need of money. And I fear that we will lose our home here if I cannot get money to pay some pressing debts. The Journal is behaving very shabily [sic]. I have been served with two summonds [sic] so you can see how bad matters really are . . . This being so helpless in a foreign country together with my fears for Mr Crane are almost driving me mad. Will you use your influence with Mr Hearst. He has no right to allow a man like Stephen Crane to be missing for over three weeks without using means to find him. And if he allows Stephen Cranes [sic] wife to be turned out of her home, while Stephen is risking his life in his service, I have told Mr Creelman I would let every correspondent in London know about it.'[27]

It took a cable from Cora to the Secretary of War to produce, in late October, the news that Crane was safe; he had only moved to a cheaper hotel without bothering to tell anybody. The report was secondhand and Cora, desperate for some assurance from him, began to imagine – how could she not? – that she had been supplanted. It fell to Jessie Conrad to comfort her and to tell her how much Crane loved her, but Cora remained wretchedly convinced that he had gone off with another woman. He would never come back! She worked herself up even more by writing stories of beautiful women who patiently waited for their beloveds only to find that they had been forgotten. In her diary, she wrote about the betrayal of love. Conrad, busy with his arrangements for moving to Pent Farm, did not do much to raise her spirits by asking whether she really believed Crane was going to return. 'Are you *sure* you can bring him back?' he tactlessly enquired after Crane had been unearthed in Havana. 'I don't doubt your influence mind! but not knowing the circumstances I do not know how far it would be feasible . . . Will he come? *Can* he come?'[28]

Crane could, but he was in no hurry to do so. Back in America, he started to house-hunt in New York and to suggest in one of his rare letters that Cora should come and join him. She had, in a moment of despair, been ready to sail to Cuba to track him down, so she could surely manage to get to New York where no tracking was required.

But from Cora's point of view, there were very good reasons to quarrel with this suggestion. She was still legally married to Stewart and Crane's absence had made her painfully conscious of the fragility of her position. The friendship of several prestigious compatriots had enabled her to achieve a fairly respectable social position in England. In America, she remained a woman with a disreputable past and an embarrassing present as Crane's common-law wife. So Cora waited for Crane to give up the battle, and she won. The New York police had not forgotten the way Crane had denounced them in court during the Dora Clark case, and they did not disguise their hostility. After being attacked on three separate occasions, twice by an unknown assailant and once by an aggressive policeman who tried to arrest him on the spot, Crane decided to go back to England – via Havana. Christmas passed without a word of his whereabouts or his plans, but on 11 January, 1899, he arrived at Gravesend on the *Manitou*, to be met by Cora. Almost his first action was to repay Conrad his loan.

Despair had not made a prudent woman of Cora. Any dreams Crane may have had of coming back to a queen of household management were dashed on arrival. The creditors were still chasing him, the household had expanded drastically to encompass the Frederic ménage, and he had been transformed from the harassed tenant of Ravensbrook into the buccaneering baron of Brede, the new and splendid home which Cora had, on Garnett's recommendation, agreed to rent from Mr and Mrs Moreton Frewen.

Socially, the move to Brede was a distinct advance; economically, it was disastrous. There were servants to be paid – the Frewens had insisted that they should all be kept on – and a huge and dilapidated house to be maintained together with a large garden and a hundred acres of parkland. And, inevitably in the case of a couple who were known to be prodigal with their hospitality, there were the guests to be entertained, the endless stream of friends and vague acquaintances who were all ready to treat Brede as a free hotel in which they could stay for as long as they pleased. And all this was at a time when Crane had not a penny to his name.

The Conrads made their first visit in June, as soon as Conrad had finished 'a rotten thing' – *Heart of Darkness*. The newly planted roses were coming into bloom and the house was looking its best in the gloriously mellow light of a Sussex summer. Crane came down the drive to meet them on one of the two vast coach-horses he had inherited with the house and which he rode every day; his appearance, Ford once remarked, was that of a frail eagle perched astride a giant elephant. He was looking dazzlingly happy, full of joy to see them, and enchanted as always by Borys. It seemed as though Brede was doing him good.

After their stay of two weeks, the Conrads changed their minds. The visit had been an exhausting one and not very enjoyable. The house was full of the strangers who lived off Crane and with whom they had nothing in common. Conrad was not above throwing a few bread pellets across the dining-room table when he was at home, but the uncouthness of the guests at Brede was of a less jocular kind. There was no sense of order or routine. As a place in which to get work done, Brede seemed a nightmare, although Conrad noticed that Crane managed to escape to his little red-walled study every day for a few hours to produce a formidable number of pages in his copperplate hand as well as finding time for endless games with Borys on the sloping lawns. Jessie, a model housekeeper and mother, was appalled by the laxness of Cora's regime. The Frederic children were allowed to run about barefoot and to appear for dinner in badly darned socks that looked absurdly out of place with their elaborate clothes. Cora had taken to wearing odd rustic costumes and to letting her hair hang loose instead of pinning it up as all respectable women did at that time. The maids were slovenly and the cook was always drunk, and refused to cook if she was not. Dinner at eight was never more than a faint hope, although the food, when it came, was usually excellent. Pent Farm might not be so grand, but a fortnight at Brede was enough to convince Jessie that Conrad was a good deal better placed than Crane. Brede had sounded enviably grand, but that illusion had faded when she saw the shabbiness of the rooms, the doors which wouldn't open, the fruit rotting in the chapel and the unpleasantly inadequate sanitary arrangements – only one lavatory in a house of that size! It was a mere ragamuffins' palace, and Jessie thought little of it.

Nor, despite his greater discretion, did Conrad. He had felt ill at ease. His friendship with Crane was, like that with Ford, one of personal intimacy. He felt uncomfortable trying to talk to him in a noisy crowd of unknown people. He postponed their next visit. A boat, *La Reine*, which the two men bought together (although Crane never paid his share), was a happy solution in an awkward situation. Sailing along the coast together, they could rediscover the easy untaxing spirit of camaraderie they had shared in their London meetings.

As a friend, Conrad remained warmly affectionate. He tried to write to Crane in the sort of language he had heard him use, calling him 'Dear old Pard.,' and telling him he was 'the greatest of the boys'. But his critical sense told him that the quality of Crane's work was beginning to diminish.

In 1898, after reading 'The Price of the Harness', published while Crane was in Cuba, Conrad had been ready to 'augur a magnificent future for his coming work'.[29] Now, in the autumn of 1899, as Crane churned out story after story in a desperate attempt to stave off the bills, he began to question that prediction. He had started to collaborate with Ford, and it may have been that their lengthy discussions about the art of the novel increased his sense that Crane was not sufficiently dedicated to his craft. Ford, for all the weakness of his early works, was in deadly earnest when it came to the idea of sacrificing a luxurious existence for the sake of your art. Conrad observed and could not approve of Crane's readiness to prostitute his talent for the sake of a pretty house and an extravagant wife.

A visit to Brede for the New Year revels of 1899–1900 confirmed Conrad's sense that Crane was leading the wrong kind of life – how could he hope to do his best work when he surrounded himself with worthless people and sat up playing poker for half the night? It was all very fine for Wells to play games which involved sliding about on a broomstick until the early hours. Wells had the stamina to work and play. Crane had not. His health had deteriorated sharply since the Cuban enterprise. He was plagued by attacks of malaria. He looked pale and drawn. But the partying still went on, and the bills accumulated. Ford mentioned having found Crane skulking in an outhouse after the New Year guests had gone, terrified that the tax-man was about to pounce and carry him off to prison for not paying his dues. Wells had asked when he was going to write another novel and had been told that he couldn't afford to do anything long. 'Short stuff' was what they wanted and where the money was. 'I got to do them,' Crane said. 'I got to do them.'

He did do them, and *Book News* was ready to say that his *Whilomville Stories* were a fine study of a boy's psychology, and the *Critic* could compare *Wounds in the Rain*, his collection of Cuban war tales, to *The Red Badge of Courage*, but Conrad had only to read 'The Blue Hotel', written at Ravensbrook in February 1898 and published in December 1899, to confirm his fears. Genius had given way to professionalism. Writing to his friend Robert Cunninghame Graham shortly after the New Year at Brede, Conrad told him that his stories of Morocco and Mexico were 'wonderful . . . perfect . . . much more of course than mere Crane-like impressionism'.[30] And yet, a month after Crane's death in June 1900, he would turn to *The Red Badge* to find the inspirational image for the last scene of *Lord Jim*.

The Introduction to Thomas Beer's biography of Stephen Crane was Conrad's last piece of writing. In it he quoted Edward Garnett's article in the *London Academy* of 17 December, 1898. 'Undoubtedly, of the young school it is Mr Crane who is the genius – the others have their talents,' Garnett had said. 'My part here being not that of critic but of private friend,' Conrad added, 'all I will say is that I agreed warmly at the time with that article.'

8

A RING OF FRIENDSHIPS: EDITH WHARTON AND THE QU'ACRE CIRCLE

Mr James left us last week, after giving us two months of a companionship unfailingly delightful, wise & kind. The more one knows him the more one wonders & admires the mixture of wisdom & tolerance, of sensitiveness & sympathy, that makes his heart even more interesting than his mind. He has gone on to Italy for a few weeks, & after that he says he returns to England *for life*.

Edith Wharton to Charles Eliot Norton,
Paris, 1907

At Queen's Acre some of the happiest hours of my life were passed, some of my dearest friendships formed or consolidated, and my own old friends welcomed because they were mine.

Edith Wharton,
A Backward Glance

I do indeed 'understand how one's heart reaches back into the past' – that incredible past in which we once lived unimagining of these horrors and not knowing that we were fantastically happy.

Henry James to Howard Sturgis,
1915

1862 Edith Jones born, possibly as the result of an affair between her mother and a young English tutor living in the house. Edith's biographer, Professor R. W. B. Lewis, suggests that he may be portrayed as M. Riviere, the young tutor in *The Age of Innocence* (1920).

1870s James makes friends with Howard Sturgis.

1878 Edith publishes *Verses*.

1882 Edith's engagement to Harry Stevens broken off, formally by her but at pressure of Mrs Stevens who wanted to keep financial control of her son's trust fund.

1883 Edith, let down a second time by Walter Berry's failure to propose to her, turns to Edward (Teddy) Wharton.

1885 Edith marries Teddy Wharton.

1890s James makes friends with Morton Fullerton.

1891 Howard Sturgis publishes *Tim*.

1895 Howard Sturgis publishes *All that was Possible*.

1897 Edith and Ogden Codman publish *The Decoration of Houses* and Berry re-enters Edith's life as friend.

1899 Edith publishes *The Greater Inclination* (short stories).

1900 Edith publishes *The Touchstone* (novella).

1901 Edith publishes *Crucial Instances* and oversees construction of her new home at Lenox, Massachusetts, The Mount.

1902 Edith publishes *The Valley of Decision* and is told by James to keep to American subjects.

1903 Edith publishes *Sanctuary* and makes friends with James.

1904 Edith publishes *The Descent of Man* and *Italian Villas and their Gardens*. James and Howard Sturgis stay at The Mount and meet Walter Berry. Howard publishes *Belchamber*.

1905 Edith publishes *The House of Mirth* and *Italian Backgrounds*.

1907 Edith publishes *The Fruit of the Tree* and *Madame de Treymes*.

1907 James visits the first of her two flats on the rue de Varenne in Paris and goes on a motor-tour of France with her and Teddy, complaining at the difficulty of keeping up with their expensive style of life. In October, on James's recommendation, Morton Fullerton visits The Mount.

1907– Edith's affair with Morton Fullerton begins.

1908 Edith publishes *A Motor-Flight through France* and *The Hermit and the Wild Woman and Other Stories*.

1909 Edith publishes *Artemis to Actaeon and Other Verse*. James publishes his parody of her, 'The Top of the Tree', as *The Velvet Glove*. Edith shows every sign of relishing the parody.

1910 Walter Berry replaces Fullerton as Edith's closest male friend. She publishes *Tales of Men and Ghosts*.

1911 The Mount is sold. Edith publishes *Ethan Frome*.

1912 Edith publishes *The Reef*.

1913 The Whartons are finally divorced. Edith publishes *The Custom of the Country*. Her main home from now on will be in France. A rupture with James over his seventieth birthday present.

1914– Edith sets up refugee hostels and
15 an *ouvroir* for unemployed seamstresses and is greatly admired by James for her courage and determination. Edith publishes *Fighting France, from Dunkerque to Belfort*. James becomes a British subject.

1916 James dies. Edith is made a Chevalier of the Legion of Honour. She publishes *Xingu and Other Stories*, but does not use her war experience for a novel until 1923, for *A Son at the Front*.

1920 Howard Sturgis dies. Edith publishes *The Age of Innocence* and is awarded the Pulitzer Prize.

1927 Walter Berry dies in his Parisian home (Edith's former flat on the rue de Varenne).

8

A RING OF FRIENDSHIPS:
EDITH WHARTON AND
THE QU'ACRE CIRCLE

I f we had been able to ask Henry James how he would most like
to spend a few days away from Rye in the early 1900s, he would
probably have suggested that Edith Wharton should come with
her chauffeur-driven car and take him to Queen's Acre (always
abbreviated to Qu'Acre), affectionately evoked here in Mrs
Wharton's autobiography, *A Backward Glance*:

> Within, profound chintz arm-chairs drawn up about a hearth on which
> a fire always smouldered; a big table piled with popular novels and
> picture-magazines; and near the table a lounge on which lay out-
> stretched, his legs covered by a thick shawl, his hands occupied with
> knitting needles or embroidery silks, a sturdily built handsome man
> with brilliantly white wavy hair, a girlishly clear complexion, a black
> moustache, and tender mocking eyes under the bold arch of his black
> brows.
>
> Such was Howard Sturgis, perfect host, matchless friend, drollest,
> kindest and strangest of men, as he appeared to the startled eyes of
> newcomers on their first introduction to Queen's Acre.[1]

Neither Wells, Crane, Ford nor Conrad held the passport to the
inner ring of James's circle: the only American among them came
from the wrong social group. To join the circle, you needed to be of
New England stock, of literary inclination and cultivated tastes; a
sharp wit was a bonus. Percy Lubbock and John Hugh Smith were
the only Englishmen who had a permanent entrée, Lubbock as a
clever if slightly sycophantic young man who was prepared to sit at
the feet of his American elders and take notes for his memoirs of
them and for his theories on the craft of fiction gleaned from their
discussions, Hugh Smith as his friend and, later, a devoted admirer
of Edith Wharton whom he met in 1908. But Mrs Wharton, James,

Gaillard Lapsley, Morton Fullerton, Walter Berry and Howard Sturgis himself, comprised a formidable and exclusive New England group.

These New Englanders abroad had as clannish an instinct as the English aristocracy when removed from home territory. Tenaciously, they clung to what they had known and defined themselves by their connections. James and his friends were drawn to Qu'Acre by the wit and charm of their host (Howard Sturgis was the man Arthur Benson chose to preserve in that savage game of which friend to strand on the dome of St Paul's, which to push off and which to save), but there was an added attraction in relaxing into a shared history, the bond of a common background in a country which, however much they loved it, remained alien. The price which snobbish England demanded of its American visitors and residents was the resignation of any sense of superiority, any freedom to mock; among themselves, the New Englanders were free to ridicule the idea of an Empress of India at Frogmore, or to refer to Edward VII as an arch-vulgarian.

Qu'Acre has lost its cosy rooms of chintz chairs and occasional tables. Externally, it remains as it was at the turn of the century. Leon Edel elevates it to the grandeur of a Georgian residence and R. W. B. Lewis, Mrs Wharton's splendid biographer, asserts that Howard Sturgis was brought up there. Both are at fault: Howard had reached middle-age before he moved to the commodious Victorian house at Windsor. (His previous country home, Tan-yr-allt in Wales, had proved inconveniently remote.) The only pseudo-Georgian feature the house possesses is a couple of œil-de-bœuf windows. White verandahs and vermilion-tinted brick walls shamelessly proclaim its modernity and ally it to the pleasant homes of maiden aunts and retired couples of the professional classes in Hastings and Hove. It was built in the 1870s by Basil Champneys, Howard's contemporary at Eton.

Qu'Acre's superiority is in its position, almost directly adjacent to Windsor Great Park, into which Mrs Wharton and James were led each morning by their brief host for a 'toddle' – Howard detested strenuous exercise – with Misery, his dog. With such a majestic landscape on the doorstep, it hardly mattered that the Qu'Acre garden was a modest acre of shaded lawn, eked out by a shrubbery and rose-beds with a coach-house to the rear. It was not nearly so grand as Mrs Wharton's American edition of Belton House in miniature and it lacked the historic interest of Lamb House, but everyone loved it. There was never a shortage of visitors to sink into the comforts of its well-run household and to relish the company of 'that dear and beloved creature' who was their host, while their needs were attended to by a famously good cook, a sturdy Scottish housemaid and the gentle anxious butler who stepped into the breach when his predecessor, Hall, regretfully departed on account of Howard's democratic distaste for summoning him in the old-fashioned way, by bell. 'I can't bear never to 'ear you ring a bell, and 'ave you always putting your 'ead out of the door and 'ollering 'all down the passage,' he mournfully explained to his amused employer.

Howard was the most English of the American circle. His Bostonian father, Russell Sturgis, had come to England as a partner in Baring Brothers' bank (in which he was known as 'the entertaining partner' on account of his lavish hospitality). He purchased a handsome house in Carlton House Terrace, overlooking the Mall. It was here and at Givons Grove at Leatherhead, their Regency country home, that Howard grew up, but the links with his New England cousins were always closely maintained. Henry James was among the constant stream of guests at the Sturgis parents' home and he affectionately remembered their 'hospitality, general bounty and benignity'.

The most influential figure in Howard Sturgis's early life was his beautiful but very dominating mother. She clung to him for company and support during Mr Sturgis's long and trying illness and after Mr Sturgis's death in 1887 Howard became, in Arthur Benson's words, a willing prisoner of the boudoir and the closed carriage. The frail, much-cosseted child developed into a sensitive young man, bearing more than a passing resemblance to James's Ralph Touchett in *The Portrait of a Lady*, whose strong and lively face contrasted strangely with a fastidious skill for embroidery. Effeminate, perhaps, he liked to say, but he preferred to keep his hands busy when he talked and, since he didn't enjoy smoking, why should he not embroider? Friends like Benson came slowly to realize that the feminine grace of manner hid an unusually acute mind and that the waspishness of which Howard frequently accused himself disguised an infinite capacity for loyalty and generosity in his friendships. He shuddered when Benson coyly addressed him as a fairy prince,* but the fairy prince's role was one he played, willingly and untiringly, to the Qu'Acre circle of New Englanders, to the Mildmays, Harcourts and Sheridans who

---

* George Santayana was another friend who chose to picture Howard in this fabulous but faintly absurd role. In *Memories and Friends* (1924), he described him as 'a figurine or voluntary caricature, sitting with his golden hair beautifully brushed, his small feet daintily crossed, in the middle of a square carpet on the emerald lawn . . . He played by turns the Fairy Prince and Disconsolate Pierrot, now full of almost tearful affection, now sitting in sky-blue silk, at the head of his sparkling table, surrounded by young dandies and distinguished elderly dames.'

came and went with the regularity of Mr Pooter's friends, and to the multitude of cousins and small nephews and nieces who knew that 'Howdie' would always make them welcome. 'I feel at times like the unctuous manager of a smart hotel,' their host ruefully observed to Benson after one particularly exhausting invasion of visitors.

Solitude was as unbearable as the prospect of choosing a wife to Howard after his adored mother's death in 1888. He took for his companion, first, his Eton tutor and then, after the move to Qu'Acre, William Haynes-Smith, a tactful, reserved and ineffably kind young man (a distant cousin) who later married Howard's relation, Maud Sturgis. Haynes-Smith's nickname of 'the Babe' encouraged Edel to perceive him as the substitute for the son Howard might have wanted to bear had he been a woman. The nickname had a more simple origin in the young man's pinkly cherubic appearance and his role was closer to that of a prudent housekeeper. If the Sturgises felt some initial uneasiness about the Babe's ambitions (Howard was too rich and too generous for ulterior motives not to be read into the devoted attentions of an impecunious young man who did, finally, inherit Howard's estate), they hid their concern and Howard's family letters are full of cheerful references to the Babe's angelic disposition and to his forbearance with his singularly tiresome old father. The family had, as it turned out, cause to be grateful to the intruder. Less extravagant than Howard who, in his relish for hospitality, had become almost as insouciantly lavish as Stephen Crane, the Babe persuaded him to curb his prodigal instincts and to make more time for his writing.

Howard put his genius into his life rather than his books, although as a critic he was unusually astute and constructive. His most shining skills were his social ones. As a host, he did as he chose and bestowed the same liberty on his guests. As a friend and intellectual sparring-partner, he was effortlessly stimulating. 'No one could outdo Howard Sturgis or ever get the better of him,' Percy Lubbock wrote in his life of Mary Cholmondley. 'He could always escape with one of his impudent turns . . . he had no shadow of shame; his mimicry of himself was as unabashed as his mimicry of us all was unsparing.' The hint of laughter-seeking cruelty is erased by Lubbock's next lines – and Lubbock, it is worth remembering, is not known for the generosity of his tributes to his friends. 'Howard who lived in affection more warmly, in sentiment more frankly, in indulgence more lavishly than anybody, he it was whose truth was the hardest and the clearest and the straightest of all.'

Julian, Howard's older brother, may have been the wiser of the two in recognizing his limitations as a writer. His comedies of manners, set in English country houses, are elegant and enjoyable without aspiring to do more than entertain the reader with witty dialogue and deftly constructed plots. Howard, in aiming higher, was made more painfully conscious of his inadequacies as a novelist. Julian asked only to amuse: Howard asked to be judged seriously. He was not and never could have been in the class of Edith Wharton and Henry James: it was his misfortune as a novelist to have chosen for his dearest friends two of the finest writers of his time, both of whom were redoubtably frank in their judgement. Howard had written two novels before they became his intimates, *Tim*, a sentimental school-story, and *All that was Possible*, an epistolary novel about a pastoral love-affair which was well enough received by the critics to encourage him to embark on something more ambitious. This was *Belchamber*, the story of an innocent and most put-upon young nobleman whose scheming wife provides him with an illegitimate heir by his rascally cousin after repelling her husband's advances in no uncertain terms. Sainty, the gentle hero with a domineering mother – the novel is transparently autobiographical – lives up to his name by behaving like a perfect gentleman at all times: he is the only person to grieve for the death of the illegitimate heir on whose small coffin a less virtuous character might have been excused a dance.

In the autumn of 1903, rather proud of his work, Howard gave the first 160 pages of proofs to James for his comments. James, evidently uneasy about causing distress, offered some mild criticisms and warned his friend that he had 'long since inevitably ceased to read with naïveté; I can only read critically, constructively, *re*constructively, writing the thing over (if I can swallow it at all) *my* way, and looking at it, so to speak, from within. But even thus I "pass" your book very – tenderly.'[2] It was a warning to desist from interrogation which Howard did not take. He wanted to know more. He wanted to be judged by the standards of Wharton and James, not to be 'passed', however tenderly. It was then that James brought the full weight of his critical armoury to bear on *Belchamber* in a series of shrewdly critical letters. Howard received the full Walpole treatment of annihilating destruction, and Howard was neither so young nor so resilient as Walpole. Sainty's toleration of his wife's behaviour was incredible, an outrage. It was excellent that Howard should have kept him as the register of consciousness, but what was he registering? What did he feel? His love for the child was most touchingly rendered, but what about his marriage, in which he appeared to have no feelings at all? What a pity it was that Howard hadn't approached him before and allowed him to help produce a character 'with a constituted and intense imaginative life of his own'. Might he not be an anonymous collaborator on the next novel?

We know that this was a line James frequently took with the works of his friends. Howard did not know it. Used only to the pleasantly whimsical malice of James in conversation, he was shattered by this unlooked-for onslaught. It was an attack not only on his hero but on himself, for it was from his own passivity and the sense which he shared with Benson of sex as something a little disagreeable that he had created Sainty's remarkable indifference. He could not but feel the criticisms of his old friend as a personal affront. He wanted to withdraw from publication at once and it took all of James's soothing skills to persuade him to continue. (Privately, James told Mrs Wharton that he thought the book 'old-fashioned and feebly Thackerayan'.)

Howard's own fears were confirmed when the reviews began to appear. James had assured him that, whatever his own opinion, *Belchamber* would be widely enjoyed. The critics, disgusted by the immorality of Sainty's wife, pronounced the book to be disagreeable, painful and unpleasant. It was of little comfort to Howard to be told by Mrs Wharton that the book was 'very nearly in the first rank'. The novel sank almost at once into obscurity. The friendship with James survived, but Howard never attempted to write another book.*

Edith Wharton, the only female member of the Qu'Acre circle, was made of stouter stuff. If James, as he frequently did, chose to take her to task over her novels and stories, she refused to allow herself to be disturbed. He 'was never to be trusted about the value of any "fiction" which was not built according to his own rigid plan' and Howard should have borne that in mind when soliciting his opinion.[3]

1903 was the year which marked, for James, the beginning of his friendship with the redoubtable Edith. He had no recollection of the earlier occasions on which she had, without success, striven to capture his attention.

Their paths had first crossed in Paris in 1887 when James went to a dinner-party given by Edward Boit, a watercolourist from Boston who was a cousin of Howard Sturgis's and an old friend of Teddy Wharton's. It was two years since the clever and eligible Miss Edith

---

* He did, however, write one unpublished short story. His subject was the appalling effect which a respected novelist's criticism has on a younger writer. The older novelist is a portrait of James, of whom Howard was well-known to be a brilliantly accurate mimic.

Jones of New York and Newport had disconcerted her friends by marrying this easy-going, unintellectual and impecunious young man, possibly on the rebound from a disappointment when Walter Berry failed to propose to her. She was a stiff and shy young woman, still very much under the influence of a formidable mother and anxious to please her by conforming to the role of the model wife. James, if he noticed the Whartons at all, saw a typical young American couple abroad, well-bred and diffident, seemingly possessed of more money than brains. He might have gleaned that they divided their time between Newport and New York when they were not travelling in Europe. A pleasant enough life for those who could afford it, he might have thought. He had met a good many such couples. He saw and heard nothing to stimulate his interest.

Poor Edith, aching for intelligent conversation and overwhelmed by the prospect of speaking to such a celebrated compatriot! She had put on her prettiest French dress in the hope that he would notice and admire her. 'I can see the dress still,' she wrote years later, 'and it *was* pretty; a tea-rose pink, embroidered with iridescent beads. But, alas, it neither gave me the courage to speak, nor attracted the attention of the great man. The evening was a failure, and I went home humbled and discouraged.'[4]

A second opportunity came in 1890 or 1891 when the Whartons were visiting Venice. James was staying at the Palazzo Barbaro, home of Ariana and Daniel Curtis since 1885 when the Bostonian Mr Curtis had left America in a towering rage after being imprisoned for punching an insulting stranger. Ralph, their son, was delighted to hear that his friends the Whartons had arrived. Knowing that Edith had literary ambitions, he arranged that they should come to dinner and meet the famous guest. Edith again put her faith in clothes to operate the necessary magic. She wore a new and very splendid hat which must surely catch Mr James's eye.

> I was almost sure it was becoming, and I felt that if he would only tell me so I might at last pluck up courage to blurt out my admiration for 'Daisy Miller' and 'The Portrait of a Lady'. But he noticed neither the hat nor its wearer – and the second of our meetings fell as flat as the first.[5]

Edith was a much less ingenuous creature by 1903 when the long-desired meeting at last took place at a London hotel. She had published six books, she had acquired a loyal literary mentor and a ready *cavaliere servente* in Walter Berry, now amply compensating for his failure to propose. She had had the satisfaction of receiving a lengthy letter from James in praise of *The Valley of Decision*. He had, with considerable good sense, suggested that she should let Italy alone and turn to the subject of American society, but he had also told her that her book was 'brilliant and interesting from a literary point of view' and expressed the hope that they might meet.

The suggestion was timely. Neither the writing of books nor the overseeing of work on her new and splendid home, The Mount, had lessened Edith's increasing sense of despair. Teddy, now fifty-four, had turned from a cheerful companion into a querulous invalid, whose collapses were as unpredictable as they were alarming. A life of constant travel and the success of his wife in an independent career had added to his sense of instability and inadequacy. Sexual relations played no part in their marriage and the intimate relations of domestic life now began to harden into stiffness and long unhappy silences. In her copy of *Madame Bovary*, Edith underlined a passage which seemed to offer a description of her own state of mind. 'Her life was as cold as a garret whose windows face north, and boredom like a spider spun its web in the shadows, to all the corners of her heart.' She needed now, far more than when she had first encountered James, to make friendships outside the claustrophobic marriage with people who would offer no threat to her emotionally insecure and ailing husband. More than the stimulus of elevated conversation, she needed laughter, raillery, the ease to be herself.

An opportunity to take up James's suggestion of a meeting presented itself when the Whartons visited London en route for a motor-flight through France. An invitation was issued and James declared himself delighted to take up their proposal of a luncheon at their Brook Street Hotel.

Edith had heard a good deal about James from Walter Berry, but nothing had prepared her for the imposing figure who presented himself at the hotel. He had grown a good deal stouter than the man she had failed to charm in Venice: 'The compact upright figure had expanded to a rolling and voluminous outline, and the elegance of dress had given way to the dictates of comfort, while a clean shave had revealed in all its sculptural beauty the noble Roman mask and the big dramatic mouth . . .'[6]

James in his turn saw a handsome strong-featured woman in fashionable and very formal dress, her reddish-brown hair pulled back into a severe chignon which was softened by a thick fringe. Her manner was a little stiff and shy but, as her nervousness receded, he noted with approval the bright flash of her wit and the acuteness of her judgements. He liked her – and she was enchanted by him. She had expected to be impressed and interested. Nothing had led her to expect what she called 'the quality of fun – often of sheer abstract "fooling" – that was the delicious surprise of his talk'. It was that, she thought later, which had made her warm to him so immediately and had over-ruled all minor irritations and misunderstandings in their long friendship.

> The real marriage of true minds is for any two people to possess a sense of humour or irony pitched in exactly the same key, so that their joint glances at any subject cross like interarching search-lights. I have had good friends between whom and myself that bond was lacking, but they were never really intimate friends; and in that sense Henry James was perhaps the most intimate friend I ever had, though in many ways we were so different.[7]

The differences mentioned here mattered less to Edith in the early years of their friendship than did the resemblances which reviewers were quick to discern in her books to those of the older novelist. James himself was ready to see as 'his almost too susceptible élève' a woman who was far too ambitious to relish being seen as his disciple. When William Crary Brownell, Edith's editor at Scribner's, sent her a collection of reviews of *The Descent of Man* (1904), her third volume of short stories, she was enraged to find that, far from praising her originality, the critics had been chiefly struck by the remarkable similarity of her work to that of James. She returned them to Brownell with her thanks and a bitter little note.

> I have never before been discouraged by criticism because when the critics have found fault with me I have normally abounded in their sense, and seen, as I thought, a way of doing better next time; but the continued cry that I am an echo of Mr James (whose books of the last ten years I can't read, much as I delight in the man), and the assumption that the people I write about are not 'real' because they are not navvies and char-women, make me feel rather hopeless. I write about what I see, what I happen to be nearest to, which is surely better than doing *cowboys de chic*.[8]

Knowledge of her friendship with James made critics quick to see Edith as his ardent follower. Percy Lubbock, who should have known better, was ready to write in 1947 that she 'had made friends with him in her books, so to speak, when she began to write – enrolled, as was evident, under his banner, a disciple of his art . . .'[9]

There is poignancy as well as irony in Millicent Bell's memorable description of Edith Wharton rising from the literary plain to find only the mountainous bulk of Henry James in sight. She had chosen to draw her characters from the same limited social circle as he and that, for most reviewers, was enough for them to discern in her his pupil. Only a few were perceptive enough to register the significant difference. Edith Wharton was first and foremost a satirist. Her finest satire was directed at the world in which James had grown up and which she, twenty years his junior, could criticize and ridicule more objectively for the funereal solemnity of its customs, the absurdity of its rigid social laws. She, rather than James, showed her characters as the prisoners of that inflexible social code and dramatized the dilemma it created for those who refused to conform to it or who were forced by circumstance to break it. Her portraits of Lily Bart in *The House of Mirth*, Ellen Olenska and Kate Clephane in *The Age of Innocence* and *The Mother's Recompense* are painted with an indignation entirely foreign to James's spirit. Society, not the individual, is the villain. The misery of her tragic heroines is rarely of their own making. James, less of a satirist and more of a psychologist, shows the unhappiness of his characters as a consequence of their relationships and of their behaviour. The implied judgement is the antithesis of Wharton's. The Baroness in *The Europeans* is condemned to leave America, Charlotte Stant to lose the Prince in *The Golden Bowl*, Daisy Miller to lose her life, because they have chosen to disobey the rules. The rules are absurd, and James recognizes their absurdity, but they are to be obeyed. For him the individual, not society, is culpable.

James, for his part, while never having to suffer the indignity of being regarded as an imitator and disciple, was envious of the substantial advances and wide readership which had eluded him and which came to Edith Wharton so easily and so early in her career. Marcia Jacobson, in *James and the Mass Market*, goes too far in attempting to prove that his subjects were chosen in an attempt to court popular taste, but there is no doubt that James longed for a wider audience. Alfred Sutro was present at a dinner during which James frankly admitted as much to another, more commercially successful novelist, W. W. Jacobs.

> We sat and talked; suddenly James leant across and said, 'Mr Jacobs, I envy you.' 'You, Henry James, envy me!' cried Jacobs, always the most modest of men. James acknowledged the compliment with a graceful wave of the hand. 'Ah, Mr Jacobs,' he said, 'you are popular! Your admirable work is appreciated by a wide circle of readers; it has achieved popularity. Mine – never goes into a second edition. I should so much have loved to be popular.'[10]

Edith Wharton was both rich and successful. James, who had once cheerfully observed that he 'could stand a good deal of gold' was not averse to enjoying the luxuries which her friendship bestowed on him. He had nothing against inherited wealth and his references to the Whartons' lavish style of life are best taken as Edith herself received them, with a pinch of salt. Mockery was a fair enough weapon to employ against the imperious nature of her kindness. He found it harder not to begrudge her seemingly effortless ascent to fame and commercial success.

James had dedicated his life to his writing, his sacred vocation. He had been rewarded by the esteem of the intelligentsia and by modest sales. Edith Wharton, to whom writing was initially a solace and refuge from a difficult and unsatisfying marriage rather than a sacred duty, had achieved without apparent hardship the dizzy twin pinnacles of bestseller status and literary acclaim. It was with mixed feelings that James registered her blithe announcement that the proceeds from her first (not very good) novel, *The Valley of Decision*, had been handsome enough to pay for her large and very expensive Panhard car. 'With the proceeds of my last novel,' he eventually remarked, alluding to *The Wings of the Dove*, 'I purchased a small go-cart, or hand-barrow, on which my guests' luggage is wheeled from the station to my house. It needs a coat of paint. With the proceeds of my next novel I shall have it painted.'

James was exaggerating the pathos of his position, but there is no doubt that he was bitterly conscious of the contrast between his new friend's primrose path to success and his own stony road to – relative – obscurity. Behind her back, he comforted himself with ironic references to her meteoric rise. So there was to be a hotel in New York called the Henry James? He could predict that it would be far too refined and elegant to be commercially viable; doubtless the management would have to close it down and re-open it as the Edith Wharton in order to recover their losses.

Heroically, James ploughed on with the most elaborate of his works, *The Golden Bowl*, published in America in 1904. The novel, to his surprise and delight, went into four editions. He had barely begun to congratulate himself on having at last achieved some measure of public success while conceding none of his literary goals when Mrs Wharton trumped his triumph.

The House of Mirth, published in 1905, established its author as one of America's finest modern writers – and one of the most widely read. Edith's literary earnings that year amounted to $20,000 (approximately $210,000 today), and that was only the beginning. In the opening months of 1906, the novel sold more copies than any other American work of fiction. Scribner's, it goes without saying, were delighted. Friends like Howard Sturgis wrote to tell the author that, with the exception of James, she was the greatest living novelist. Fans wrote in to grieve that she had not allowed the beautiful Lily Bart to live and marry Laurence Selden, but an unhappy ending had not lessened their delight in the book. One reader raved that he had loved 'not every word in the book, but every period and comma'. Amusedly noting the omitted 'only' in a well-intended burst of enthusiasm, Edith added that she was finding all this adulation 'great fun'.

'I am not sure that Henry James had not secretly dreamed of being a "bestseller" in the days when that odd literary form was at its height,' Edith wrote years later as if the thought had only just struck her. Perhaps it had. Perhaps it never occurred to her that Henry James might have envied her easy conquest of the audience he had conspicuously failed to captivate. The success of *The Golden Bowl* was trifling by comparison. He had never been able to boast that he had sold 140,000 copies of one of his books in two months, as Edith could. Not even Daisy Miller, his 'most prosperous child', had done that for him. $200 was all he made from the American edition after a transatlantic pirating of the English *Cornhill* publication.

James was frankly astonished by *The House of Mirth*'s runaway success. He had thought it 'better written than composed'. The story struck him as confused. The picture of Lily had been kept 'very big and true', but the portrait of Selden had been too shadowy for the good of the novel.[11] His praises for it amounted to a courteous nod compared to the great slap of applause he hurried to offer to Wells the next week for *Kipps*. Here was 'a diamond of the first water, from start to finish, exquisite and radiant . . . if we had any other than skin-deep criticism . . . it would have immense recognition'.[12]

If Edith was hurt by James's measured praises, pride forbade that she should admit to it. Friendship would never prevent him from being brutally honest about her work and she was quick to realize that her best defence was to seem to accept his criticisms with grace and good-humour. 'He knew I enjoyed our literary rough-and-tumbles,' she wrote in her autobiography, 'and no doubt for that reason scrupled the less to hit straight from the shoulder.'[13] But the clarity with which, in 1934, she could recall his most cutting literary judgements suggests that the hit was usually a palpable and painful one.

Recollections often end by revealing more than the author had originally intended. Ford, when he set out to portray James as 'the most lovable of men', found himself remembering instances of suave discourtesy and brutal snubs. Edith, preparing to offer examples of the 'mere chaff and malice' of her old friend, found herself writing about the occasions when she had cringed under the whip of his scorn. She remembered the time when he told her that her subject was 'totally unsuitable' and grieved that she had given it 'so curiously conventional a treatment'. She remembered, too, how he had seized on the chance to ridicule her in public when she dared to write a story in French. 'He swung round on me slowly. "I congratulate you, my dear, on the way in which you've picked up every old worn-out literary phrase that's been lying about the streets of Paris for the last twenty years, and managed to pack them all into these few pages."'[14] She remembered how he had condemned one of her finest works, *The Custom of the Country*, seeing in it only the germ of the great novel she could have written if she had taken his advice, and the lectures she had been given every time she failed to use an American location. She, of course, was expected to submit to these attacks without a murmur while James himself collapsed at the first whisper of disapproval, 'miserably alive to the least hint of criticism, even from those who most completely understood, and sympathized with, his later experiments in technique and style'.[15]

Edith herself was not an admirer of James's later style and it is apparent that she could match him, when she chose, in lethal comment. There was not much sweetness in her request that he should explain to her one of his paragraphs which, she told him, she had found 'after repeated reading . . . unintelligible'. She asked him, too, why he had chosen to strip *The Golden Bowl*'s characters 'of all the *human fringes* we necessarily trail after us through life' and remembered with some satisfaction that James had been horrified to learn of a fault of which he had been completely unconscious.[16] She fastened like a leech on to his much-discussed refusal to treat of the financial and industrial worlds and used it, in *A Backward Glance*, to reduce his stature. 'Henry James,' she wrote, 'was essentially a novelist of manners, and the manners he was qualified by nature and situation to observe were those of the little vanishing group of people among whom he had grown up, or their more picturesque prototypes in older societies.'[17]

This is hardly the note of friendship and high esteem, but this was no ordinary friendship and it is a tribute to its strength that it survived the malice, envy and irritation which it contained.

Annoying though it was to learn that Edith had made enough money from a mediocre novel to buy herself a magnificent new car, James was not averse to availing himself of every possible opportunity to be driven about in it. Back from their French expedition in May, 1904, the Whartons wasted no time in making their way to Rye to visit their new friend and putting the Panhard at his disposal in return for his hospitality.

James was entranced. Sussex was delightful when viewed from a bicycle, but to look down on it from Edith's gleaming machine was to feel like a Napoleon of the road. He had already decided that he liked this lively strong-minded woman. He was captivated by her new aspect as a tireless and exuberant chauffeur who enjoyed exploring the countryside as much as he did himself. When she and Teddy insisted that he must visit them at The Mount during his American visit that autumn and promised that he would be driven anywhere he wanted to go, he accepted with alacrity.

Edith and her car, in the mythology of James, were as inseparable as Hispano from Suiza or Mercedes from Benz. Cynicism is tempting: would he have been as fond a friend if Edith had not been so ready to put her succession of splendid cars so unfailingly at his disposal? James was anxious that his friends should not think badly of him for living – on the road, at least – in a rich woman's pocket. His letters were neatly dedicated to conveying the opposite view. Fancifully, he endowed Edith with names intended to suggest the imperious nature of her summons to a motor-flight. Untruthfully, he represented himself as the helpless mouse snatched up in the eagle's talons. In his letters to their mutual friends of the Qu'Acre circle, he mockingly deified her as the Angel of Devastation, the Firebird, the high-flying Kite, the bird o'Freedom, carrying a timid old gentleman away from his humble home on some new and deplorably luxurious tour. A visit to Qu'Acre contrived by James was frequently prefaced by a mournful epistle from Lamb House, protesting that the threatened invasion was all Edith's idea. He was only her embarrassed slave, incapable of resisting her will. A letter to Edith expressing a wish to visit Howard and to be driven to Windsor by her ('Don't fail me of this.') would be followed by a letter to Howard announcing that the dreaded Firebird was about to cull him and fling him down at Qu'Acre 'as a limp field-flower . . . But let me, while even in the coruscating claws, let me make you this small squirming sigh – let me wish you to have it from myself too at least that I am thus to be hurled on your hospitality.'[18] Howard, highly entertained at this extravagant hypocrisy, encouraged it and James soared in a most un-mouselike fashion to new heights of misrepresentation.

> She has already left us . . . ground to powder, reduced to pulp, consumed utterly, and she with her summer practically still to some-how constitute. That is what fairly terrifies me . . . All thanks for your wishes and inquiries about my pectoral botherations. They will be

> better enough, I feel sure, when a sordid peace again reigns. All I want
> for that improvement is to be *let alone*, and not to feel myself far aloft
> in irresistible talons and under the flap of mighty wings – and about
> to be deposited on dizzy and alien peaks.[19]

One of the circle kept Edith well-informed, despite James's understandable entreaties that his letters about her should be immediately
destroyed. Not unamused by the elaborate nature of his social duplicities, she waited until writing her autobiography to offer her own
version of life as James's satellite, an image she had sometimes used
in her letters. She expanded it in *A Backward Glance* to present herself
as James's resigned victim, seeking only to comply with his wishes
and to gratify his appetite for the free and luxurious travel which she
could provide.

> [He] took advantage, to the last drop of petrol, of the travelling capacity
> of any visitor's car . . . as soon as luncheon was over we were always
> whirled miles away, throwing out over the countryside what he called
> our 'great loops' of exploration . . . James was as jubilant as a child.
> Everything pleased him – the easy locomotion (which often cradled
> him into a brief nap), the bosky softness of the landscape, the discovery
> of towns and villages hitherto beyond his range, the magic of ancient
> names, quaint or impressive, crabbed or melodious. These he would
> murmur over and over to himself in a low chant, finally creating
> characters to fit them . . . such as the Dymmes of Dymchurch, one
> of whom married a Sparkle, and was the mother of little Scyntilla
> Dymme-Sparkle, subject of much mirth and many anecdotes.[20]

The truth, as always with these adroit fencing partners, lay somewhere between the two accounts. James loved being driven and, for
the price of a drive, Edith was more than ready to exchange the
'anxious frugality' of Lamb House for the 'cheerful lavishness' of
Qu'Acre. Howard's father had taught him to take food seriously
(Russell Sturgis's own chef, Monsieur Lanou, was said to be the best
in London) and Mrs Lees, the cook at Qu'Acre, was the envy
and delight of Howard's friends. James offered by contrast a most
wretched table, usually adorned, Edith noted with distaste, with a
tepid and dreary pie of which half had served as their dinner the
previous day. She noted too, with the eye of a woman whose own
homes were always impeccably kept-up, that the lawn of the Lamb
House garden was thin and worn, the flower-beds unkempt and the
steps up to the garden-room rickety and unsafe. The owner, she
added for good measure, was regrettably neglectful of his appearance,
only 'spasmodically fastidious about his dress, and about other trifling
social observances'.

James could hardly criticize The Mount for being neglected or rickety when he took up his invitation to stay there in the autumn of 1904, bringing with him Howard Sturgis, then only distantly acquainted with their hostess. Howard, primed with ecstatic reports of its luxury by Gaillard Lapsley, was immediately at home. James, as always, was too afraid that anyone might think he could revel in luxury to be honest. Friends like Jessie Allen were informed that it was all too 'oppressively rich' for his liking.

Nothing could have described his pleasure so misleadingly. Life at The Mount suited him perfectly. Walter Berry was the most congenial of fellow-guests. There was an excellent library at his disposal and a beautifully landscaped garden in which to ramble. Best of all, a car was at his service every afternoon, ready to convey him to the remembered haunts of his youth and further afield, to 'explorations among villages still bedrowsed in a decaying rural existence, and sad slow-speaking people living in conditions hardly changed since their forbears held those villages against the Indians'.[21] A heatwave made these daily excursions essential for James's comfort. 'Electric fans, iced drinks and cold baths seemed to give no relief,' Edith remembered. '. . . the only panacea was constant motoring . . . daily, incessantly, over miles and miles of lustrous landscape lying motionless under the still glaze of heat.'[22] Refreshed by the wind of movement, James was able to enjoy his hostess's riveting stories of sexual violence, incest and murder in the remote homesteads of Massachusetts, the stories which gave her the background against which to set Ethan Frome and Summer. In the evening, when the heat had dropped to a bearable level, he offered ample compensation for his complaints to an enchanted audience. He enthralled them with Balzacian stories about the vast tribe of his Emmet and Temple cousins; he astonished them with the unfaltering beauty of his poetry-reading. The stammer vanished and the rich and flexible voice filled the room with an organ-like adagio, chanting the hypnotic rhythms of Whitman's 'Leaves of Grass'. 'I have never before heard poetry read as he read it,' Edith wrote, 'and I never have since . . . He read from his soul,' and no one who never heard him read poetry knows what that soul was. I think,' she added, 'that Henry James was never so good as with this little party at The Mount, or when some of its members were reunited, as often happened in after years, under Howard Sturgis's welcoming roof at Windsor.'[23]

James visited another of Edith's homes in the New Year of 1905, a tiny house in New York at 884 Park Avenue in which the unhappiness of the Wharton marriage was inescapably apparent. Edith found him a restless and uneasy guest. She thought, rightly, that he was múch more at home in New England where there was always an uncle or a cousin to provide a common link in conversation. In New York, there were no such connections. The New Yorkers showed no great enthusiasm for his works and little taste for the laborious hesitant oddity of his talk. He was honoured only as Edith's guest.

If he wilted in New York, he blossomed in Paris where, after 1907, Edith had a flat on the rue de Varenne in the fashionable 7th *arrondissement*. The Mount was sold in 1911, partly as a result of Teddy's disastrous investments and partly because he was making it clear that he no longer wished to live with Edith. (He had been wildly promiscuous since 1908, but it was not until 1913 that Edith agreed to release him with a decent settlement.) As the marriage deteriorated, the rue de Varenne increasingly became her refuge and the fixed point in the turmoil of her travels.

Walter Berry, Bernard Berenson and James were immediate converts to the charms of the rue de Varenne. 'Nobody knows our Edith who has not seen her in the process of making a habitation for herself,' James said to Percy Lubbock. He spoke, for once, in genuine admiration. The flat was spacious and charmingly furnished and James was particularly taken by the crimson Aubusson carpet Edith had spread on the drawing-room floor. He was taken, too, by the new circle of friends Edith acquired there through Rosa, the Comtesse Robert de Fitz-James (nicknamed Rosa Malheur for her handsome husband's infidelities), and Jacques-Emile Blanche, whom Edith commissioned to paint James on his last visit in 1908. The names which flit through the Parisian pages of *A Backward Glance* are material for the Proustian novel Edith never wrote: Consuelo Vanderbilt, Count Keyserling, Anna Comtesse de Noailles, the Marquis de Ségur, the Comte d'Haussonville (great-grandson of Madame de Staël and one of Proust's models for the Duc de Guermantes) and, most dear of all to her, the witty cherubic Abbé Mugnier, so loved in the Faubourg St Germain that they paid for a daily taxi to bring him back to them when he was demoted to the 14th *arrondissement* for attempting to reconvert an unfrocked and married priest.

Another visitor to the rue de Varenne and to Qu'Acre goes unmentioned in *A Backward Glance* for reasons of discretion. It was James who brought him into Edith's home and, unwittingly, instigated the first and last passionate sexual relationship of her life.

James had been on affectionate terms with Morton Fullerton since the early nineties when the young New Englander was working for *The Times* in London before being appointed to the Paris office. Slight, dandified and with a religious idealism inherited from his clergyman father, Fullerton was a bisexual whose sexual magnetism was at odds with his modest appearance. Only the drooping moustache and heavy eyes hint at the impressive thoroughness of his many conquests. Women swooned over him, men adored him. Henry James's letters are full of squeezes and tender pressures and yearnings; ladies called him Adonis and begged for the opportunity to visit his rooms.

In England, Fullerton had successfully laid siege to Lord Ronald Gower and Margaret Brooke, the corpulent Ranee of Sarawak. The Ranee, like all Fullerton's mistresses, was expected to resign with grace when her lover found a new object of desire. Unusually, she complied with his expectations without a murmur of reproach. In Paris, he began an affair with another older woman of a more troublesome kind, Henriette de Mirecourt – and embarked on a brief and highly unsatisfactory marriage to a pretty young *chanteuse*, Camille Chabert, possibly because she was pregnant by him. It is a striking testament to Fullerton's charm that, although the marriage lasted for little more than a year, Camille was still writing to him ten years later as 'Camille, qui t'adore'.

Fullerton came into Edith's life in 1907, a year when his own life was in a state of considerable confusion. The irrepressible and passionate Henriette was making it clear that she was ready to cause a good deal of trouble if he failed to commit himself to her. At the same time, he was trying to decide what he should do about Katherine Fullerton who, having been brought up as his adoring sister, had recently been overjoyed to discover that she was his first cousin. Even as his sister, she had been brave enough to say that she could not love him platonically and now that the marriage to Camille was over, she saw no obstacle to their life together. Had he not said that he shared her feelings? He had, and probably meant it. He always did.

In October 1907, on his way to The Mount with a warm letter of recommendation from Henry James in his pocket, Fullerton visited Katherine in her rooms at Bryn Mawr College where she was a Reader in English. He told her, as he had told many before her, that life without her would be unbearable and, since a proposal was expected, he made one. Katherine, overwhelmed with joy, was untroubled by her suitor's murmur of a few minor problems to be sorted out in Paris before the wedding could take place. It could only be a matter of a few months: she was content to wait. Promises and reassurances were the meagre diet on which she survived as his invisible fiancée for the next year, and the next. In 1910, sure that Fullerton would be heartbroken, she sent him a message – 'Courage, dear' — with the news that she was marrying a Mr Gordon Gerould.

With Katherine's fears allayed, Fullerton cheerfully proceeded to The Mount where, in a few days, he succeeded in reducing the proud and indomitable Edith to a condition of trembling hope. She had been looking forward to his visit, remembering how much she had liked him when, some six months earlier, he had visited her in Paris (most probably at the suggestion of his friend James, who was staying with her at the time) to discuss the possible magazine translation of *The House of Mirth*. What she had not expected was that she would fall in love with him. Only looks were exchanged and a plucked sprig of wych-hazel endowed with mysterious significance, but it was enough. Three days after Fullerton's departure, Edith started writing a secret journal addressed to him. She also changed her schedule so as to leave for Paris a month earlier than she had previously planned. It was not an unmixed joy to her to learn that Teddy had decided to accompany her.

Teddy's substantial presence in the rue de Varenne and problems with Henriette de Mirecourt kept Fullerton from furthering the relationship with Edith during the first weeks of her visit. He was more concerned with soliciting James's advice as to how he was to extricate himself with dignity from an increasingly disagreeable situation. (Henriette, raging with all the fury of the discarded mistress, had managed to lay hands on a batch of letters which related to Fullerton's sexual relations with the Ranee and with Ronald Gower and was threatening to publish them: James, full of commiseration, advised him to get on with his work and ignore her.) Edith, bewildered by Fullerton's apparent indifference, decided that there was nothing for it but to take the initiative herself. A month after her arrival, she wrote to invite him to come to an Italian play with her and did not fail to make it clear that Teddy, who hated Italian, would not be coming with them.

The strategy, if such direct tactics can be called that, worked. By the end of another month, Fullerton was her 'cher aimé', and her 'cuor mio'. By mid-April, Teddy, after suffering his worst nervous collapse for five years, had decided to go home. Henriette had subsided and Edith had moved from the gossiping Faubourg to her brother's empty home at 3, place des Etats-Unis, a discreet residence in which to continue the affair. A passionate letter was carried from the thoughtful Fullerton's office every day to be laid on her breakfast tray, and she responded in kind, telling him that 'you can't come into the room without my feeling all over me a ripple of flame . . . all the words in me seem to have become throbbing pulses . . .' At the age of forty-five, she was deeply and helplessly in love for the first time in her life. The brusque middle-aged gentlewoman had blossomed into an erotic adventuress who revelled in every form of sensual pleasure, by Fullerton's account. A disconcertingly pornographic fragment of her abandoned novel, 'Beatrice Palmato', suggests that he did not exaggerate.

It was not what James had planned or anticipated when he sent Fullerton to The Mount. No revelations had been made, but he was uneasily aware that something was afoot when Edith airily told him that Fullerton would be with them when he came to visit her in Paris in April 1908. Puzzled but polite, James responded that it would be 'adorable to have W.M.F.' with them.

It was a brief visit and, for James, a less comfortable one than he allowed his hostess to guess. She was transparently besotted. She evidently knew nothing about Henriette or Katherine Fullerton or her lover's chequered past. Glumly, he resigned himself to being packed off to parties alone so that Edith could steal a precious two hours with Fullerton. Sympathetically aware of the wretchedness of her marriage and of her unfulfilled longing for a grand passion, he was not at all sure that Fullerton could match up to her expectations. It was not entirely clear to him how far the affair had gone. He could only hope that Edith would be prudent and discreet.

James was also a little jealous. He was deeply attached to Fullerton and had been looking forward to seeing him. The circumstances took much of the pleasure out of the meeting. There was no opportunity for enjoyable gossip of the kind Fullerton could always be relied on to provide. Edith was always with them. Pleasant though it was to live 'in gorgeous bondage, in breathless attendance and luxurious *asservissement*', he felt superfluous. He did not visit Edith in Paris again.

Relations were not at their easiest between James and Edith at this time. He had shown no great enthusiasm for her last novel, *The Fruit of the Tree*, and had, very charmingly, turned down her suggestion that he might like to write an article in praise of her work. (James was always unpredictable on such occasions; he was infuriated when Edith was asked to write a piece about Conrad, whose works she greatly admired, while nobody seemed to have thought that he would do it very much better.) She did not yet know it, but the novel and her suggestion had prompted James to write about her in a very different way, parodying her as a pushing authoress in 'The Velvet Glove', a story which he originally and more cruelly called 'The Top of the Tree'. He was, nevertheless, Edith's friend and confidant and the one who seemed most likely to understand the feeling Fullerton had inspired in her. In October 1908, she broke down the delicate barrier of reticence which she had hitherto maintained.

She had dreaded leaving Paris. ('I am mad about you Dear Heart and sick at the thought of our parting and the days of separation and longing that are to follow.') In May, she had returned to the prison-house of her marriage, solaced only by the love-letters which arrived by every steamer – for the first three months. Fullerton had already mentioned that he was leaving the Paris office and would be unlikely to visit America until the following year. Now, without explanation, the letters stopped and her pleas for explanations went unanswered. All that had seemed possible was in doubt. Wretchedly, Edith unburdened herself to James. What should she do? Her marriage was intolerable. Life without Fullerton was something she could not bear to contemplate. What choice did he think she should make?

James knew desperation when he heard it. He knew Fullerton too well to have much faith in his staying power, but to advise Edith to give up all hope was too cruel. 'Don't *conclude!*' he wrote. 'Some light will *still* absolutely come to you – I believe – though I can't pretend to say what it conceivably may be . . . Only sit tight yourself and *go through the movements of life* . . . Live it all through, every inch of it – out of it something valuable will come – but live it ever so quietly, and – *je maintiens mon dire* – waitingly! I have had but that one letter, of weeks ago – and there are *kinds* of news I can't ask for . . .'[24] To Howard Sturgis, he wrote sadly: 'What an incoherent life . . .' and urged him to be particularly kind to Edith when she arrived in England the following month.

Howard rose to the occasion splendidly. He and the Qu'Acre circle gathered around to comfort their desolate Firebird and when she set off for France in December, Howard laid down his rugs and embroidery and, accompanied by the Babe, went with her, to find that, after all the storm was only of teacup proportions. The threatened move from Paris had not taken place and Fullerton was ready to resume the affair. Edith glowed, the Babe was an unqualified success – 'ce charmant Enès-Smith' – and Howard was permitted, most thankfully, to retire to report the good news. 'Fly your flight – live your romance – drain the cup of pleasure to the dregs,' he urged her.

Edith needed no encouragement. Cradled in Fullerton's arms, she felt secure enough to listen to his confessions without resentment or alarm. She heard for the first time about Henriette and about the threats which she was now making with renewed ferocity. Eloquence was a part of Fullerton's charm. We can be sure that his explanation was a moving one. If only he could be rid of this terrible fear of Henriette, how much more would he be able to concentrate on the woman he really loved. He was only telling her because he knew that she would understand how little Henriette had ever meant to him. But what could he do? He had no resources. No, he should not have troubled her. He had so wanted her to understand. The lines are invented, but probably not far from the truth.

The role of benefactress always had an appeal for Edith. She was deeply moved, and anxious to help. Fullerton's pride could not be insulted by a direct gift of money. Instead, she turned to James and, with his warm approval, concocted a fantastically labyrinthine plot whereby she would get Macmillan to commission Fullerton to write a book on Paris and send a cheque of £100 herself to James, who would then send the cheque to Macmillan, who would then offer it as a second advance. If she were to send them the cheque, it would inevitably lead to an undesirable public linking of names.

James readily complied. He had modified his own view of the relationship as reports of Teddy's behaviour grew more and more disturbing. When Edith and Fullerton arrived in England together, he took what was for him the unusual step of treating them as a couple, dining, lunching and going on excursions with them. When they spent a night together at the Charing Cross Hotel, he dined with them in their suite. For a man who went to unusual lengths to observe the social niceties, it was generous behaviour.

The affair continued in a sporadic manner until the end of 1910 and the choice to end it was more hers than his. Edith's journals and poems betray her as a romantic and Fullerton had over-estimated her worldliness in expecting her not to be disillusioned by his confessions. He had certainly told her about the affair with Henriette de Mirecourt and one of Edith's short stories makes it apparent that she had a pretty clear picture of his relationship with Katherine Fullerton. In 'The Letters' she portrayed Fullerton as Deering, a plausible liar who marries for the sake of a legacy while swearing to the heiress that he perused every loving line of the letters she wrote him before she became rich. The lie is exposed when she finds her letters lying unopened in a trunk. The fictitious letters are remarkably similar to those written by Katherine when she believed that Fullerton was going to marry her.

Edith could accept the revelation of a discarded mistress and even help to pay her off. She could steel herself to endure the periods when Fullerton would slide out of reach and offer neither excuses nor explanations. She is unlikely to have tolerated the thought that

Fullerton had been promising to marry another woman while making love to her. Stripped of romance, the affair seemed as ugly as Teddy's infidelities and Fullerton stood revealed as the charming, flexible womanizer that he was. The price that he demanded, that she would always be cheerful and uncomplaining, that she should not ask awkward questions, that she should never expect more than he was prepared to give, was too high. Her future lay elsewhere. She remained on fond and easy terms with Fullerton, but there was never a question of reviving the more intimate relationship.

An intriguing postscript to the affair was added in the summer of 1912 when James and Howard Sturgis took Edith off to Ascot to have tea with the Ranee of Sarawak, now an imposing and eccentric matriarch who lived up to her exotic title by reclining in vast armchairs with a vociferous scarlet macaw perched on her wrist. It was an occasion which promised to be enthralling. Which of the two strong-minded ladies would be the first to introduce Fullerton's name? The two men waited with bated breath. Alas for their hopes! Edith matched the Ranee's courteous reticence and his name was never spoken.

It was as the Fullerton affair came to an end that Edith was most in need of support and friendship. She had only recently had the double-blow of discovering that Teddy had been embezzling and spending her Trust funds and that part of the money had gone towards purchasing a home for his mistress in Boston. She now learned from the doctors that he was suffering from what we have since named manic depression and that recovery could not be guaranteed. Sanatoriums worked only a temporary improvement. She was advised that he should be kept under restraint, a suggestion which neither she nor Teddy were prepared to accept although Edith understood well enough the imperative need to take all financial control into her own hands. She proposed that he should have sole charge of The Mount and accept an allowance of $500 a month on condition that he resigned all his rights as co-trustee: to Teddy, who had been brought up to believe in male supremacy, it was the final insult. She had spent the whole of their married life making him feel miserably conscious of his intellectual inferiority and orchestrating his life to suit her plans. She had done her best to have him locked up and now she was trying to reduce him to the status of a well-paid housekeeper. James was staying at The Mount in 1911 when Teddy arrived to have the matter out with his wife. He was horrified. 'One's pity for her is at the best scarce bearable,' he wrote to Gaillard Lapsley, who had just left. 'The violent and scenic Teddy is negotiable in a measure – but the pleading, suffering, clinging, helpless Teddy is a very awful and irreducible measure indeed.'[25] Much though he admired Edith's determination to see the marriage through, the visit convinced him that the only possible solution was for her to sell The Mount and leave her husband. She could not bring herself to do it. The sale of the house went through later that year, at Teddy's wish and with his wife's reluctant consent. The question of a divorce remained in the balance for another two years.

As Fullerton receded into the shadowy fringes of Edith's European life, Walter Berry came forward to take his place, not as her lover, but as her most constant companion, adviser and friend. She could not have chosen a man more congenial to James and the Qu'Acre circle. James had taken to him at their first meeting at The Mount and Lapsley and Howard Sturgis were devoted to him. Only Lubbock had reservations about the elegant and acidly sarcastic New Englander; years later, he wrote in his biography of Edith that Berry's effect on her had been disastrous.

There had been a fourteen-year gap between the time when Walter van Rensselaer Berry had decided not to propose to Edith (perhaps because she was not then quite rich enough for a man who was never impervious to the charms of wealth), and the time when he had re-entered her life as her ally and literary mentor. From 1910 until his death in 1927, Berry played the part of the husband he had chosen not to be to her.

An international lawyer who was at one time President of the American Chamber of Commerce, Berry was a distinctive figure, tall and very thin with a prominent aquiline nose and disquietingly penetrating blue eyes. As much of a stickler for convention as James and Edith, he exceeded them in his relish for aristocratic society. Proust, who shared that weakness, adored him, but women were often put off by his coldly sarcastic manner. His knowledge about and enthusiasm for literature, combined with a New England background and an incisive wit, ensured him of a warm welcome among Edith's friends in England. They already knew what he had meant to her in the lonely early days of her writing career when his astute criticisms and unflagging enthusiasm for her work had been her inspiration and solace. It seemed to them now that nobody was better suited than Berry to the task of keeping her amused and entertained and holding her depression about Teddy at bay.

Berry had another advantage in that he was an enthusiastic motor-ing companion. Edith could not be expected to go racing around Europe with only Cook, the chauffeur, for her escort, but James was growing too old to submit to the exhausting nature of her tours and

Howard Sturgis was unwilling to be lured further than an hour's journey from his doorstep. John Hugh Smith's embarrassing ardour ruled him out and Lapsley and Lubbock were both too young not to look rather bizarre as companions for a middle-aged lady. Berry, three years older than herself and quite as gallantly indefatigable a traveller, was ideal.

It was as well that Berry was intrepid. Their whirligig rushes around Europe were not of a kind to suit the fainthearted. A hair-raising trip to a monastery high in the Appenines (La Verna, where St Francis received the stigmata) had been crowned by a nightmarish scene in which the car, with Cook at the wheel, was attached to ropes and lowered over the side of a precipice onto the narrow mountain road below. Even Edith was forced to admit that she would not care to repeat the experience.

Berry, as much as Edith, was responsible for the plan which, in 1913, the year of James's seventieth birthday, bade fair to deprive them both of his friendship. Word had reached them of the plans that were afoot in England where a sum of money was being collected for James to commission a portrait by Sargent. They felt that their old friend should be honoured in a similar way by his own country. Pride was involved. It would not do for the English to seem more appreciative than the Americans of James's worth. W. D. Howells was drawn into the plan and persuaded to add his name to the circular sent out by Edith in mid-March. It proposed that $5,000 should be raised and given to James to spend as he wished. (Later, too late, Edith would protest that she had always meant it to be for a piece of furniture for Lamb House; the circular suggested only a fat sum of money.)

Two weeks later, James's nephew, Billy, wrote to his uncle to express the anxious hope that he would not accept such a humiliating present, humiliating to all the family in that it seemed to suggest that his own family were allowing him to live in poverty. It was the first James had heard of it, and he was furious, far more so than he had been about the English fund. His prompt cable to Billy requested that he should take immediate steps to prohibit any money being collected. His letter of the next day was still more forceful.

> The thing is for you to give it out as strongly and emphatically as possible, to all such persons about you as may have been deplorably approached, and may be bewilderedly intending, that you have it from me, straight and strong, that the idea . . . fills me with unmitigated horror, and that should it most accursedly push forward to any practical effect, every cent of the money would be instantly and ruthlessly, and

be even quite resentfully, returned. A more reckless undertaking . . .
I cannot possibly conceive . . .[26]

A few days later, Edith received a brusque order to drop the project, followed by an irate letter from James expressing his regret that such a vulgarly commercial tribute could have been deemed likely to please him.

It is not an episode in which either James or his nephew appear to advantage. Billy was being absurdly pompous and officious and James might have thought twice before behaving with such vehement ungraciousness to a well-meaning friend who had only just emerged from the devastating experience of a divorce.

It was Edith's misfortune to have unwittingly touched James on his most sensitive spot. He was perfectly happy to make jokes about the impoverished style of his life, but not to have them taken seriously and used to exhibit him as an object of pity. He could see a gift of money in no other light. It was difficult enough for him to smile and applaud Edith's larger earnings and her unmatchable sales; he was not prepared to let her have the additional kudos of being known as Henry James's benefactress. The friendship between them was renewed after a brief and painful hiccup, but the subject was never raised again and James never offered an apology for his violent repudiation of her kindness.*

Edith Wharton had never been the kind of woman to take defeat easily and she remained convinced that money was the answer to James's problems. She had already unsuccessfully tried to secure him the Nobel Prize in 1911. She had been deprived of the chance to make a grand gesture for his birthday. Made cunning by experience, she found another and more devious way to put money into his hand. James was at work on a new novel, *The Ivory Tower*. Edith entered into an arrangement with Scribner's, who had published *The Golden Bowl*, whereby she would supply the funds for them to offer James an advance of $8,000 for 'another great novel' to balance it, half of which would be released as soon as he signed the contract.

The plan worked. James, astonished and delighted by such a handsome and unexpected offer, accepted it without demur and Scribner's were able to inform Edith that the money had been sent. The second payment was never made as James died before completing the novel, but Edith was able to rejoice in the sense that she had outwitted her old friend and made his life a little easier.

* Edith salvaged her pride by laying the blame on James's over-officious family and declaring to her friends that he himself had only been upset by their presentation of the facts.

The outbreak of war the following year brought an end to motor-tours and visits to Qu'Acre and the leisurely chatter of books and friends. To Howard, it was dreadful and harrowing and too horrible to talk about. To James, it was the beginning of the end of civilization. To Edith, the declaration of war was a clarion-call which brought to the fore all of her energy and her awesome powers of organization. Her friends looked on with amazement as she responded to the summons. Within two weeks of the declaration, she had set up an *ouvroir* in the rue de l'Université for the several dozen seamstresses put out of work by the enthusiasm their former employers showed for sewing shirts for the troops. She set up a chain of refugee hostels, she took hospital supplies out to the front lines at Verdun, she set up a rescue committee for the Children of Flanders, victims of the onslaught on Belgium, and she persuaded Scribner's and Macmillan to publish *The Book of the Homeless*, an anthology of poetry, prose and illustrations collected by her from, among others, Claudel, Cocteau, Bakst and Monet, to raise money for her hostels and committees.

James had never admired her so much. Her zeal and determination were, he thought, an inspiration to them all. Stravinsky's firebird seemed too frivolous an image for such a heroine. He looked for a new image and settled on Joan of Arc, 'so golden-plated you shine straight over at me – and at us all!' He wept over her accounts of the scenes she had witnessed at Verdun. He signed himself 'more devotedlier than ever' and he urged her on: 'do it, *do* it, my blest Edith, for all you're worth: rather, rather – "sauvez, sauvez la France."'[27] He did all that he could to help her, sending blankets and newspapers for her refugees and spreading the news of her work and the need for funds to support it, soliciting contributions from Hardy and Sargent for her anthology.

Among the praises for her courage, he found space for a reference to their mutual friend, Morton Fullerton. James had, too often, made judgements of Edith behind her back. Now, as she rose to the status of 'Chère Madame et Confrère', she became the recipient of his final judgement on the man who had never quite lived up to their expectations. In 1915, Fullerton made a brief and ill-starred attempt to start a new career in America. Edith reported his return to Paris in a little less than six months. It broke his heart to hear it, James replied, and yet he was not surprised. It only obliged him again to confront 'that exquisite art in him of not bringing it off . . .' She could only agree.

Edith had recovered from the unpleasant shock of hearing that James had chosen to become a British subject – a decision which she, like many Americans, regarded as a betrayal of his roots – when the news came of his collapse towards the end of 1915. He seemed to have been thinking about her. One of his last dictations, given when his mind was no longer clear, was about a motor-car trip. Howard Sturgis wrote to her in anguish: 'Oh, it is going to be terrible to lose him . . . I'm all dissolved in grief, Edith, and I know what you are feeling too. We both adored him.'28 Edith in her turn wrote to Lapsley of the Henry they had all shared, the Henry no one else knew, their malicious, chaffing, jubilant friend, 'the jolliest of comrades' whom she would evoke in the most tender passages of *A Backward Glance*. 'Dearest Gaillard,' she wrote, 'let us keep together all the closer now, we few who had him at his best.'29

James died in the New Year of 1916. Death inexorably began to thin the circle. Howard Sturgis died in 1920, after two years of illness. Walter Berry, then living in Edith's old flat on the rue de Varenne, died in 1927 and was given a funeral appropriate to one of France's most devoted supporters in the war. Edith, who had been a constant visitor during his final days, paid him a last farewell in her journal: 'The love of all my life died today, and I with him.'30 Teddy had gone the following year, old, sad and muddled, still querulously resentful of the divorce he had never quite comprehended. Only Lubbock and Lapsley and Hugh Smith remained to Edith, bound to her by affection and respect, but also by the strong bond of their common memories. Gathering together at Hyères, Edith's last French home, they could summon up the badinage and the elaborate plots, the duplicities and complicities, the love affairs and the losses, all that had been theirs and is now ours through their letters and memoirs.

THE BENCH OF DESOLATION: JAMES AT SEVENTY

I am in town, you see – not at Rye, having gone back there definitely, three weeks ago, to the questionable experiment of taking up my abode there for the season to come. The experiment broke down – I can no longer stand the solitude and confinement, the *immobilisation*, of that contracted corner . . . These things have the worst effect upon me – and I fled to London pavements, lamplights, shopfronts, taxis – and friends; amid all of which I have recovered my equilibrium excellently, and shall do so still more.

> Henry James to Mrs Frederic Harrison, 1911

We eat and drink, and talk and walk and think, we sleep and wake and live and breathe only the War, and it is a bitter regimen enough and such as, frankly, I hoped I shouldn't live on, disillusioned and horror-ridden, to see.

> Henry James to Mrs Thomas Sergeant Perry, 1914

I have never seen anyone else who, without a private personal stake in that awful struggle, suffered from it as he did . . . His devouring imagination was never at rest, and the agony was more than he could bear.

> Edith Wharton,
> *A Backward Glance*

I never dreamed of such duties as laid upon me.

> From the last dictation of Henry James, December 1915

HENRY JAMES   1843 – 1916
JOSEPH CONRAD   1857 – 1924
H. G. WELLS   1866 – 1946
STEPHEN CRANE   1871 – 1900
FORD MADOX FORD   1873 – 1939

This picture used to hang, framed with a thin ebony wood, in the corridor upstairs
at Lamb House, Rye.

THE BENCH OF DESOLATION:

JAMES AT SEVENTY

'London, and London alone, is so excellently good for me – better than any other place in the world,' James wrote to Edith Wharton in the autumn of 1911.[1] He expressed himself more strongly two days later to his secretary, Theodora Bosanquet, admitting that he was 'bolting – in horror and loathing' from Rye. What provoked James to express such a powerful antipathy for his sedate and orderly existence in pretty, tranquil Lamb House?

The decision to bolt was made within two months of his return from America where he had lingered on for a year after William's death and where he had dwelt longingly on the prospect of returning to his 'beloved little corner' of England. He had scarcely stepped off the *Mauretania* before changing his mind.

Several reasons can be put forward for James's sudden aversion to his house in Rye. A year of vigorous social activity had revived his affection for urban life. Most of his English friends lived in or had moved to London and he was too old to want to expose himself to any more travelling than was strictly necessary. He was almost seventy and this, in itself, may have contributed to his wish to be in London. The bicycle-rides and long walks in which he had delighted when he first moved to Sussex were now more of a test of endurance than a relaxation; age and failing health may have made him feel that it would be comforting to be within easy distance of loyal friends and the best available medical attention. He was devoted to Dr Skinner of Rye, but he put more faith in the London practitioners who had examined him in the past two years. It is also reasonable to suppose that Lamb House stirred up memories which he would have preferred to lay to rest. He had begun to compose the opening chapters of his autobiography, summoning up scenes of his childhood and the years when William, the older brother, had bulked like a giant of strength and wit and boldness beside his timid sibling. His mind was full of William and Lamb House was full of painful associations with William's last visit. He had made the journey to

Rye, as James was now unhappily aware, to look after his ailing brother when he himself was dying. Was James now all too conscious of his own selfishness in clinging to Alice James and seizing for himself the role of the tragic invalid? Or did the combination of Lamb House and the writing of the memoirs make him shrink from any close interrogation of his own behaviour? Memories must surely have played some part in provoking him to such a violent description of his need to escape. Neither loneliness nor old age alone could have driven him to such an emotional statement.

1911 marked his return to the city, and Lamb House reverted to what he had originally intended it to be, a brief summer refuge.

The room which he had retained since 1900 at the grimly grand Reform Club in Pall Mall solved the immediate problem of habitation, but not of work. His secretary's sex prohibited her from entry. Always resourceful, Miss Bosanquet met that difficulty by securing two rooms behind her flat in Lawrence Street, Chelsea, to which James repaired each morning to dictate *A Small Boy and Others*. It was not an ideal arrangement. The Reform Club's gloomy elegance was not uplifting and James had grown too used to living in a home of his own to relish the exchange of relaxed domesticity for the dreary formality of the club. In 1912, he made the sensible decision to take a three-year lease on a flat in Cheyne Walk.

21, Carlyle Mansions was ideally suited for James's needs. Sunny, modern and spacious enough to house an occasional guest as well as the cook, Minnie Kidd the maid and Burgess the valet, its two main rooms offered wide views of the river and the Albert Bridge, while those to the rear overlooked the well-kept gardens on the north side of the block. It was, he told his friends, just the right thing for him and the pleasure of looking out on the river as he worked remained an unfailing delight.

James's daily engagement-books for the first nine months of 1912 show him happily falling back into the frenetically social habits of his early years. Hugh Walpole and Jocelyn Persse's names feature frequently among his list of luncheon companions; the afternoons were rounded off by tea with Lucy Clifford or Mrs Ward or the Ranee of Sarawak. He dined out almost every night, sometimes with a party but more often with an old friend like Howard Sturgis. There were plays (*Coriolanus, The Playboy of the Western World* and Beerbohm Tree's 'awful, unspeakable *Othello*' featured among the performances he attended); there were concerts and musical parties and the Russian ballet which was all the rage in London that year. There were wearyingly long journeys up to Hampstead Drill Hall for the fancy-dress balls given by Mr and Mrs Wells. (James did not enjoy these last so much as his host who gloried in appearing as a barbarian or an unlikely pasha; for his guest they were an ordeal best endured by staying safely in a corner while Hugh Walpole capered about the floor. Mrs Wells's entreaties to Mr James to join her in dancing the Sir Roger de Coverley were politely and firmly resisted.)

It was a taxing schedule for an elderly man with a weak heart to set for himself and payment was duly made when James collapsed in the autumn with a severe attack of *herpes zoster* (shingles), the effects of which lingered on well into 1913. The spasmodic nature of the diary entries from this time on suggests that James had realized the folly of trying to live at the lively pace of the younger and healthier men to whom he attached himself.

1913 was the year in which James's English friends joined together to celebrate his seventieth birthday by raising £500 for a portrait of him by John Singer Sargent (whose name featured with embarrassing prominence among those friends who were soliciting the donations). James was being honoured for his work and for the affection and respect he inspired, but also for having reached a venerable age. The time was long past when he could claim to feel forty, clean and light when he looked at his newly shaven face in the glass. James at seventy looked what he was, a grand old man set in his habits and his judgements and no longer very much in touch with the present. His niece Peggy noted with regret that he was becoming increasingly unreal, revelling in his own singular and ever more fantastic style of delivery. He told her frankly that he detested American simplicity and that if he only knew a more elaborate way to pronounce his own name he would glory in using it.

Peggy endured her uncle's circumlocutions and grandiose speeches, but strangers were irritated and bored by them – although Ezra Pound was thrilled when James paused to greet him in a street in 1914 and to speak in a way which confirmed Pound's sense of himself as James's literary heir. The young found him faintly absurd, a massive relic of the past to be viewed with interest but not, perhaps, regarded with so much respect as James would have wished. Lytton Strachey; peering through James's window, thought he looked like a solemn and anxious tradesman trying to placate a client. Virginia Woolf was baffled by his ponderous allusions to her as the descendant of ink and pen when he only needed to mention her father, Sir Leslie Stephen, to make the point. E. M. Forster gleefully related the occasion on which James had paused and gravely patted his back while telling him that he was G. E. Moore. James was an important figure and they were all eager to meet him – but he was not of their world.

Age did not broaden James's mind – he could not bring himself to approve of the suffragettes – and the snobbishness which had always been present in his nature grew more pronounced. He was appalled when Lady Ottoline Morrell announced that she would like to meet Joseph Conrad and to introduce him to Bertrand Russell. What could she be thinking of, James wondered? She could not hope to extract any pleasure from meeting such a man. He had led such a rough and peculiar life. He could not advise her to persist with the idea. Lady Ottoline, a woman of character, ignored him and was immensely impressed by 'the super-subtle Pole', while Russell was enthralled. 'We looked into each other's eyes, half appalled and half intoxicated to find ourselves in such a region,' he remembered. 'The emotion was as intense as passionate love, and at the same time all-embracing. I came away bewildered, and hardly able to find my way among ordinary affairs.'[2]

There was a certain irony in the fact that the suffragette who entered the 1914 exhibition at the Royal Academy armed with a meat-cleaver should have chosen Henry James for her target. She had no personal axe to grind against the portrait-sitter, but her random choice was an appropriate one. Snugly ensconced in his new eyrie above the Thames, James might as well have been in Rye for all the impact that events of the rebellious pre-war years made on him. Nearly a million people were out on strike over their jobs and their poor housing conditions in 1911, and many more were ready to follow them in 1912. But while Shaw was haranguing the lecture halls and Wells was calling on the government to face up to 'the great task of social reconstruction which lies before us all', James was reproaching the American Academy of Arts and Letters for expecting him to vote for members whose names were, to him, at least, unknown. His friendship with the Liberal Prime Minister, Herbert Asquith, failed to stimulate any interest in the welfare of his adopted country until the outbreak of war finally shocked him into action.

As with politics, so it was with the worlds of arts and letters. 1910 marked the beginning of a cultural revolution in England. It had been presaged on the continent by the 1909 Italian Futurist Manifesto's raucous celebration of war and the triumph of the machine. In 1910 Roger Fry organized an exhibition of works by Matisse, Gauguin, Picasso, Cézanne, van Gogh and the Fauves, shattering the Edwardian concept of high art (delicate brushwork, lushly suggestive forms, fragile well-bred faces) with strong primary colours and distorted shapes conjuring up images of chaos and violence. Admirers of Lord Leighton's yearning nudes reacted with bewilderment to the grim offerings of Brancusi and Epstein. Paintings like Picasso's *Poor People by the Sea* (1903) made no concession to the sentimental taste of a public who had been taught that poverty always wore her rags with a sweetly submissive smile. D. H. Lawrence gave the literary pendulum of taste a vigorous swing in the same direction with *Sons and Lovers* (1913). The Vorticists, headed by Wyndham Lewis, used *BLAST* magazine to celebrate the birth of a new age of discordancy and rage.

Ford, who had encouraged Lewis and had published Lawrence in the *English Review*, was an enthusiastic supporter of the new avant-garde, regardless of the fact that its pioneers thought of him as a pompous old wind-bag. James, having ventured so far as to make a visit to Fry's exhibition at the Grafton Gallery, decided to close his eyes. He had presented his literary credo in the *Prefaces* to the New York Edition of his works. They contained his considered and final judgement. He had been regarded as the Master and had accepted his right to that position for too long for any concessions to be made to the undisciplined bravado of youth. To old friends like Lucy Clifford, he sighed over the sloppiness of modern fiction and added that 'the young, on the whole, make me pretty sad – the old themselves don't'.[3]

It was not in sadness but in the spirit of a complacent schoolmaster that James sat down in 1913 to offer his judgement on the younger generation of novelists in a two-part article for The *Times Literary Supplement*. It was, as has been stated in an earlier chapter, an unfortunate undertaking. It caused considerable hurt to Conrad and infuriated Bennett and Wells, none of whom were, by any stretch of the imagination, members of the younger generation of novelists James was supposedly assessing. D. H. Lawrence, the only significant writer to be singled out in the article, was dismissed with a sneer while Mr Gilbert Cannan, a charming and fashionable translator and novelist whose present obscurity is not undeserved, was elevated with Hugh Walpole to the ranks of those who might hope, one day, to wear James's crown. If James was aware that the wind was blowing strongly in a new direction in 1913, he went to considerable lengths to present his back to it, conveying by his stance his belief that the new movement away from his own mannered style was unworthy of his attention.

James's criticism of Wells was directed at *Marriage* (1912) and in particular at a scene which the author had neglected to describe with the richness of detail James considered due to it. The scene was one during which a young woman, Marjorie Pope, falls in love with Trafford, a physicist; to Wells, it had seemed sufficient to send the two of them off to sit in a country lane for three hours and bring them out of it in a state of enamoured bliss. He had cheerfully shirked his duty to the reader in order to hurry on to the topic which interested him, a marriage which would represent the triumph of intellect over materialism. The omission was, from James's point of view, a 'peculiarly gratuitous sacrifice to the casual' which made the reader wince 'as at seeing some fine and indispensable little part of a mechanism slip through profane fingers and lose itself'. Was this not 'a well-nigh heartbreaking miscarriage of "effect"?' The instance, he conceded, was a trifling one, but it represented a flaw in Wells's work which was only partially redeemed by his virtues of 'large assurance and incorrigible levity'.[4] He went on, at length, to rebuke Wells and Bennett for having failed to do more than 'squeeze the orange' (an image to which James was addicted) when saturation was required.

Twenty years later, Wells was prepared to acknowledge that Miss Pope and her suitor had not behaved convincingly and to add that he doubted if any of his novels complied with James's theory of fiction. 'Henry James was quite right,' he wrote, '. . . but my defence is that that did not matter, or at least that for the purposes of the book it did not matter very much.'[5] But the criticism still rankled, enough for him to add that he had never attempted such an attack on James's work.

James's criticism of Wells was unjustified in that it assumed that there was only one way to write a novel and only one set of rules by which it could be judged to have failed or succeeded. Wells had already made it abundantly clear that, for him, fiction was a means to a political end. He had never regarded literary technique as being in itself a sufficient goal. He had, in 1911, given a talk which made it plain that he saw fiction as an instrument to be used for social reform. 'The success of civilization amounts ultimately to a success of sympathy and understanding . . .' he had declared then. 'We must have not only the fullest treatment of the temptations, vanities, abuses, and absurdities of office, but all its dreams, its sense of constructive order, its consolations, its sense of service, and its nobler satisfactions. You may say that is demanding more insight and power in our novels and novelists than we can possibly hope to find in them. So much the worse for us.'[6] He felt then as he felt in 1934 when he reviewed the literary battlefields of his past that James was mistaken in choosing one standard by which to judge all novels. There was room for more than one kind of fiction in the world and 'the novel of completely consistent characterisation arranged beautifully in a story and painted deep and round and solid, no more exhausts the possibilities of the novel, than the art of Velasquez exhausts the possibility of the painted picture . . . I had a queer feeling that we were both incompatibly right.'[7]

Such a fair-minded view was beyond Wells in 1914, however. He had accepted James as a self-appointed mentor in the private world of letters; it was quite another matter for James to offer public reproof, as though he was a naughty schoolboy to be slapped on the hand for careless work rather than a novelist whose name meant much more to the common reader than that of Henry James. Until now, he had played along with James and allowed himself to be patronized. In his private correspondence with him over *Marriage* in 1912, he had meekly thanked him for 'the wisest, most penetrating and guiding of criticism and reproof' and had promised that he would 'seek earnestly to make my pen lead a decent life, pull myself together, think of Form'.[8] The *Times Literary Supplement* article put an end to his wish to continue with this pleasantly empty form of homage.

Wells had, since 1905, been sporadically working on a satirical investigation of the literary world, written in a broad approximation of the elegant style of Thomas Love Peacock's novels of debate. *Boon* was presented as a collection of the private papers of a successful novelist, George Boon, a man in restless thrall to the genteel sensibility of his secretary. Miss Bathwick will only consent to transcribe the romantic fiction she considers fit for public consumption; her employer finds private solace in shredding the reputations of his literary colleagues. 'Reginald Bliss' purports to be the editor of Boon's posthumously published papers to which Wells provided 'An Ambiguous Introduction'.

Boon, as it stood in March 1914, was a transparently personal attack on the works of Belloc, Chesterton, Conrad, Ford, Shaw and Walpole with only a glancing reference to James. It was formless and feeble with all the marks of being hastily written and carelessly contrived. Had Wells not decided to add a further chapter after reading 'The Younger Generation', *Boon* would have sunk into obscurity. It was not only reasons of delicacy that made Wells shrink from mentioning it in his autobiography.

The new chapter was entitled 'Of Art, Of Literature, Of Mr Henry James' and its object was to expose both the man and his work to public ridicule. Fuelled by rage, Wells produced a cruel and occasionally devastating critique which was, unfortunately for James, rich in irresistibly quotable lines. Ford and Conrad received, by comparison, a friendly cuff on the head. James was put up against a wall and given a firing-squad execution.

Wells started from the premise that the novel should be a truthful representation of life and that digression and irrelevance are a necessary part of fiction. Life is not orderly – why should a novelist lie by making it seem to be so? He then proceeded to castigate James (as Edith Wharton had done) for stripping the human fringes from his characters in order to create a false unity. 'He sets himself to pick the straws out of the hair of life before he paints her. But without the straws she is no longer the mad woman we love . . . He omits everything that demands digressive treatment or collateral statement.' Void of any human impulses other than 'a certain avidity and an entirely superficial curiosity', James's eviscerated characters focus minds of a Jamesian calibre on the task of discovery of the gruesome or absurdly trivial. A James novel, he announced, was 'like a church lit but without a congregation to distract you, with every light and line focused on the high altar. And on the altar, very reverently placed, intensely there, is a dead kitten, an egg-shell, a bit of string . . . Like his "Altar of the Dead", with nothing to the dead at all.'[9]

The intricacies of James's style were Wells's next target and for these he reserved his cruellest cuts. How wonderful, he exclaimed, that so much intellectual effort should be expended on the expression of emptiness! 'He spares no resource in the telling of his dead inventions . . . His vast paragraphs sweat and struggle; they could not sweat and elbow and struggle more if God himself was the processional meaning to which they sought to come. And all for tales of nothingness . . . It is leviathan retrieving pebbles.'[10]

The attack was rounded off with Boon's story, 'The Spoils of Mr Blandish' in which James features as a bloodless bachelor whose private means enable him to live 'freely and delicately and charmingly . . . avoiding ugliness, death, suffering, industrialism, politics, sport, the thought of war, the red blaze of passion . . . Chiefly he visited interesting and ancient places, putting his ever more exquisite sensorium at them, consciously taking delicate impressions upon the refined wax of his being.'[11] The descriptions of Blandish's acquisition of Samphire House, his pleasure in its history and in the furnishing of it, together with his undisguised satisfaction in having a butler ('unquestionably early Georgian') are an uncharitable portrait of James in the early years of his friendship with Wells. Resentment which had been stored up for ten years came bubbling to the surface. Reading this passage, it becomes clear how much the English parvenu in his spanking new home at Sandgate had been riled by James's air of kindly superiority – and how many times he must have been compelled to listen to the story of James's first visit to Rye, his sighting of Lamb House, the thrill of its suddenly falling into his hands. It is all here, and the voice of James is immediately recognizable.

Reverting to his mockery of James's style, Wells succeeded in hitting off the dialogues of tentative exploration with considerable neatness.

> On that the mind of Mr Blandish played for a time.
>   'Then it isn't altogether tangible yet?'
>   'It isn't tangible enough for him to go upon.'
>   'Definitely something.'
> Her assent was mutely concise.
>   'That we on our part –?'
> The *we* seemed to trouble her.
>   'He knows more than you do,' she yielded.[12]

Had Wells only settled for a chapter in that vein of smart parody, hurt might have been avoided. James, contrary to Edith Wharton's belief that he could not endure any form of criticism, had no objection to being teased. He had positively relished Max Beerbohm's 'The Mote in the Middle Distance' and had sent reassurances to its nervous author that nobody had more enjoyed this entertaining skit on the Jamesian style than he himself. But Wells's representation of late Jamesian dialogue offered only a moment of light relief in a vicious and sustained attack on his personality, his beliefs and his works, an attack which was conspicuously lacking in Max's tender affection and very real esteem for James's achievement.

It is difficult to suppose that it was in a spirit of good-will that Wells wrapped up one of the first published copies of *Boon* and took it across London to the Reform Club, where he left instructions that it was to be handed to Mr James on his next visit. It was presented to James on July 5 and, always curious to read a new work by Wells, he embarked on it that day. His response, written on July 6, suggests that nobody had warned him of its nature. The greatest hurt was in the shock. Taking Wells to task had become a habit which he always supposed that Wells took in good part; nothing had prepared him for the cruelty of a riposte of this kind. He had not, he wrote with masterly understatement, been filled with 'a fond elation' to find himself an object of contempt, although he had done his best to look at himself through Wells's eyes and see how it was that he could have been judged as such 'an unmitigated mistake'.

> It is difficult of course for a writer to put himself *fully* in the place of another writer who finds him extraordinarily futile and void, and who is moved to publish that to the world – and I think the case isn't easier when he happens to have enjoyed the other writer enormously, from far back . . . I am aware of certain things I have, and not less conscious, I believe, of various others that I am simply reduced to wish I did or could have; so I try, for possible light, to enter into the feelings of a critic for whom the deficiencies so preponderate.

Gently and courteously, he stuck to his guns. It was true that there were many things which Wells could do and he could not, but he still held to what he had always believed, that 'interest may be, *must* be, exquisitely made and created' and no criticism would persuade him to abandon his hunt after that perfection, 'my constant wish to run it to earth'. James did not, however, feel that Wells's criticism had been searching enough to merit any further elaboration of his literary creed; he remained glad that there was room in the house of fiction for such 'widely different windows of attention'.[13] It was a letter designed to make the recipient squirm – and Wells grovelled. *Boon* was nothing, a mere waste-paper basket of old notes which he had taken up to escape from the obsession of war. He had always been a warmly appreciative admirer of James's work. His 'sparring and punching' had been undertaken in fear that he would be over-whelmed by his own respect for James's literary judgement. He had regretted a hundred times his failure to express the difference between them in a more graceful way and he remained, gratefully and affec-tionately, a keenly appreciative reader of James's novels.

James knew hypocrisy when he heard it. His letter of reply was magnificently glacial. Writers did not publish what they put in their waste-paper baskets. No excuses could justify what he could only bluntly call 'the bad manners of *Boon*, so far as your indulgence in them at the expense of your poor old H.J. is concerned'. The letter rose with an orchestral grandeur to sweep away Wells's clumsy attempt to formulate the difference between their attitudes as the distinction between painting (fiction as an end in itself) and architec-ture (fiction with a use). The dilemma of building for service or building for art has been present for far longer than the tension between form and function in the novel. The analogy was absurd and James said so. He ended the letter with what has become his most famous statement about the social role of fiction.

> Far from . . . literature being irrelevant to the literary report upon life, and to its being made as interesting as possible, I regard it as relevant in a degree that leaves everything else behind. It is art that *makes* life, makes interest, makes importance, for our consideration and application of these things, and I know of no substitute whatever for the force and beauty of its process.[14]

Wells could only answer with sullen defiance that he did not under-stand what James meant when he talked about art making life and that he supposed his incomprehension defined the unbridgeable gap between their attitudes. It was impossible for him to accept that art, however exquisite, could be an end in itself or that its influence could be indirect. It had to have an explicit social purpose.

There, unresolved, the dispute rested. James died six months later without having disclosed his feelings about *Boon* to anyone. Wells, when he returned to the attack in his autobiography, mentioned neither the book nor the exchange of letters. He did, however, feel guilty enough to offer Hugh Walpole a bizarre defence of his behaviour in 1917. He was furious that The *Times Literary Supplement* had neglected to review Rebecca West's highly critical biography of James, published in 1916. James's friends and admirers had closed ranks against a book which described *The Golden Bowl* as 'an ugly and incompletely invented story about some people who are sexually mad' and a Jamesian sentence as 'a delicate creature swathed in relative clauses as an invalid in shawls'.[15] James's death was still being mourned and the book seemed to them to be in very poor taste.

Raging at this 'boycotting' of his mistress's book, Wells chose to see the critics' behaviour as indicative of the same prejudicial attitude which had been shown to *Boon*. (The book had not been reviewed with any degree of enthusiasm.) He now defended himself for writing it on the curious grounds that he had not behaved nearly so badly as the non-reviewers of Miss West.

> The old man was a little treacherous to me in a very natural sort of way and the James cult has been overdone. Anyhow nothing I've ever written or said or anything anyone has ever written or said about James can balance the extravagant dirtiness of Lubbock and his friends in boycotting Rebecca West's book on him in The *Times Literary Supplement*. My blood still boils at the thought of those pretentious academic greasers conspiring to down a friendless girl (who can write any of them out of sight) in the name of loyalty to literature. It makes the name of James stink in my memory.[16]★

It was Wells, we remember, who observed that he was conscious

★ The outburst was characteristic of Wells's readiness to champion the cause of writers he admired. In *Boon*, he had been almost tender in his references to Ford, 'the only Uncle of the Gifted Young'. When G. K. Chesterton's *New Witness* paper printed a vicious correspondence about *The Good Soldier* in 1916, Wells was quick to rebuke Chesterton for giving space to 'that disgusting little greaser [who] has been allowed to insult old F.M.H. in a series of letters which make me ashamed of my species. Hueffer has many faults no doubt, but first he's poor, secondly he's notoriously unhappy and in a most miserable position, thirdly he's a better writer than any of your little crowd and frankly, instead of pleading his age and his fat and taking refuge from service in a greasy obesity as your brother has done, he is serving his country. His book is a great book . . .' (Quoted by Maisie Ward in *G. K. Chesterton* (London, 1944).) It is only fair to add that Chesterton's brother Cyril, far from pleading age and excess weight, enlisted as a private and was killed in action.

of a ring of foreign conspirators plotting against British letters in the region of Rye and Ford who, pleased by the image, repeated it and even drew a little map of the supposed invasion in *Return to Yesterday*. There were collaborations, but the only conspiracy which suggests itself here is between two British writers against a foreigner. There can be no doubt at all that Rebecca West read *Boon* and there can be very little doubt that, during the closest years of their relationship, she and Wells talked about James and found themselves sharing the view that he was greatly over-esteemed. West's book is not entirely ungenerous to him. Even when she is bent on ridiculing *The Golden Bowl*, she is ready to acknowledge that 'the great glow at the back, the emotional conflagration, is always right'.[17] But there are passages of criticism in which she appears to have picked up the sword where Wells dropped it in order to deliver another stab to the corpse. Her discussion of *The Sacred Fount* is a manipulation of contrasts between the sublime and the ridiculous which owes much to Wells's image of the dead kitten on the altar. 'With sentences cast as the granite blocks of the Pyramids and a scene that would have made a site for a capital he set about constructing a story the size of a hen-house.'[18] That is pure Boonery and so is the vicious injustice of the declaration that 'the homage which England loves to pay to the unread is responsible for half Mr James's reputation as a critic'.[19] Neither West nor Wells should have wondered that their efforts to reduce James's literary stature were met by a disapproving silence.

Among the many injustices done to James in *Boon* was the suggestion that he shunned all thought of war. The passive role which James had played as a young man in the American Civil War had been forced upon him, possibly because of his mysterious 'obscure hurt' and more probably because Henry James Senior flatly refused to let his two eldest sons volunteer. The letters of that period do not suggest that James wanted to stay at home. His father cheerfully noted that his two boys 'vituperate me beyond measure because I won't let them go'. For a young man, it had been humiliating to be reduced to the role of comforter to the wounded; in his seventies, he committed himself to helping in every way that was open to him. It would be as misleading to say that he rejoiced in the war as to say that he shunned it, but he entered into the spirit of it with an energy and wholeheartedness which won the admiration of all those who met the old man in his last years.

In 1910–1914, James had withdrawn into his ivory tower. The first hint of war came, as Ford remembered, with a discreet little announcement a long way from the headlines, to the effect that the archduke had been murdered. The declaration of war on 4 August stunned those who had shared Ford's profound faith in the Germans as a peace-loving nation. For James, the greater shock and shame was in America's non-involvement. He could not from that moment on take any pride in his American nationality. He emerged from the ivory tower with a sense of total identification with the British people and their cause. His naturalization as a British subject in 1915 was the logical conclusion of the transition he had already mentally undertaken. 'You see how I talk of "we" and "our" – which is so absolute and irresistible with me that I should feel quite abject if I didn't,' he wrote to his nephew Harry in America only two months after war had been declared.[20]

Much of James's life had been devoted to distancing himself from the uglier aspects of reality. Wells was not wrong about that. The change took place almost overnight. The letters in which, until then, the most unthinkable horror had been an ill-judged birthday offering, were now unflinchingly turned towards the gruesome face of war as James followed its course with passionate anxiety. '. . . to be old and doddering now is for a male person not at all glorious,' he wrote to his friend Rhoda Broughton. 'But if to *feel*, with consuming passion, under the call of the great cause, is any sort of attestation of use, then I contribute my fond vibration.'[21] To Edith Wharton in Paris, he let it be known that all of his affections were taken up by it. 'They grow more and more – and my soul is in the whole connection one huge sore ache.' All that he had known or experienced before seemed to have vanished into 'the grey mists of insignificance'.

It is difficult not to smile at the picture evoked by James addressing poor, terrified Howard Sturgis as 'we warriors' and trumpeting England's cause to old ladies in Belgravia like a general rallying his troops, but the urgency and depth of feeling expressed in the war-letters inspire more admiration than amusement. Both of the editors of James's correspondence have shown a deep respect for the war letters, Lubbock by devoting more than a hundred pages to them in his second volume, Edel by declaring them to be 'among the most eloquent he ever wrote'.[22] They reveal James in a new light. The chaff and malice have gone and in their place is a tender and profound concern for humanity.

To be deeply involved and too old and infirm to participate was frustrating. Walking in St James's Park one day in 1915, James ran into Ford, smartly turned out in the uniform of the Welch Regiment. Ford was in the best of spirits. He was anticipating being sent off to France at any moment and being allowed to prove that he was not the old duffer he was taken for by his young friends on *BLAST* magazine. Rancour was forgotten as James looked at him with wistful envy. *'Ah, tu vas te battre pour le sol sacré de Madame de Staël!'* he exclaimed before walking slowly on.

England had become a country for old men. All the young were gone, many, like Wilfred Sheridan, to their deaths. James had become very fond of Wilfred and Clare, his wife. Wilfred was witty, handsome and charming. Clare, the daughter of Mr and Mrs Moreton Frewen, was quick and clever and devoted to her husband. James had been at Qu'Acre with them shortly after their wedding and had often visited them both at Brede and their London home. He had written to Clare shortly before Wilfred's death that their happiness was of the kind that brought tears to his eyes and that he loved them both for their beauty and their courage. Their baby son was born three days before Wilfred died leading a grenade attack on the German Front and James could only write of 'how absolutely I adored him! . . . I can't pretend to utter to you words of "consolation" – vainest of dreams; for what is your suffering but the measure of his value, his charm and his beauty? everything we so loved him for. But I see you marked with his glory too . . .'[23] Rupert Brooke, who had dazzled James in his brief encounter, was gone and James sadly predicted the glorious legend that would be woven around his name. Even little Burgess Noakes, 'my invaluable and irreplaceable little Burgess', had gone to the Front, from which he reported that he was doing pretty well at keeping pace on the long marches – his legs were very short, so this was an achievement worthy of congratulation. James was full of concern for his small valet, frequently sending him chocolate and food parcels and ointment for his sore feet and urging him to keep up his 'jolly plucky spirit' and to 'notice and observe and remember all you can – we shall want to have every scrap of it from you on your return'.[24] Edith Wharton thoughtfully sent over one of her own servants to act as a substitute.

James had discovered during the American Civil War that he had a good bedside manner; it had been of some solace to know that he could comfort the wounded soldiers. Now, he put that gift to use again as he visited the London hospitals. His fluency in French gave him immediate access to the Belgian invalids at St Bartholomew's and his diaries show that he became an assiduous visitor. He wrote to Hugh Walpole in Russia that he had 'hereby almost discovered my vocation in life to be the beguiling and drawing-out of the suffering soldier . . . The Belgians get worked off, convalesce, and are sent away etc.; but the British influx is steady, and I have lately been seeing more (always at Bart's) of *that* prostrate warrior, with whom I seem to get even better into relation. At his best he is admirable – so much may be made of him; of a freshness and brightness of soldier-stuff that I think must be unsurpassable.'[25] His admiration for them was large and unqualified. He wanted to help them in every way he could. Some, who became his friends, were taken out to tea and given presents of chocolates or cigarettes. Others, unknown, were stopped in the street while James plunged his hands into his pockets to present them with whatever change he had on him at the time. They liked him. The James they saw was a large, gentle, softly spoken man who talked of ordinary, everyday things or listened tranquilly to whatever story they had to tell. 'The Long Wards', his contribution to Edith Wharton's war anthology, clearly shows this other aspect of James; reliable, matter-of-fact and always sympathetic.

James was, in addition to his round of visits to the London hospitals – St George's and St Thomas' had been added to Bart's – busily raising funds for the American Volunteer Motor Ambulance Corps and writing appeals on their behalf. Lucidity had, for once, been of greater concern to him than style. Violet Hunt, to whom he read his appeal, was asked to tell him frankly if it was incomprehensible. '"They tell me" – he turned his head away – "that I am obscure."' When he had finished reading, Violet exclaimed that she had never known him to be so passionate, to which James responded, '"Ah, madam, you must not forget that in this article I am addressing not a Woman, but a Nation."'[26] He had, in his capacity as chairman of the Corps, dined with various eminent politicians including Winston Churchill who, although he didn't care for James and thought him maddeningly verbose, seems to have borrowed some of his finest flourishes of rhetoric for his own splendid speeches.

The war, rather than London, had perversely turned out to be excellently good for James. It restored to him his old enthusiasm and vitality. More importantly, it occupied his mind at a time when his private life was full of sadness. The shock of *Boon* could be courageously faced when greater issues were at stake and he only allowed himself a moment in August 1915 to brood on the tragic failure of his largest endeavour, the great New York edition of his works. He tried to make a joke of it to Edmund Gosse, comparing his neglected literary empire to that of a lesser Ozymandias, but there was no disguising the fact that the edition had been 'a complete failure; vulgarly speaking, it doesn't sell – that is, my annual report of what it does – the whole twenty-four volumes – in this country amounts to about £25 from the Macmillans; and the ditto from the Scribner's in the US to very little more. I am past praying for anywhere; I remain at my age (which you know), and after my long career, utterly, unsurmountably, unsaleable.'[27]

Not even the loss of his favourite tree at Lamb House, a splendid old mulberry which was brought down by a gale in the winter of 1915, could stir up the passion of grief to which, in peacetime, James would undoubtedly have allowed himself to surrender. Now, answering a neighbour who had written to sympathize on his loss, he could only reproach himself (not her) for wasting a moment in lamenting it. 'But what a folly to talk of *that* prostration, among all the prostrations that surround us! One hears of them here on every side – and they represent (of course I am speaking of the innumerable splendid young men, fallen in their flower) . . . the irreparable dead loss of what is most precious, the inestimable seed of the future.'[28]*

James was an infrequent visitor to Rye at this time, but it was his residence there which prompted him, in the summer of 1915, to become a British subject. He was told that, if he wished to visit Lamb House, he would have to be registered as an alien and kept under police supervision. It was a humiliating prospect for a man who had so passionately identified himself with the English cause. Logan Pearsall Smith, the American-born brother of Mary Berenson who had already chosen to become a British subject, had for some time been urging James to follow his example. A painful reminder of his alien status was all that was needed to tip the balance. Conscious that his family and American friends would be puzzled and distressed, James warned them in advance of his decision, explaining in a letter to his nephew, Henry, that he was simply rectifying a position which had become 'inconveniently and uncomfortably false'. He went on to justify his choice. He had spent nearly forty years – 'the best years of my life' – in England. There was no possibility of his returning to America 'or taking up any relation with it as a country. My practical relation has been to this one for ever so long, and now my "spiritual" or "sentimental" quite ideally matches it.' He ended the letter, fearing that Henry might have inherited his father's taste for frank utterance, with a plea to him not to raise any objections to 'my own absolute need and passion here; which the whole experience of the past year has made quite unspeakably final.'[29]

Four sponsors were required to endorse his eligibility for British

* The stately old tree was often mentioned in the reminiscences of visitors to Lamb House and I am inclined to think that Ford Madox Ford had its demise in his mind when he came to write the last book of his tetralogy, *Parade's End*, in which the fall of the great tree at Groby, the Tietjens' country home, is made to symbolize the fall of pre-war civilization.

citizenship. James's agent, Pinker, Sir George Prothero, his old friend from Rye who was now also based in London, and Edmund Gosse, made a highly respectable trio. His fourth and grandest sponsor was the Prime Minister, grinning faintly at the prospect of subscribing to the proposition that 'he could both write and talk English'.[30] On 26 July, James formally became a British subject. The process, he told Gosse afterwards, was only nominal. It had simply confirmed a mental identification.

James's health had been precarious for some years. It started to deteriorate that summer. Both Dr Skinner in Rye and Sir James Mackenzie in London diagnosed a cardiac weakness. When Edith Wharton came to England in September with the idea of giving James one of his favourite treats, a visit to Howard Sturgis at Qu'Acre, she was disturbed by his sorrowful confession that he wasn't well enough to contemplate it, even though Qu'Acre was only half an hour's journey from London. Edith was worried, and more so when James refused to tell her what was wrong with him. Pretending that she needed some typing done, she persuaded him to lend her Miss Bosanquet for the day and interrogated her about the precise nature of James's illness. The report was not reassuring. Edith had learnt the danger of seeming to force her magnanimity on James. Instead, she extracted a promise from his secretary that she would be informed if there was a lapse. Miss Bosanquet, who did not like Mrs Wharton's imperious manner or her display of naked flesh (her arms, she disapprovingly noted after this encounter, had been very freely exposed), said coldly that she would keep her informed. Edith returned to France, blaming an eccentric diet and the sorrows of war for her old friend's decline. His heart condition did not seem, to her, a relevant factor.

'So here it is at last, the distinguished thing.' Those, James was convinced, were the words he heard spoken just before he slipped to the floor of his bedroom on the morning of 2 December, 1915. Minnie Kidd, the maid, found him lying there and, with the help of Burgess, back on leave from the Front, managed to get him back into bed. A second stroke the following evening confirmed the seriousness of his condition. Telegrams were despatched by Miss Bosanquet after the doctors had submitted a pessimistic view of his chances of recovery. Mrs James, who had promised William that she would look after his brother when the time came, made arrangements to leave for England immediately. James was still alert enough to call for a dictionary and announce that paralysis didn't precisely describe his condition.

He had taken a turn for the worse by the time Mrs James arrived on 13 December. Embolic pneumonia had been diagnosed after the discovery of a blood clot on the lung and another on the brain. His mind was no longer stable. He was only waveringly conscious of his identity and of his whereabouts. He spoke of going out to dinner with Lady Hyde at 21, Carlyle Mansions and was puzzled to be told that this was his own address. He wanted to take Burgess to dine with her. But he seemed pleased to see Alice, although it was not clear that he knew who she was.

Alice and the admirable Miss Bosanquet were constantly on hand to soothe and reassure James during the last lingering month of his existence. Confusion now ruled his mind and he was, unhappily, conscious of it until the last two weeks. Increasingly, he worried about seeming mad and asked if it didn't make people laugh when they came to see him. No, Alice told him gently. Nobody felt any wish to laugh. Sometimes, he fell into a deep depression and would spend all day calling in his servants to wish them goodbye. On other occasions, he grew uncontrollably angry, shouting down any attempt to calm him. Confined to his bed for all but a few 'good' days, he removed himself from it on an endless round of imaginary visits. One day, he was in Rye, on another, he was in a theatre, directing a play, or in Ireland, at Cork, where he had briefly stayed on his return journey to England after his mother's death.

Out of the confusion and bewilderment, a new personality emerged. James's character did not change, but he had fallen prey to the belief that he was Napoleon. Miss Bosanquet and his niece, Peggy, were called in to take down letters which, while retaining strong elements of James's distinctive style, related in their content most precisely to the activities of the Emperor and his family. As Napoleon, James ordered the decoration of the Tuileries and the Louvre and urged his 'dear brother and sister' to turn to good account their position as residents of the Republic and to live up to the high reputation he had made sure to give them. The accuracy of detail can be explained by the fact that James had been for many years an enthusiastic reader of Napoleonic memoirs, but that hardly explains why, in his muddled state, he should have become convinced that he was Bonaparte.

The clue may lie in Napoleon's role as a leader of troops; the last letters contain a strong military element. Throughout the war, James's letters had been written in the spirit of a leader rather than a subject and, while he was chiefly concerned with England's progress towards victory (he never doubted that it would be a victory), he had also been passionately concerned for the welfare of France. 'I rejoice in all expressions and testaments about the French, wonderful

and genial race,' he had written in March 1915; 'all generous appreciation of the way they are carrying themselves now seems to me of
the highest international value and importance, and, frankly, I wish
more of that found its way into our newspapers here, so prodigiously
(even if erratically) copious about our own doings. We ought to
commend and commemorate and celebrate them . . . but the want
of imagination hereabouts . . . is almost a painful impression.'[31] Was
it that painful impression which James, in his delirium, was struggling
to rectify? Was it so very surprising that he should make the mental
adjustment from armchair leader to imperial tyrant? Or, remembering his mocking reference to himself as Ozymandias, should we
content ourselves with seeing the Napoleon persona as an extension
of his private sense of himself as a literary leader, a conqueror of new
regions of fiction? We can only speculate. There is no answer that
can be defended by more than conjecture.

On 28 December, Edmund Gosse brought word to James that he
had been given the Order of Merit, hitherto only awarded to two
novelists, Meredith and Hardy. It was the greatest civilian distinction
which could be bestowed on a British subject by a monarch. James
was clearly unfit to receive the order in person at Buckingham
Palace, but he was sufficiently alert to be pleased by the gesture of
recognition. Gosse did not see any sign that James had taken in the
good news, but when he had left the room, James asked the maid
to turn off the light 'to spare my blushes'. He was shown the
congratulatory messages which flooded in, including one from
George Alexander to say, most hypocritically, how proud he had
been to present *Guy Domville*. On this, James made no comment,
but the felicitations appeared to please him.

It looked at first as though official recognition had worked a
miracle. For two weeks, James appeared to be making a remarkable
recovery. It was not maintained. Confused and drowsy but not in
any pain, he slowly sank into unconsciousness. Mrs James was sitting
with him on the evening of 28 February, 1916 when, with three brief
sighs, he died. His face, in death, struck many of his friends as being
uncannily similar to that of Napoleon.

It rained on the day of the funeral, but Chelsea Old Church was
packed with James's friends and admirers, including Jessie Allen,
Lucy Clifford, Howard Sturgis, Sargent and Kipling. The congregation sang the old stalwarts, 'For all the saints who from their
labours rest' and 'O God, our help in ages past', before the body
was transported to Golders Green on the other side of London for
cremation. The ashes were taken back to America to be buried in the
family plot at Cambridge. At Lamb House, which had been willed

to James's nephew, Harry, a commemorative plaque was put up announcing that 'Henry James, author, lived here 1898–1916'. Harry James let the house to various Americans before presenting it to the English National Trust 'as an enduring symbol of the ties that unite the British and American peoples'. James's friend, Arthur Benson, inhabited it with his brother, the author of, among many other works, the Mapp and Lucia books set in Rye. E. F. Benson continued to live there after Arthur's death and the house has, to this day, been the home of people closely connected to the literary world.

One wonders whether James would have approved of his nephew's quietly retrieving him for America in his statement to the National Trust. Lamb House had, after all, represented a crucial step in his journey towards British citizenship. His life there had been that of an English country gentleman. Lamb House had symbolized his severance from America, not the ties that held him to it. I think he would have preferred Gosse's letter to *The Times* in which his old friend described him as a soldier and an Englishman. 'No one has suffered more in spirit, no one was more tensely agitated by the war, than Henry James,' Gosse wrote. 'He was a volunteer in our great cause . . . he was an English hero of whom England shall be proud.'[32]

POSTSCRIPT

Conrad did not attend the funeral, although he was a fairly frequent visitor to London at this time. There had been no rift on the scale caused by Wells's *Boon*, but Conrad had not found it easy to forgive James for saying in 'The Younger Generation' that *Chance* was artificially constructed and that its author had put form before content. Coming from James, the writer he esteemed above all others, the criticism had been particularly hard to accept with grace.

Conrad and his family had, since 1910, been living at Capel House, a pretty seventeenth-century house at Orlestone, eight miles from The Pent. *Victory* had been published and very well-received in 1915. At the time of James's death, Conrad had just completed *The Shadow Line*, spurred on by the likelihood that his son Borys was likely to be despatched to the Front in France at any moment.

Conrad had revisited Poland just before the outbreak of war, and it was Poland's fate which dominated his thoughts during the course of the war. The proposals he put forward were for a Polish Commonwealth of Nations under a joint Anglo-French protectorate which would last for twenty years. Always sceptical, he remained deeply pessimistic about his homeland's future: President Wilson's famous declaration seemed to him to offer no more than fine words and empty promises.

Conrad's friendship with Ford was tentatively renewed during the war. Ford, like Borys, took part in the Battle of the Somme. He sent Conrad three long descriptive letters, exorcising his fear of the shrill, spasmodic sounds of battle by concentrating on finding the words which would best convey them. He wrote again in December 1916 from the Red Cross Hospital in Rouen, to say that he had been gassed. This was not true, but he had cracked up under a harsh commander and was not exaggerating when he described his life as a hell of fear and hallucinations. In 1921, he sent another less friendly letter, demanding that old accounts should be paid, and was answered promptly with a cheque for £20. In 1924, having failed to persuade Conrad to contribute an article to the *transatlantic review*, Ford visited him at Oswalds near Canterbury, where the Conrads had been living since 1919. The meeting was affable enough but, while Ford was telling himself that the old friendship was quite restored, his host was watching him cynically, wondering 'when would the kink come?' It was a relief to him to learn that Ford now spent most of his time in Paris; there was no great risk of his becoming a frequent visitor.

Conrad died on 3 August, 1924 and was buried in the Roman Catholic church of St Thomas's, Canterbury. The crowds who filled the streets of Canterbury that day had not come to mourn the death of a great novelist but to enjoy the town's Cricket Festival. Only a few family friends were there to see Konrad Korzeniowski laid to rest in a modest grave at the edge of the cemetery.

Ford was full of enthusiasm for his new role as an officer of the 9th Welch Regiment when James met him in St James's Park. He had not waited for his appointment to be gazetted to don his uniform. He also deemed it an opportune moment to bury a little of his German parentage by exchanging his middle name of Hermann for Madox. War offered the kind of social position which he craved. It also offered an escape from Violet Hunt who, terrified of losing him and fearful that she already had, persuaded Wells to write and ask Ford why he was angry with her. The answer, while conciliatory, was not reassuring. Ford had no intention of quitting regimental life for civilian domesticity. Violet's meagre comfort was the knowledge that she shared with Conrad the responsibility of being Ford's literary executor if he died in action. Ford did not die, but he soon came to the view that death had no worse horrors to offer than he was enduring in life. Constant shelling, unceasing apprehension and concussion after a near-miss reduced him to a condition of jittering nervous terror and to temporary amnesia. The C.O. of the 9th Welch told him bluntly that he was inefficient and too old for the job, which it was his duty to resign. Neither the C.O. nor Ford was overjoyed when, after a brief respite in North Wales, Ford was ordered back to France and reassigned to the 9th Welch. It was probably as well for both of them that Ford collapsed at this point and had to be hospitalized in Rouen. After a brief spell as commander of a Canadian casualty battalion, he was put in charge of a prisoner-of-war camp at

Abbeville, a thankless job from which a lung infection gave him a merciful escape. He was invalided home in March 1917.

Violet's fears were soon confirmed. In 1918 Ford met a shy young Australian artist called Stella Bowen. In 1919, she and Ford set up home together in a Sussex cottage and, with the intention of sparing Stella the awkwardness of being called Mrs Hueffer (Elsie Hueffer was alive and hostile and still, technically, his wife), he changed his name to Ford.

'My life through I seemed to have been mixed up in terrific rows with people who appeared singularly touchy,' Ford wrote in *Return to Yesterday*. Given the nature of Ford's post-war reminiscences, their touchiness was not surprising. Wells was furious when Ford informed his public that only he had been concerned with the 'how' of writing and that he had squashed Wells with a devastating retort when the latter had tried to lecture him on his art. Jessie Conrad was less justifiably enraged when Ford published his tribute to her husband and failed to show any respect for her role as the author's wife and loyal assistant. Violet Hunt, still devoted to Ford, was more intrigued than irritated to discover how much of her own behaviour was mirrored in that of Sylvia Tietjens, persecutor of a noble and astonishingly tolerant man, in the first three volumes of *Parade's End*. Ford himself steadily refused to acknowledge any sense of shame or embarrassment. He had always told the significant truths. What did it matter if he improved his stories by altering the unimportant details? Accused of lying, he could always resort to saying that he had been poking a little mild fun. 'I suppose I have always rather liked teasing public characters and public characters must dislike being teased more than I had imagined,' was his airy defence of his webs of truth and fantasy.

The history of Ford's years in Paris, his editorship of the *transatlantic review*, his friendships with Hemingway, Joyce, Pound and Stein, his ménage à trois with Stella and Jean Rhys, his experiences as a lecturer in America and the serenity of his life in a Provençal villa with his last love, Janice Biala, can be found in Arthur Mizener's appropriately titled *The Saddest Story*. There is a good deal of sadness in Ford's story, not all of his own making. Reading his books, it is apparent that the years which he remembered as his happiest were those he spent at Winchelsea, Aldington and The Pent. In *Return to Yesterday*, he was writing about a golden age of hope and high ambition to which he could never return.

Ford died in Janice's arms on 26 June, 1939. He was buried, with only three friends to mourn him, at Deauville cemetery, on a hill overlooking the sea.

Wells had been prophesying catastrophe for years, but the declaration of war in 1914 still took him by surprise. 'I let my imagination play about it, but at the bottom of my heart I could not feel and believe it would really be let happen,' he wrote many years later.

Too old, at forty-eight, to participate, he devoted himself to hammering home the idea that this war must be the last. For the pacifists, he had nothing but scorn. He wanted peace as much as they did and was prepared to set out his proposals for disarmament, but in the meantime, there was a war to be fought and won! The Bloomsbury Group recoiled in disgust, united in the view that Wells was a belligerent vulgarian. The public read him more avidly than ever.

Influential writers were sent out to the Front and in 1916 Wells accepted the government's invitation to tour the battlefields of France. The real thing, oddly, affected him less than what he had read about it. His letter to his wife from 'Poor bored Daddy' complained that he had seen it all before in the newspapers and magazines at home. In *Mr Britling Sees It Through*, he seemed to have found a new and – for an agnostic – surprising answer to the horrors of war. Britling, a thinly disguised portrait of Wells himself, comes to the conclusion that the only hope is for man to put his faith in God. In his next book, Wells presented himself as God's spokesman on earth. It took considerable ingenuity for Wells to explain away this religious phase in later years.

By the end of the war, Wells had reverted to his role of The Great Educator. He spent three years toiling over *The Outline of History*, a 750,000 word rewriting of the past in terms which accommodated his vision of the future. *The Outline* made Wells a fortune, selling over two million copies in England and America alone. It was the book which brought him international fame.

In 1914, Rebecca West had given birth to a son by Wells who, while very ready to continue the liaison, showed no inclination to abandon his devoted and astonishingly tolerant wife. By 1923, Rebecca had had enough of her role as part-time mistress. She left for America and by the following year Wells had replaced her with Odette Keun, a witty, quarrelsome, warm-hearted woman who was ready to fit in with the double life which marriage obliged Wells to lead. The arrangement suited everybody reasonably well. At Lou Pidou near Grasse, Odette had Wells to herself. At Easton Glebe, in Essex, Wells was a fond husband and father to Jane and the two boys. He had never ceased to love Jane. When cancer was diagnosed in 1927, Jane left it to her sons to inform their father. 'My dear dear wife . . .' Wells wrote to her. 'I love you much more than I have loved anyone else in the world & I am coming back to you to take care of you & to do all I can to make you happy.' He kept his word and the mourners at her funeral were moved and embarrassed to see Wells sobbing like a child. Although he was back at Lou Pidou within a few days, his next work was a touching personal tribute to his wife, only marred by the author's anxiety to justify his own unhusbandly behaviour.

The 1930s saw Wells involved in a new affair, with Moura Budberg, taking up the role of international president of the PEN clubs which were set up to promote wider understanding – and protection – for writers in different countries, and doing his best to wake Russia from 'the dope-dream of Sovietic self-sufficiency' into which he saw it sinking when he talked to Stalin and toured the country. His *Autobiography* was published and well-received. A little ominously, he explained his choice of a new London home, a splendid Nash house overlooking Regent's Park, by saying he was 'looking for a house to die in'. When the PEN Club gave him a seventieth birthday dinner in 1936, Wells ended his speech to them on an apprehensive note. 'Few of my games are nearly finished and some of them I feel I have hardly begun.'

Despair had started to take the place of his old ebullience. It depressed him to be made aware of his power to terrify people when he heard of the millions of Americans who had been frightened out of their wits by Orson Welles's radio broadcast from *The War of the Worlds* in October 1938. It depressed him to think that nothing he had written could alter the course of destiny. It depressed him when he travelled to Australia to find it in the grip of the same panicky extremism which governed European thinking at that time. Modern technology had moved beyond Wells and his large, vague dreams of a world order. All he could do now was prophesy that catastrophe was on its way and that the human race would prove 'a walk-over for disaster'.

Hope, rather than threats of disaster, was what readers craved during the war. Wells had none to offer, only his old and cherished dream of a new world order which could emerge like a phoenix from the flames of destruction. If people were not prepared to share in his dream, he could promise them nothing more encouraging than 'disaster and extinction'. It was not what people wanted to hear. Thousands had taken comfort in Mr Britling's vision. Only a loyal few struggled through to the confused conclusions of *Phoenix*.

Wells's last years were spent in launching attacks at all visible targets. Roman Catholicism was 'the most evil thing in the whole world'. Communism was 'the identical twin of Catholicism', hide-bound by its own dogma. Monarchists were derided alongside the narrow-minded, trade-union dominated Labour Party. His last work was to have been a screenplay for Alexander Korda, a revised and updated version of *Things to Come* which would have at its heart the horror of the bomb which had just been dropped on Hiroshima. The ingredients had changed, but the message had not altered since Wells's apocalyptic fictions of fifty years before.

Wells died on 13 August, 1946 and was cremated at Golders Green. The farewell address by J. B. Priestley was a tribute to a friend who had been not only 'the great prophet of our time' but the most mischievous, inventive, friendly and outspoken of men.

Wells, the last survivor, had been the first to introduce the notion of a group of literary conspirators who had succeeded in transforming the face of English fiction. It was Wells, too, who on another occasion had pointed out that they had done so, not as a group, but as individuals of markedly dissimilar talents and beliefs; 'impulsive, unco-ordinated, wilful'. Had they been exposed to and enthused by the 'expert and scientific educational process' which Wells would have liked to put into operation, there might have been a conspira-torial group, a group dedicated to turning fiction into a vehicle for social reform. It did not happen and, given the characters of the writers involved, it is safe to say that under no circumstances could it have happened. It has been part of my intention in this book to convey the unusual degree to which the opposite was true. Neither criticism, praise nor collaboration could influence any one of the writers away from their chosen approach and style.

The conspiracies which I have tried to unravel were of a different kind, the product of ambivalence exemplified in James's response to Wells's writings, of hypocrisy, exemplified in Conrad's private mockery of the book which he fulsomely praised to Ford's face. There was also a conspiracy of wishful thinking, as Wells set about diminishing the past and the closeness of the friendships which had existed and as Ford set about embroidering on and exaggerating them, and another of rank bitterness, as Jessie Conrad set out to undermine the role Ford claimed to have played in her husband's life.

The most important conspiracy of all, as far as James's attitude to his literary neighbours was concerned, has perhaps been too obliquely conveyed. It was the conspiracy of class. There is no doubt – in my mind, at least – why James would have been perfectly content to hear himself described as part of the Qu'Acre circle of well-born New Englanders and furious to hear that he was thought to have been on equally intimate terms with Wells, Conrad, Ford and Crane. Snobbery had played no part in James's upbringing and education and it was not a vice which escaped mockery in his fictions. But life as an expatriate had, nevertheless, given him a taste for what we still, old-fashionedly and unforgivably, call the upper classes. To be accepted by them was not only important for his writing, but for his sense of security in a country which was not his own. When, in 1903, he chided Howard Sturgis for writing about an English Marquis without seeking his advice on how an aristocrat would behave (an odd criticism from a man who was aware that Sturgis, with a Marquis for a brother-in-law, was amply informed on such fine points), the reader needs little perception to pick up the complacent note. James had received his passport into English aristocratic society, and he did not intend to forgo it by seeming to move in less precisely ordered and recorded circles. Ford could boast of his grand German relations, but James had already firmly placed him as a young man who was to be pitied for having grown up in the altogether too bohemian circle of the Pre-Raphaelites. Conrad, too modest to suppose James could be interested in his Polish ancestry, had lowered himself by his marriage. Lady Ottoline Morrell could afford to go slumming and enthuse over the 'super-subtle Pole' she had found at The Pent. James, acutely sensitive to social judgement, could not. Physically, Lamb House occupied an elevated position in Rye. Socially, James did not neglect the challenge to live up to it. His relations with his literary neighbours were courteous and cordial, but it was cordiality tempered by the prudent caution of a man unusually alert to the value of his social position.

POSTSCRIPT TO
THE PAPERBACK EDITION

Looking back across sixteen years, I wonder at the innocence and arrogance with which I embarked on this book. Never having published a work of non-fiction, I might have chosen to begin with a less ambitious project had I realised what it entailed. To write about Henry James in his last twenty years clearly required a knowledge of the life and the work that had gone before. To create a plausible network of connections between The Master and his literary neighbours, his family and his American friends in England, required easy familiarity with all their writings, both private and public. Given that the figures involved were prolific authors, this was a tall order: Ford Madox Ford alone had written enough books to stock a small library; H. G. Wells, Joseph Conrad and Edith Wharton didn't lag far behind.

Now, many universities offer biography courses; back in the 1980s, no one could advise me on how best to construct a work which aimed to reveal these authors by examining their literary and personal relationships. Inexperienced and uninformed in the usual tricks of the trade – record cards, subject indexes, chronology charts – by which biographers make their lives a little easier, I filled bulky files with handwritten notes, marking up the connections in different coloured pens in a way which now, in the age of the computer, seems marvellously primitive. I filled novels with notes on loose leaves of paper and then lost them. I had no idea how to sift information, how to conduct interviews or how to set about identifying the holders of copyrights. It was all a mystery.

The process was long: seven years from beginning to completion, largely due to my own ineptitude. Even so, I am not sure that I would choose to write the book again by any other method. I did, for all my inefficiency, reap the reward of familiarity with my subject; I did, I believe, achieve my aim. I wanted to show that, despite the sometimes comical courtesy and deference with which this disparate group of authors dealt with each other in meetings and in correspondence, each writer guarded his individuality and resisted the influence of his literary neighbours. Conrad and Ford Madox Ford collaborated for a time, but no admirer of *The Secret Agent* and *The Good Soldier* would ever suspect it. H. G. Wells expressed almost obsequious gratitude to Henry James for his tips on how to write, while James himself thanked his brother William for advice on how best to please his readers. Neither writer deviated by a hair's breadth from his chosen course as a result of these well-intended tips, and we can be thankful for their strength of mind.

I have a special affection for this book. I still read Henry James with untiring pleasure; the only marked change is that I have grown more alert to the subtle but devastating wit which glances through some of his most demure observations. Perceptive, meticulous and assured in his prose, James was also a master of comic detail. He must have been a wonderfully entertaining companion.

Many excellent books have been written about James, but he still retains the power and fascination of an enigma. In correspondence, he could be richly malicious; in life, he was almost invariably kind and gentle-hearted, fierce only in the guarding of his privacy. The notion that he was a homosexual – by instinct at least – doesn't begin to explain James's horror of revelations. No such disclosures are likely to have been made in the letters which he took such pains to destroy after the suicide of his friend Constance Fenimore Woolson. When he wrote his celebrated story about the theft of a writer's private manuscripts, *The Aspern Papers*, James made it clear that illumination of the work was an insufficient reason for any critic or biographer to violate the privacy of their subject.

My own book might have escaped James's disapproval, since it largely relies on published sources. Since 1988, however, I have come across a small cache of letters, buried in a family archive and published in this new Postscript for the first time. Since they contain nothing incriminating, I doubt if James would object. They are addressed to members of the Sturgis family, who provide my only personal link to James.

The modest interest of these letters lies in the way they underline the degree to which Henry James relied on the friendship of fellow expatriates during his years in Europe. The Sturgis family – not to be confused with James's friend, Jonathan Sturges – originated from Boston. Their homes abroad, in London, Surrey and Middlesex, were hospitable meeting-places for fellow Americans living abroad. In Venice, James often enjoyed the hospitality of another Bostonian family, the Curtises, owners of the Palazzo Barbaro; in Paris, he stayed with their American friend Edith Wharton, whom he first encountered at a dinner party given by Edward Boit, another New Englander and a relation of the Sturgises. When we remember that Morton Fullerton and Walter Berry, both of whom were closely attached to Henry James and to the Whartons, were also New Englanders, it becomes clear that James worked hard at retaining close links to his past. This was a small world of intimate friendships and shared memories, reassuring to all the expatriates, and to none more so than a middle-aged and sometimes lonely bachelor. James made a point of never spending more time than he could help in the homes of his English friends; he was a frequent guest in the homes of his fellow Americans.

The first of these newly discovered letters is addressed to the mother of Howard Sturgis. James wrote it in 1881 as he prepared to return to America and see his family after six years of separation. 'Mr Sturgis' was Russell, a partner in Baring Brothers' bank; 'Julian' was Howard's married brother, a playwright and novelist.

The Adelphi Hotel, Liverpool
20 October, 1881

My dear Mrs Sturgis
    I *will* snatch a moment, though I embark for the U.S. in half an hour, to do what I ought to have done – and was a dozen times on the brink of doing – a fortnight ago: i.e. bid you and your dear family a tender farewell and tell you how sorry I was that I never offered you my company at the Farm before my little journey. I heard from Mrs Brett in Scotland that you were moving to Brighton and your house was still being further embellished and I didn't feel at liberty – familiar as I am with your generous hospitality – to come down on you at the former place as I should have done at the latter. I visit my native land for as short a time as possible, and shall be back in Bolton Street, which is always my address, while the New Year is yet young. I latterly made two attempts to see Mr Sturgis in the City – to say all sorts of affectionate things to him – but he was represented as absent. I should have liked to see Julian also, of whom I am as fond as he will let me be; which isn't much. Goodbye, and receive my kindest wishes for your health and happiness. I shall be both seasick and homesick!
    Very faithfully
    H James

The second, undated, letter is to Howard Sturgis's sister May, the wife of Leopold Seymour, my great-grandfather. The tone is slightly less affectionate; May was a handsome woman, but cold. The fact that James wrote from Bournemouth suggests that this was written in 1885, when his sister Alice was dying there. This would explain James's muted allusion to the need to do 'dismal things'.

Bath Hotel, Bournemouth
Saturday [undated, but evidently close to Christmas]

Dear Mrs Seymour

How more than kind your note – and how horrible to be of a habit so perverse and unworthy that I don't reply to it by straightway knocking at your door! I am greatly touched by the generosity of your thought of me and the altogether noble accent of your hospitality. I have fled from town, but to occupations that preclude visiting and make me now as one who does dismal things. The Victorian Saturnalia appal me – and I am beside the sounding sea and listening to winds and waves – an ominous persistence of the former. Some day I shall be delighted – impracticable wretch as I am – to come and spend a Sunday with you – the poor predestined limit of my rare country visiting. Please believe in the appreciation which I meanwhile have of your liberality, which I like to think owes something (I mean the liberality itself) to the very old time attachments for so many of *les vôtres* that will perhaps enable you to let me call myself your very faithful old friend

Henry James

The third letter is to Howard Sturgis's older brother Julian. The content suggests that it was written during the early 1890s, when Henry James was living in De Vere Gardens, Kensington, and taking a keen interest in theatricals. It is likely that he consulted Julian, a successful playwright, as he began to write plays of his own. 'Mrs Seymour' is Julian's sister May.

34 De Vere Gardens
Wednesday [undated]

My dear Julian,

I am equally indebted to the old Etonian and to the new. 'Sneak' will bring down the house – I [mean?] alas, sell the edition. I shall reserve 'Wolf' for tragedy, and bring in a baron on purple [sic] – a wolfing baron is grand. But we must let the baronets of comedy only sneak or at most 'shark'.

Many thanks all round. Won't you say something quite extraordinarily friendly to Mrs Seymour for me?

Yours ever
Henry James

The fourth letter from this archive is from E. F. Benson, who rented Lamb House from Henry James's nephew and namesake. The recipient is Howard and Julian Sturgis's sister May, who had by this date remarried.

She had recently secured a peerage for her second husband, Bertie Falle, by selling some substantial pieces of jewellery.

> Lamb House
> 18 June 1939
>
> Dear Lady Portsea
>   I was delighted to get your letter first because it was *yours*, and secondly because I was very glad to know that you approved of the 'Daughters'. It had a great success in America and is doing well here, but I value personal appreciations more than editions. It was difficult to work several private lives simultaneously into a background of historical events (this when stated sounds rather a truism).
>   I am stopping down here yet awhile, for Henry James, my landlord, wants to come here for a day or two early in July, and I don't expect to get up to London till after his visit. But I have the firmest intention of letting you know when I arrive.
>   Yours very sincerely
>   E. F. Benson

My warm thanks to my cousin Sarah Ducas, who found these original letters in an album which was compiled by our great-grandmother, Lady Portsea, and was given by her son Richard Sturgis Seymour to his oldest son, Leo.

This is a re-issue rather than a revised edition. I would like to use this new Postscript to make a few brief comments. I was not aware when I first wrote the book that the bookplate drawn for Henry James by Edward Gordon Craig (reproduced on page 11) represented the old mulberry tree in the garden of Lamb House. As I have now noted in the revised caption, the tree was brought down by winds in 1915, shortly before James's death. The hopes I expressed in 1988 for the construction of a new Garden Room at Rye to replace the airy pavilion in which Henry James dictated his later novels have not been fulfilled; the Garden Room project has been abandoned through lack of resources.

Times have moved on since 1988. I would not now dream of writing of 'maiden aunts' or of 'the upper classes' as if these expressions were still in use. They aren't.

The chapter on Henry James's American friendships in England contains a few details taken from R. W. B. Lewis's biography of Edith Wharton, which have since been shown – by Lewis's researcher, Marian Mainwaring – to be mildly inaccurate. I should have spelled the name of

Fullerton's wife as Camille Chabbert, not Chabert, and identified Madame Mirecourt as Adele, rather than Henriette Mirecourt. Mainwaring has shown that against Henry James's advice, Fullerton continued to lodge at Mirecourt's home in Paris after she attempted to blackmail him with compromising letters stolen from his rooms. Fullerton had been close to Lord Ronald Gower, a homosexual; homosexuality was a criminal offence at the beginning of the twentieth century. This would explain why Fullerton was still making blackmail payments to Madame Mirecourt when she died in 1924.

The census for New Windsor in 1901, recently shown to me by the current tenants of Lamb House, enables us to put a little more colour into the portrait of life at Qu'Acre, where Henry James was a guest when the census was taken. James was fifty-seven at the time of the visit; his host, who identified his own profession as 'Income' and his birthplace as Kilburn, in north London, was forty-five. Howard Sturgis's closest male friend, and cousin, William Haynes-Smith, then thirty, was also staying; Julian Sturgis, Howard's older married brother, was also a member of the party. No mention of this visit appears in the published letters of Henry James, but it is worth noting that this was a year in which the tranquillity of Lamb House was shaken by the obstreperous behaviour of Mr and Mrs Smith, James's alcoholic servants. The Qu'Acre guests in 1901 were cared for by two housemaids, a kitchen maid, a scullery maid, a hall boy, a footman and a talented female cook; it isn't surprising that James was happy to take refuge there while he completed work on *The Ambassadors*.

My thanks to my agent, Anthony Goff, and my editor, Andrew Gordon, for their enthusiasm about re-issuing a book to which I am so warmly attached. I hope it may help to introduce some new readers to Henry James and the circle of writers who lived, not always graciously, in the shadow of the greatest master of prose of his time, and of ours.

MIRANDA SEYMOUR
June 2004

LIST OF ILLUSTRATIONS

Henry James and Howard Sturgis (reproduced by kind permission of Mrs Katherine Sturgis Goodman)

Henry James at Qu'Acre (reproduced by kind permission of Mr and the Hon. Mrs George Seymour)

Cora Crane and Henry James (photo at Colombia University Library)

Howard Sturgis and William Haynes-Smith (photo at Beinecke Rare Book and Manuscript Library, Yale University)

An engraving of Rye by Hollar after van Dyck (reproduced by courtesy of the Master and Fellows of Magdalene College, Cambridge)

Henry James at Lamb House

NOTES

NOTES

Introduction pp. 13–21

1. A glance at the social history of the British arts shows a striking lack of groups of novelists. There are innumerable examples of groups of poets and artists – Pope and his circle, the Lake poets, the East Anglian School of painters, to cite a few – but there are none of novelists. Coteries of writers have often formed but a coterie is not a group with a defined artistic purpose. The Bloomsbury Group, while including many novelists, was an aggregation of philosophers, historians, poets and painters.

2. H. G. Wells, *Experiment in Autobiography,* II (London, 1934*),* p. 620.

Chapter 1 – Imaginative Truths: The Cranes pp. 23–44

1. Cora Crane to Edward Garnett, 19.1.1899, *Stephen Crane: Letters,* ed. R. W. Stallman and Lillian Gilkes (London, 1960)
2. *ibid.,* James B. Pinker to Stephen Crane, 24.10.1899
3. *ibid.,* Cora Crane to James B. Pinker, 26.10.1899
4. Stephen Crane to John N. Hilliard (1897?). First published in the *New York Times,* 14.7.1900.
5. Stephen Crane to H. B. Marriott-Watson, 15.11.1899. *Letters, op. cit.* Marriott-Watson, a prolific author, had written an influential and highly favourable review of *The Red Badge of Courage* just before its English publication in 1896. The two men subsequently became cordial friends.
6. C. Lewis Hind, *Authors and I* (London, 1921) p.72
7. *Manchester Guardian,* 13.1.1900
8. H. G. Wells, *Experiment in Autobiography,* II, *op. cit.,* p. 615
9. Quoted in *Stephen Crane: Letters, op. cit.* The only source given is an English newspaper, 16.6.1900.
10. Quoted by John Berryman in *Stephen Crane* (London, 1951) as an undated letter from Crane.
11. H. G. Wells to Stephen Crane, 22.4.1900, *Stephen Crane: Letters, op. cit.*
12. Quoted by R. W. Stallman in *Stephen Crane* (New York, 1968), p. 512, from an undated letter from H. G. Wells to a friend.

13. *ibid.*, p. 465, from an undated letter from Stephen Crane to a friend.
14. Ford Madox Ford, *Return to Yesterday* (London, 1931), p. 31
15. H. G. Wells, *Experiment in Autobiography*, II, *op. cit.*, p. 617
16. *ibid.*, p. 623
17. H. G. Wells to Henry James, 20.3.1907, *Henry James & H.G. Wells*, ed. Leon Edel and Gordon N. Ray (London, 1958)
18. Quoted by R. L. Megroz in *A Talk with Joseph Conrad: A Criticism of his Mind and Method* (London, 1926), p. 54

Chapter Two – A Provincial Gentleman: James at Rye pp. 45–71

1   Henry James to Francis Parkman, 24.8.1884, *Henry James Letters,* III, ed. Leon Edel (London, 1980)
2. Ford Madox Ford, *Return to Yesterday, op. cit.,* p. 14
3. Henry James to Mrs William James, 1.12.1897, *Henry James Letters,* IV, ed. Leon Edel (Harvard University Press, 1984)
4. Henry James to Miss Muir Mackenzie, 1.6.1901, *ibid.*
5. Henry James, *The Awkward Age,* 1899. This quotation has been taken from the New York revised edition of 1908, p. 275
6. Henry James to Mrs William James, 26.9.1901, *Henry James Letters,* IV, *op. cit.*
7. Henry James to Miss Louise Horstmann, 12.8.1904, *ibid.*
8. Quoted by H. M. R. Hyde in *Henry James at Home,* ch. iv (London, 1969)
9. *ibid.*
10. Theodora Bosanquet, *Henry James at Work* (London, 1924), pp. 244–55
11. C. Lewis Hind, *Authors and I,* London, 1921, p. 163
12. Henry James to Grace Norton, 18.12.1902, *Henry James Letters,* IV, *op. cit.*
13. Henry James to Mrs Francis Bellingham, 31.12.1902, *ibid.*
14. Henry James to Edward Warren, 24.5.1903, *ibid.*
15. Henry James to Grace Norton, 18.12.1902, *ibid.*
16. Waterlow Diary, Berg Collection, New York Public Library, 'Memories of Henry James', *New Statesman,* 6.2.1926
17. Henry James to Mrs J. T. Fields, 5.9.(1898), *Henry James Letters,* IV, *op. cit.*
18. Edmund Gosse, 'Henry James', *London Mercury* 11(1920), pp. 32–4
19. Hamlin Garland, *Roadside Meetings* (London, 1931), pp. 459–65
20. Henry James to Mrs W. K. Clifford, 24.1.1900, *Henry James Letters,* IV, *op. cit.*
21. Henry James to Henrietta Reubell, 15.12.1901, *ibid.*

Chapter Three – The Master and the Prophet: James and Wells pp. 73–106

1. H. G. Wells, *Experiment in Autobiography,* II, *op. cit.,* p. 534
2. H. G. Wells, *Guy Domville* at the St James's, *Pall Mall Gazette,* 7.1.1895

3. H. G. Wells, *Experiment in Autobiography*, II, *op. cit.*, p. 536
4. Violet Hunt, *The Flurried Years* (New York, 1926), p. 41
5. Dorothy Richardson, *The Tunnel* (London, 1919), ch. 6, vii
6. Frank Swinnerton, *An Autobiography* (London, 1935), ch. 9, ii
7. H. G. Wells, *Experiment in Autobiography*, II, *op. cit.*, p. 592
8. H. G. Wells, *Kipps: The Story of a Simple Soul* (London, 1905), Bk 3, iii
9. Joseph Conrad to H. G. Wells, 11.10.1898, *The Collected Letters of Joseph Conrad*, II, ed. Frederick R. Karl & Laurence Davies (London, 1986)
10. H. G. Wells, *Experiment in Autobiography*, II, *op. cit.*, p. 618
11. *ibid.*, pp. 488–9
12. Henry James to H. G. Wells, 9.12.1898, *Henry James Letters*, IV, *op. cit.*
13. H. G. Wells to Henry James, 16.1.1899. *Henry James & H.G.Wells*, ed. Leon Edel & Gordon N. Ray (London, 1958). Full versions of the letters between Wells and James from which I quote in this chapter are given in this book, and many of them are reprinted in Leon Edel's fourth volume of the Henry James Letters.
14. H. G. Wells, *An Englishman Looks at the World* (London, 1914), pp. 148–69
15. Henry James, *The American Scene* (London, 1907), ch. 2. Quotations from *The American Scene* in this chapter are drawn from chapters 2 and 3.
16. H. G. Wells, *The Future in America: A Search after Realities* (London, 1906), ch. 3. Quotations from *The Future in America* in this chapter are taken, in order, from chapters 13, 11, 10, 8, 3, 8, 8.
17. Henry James to H. G. Wells, 8.11.1906, *Henry James & H.G.Wells*, *op. cit.*
18. H. G. Wells to Henry James, 20.3.1907, *ibid.*

Chapter Four – The Brothers: Henry and William pp. 107–130

1. William James to H. G. Wells, 6.6.1905, *The Letters of William James*, II, ed. his son Henry James, 1920.
2. H. G. Wells to Henry James, 31.8.1910, *Henry James & H.G.Wells*, *op. cit.*
3. Henry James to William James, 9.8.1899, *Henry James Letters*, IV, *op. cit.*
4. William James to Mrs Henry Whitman, 5.10.1899, *The Letters of William James*, II, *op. cit.*
5. William James to Miss Frances R. Morse, 23–24.12.1899, *ibid.*
6. Henry James to Mrs W. K. Clifford, 24.1.1900, *Henry James Letters*, IV, *op. cit.*
7. Henry James to Miss Margaret Mary James, 24.9.(1900), *ibid.*
8. Miss Margaret Mary James to William James III, 26.4.1901. Quoted

by Leon Edel in *The Life of Henry James,* II (Penguin, 1977), and in the abridged *Life* (Collins, 1987). The quotation does not feature in the original edition of 1972.

9. William James to Henry James, 3.5.1903. *The Letters of William James,* II, *op. cit.*

10. William James to Miss Margaret Mary James, 6.5.1903, *ibid.*

11. William James to Miss Pauline Goldmark 21.9.1904, *ibid.*

12. 17.8.1909, *The Letters of Henry James,* II, ed. Percy Lubbock (1920).

13. Henry James to William James, 12.5.1900, *Henry James Letters,* IV, *op. cit.*

14. Quoted by Ralph Barton Perry, *The Thought and Character of William James* (New York, 1935), p. 371.

15. William James to Henry James, 9.5.1886, *The Letters of William James,* I, *op. cit.*

16. William James to Henry James, 11.7.1888, *ibid.*

17. Diaries of Arthur Benson, vol. 65, Jan–Feb, 1905 (Magdalene, Cambridge)

18. William James to Henry James, 22.10.1906 (Ms. Harvard)

19. Henry James to William James, 23.11.1905, *Henry James Letters,* IV, *op. cit.*

20. William James to Henry James, 1.2.1906, *The Letters of William James,* II, *op. cit.*

21. William James to Henry James, 9.5. 1906, *ibid.*

22. William James to Henry James, 7.5.1907, *ibid.*

23. Henry James to William James, Jr., 30.5. 1907, *Henry James Letters,* IV, *op. cit.*

24. Henry James to William James, 31.10.1909, Lubbock, II, *op. cit.*

25. Henry James to William and Alice James, 8.2.1910, *Henry James Letters,* IV, *op. cit.*

26. Henry James to Edith Wharton, 10.6.1910, *ibid.*

27. Henry James to Edith Wharton, 29.7.1910, *ibid.*

28. 11.8.1910, *The Complete Notebooks of Henry James,* ed. Leon Edel and Lyall H. Powers (New York, 1987)

29. Henry James to Grace Norton, 26.8.1910, *Henry James Letters,* IV, *op. cit.*

30. Henry James to Thomas Sergeant Perry, 2.9.1910, *ibid.*

31. Henry James, *A Small Boy and Others,* 1913, p. 4

32. Henry James to Henry James, Jr., 15–18.11.1913, *The Letters of Henry James,* II, Lubbock, *op. cit.*

Chapter Five – The Collaborators: Ford and Conrad pp. 131–166

1. Ford Madox Ford, *Return to Yesterday,* 1931, p. 152, quoted in *Your Mirror to My Times: The Selected Autobiographies and Impressions of Ford Madox Ford,* ed. Michael Killigrew, 1971, p. 113. (Hereafter referred to as *Mirror.*)

2. *ibid., Mirror,* pp. 104 and 114

3. *ibid., Mirror,* p. 196

4. Arthur Mizener, *The Saddest Story: A Biography of Ford Madox Ford* (London, 1972), p. 64

5. Ford, *Return to Yesterday, Mirror,* p. 199

6. *ibid., Mirror,* p. 203

7. *ibid., Mirror,* p. 209

8. Henry James, Preface to *The Spoils of Poynton,* the New York Edition, 1909. (The 1897 edition was, of course, issued without a preface.)

9. Violet Hunt, *The Flurried Years, op. cit.,* p. 79

10. *Daily Mirror,* 21.10.1911, p.3

11 Henry James to Violet Hunt, 31.10.1909 (quoted by Hunt in *The Flurried Years, op. cit.,* pp. 86–7)

12. Henry James to Violet Hunt, 2.11.1909, *Henry James Letters,* IV, *op. cit.*

13. Henry James to Violet Hunt, 5.11.1909, *ibid.*

14. Henry James to Ford Madox Ford, 8.11.1909, *ibid.*

15. Violet Hunt, *The Flurried Years, op. cit.* p. 105.

16. Ford, *Return to Yesterday, Mirror,* p. 211

17. Ford Madox Ford, *Joseph Conrad,* 1924, *Mirror,* pp. 215–16

18. Joseph Conrad to W. E. Henley, 18.10.1898, *Letters,* II, *op. cit.*

19. Joseph Conrad to Ford Madox Ford, 18.1.1907. Copy at Cornell University Library, Ithaca, N.Y.

20. Joseph Conrad to H. G. Wells, 23.12.1898, *Letters,* II, *op. cit.*

21. Ford, *Return to Yesterday, Mirror,* pp. 217–18

22. H. G. Wells, *Experiment in Autobiography,* II, *op. cit.,* p. 622

23. Edward Garnett, *The Golden Echo* (London, 1954), p. 64

24. Ford, *Joseph Conrad, op. cit., Mirror,* p. 215

25. Joseph Conrad to Ford Madox Ford, [12].11.1899, *Letters,* II, *op. cit.*

26. Joseph Conrad to Ford Madox Ford, 17.2.1900, *ibid.*

27. Jessie Conrad, *Conrad as I Knew Him* (London, 1926), p. 113

28. Joseph Conrad to Ford Madox Ford (25.3.1900), dated by post-office stamp. *Letters,* II, *op. cit.*

29. Joseph Conrad to Edward Garnett, 26.3.1900, *ibid.*

30. *Daily Telegraph,* 14.7.1901

31. Joseph Conrad to the *New York Times* 'Saturday Review', 2.8.1901, *Letters,* II, *op. cit.*

32. Joseph Conrad to James B. Pinker, 6.1.1902, *ibid.*

33. Jessie Conrad, *Joseph Conrad and his Circle,* (London, 1935) p. 71

34. Joseph Conrad to John Galsworthy, 19.9.1900, *Letters,* II, *op. cit.*

35. Joseph Conrad to Ford Madox Ford (13.6.1901), *ibid.*

36. Jessie Conrad, *Joseph Conrad and his Circle, op. cit.,* p. 66

37. Ford, *Joseph Conrad, op. cit., Mirror,* p. 218

38. Joseph Conrad to James B. Pinker, 7.11.1901, *Letters,* II, *op. cit.*

39. Joseph Conrad to John Galsworthy, 10.3.1902, *Letters,* II, *op. cit.*
40. Joseph Conrad to Ford Madox Ford, Monday (24.3.1902), *Letters,* II, *op. cit.*
41. Joseph Conrad to Ford Madox Ford, 15.4.1902, *Letters,* II, *op. cit.*
42. Joseph Conrad to Edward Garnett, 10.6.1902, *ibid.*
43. Ford, *Joseph Conrad, op. cit., Mirror,* p. 220
44. Jessie Conrad, *Joseph Conrad and his Circle, op. cit.,* p. 114
45. Henry James to Joseph Conrad, 1.11.1906, *Henry James Letters,* IV, *op. cit.*
46. Joseph Conrad to Henri-Durand Davray, 8.11.1906, *Lettres françaises,* ed. Jean-Aubry (Paris, 1929)
47. Zdzislaw Najder, *Joseph Conrad: A Chronicle* (Cambridge, 1983), p. 343
48. Jessie Conrad, *Conrad as I Knew Him, op. cit.,* p. 57
49. Joseph Conrad to Ford Madox Ford, (28.4. 1909 or 5.5.1909). Najder dates the letter by its references to the *English Review* May issue. Najder, *Joseph Conrad, op. cit.,* p. 349
50. Joseph Conrad to Ford Madox Ford, 20.5.1909, Berg Collection, New York Public Library, N.Y.C.
51. Joseph Conrad to James B. Pinker, Wednesday (4.8.1909), Berg Collection, *loc. cit.*
52. Joseph Conrad to James B. Pinker, 3.2.1924, Berg Coll., *loc. cit.*
53. Jessie Conrad to James B. Pinker, 30.4.1924, Berg Coll., *loc. cit.*
54. Joseph Conrad to Ford Madox Ford, 21.12.1911, Berg Coll., *loc. cit.*

Chapter Six – Living Prudently: James's Friendships pp. 167–197

1. Henry James to Mrs William James, 26.3.1870, *Henry James Letters,* I, Edel, *op. cit.*
2. *ibid.*
3. Henry James to William James, 29.3.1870, *ibid.*
4. *ibid.*
5. *The Complete Tales of Henry James,* vol. 9, p. 242 (London, 1964*).* First published in *Terminations,* 1895
6. Henry James, *The Wings of the Dove,* 1902, Bk 10, vi
7. Entry for 9.2.1882. *The Notebooks of Henry James,* edited by F. O. Matthiesson and Kenneth B. Murdoch (Oxford, 1945), p. 41
8. Mrs William James to Henry James, 3.6.1874. Quoted by Jean Strouse in *Alice James: A Biography* (London, 1981), p. 25
9. Henry James to Mrs William James, 3.6.1874, *ibid.,* p. 25
10. Henry James to William James, 6.5.1904, *Henry James Letters,* IV, *op. cit.*
11. Unpublished extract from Arthur Benson's *diary,* 12.11.1905–16.12.1905, vol. 76, *loc. cit.*
12. Henry James to Mrs W. K. Clifford, 17.2.1907, *Henry James Letters,* IV, *op. cit.*

13. Henry James to Violet Hunt, 28.2.1906. Quoted by Robert Secor in 'Henry James and Violet Hunt, "the Improper Person of Babylon"' (*Journal of Modern Literature*, vol. 13, no. 1, 1986), p. 18

14. *ibid.*, p. 19

15. Violet Hunt, *The Flurried Years*, English edition, *op. cit.*, p. 40

16. *ibid.*, American edition, p. 41

17. *ibid.*, American edition, p. 95

18. *ibid.*, American edition, p. 46

19. *ibid.*, English edition, p. 105

20. H. Montgomery Hyde, *Henry James at Home*, (London, 1969), p. 153

21. Lady Maud Warrender, *My First Sixty Years* (London, 1933), p. 72

22. Henry James to Jessie Allen, 19.9.1901, *Henry James Letters*, IV, *op. cit.*

23. Henry James to Mrs Humphry Ward, 25.9.1906, *ibid.*

24. Henry James to Mrs Humphry Ward, Sunday (July, 1899), *Letters of Henry James*, I, edited by Percy Lubbock, *op. cit.*

25. Ann Thwaite, *Edmund Gosse: A literary landscape* (OUP, 1985, paperback edition), p. 222. The letter is quoted without date.

26. Unpublished extract from Arthur Benson's *Diary*, December–March, 1924, vol. 173, *loc. cit.*

27. *ibid.*, 14.4.1913

28. Henry James to Hendrik Andersen, 27.7.1899, *Henry James Letters*, IV, *op cit.*

29. Henry James to Hendrik Andersen, 7.9.1899, *ibid.*

30. Henry James to Hendrik Andersen, 9.2.1902, *ibid.*

31. Henry James to Hendrik Andersen, 28.2.1902, *ibid.*

32. Henry James to Hendrik Andersen, 10.8.1904, *ibid.*

33. Henry James to Hendrik Andersen, 6.8.1905, *ibid.*

34. Henry James to Hendrik Andersen, 2.9.1913, *ibid.*

35. Unpublished extract of Arthur Benson's *Diary*, October–December, 1909, vol. 108, *loc. cit.*

36. Rupert Hart-Davis, *Hugh Walpole* (London, 1963), p. 68

37. *ibid.*, p. 68

38. Unpublished extract from Arthur Benson's *Diary*, October–December 1909, vol. 108

39. Henry James to Hugh Walpole, 13.5.1910, *Henry James Letters*, IV, *op. cit.*

40. Unpublished extract from Arthur Benson's *Diary*, January–March 1902, vol. II, *loc. cit.*

41. Henry James, 'The Younger Generation', in *The Times Literary Supplement*, 19.3.1914 and 2.4.1914, pp. 133–4 & 137–58

42. Henry James to Charles Sayle, 16.6.1909, *Henry James Letters*, IV, *op. cit.*

43. Henry James to Gaillard Lapsley, 17.3.1908 *(Letters*, II, Lubbock), and 15.9.1902 *(Letters*, IV, Edel)

44. Henry James to Hugh Walpole, 19.5.1912, *Henry James Letters*, IV, *op. cit.*

45. Henry James to Hugh Walpole, 14.10.1913, *ibid.*

Chapter Seven – Living Dangerously: The Cranes pp. 199–223

1. Thomas Beer, *Stephen Crane: A Study in American Letters* (London, 1924), p. 142

2. Edith Ritchie Jones, 'Stephen Crane at Brede', *Atlantic Monthly* (July, 1954)

3. Henry James to Cora Crane (4.9.1899), *Henry James Letters*, IV, *op. cit.* I have followed the editors of Stephen and Cora's letters in giving her the name, to which she was not technically entitled, of Cora Crane.

4. Henry James to James B. Pinker, 9.8.1900, *ibid.*

5. Robert W. Stallman, *Stephen Crane, op. cit.*, p. 62

6. *ibid.*, p. 93

7. Thomas Beer, *op. cit.*, p. 160

8. Ford Madox Ford, *Return to Yesterday, op. cit.*, p. 50

9. *ibid.*, p. 29

10. Robert W. Stallman, *Stephen Crane, op. cit.* pp. 299–300. Two variants of this observation on Crane are to be found in Ford Madox Ford's *Mightier than the Sword* (New York, 1938) and Douglas Goldring's *The Last Pre-Raphaelite* (New York, 1948).

11. Joseph Conrad to Edward Garnett, 14.10.1897, *Letters*, I, *op. cit.*

12. Joseph Conrad's *Introduction* to Beer's biography of Crane, *op. cit.*, pp. 12–13

13. Stephen Crane to Joseph Conrad, 11.11.1897, *Stephen Crane: Letters, op. cit.*

14. Joseph Conrad to Crane, 16.11.1897, *Letters*, I, *op cit.*

15. Joseph Conrad to Stephen Crane, 1.12.1897, *ibid.*

16. Joseph Conrad to Henry James (30.11.1897), *ibid.*

17. Joseph Conrad to Edward Garnett, 5.12.1897, *ibid.*

18. Joseph Conrad's *Introduction* to Beer's biography of Crane, *op. cit.*, p. 31

19. Joseph Conrad to Stephen Crane (12? 1.1898). See footnote to ch 7. p. 276, *Letters*, II, *op. cit.*

20. Joseph Conrad's *Introduction* to Beer's biography, *op. cit.*, p. 31.

21. Joseph Conrad to Stephen Crane, 16.1.1898, *Letters*, II, *op. cit.*

22. Joseph Conrad's *Introduction* to Beer's biography, *op. cit.*, p. 22

23. *ibid.*, p. 23

24. *Letters from Conrad*, 1895–1924, ed. Edward Garnett (London, 1928), pp. xv–xvi

25. Joseph Conrad to Stephen Crane, 5 (March) 1898. *Letters*, II, *op. cit.* Conrad mistakenly dated this letter as 5.2.1898, but Najder points out that the letter clearly follows the February visit to Ravensbrook, and the editors of Conrad's letters have followed him in correcting the month to March.

26. Joseph Conrad's *Introduction* to Beer's biography, *op. cit.*, p. 34

27. Cora Crane to Paul Revere Reynolds, 25.8.1898, *Stephen Crane: Letters, op. cit.*

28. Joseph Conrad to Cora Crane, 28.10.1898, *Letters,* II, *op. cit.*
29. Joseph Conrad to Cora Crane, 4.12.1898, *ibid.*
30. Joseph Conrad to Robert Cunninghame Graham, 19.1.1900, *ibid.*

Chapter Eight – A Ring of Friendships: Edith Wharton . . . pp. 225–254

1. Edith Wharton, *A Backward Glance* (New York, 1934), p. 225
2. Henry James to Howard Sturgis, 8.11.1903, *Henry James Letters,* IV, *op. cit.*
3. *A Backward Glance, op. cit.,* pp. 234–5
4. *ibid.,* p. 172
5. *ibid.,* p. 172
6. *ibid.,* p. 173
7. *ibid.,* p. 173
8. R. W. B. Lewis, *Edith Wharton* (London, 1975), p. 132
9. Percy Lubbock, *A Portrait of Edith Wharton* (London, 1947), p. 137
10. Simon Nowell-Smith, *The Legend of the Master* (London, 1947), p. 134
11. Henry James to Edith Wharton, 8.11.1905, *Henry James Letters,* IV, *op. cit.*
12. Henry James to H. G. Wells, 19.11.1905, *ibid.*
13. *A Backward Glance, op. cit.,* p. 184
14. *ibid.,* p. 183
15. *ibid.,* p. 192
16. *ibid.,* p. 191
17. *ibid.,* p. 176
18. Henry James to Howard Sturgis, 2.8.1910, *Henry James Letters,* IV, *op. cit.*
19. Henry James to Howard Sturgis, 9.8.1912, *ibid.*
20. *A Backward Glance, op. cit.,* pp. 248–9
21. *ibid.,* pp. 153–4
22. *ibid.,* pp. 186–7
23. *ibid.,* p. 192
24. Henry James to Edith Wharton, 13.10.1908, *Henry James Letters,* IV, *op. cit.*
25. R. W. B. Lewis, *Edith Wharton, op. cit.,* p. 304
26. Henry James to William James III, 29.3.1913, *Henry James Letters,* IV, *op. cit.*
27. Henry James to Edith Wharton, 17.10.1914, *Henry James Letters,* II, ed. Percy Lubbock, *op. cit.*
28. R. W. B. Lewis, *Edith Wharton, op. cit.,* p. 383
29. *ibid.,* p. 383
30. Quoted by Cynthia Griffin Wolff, *A Feast of Words* (London, 1977), from *Quaderno dello Studente,* 8.

Chapter Nine – The Bench of Desolation: James at Seventy pp. 255–276

1. Henry James to Edith Wharton, 25.10.1911, *Henry James Letters*, IV, *op. cit.*
2. Bertrand Russell, *Autobiography, 1872–1914* (New York, 1968), pp. 278–9
3. Henry James to Mrs W. K. Clifford, 18.5.1912, *Henry James Letters*, IV, *op. cit.*
4. 'The Younger Generation', quoted in *Henry James and H. G. Wells*, Edel & Ray, *op. cit.*, pp. 191–2
5. H. G. Wells, *Experiment in Autobiography*, *op. cit.*, p. 490
6. 'An Englishman Looks at the World', quoted in *Henry James and H. G. Wells*, Edel & Ray, *op. cit.*, p. 191
7. H. G. Wells, *Experiment in Autobiography*, *op. cit.*, p. 493
8. H. G. Wells to Henry James, (9).10.1912, *Henry James and H. G. Wells*, Edel & Ray, *op. cit.*
9. H. G. Wells, *Boon, The Mind of the Race, The Wild Asses of the Devil* and *The Last Trump* (London, 1915), quoted in *Henry James and H. G. Wells, ibid.*, p. 248
10. *ibid.*, p. 249
11. *ibid.*, p. 250
12. *ibid.*, p. 257
13. Henry James to H. G. Wells, 6.7.1915, *Henry James Letters*, IV, *op. cit.*
14. Henry James to H. G. Wells, 10.7.1915, *ibid.*
15. Rebecca West, *Henry James* (London, 1916), p. 107
16. H. G. Wells to Hugh Walpole (1917), quoted by Norman and Jeanne Mackenzie in *The Time Traveller, op. cit.*, p. 292
17. Rebecca West, *Henry James, op. cit.*, p. 41
18. *ibid.*, p. 107
19. *ibid.*, p. 64
20. Henry James to Henry James, Junior, 30.10.1914, *Henry James Letters*, II, Lubbock, *op. cit.*
21. Henry James to Rhoda Broughton, 1.10.1914, *ibid.*
22. Leon Edel, *Henry James Letters*, IV, *op. cit.*, p. 570
23. Henry James to Clare Sheridan, 4.10.1915, *Henry James Letters*, IV, *op. cit.*
24. Henry James to Burgess Noakes, 22.3.1915, *ibid.*
25. Henry James to Hugh Walpole, 21.11.1914, *ibid.*
26. Violet Hunt, 'The Last Days of Henry James', *Daily Mail*, 1.3.1916, p. 4
27. Henry James to Edmund Gosse, 25.8.1915, *Henry James Letters*, IV, *op. cit.*
28. Henry James to Mrs Dacre Vincent, 6.1.1915, *Henry James Letters*, II, Lubbock, *op. cit.*
29. Henry James to Henry James, Junior, 24.6.1915, *Henry James Letters*, IV, *op. cit.*
30. J. A. Spender & Cyril Asquith, *Life of Henry Herbert Asquith, Lord Oxford and Asquith* (London, 1923), p. 216

31. Henry James to the Hon. Evan Charteris, 13.3.1915, *Henry James Letters,* II, Lubbock, *op. cit.*
32. Edmund Gosse, *The Times,* 4.3.1916

BIBLIOGRAPHIES

GENERAL BIBLIOGRAPHY

Gay Wilson Allen, *William James,* London, 1967

Quentin Anderson, *The American Henry James,* London 1957

Louis Auchincloss, *Edith Wharton: A Woman in her Time,* New York, 1971

—— 'Henry James's Use of his American Tour, 1904'; *South Atlantic Quarterly* (74), pp. 45–52

Geoffrey Spink Bagley, *The Book of Rye,* London, Barracuda Books, 1982

Jocelyn Baines, *Joseph Conrad: A Critical Biography,* London, Penguin, 1986

Consuelo Vanderbilt Balsan, *The Glitter and the Gold,* London, 1953

Harold Beaver, 'In the Land of Acquisition: H. G. Wells, The Future in America and Henry James, The American Scene,' *The Times Literary Supplement,* September 1987, p. 1020

Thomas Beer, *Stephen Crane,* London, 1924

Max Beerbohm, *A Book of Caricatures,* London, 1907

—— *Fifty Caricatures,* London, 1913

—— *Around Theatres,* London, Greenwood Press, 1969

—— *Letters to Reggie Turner,* ed. Rupert Hart-Davis, London, 1953

Millicent Bell, *Edith Wharton and Henry James,* New York, 1966

—— 'Henry James: The Man Who Lived', *Massachusetts Review* (14), Spring 1973, pp. 391–414

Arthur Benson, *Memories and Friends,* London, 1924

—— *The Diary of Arthur Benson,* ed. Percy Lubbock, London, 1926

E. F. Benson, *As We Were,* London, Hogarth Press, 1985

—— *As We Are,* London, Hogarth Press, 1985

Bernard Berenson, *Sketch for a Self-Portrait,* London, 1949

Bernard Bergonzi, *The Early Life of H. G. Wells,* London, 1961

Alwyn Berland, *Culture and Condition in the Novels of Henry James,* Cambridge, Cambridge University Press, 1981

John Berryman, *Stephen Crane,* London, Aquila Pub. Co., 1981

Marius Bewley, *The Eccentric Design,* London, 1959

David Bone, 'Memories of Conrad', *The Saturday Review of English Literature* (7), November 1925

H. R. Pratt Boorman, *Kent and the Cinque Ports,* London, 1957

Elmer Borklund, 'Howard Sturgis, Henry James, and *Belchamber'*, *Modern Philology,* Vol. 58, No. 4, May 1961

Theodora Bosanquet, *Henry James at Work,* Haskell House Pub., 1982

—— 'As I remember Henry James', *Time and Tide,* Vol. 35, No. 27, July 1954

Percy Boynton, *Some Contemporary Americans,* Chicago, 1924

Margaret Brentnall, *The Cinque Ports and Romney Marsh,* London, 1972

Vincent Brome, *H. G. Wells,* London, Greenwood Press, 1951

Van Wyck Brooks, *The World of H. G. Wells,* Haskell House Pub., 1982

—— *The Confident Years,* London, 1952

E. K. Brown, 'James and Conrad', *Yale Review* (35)' Winter 1946

G. F. Chambers, *Tourists' Guide to East Sussex,* London, 1891

G. K. Chesterton, *Autobiography,* London, Hamish Hamilton, 1986

Richard Church, *Kent,* London, Hale, 1966

Jill Colaco, 'Henry James and Mrs Humphry Ward: a Misunderstanding', *Notes and Queries* (23), pp. 408–10

Cyril Connolly, *Les Pavillons,* London, 1962

Borys Conrad, *My Father, Joseph Conrad,* London, J. Calder, 1970

—— *A Tour of Joseph Conrad's Homes,* London, 1974

Jessie Conrad, *Joseph Conrad as I Knew Him,* London, 1924; revised version, 1926

'Recollections of Stephen Crane', *Bookman,* April, 1926

—— *A Handbook of Cookery,* London, 1933

—— *Joseph Conrad and his Circle,* London, 1935

John Conrad, *Joseph Conrad: Times Remembered,* Cambridge, Cambridge University Press, 1981

Joseph Conrad, *Lettres françaises,* ed. Jean-Aubry, Paris, 1929

—— *Letters from Joseph Conrad,* 1895–1924, edited by David Garnett, London, 1928

—— *Collected Letters,* ed. Frederick R. Karl & Laurence Davies, vols. 1, 2 and 3 (1861–1907), Cambridge, Cambridge University Press, 1983, 1988

George Core, 'Henry, Leon & other Jamesians', *Michigan Quarterly Review* (12), Winter 1973, pp. 82–8

Stephen Crane, *Letters,* ed. R. W. Stallman & Lillian Gilkes, London, 1960

Stephen Crane, *The Critical Heritage,* ed. Richard M. Weatherford, London, Routledge, 1973

Fred A. Crawford, 'Hemingway & Brooks: the mystery of 'Henry's Bicycle', *Studies in American Fiction* (6), 1978, pp. 106–9

Nicholas Delbanco, *Group Portrait*, London, 1982

Lovat Dickson, *H. G. Wells: His Turbulent Life and Times*, London, 1969

R. Downey, *Some Errors of H. G. Wells*, London, 1933

F. W. Dupee, *Henry James*, New York, 1956

Leon Edel, *Henry James*, 5 volumes, London, 1953–1972; *Life of Henry James*, 2 volumes (paperback, condensed and revised), London, Penguin, 1977

—— *Henry James: A Life* (hardback, condensed and revised), London, 1987

—— *Stuff of Sleep and Dreams: Experiments in Literary Psychology*, London, 1982

Leon Edel and Dan Laurence, *Henry James: A Bibliography*, London, 1961

Susan Edmiston & Linda D. Cirino, *Literary New York*, Boston, 1976

Iain Finlayson, *Writers in Romney Marsh*, London, Severn House, 1986

Simon Fleet, 'In Search of Henry James at Rye', *Modern Age* (9), Winter 1964, pp. 69–76

Hamlin Garland, *Roadside Meetings*, London, 1931

David Garnett, *The Golden Echo*, London, 1954

Maxwell Geismar, *Henry James and his Cult*, London, 1964

Lillian Gilkes, *Cora Crane*, London, 1962

Richard Gill, *Happy Rural Seat: The English Country House and the Literary Imagination*, Yale, 1972

Douglas Goldring, *South Lodge*, London, 1943

—— *The Last Pre-Raphaelite: A Record of the Life and Writings of Ford Madox Ford*, London, 1948

John Gordon, 'The Ghost at Brede Place', *Bulletin of New York Public Library*, December 1952

Edmund Gosse, *Aspects and Impressions*, London, 1922

C. Hartley Grattan, *The Three Jameses*, London, 1932

Cynthia Griffin Wolff, *A Feast of Words: The Triumph of Edith Wharton*, Oxford, Oxford University Press, 1979

—— 'Lily Bart and the Beautiful Death', *American Literature* (46), 1974, pp. 16–40

Augustus Hare, *Sussex*, London, 1896

Rupert Hart-Davis, *Hugh Walpole*, London, 1952

John Harvey, 'Contrasting Worlds: A Study in the novels of Edith Wharton', *Etudes Anglaises* (7), 1954, pp. 190–8

Christopher Hassall, *Edward Marsh*, London, 1959

—— *Rupert Brooke*, London, Faber, 1972

Richard A. Hocks, *Henry James and pragmatistic thought: a study in the relationship between the philosophy of William James and the literary art of Henry James*, University of North Carolina, 1974

William Hollaway, *The History of Romney Marsh*, London, 1849

H. Montgomery Hyde, *The Story of Lamb House, Rye*, London, 1966

—— *Henry James at Home*, London, 1969

BIBLIOGRAPHIES

Samuel Hynes, *The Edwardian Turn of Mind*, London, 1968

Violet Hunt, *I Have This to Say: The Story of my Flurried Years*, London and New York, 1926

—— 'The Last days of Henry James', *Daily Mail*, 1.3.1916

Marcia Jacobson, *Henry James and the Mass Market*, Alabama, University of Alabama Press, 1984

Alice James, *The Diary of Alice James*, ed. Leon Edel, New York, 1964

Henry James, *Letters*, 4 vols. ed. Leon Edel, London and Harvard, Macmillan and Harvard University Press, 1975–1984

—— *Letters*, 2 vols, ed. Percy Lubbock, London, 1920

—— *The Complete Notebooks*, ed. Leon Edel and Lyall H. Powers, Oxford, Oxford University Press, 1987

—— *The Complete Plays*, ed. Leon Edel, London, 1949

—— *Henry James & H. G. Wells: A Correspondence*, ed. Leon Edel and Gordon N. Ray, London, 1959

—— *Henry James: Fiction as History*, ed. Ian Bell, London, 1984

—— *Interviews & Recollections*, ed. Norman Page, London, 1984

—— *The Critical Heritage*, ed. Roger Gard, London, 1968

—— *The Henry James Review*, three-yearly, ed. Daniel Mark Fogel, first published, 1979

William James, *Letters*, 2 vols, ed. Henry James, his son, London, 1920

Edith Ritchie Jones, 'Stephen Crane at Brede', *Atlantic Monthly*, July, 1954

Frederick Karl, *A Reader's Guide to Joseph Conrad*, New York, 1969

—— *Joseph Conrad: The Three Lives*, New York, 1979

—— 'Conrad and Pinker' in *Joseph Conrad: A Commemoration*, ed. Norman Sherry, London, 1976

Alfred Kazin, *On Native Grounds*, New York, 1942

Grace Kellogg, *The Two Lives of Edith Wharton*, New York, 1965

David K. Kirby, 'Henry James: Art and Autobiography', *Dalhousie Review* (52), Winter, 1972, pp. 637–44

Anita Leslie, *Mr Frewen of England*, London, 1966

John S. Lewis, 'Conrad in 1914', *The Polish Review*, Nos. 2 and 3, 1957

R. W. B. Lewis, *The American Adam: Innocence and Tragedy and Tradition in the Nineteenth Century*, Chicago, University of Chicago Press, 1955

—— *Edith Wharton*, London, Constable, 1975

R. W. B. Lewis and Nancy Lewis (eds.), *The Letters of Edith Wharton*, New York, Charles Scribner's Sons, 1988

C. Lewis Hind, *Authors and I*, London, 1921 *More Authors and I*, London, 1921

Gary H. Lindberg, *Edith Wharton and the Novel of Manners*, New York, 1976

Percy Lubbock, *Portrait of Edith Wharton*, London, 1947

—— *Mary Cholmondley*, London, 1928

Desmond Macarthy, *Portraits*, London, 1931

Kristin Pruitt McColgan, *Henry James: A Reference Guide*, London, 1979

Margaret Blame McDowell, 'Viewing the Custom of the Country: Edith Wharton's Feminism', *Contemporary Literature* (15) 1974, pp. 521–38

—— *Edith Wharton: A Bibliography*, Boston, Massachusetts, 1976

Sir Compton Mackenzie, *My Life and Times*, 6 vols, London, 1963–7

Norman and Jeanne Mackenzie, *The Time Traveller: The Life of H. G. Wells*, London, 1973; Hogarth Press, London 1987

Katherine Mansfield, *Novels and Novelists*, ed. J. Middleton Murry, London, 1930

Edward Marsh, *A Number of People*, London, 1939

A. E. W. Mason, *Sir George Alexander and the St James's Theatre*, London, 1935

F. O. Matthiessen, *The James Family*, New York, 1947

R. L. Megroz, *A Talk with Joseph Conrad: A Criticism of his Mind and Method*, London, 1926

H. L. Mencken, *The American Language*, New York, 1926

Mathilde Meyer, *H. G. Wells and his Family*, London, 1956

Arthur Mizener, *The Saddest Story: A Biography of Ford Madox Ford*, London, 1971

Modern Fiction Studies, *Henry James Number* (12), Spring 1966

Lady Ottoline Morrell, *Memoirs: A Study in Friendship*, ed. R. Gathorne-Hardy, New York, 1964

Zdzislaw Najder, *Joseph Conrad: A Chronicle*, Cambridge, Cambridge University Press, 1984

Blake Nevius, *Edith Wharton: A Study of her Fiction*, University of California Press, 1976

Simon Nowell-Smith, *The Legend of the Master*, London, 1947

Hajime Okita, 'Henry James's Contribution to American Literature', *Timbun* (4), Kyoto Prefecturial University, October 1962, pp. 51–73

Stanley Olsen, *John Singer Sargent*, London, 1986

Ralph Barton Perry, *The Thought and Character of William James*, London, 1953

Stow Persons, *The Decline of American Gentility*, New York, 1973

Lyall H. Powers, *Henry James: An Introduction and Interpretation*, New York, 1970

Jonathan Rose, *The Edwardian Temperament 1895–1919*, Ohio University Press, 1986

Daniel N. Roselli, 'Max Beerbohm's Unpublished Parody of Henry James', *Review of English Studies*, February 1971, pp. 61–3

Bertrand Russell, *Portraits from Memory*, London, Allen & Unwin, 1956

—— *Autobiography*, 1872–1914, London, Allen & Unwin, 1967

E. W. Said, *Joseph Conrad and the Fiction of Autobiography*, Cambridge, Massachusetts, 1966

Vittoria Sanni, 'I romanzi di Edith Wharton e la narrativa jamesiana', *American Studies* (studi americani) (10), 1964, pp. 229–91

George Santayana, *Winds of Doctrine,* New York, 1926

Robert Secor, 'Henry James and Violet Hunt, "The Improper Person of Babylon"', *Journal of Modern Literature,* vol. 13, (1) March 1986, pp. 3–36

Henry Dwight Sedgwick, *The New American Type and Other Essays,* Boston, 1908

Norman Sherry, *Conrad's Eastern World,* Cambridge, Cambridge University Press, 1977

—— *Conrad's Western World,* Cambridge, Cambridge University Press, 1971

—— (ed.) *Joseph Conrad: A Commemoration,* London, Macmillan, 1976

—— (ed.) *Joseph Conrad: The Critical Heritage,* London, 1973

Logan Pearsall Smith, *Unforgotten Years,* London, 1938

Eric Solomon, *Stephen Crane in England,* Columbus Ohio St University

J. A. Spender & Cyril Asquith, *Life of Henry Herbert Asquith, Lord Oxford & Asquith,* London, 1932

R. W. Stallman, *Stephen Crane,* New York, 1968

August W. Staub, 'The Well-Made Failures of Henry James', *Southern Speech Journal* (27), Winter 1961, pp. 91–101

Michael Swan, *Henry James,* London, 1952

Frank Swinnerton, *An Autobiography,* London, 1935

William Makepeace Thackeray, *Denis Duval,* London, 1869

Ann Thwaite, *Edmund Gosse: A Literary Landscape,* Oxford, Oxford University Press, 1985

Adeline R. Tintner, 'Landmarks of "the terrible town": the New York scene in Henry James's last stories', *Prospects* (2), 1976, pp. 399–435

Janet Penrose Trevelyan, *The Life of Mrs Humphry Ward,* London, 1923

Lionel Trilling, *A Gathering of Fugitives,* London, 1957

James W. Tuttleton, 'Henry James and Edith Wharton: Fiction as the House of Fame', *Midcontinent American Studies Journal* (7), Spring 1966, pp. 25–36

Thorstein Veblen, *The Theory of the Leisure Class: An Economic Study of Institution,* New York, 1899

Geoffrey Walton, *Edith Wharton: A Critical Interpretation,* Fairleigh Dickinson UP., 1983

Mrs Humphry Ward, *A Writer's Recollections,* New York, 1918

Lady Maud Warrender, *My First Sixty Years,* London, 1933

Ian Watt, 'Conrad, James and "Chance"' in *Imagined Worlds: Essays on Some English Novels and Novelists in Honour of John Butt,* ed. Maynard Mack and Ian Gregor, London, 1968

Stanley Weintraub, *The London Yankees,* New York, 1979

G. P. Wells, *H. G. Wells in Love,* London, 1984

H. G. Wells, *Interviews and Recollections,* ed. J. R. Hammond, London, 1980

Carol Wershovan, *The Female Intruder in the Novels of Edith Wharton,* Fairleigh Dickinson UP., 1983

GENERAL BIBLIOGRAPHY

Dame Rebecca West, *Henry James*, Haskell House Pub., 1982

Edith Wharton, *A Collection of Critical Essays*, ed. Irving Howe, London, 1962

Morton and Lucia White, *The Intellectual versus the City*, London, Greenwood Press, 1981

Edmund Wilson, *The Wound and the Bow*, New York, 1947

WORKS WRITTEN BY THE AUTHORS, 1895–1915

This is not a full list of each writer's works but of those published in the period covered in this book. I have, however, included those few exceptions to which reference has been made in the text.

The date of first publication is given with every title.

Joseph Conrad
Almayer's Folly, London, 1895
An Outcast of the Islands, London, 1896
The Nigger of the 'Narcissus', London, 1897
Tales of Unrest, London, 1898
Lord Jim, London, 1900
The Inheritors, London, 1901 (in collaboration with Ford.)
Youth and Two Stories, London, 1902
Typhoon and Other Stories, London, 1903
Romance, London, 1903 (in collaboration with Ford.)
Nostromo – A Tale of the Seaboard, London, 1904
The Mirror of the Sea – Memories and Impressions, London, 1906
The Secret Agent – A Simple Tale, London, 1907
A Set of Six, London, 1908
Under Western Eyes, London, 1911
Some Reminiscences (later renamed *A Personal Record*), London, 1912
'Twixt Land and Sea – Tales, London, 1912
Chance – A Tale in Two Parts, London, 1913
Within the Tides – Tales, London, 1915
Victory – An Island Tale, London, 1915
Conrad's pamphlet on *Henry James* was published in 1919

Stephen Crane

Maggie: A Girl of the Streets, New York, 1893, under pseudonym of Johnston Smith

The Black Riders and other Lines, Boston, 1895

The Red Badge of Courage, New York, 1895

George's Mother, New York and London, 1896

The Little Regiment and Other Episodes of the American Civil War, New York, 1896

The Third Violet, New York and London, 1897

The Open Boat and Other Stories, New York and London, 1898

The Monster and Other Stories, New York and London, 1899

War is Kind, New York, 1899

Active Service, New York and London, 1899

Whilomville Stories, New York and London, 1900

Wounds in the Rain: A Collection of Stories relating to the Spanish–American War of 1898, New York and London, 1900

Great Battles of the World, New York and London, 1901 (posthumous)

Last Words: A posthumous collection of Crane's stories and articles, London, 1902

The O'Ruddy: A Romance, completed by Robert Barr, London, 1903

Ford Madox Ford

Ford Madox Brown: A Record of his Life, London, 1896

The Cinque Ports, London, 1900

Poems for Pictures, London, 1900

Rossetti, London, 1902

The Face of the Night (Poems), London, 1904

The Soul of London, London, 1905

The Benefactor, London, 1905

Hans Holbein the Younger, London, 1905

The Fifth Queen, London, 1906

The Heart of the Country, London, 1906

Christina's Fairy Book, London, 1906

Privy Seal, London, 1907

From Inland (Poems), London, 1907

An English Girl, London, 1907

The Spirit of the People, London, 1907

The Pre-Raphaelite Brotherhood, London, 1907

The Fifth Queen Crowned, London, 1908

Mr Apollo, London, 1908

The Half Moon, London, 1909

Songs from London, London, 1910

A Call, London, 1910

The Portrait, London, 1910

Ancient Lights, London, 1910

The Simple Life Limited, under pseudonym of Daniel Chaucer, London, 1911
Ladies Whose Bright Eyes, London, 1911
The Critical Attitude, London, 1911
High Germany (Poems), London, 1912
The Panel, London, 1912
The New Humpty-Dumpty, under pseudonym of Daniel Chaucer, London, 1912
The Monstrous Regiment of Women (Pamphlet), London, 1913
Mr Fleight, unpublished, London, 1913. The publishers, Latimer and Byles, were unable to pay the printer's bill.
The Young Lovell, London, 1913
Collected Poems, London, 1913
Henry James, London, 1913
The Good Soldier, London, 1915
When Blood is their Argument, London, 1915
Between St Dennis and St George, London, 1915
Antwerp, Poems, illustrated by Wyndham Lewis, London, 1915

Harold Frederic
The Damnation of Theron Ware, London and New York, 1896

Henry James
Guy Domville, 1895, Play
The Next Time, 1895, Short story
The Altar of the Dead, 1895, Short story
The Figure in the Carpet, 1896, Short story
Glasses, 1896, Short story
The Friends of the Friends, 1896, Short story
What Maisie Knew, 1897, Novel
The Spoils of Poynton, 1897, Novel
The Turn of the Screw, 1898, Novella
In the Cage, 1898, Short story
Covering End, 1895, Short story adapted from the play, *Summersoft,* 1895
The Given Case, 1898, Short story
John Delavoy, 1898, Short story
The Awkward Age, 1899, Novel; Oxford, Oxford University Press, 1984
The Great Condition 1899, Short story
Europe, 1899, Short story
Paste, 1899, Short story
The Real Right Thing, 1899, Short story
The Great Good Place, 1900, Short story
Maud Evelyn, 1900, Short story
Miss Gunton of Poughkeepsie, 1900, Short story
The Tree of Knowledge, 1900, Short story
The Abasement of the Northmores, 1900, Short story

The Third Person, 1900, Short story
The Special Type, 1900, Short story
The Tone of Time, 1900, Short story
Broken Wings, 1900, Short story
The Two Faces, 1900, Short story
Mrs Medwin, 1900, Short story
The Beldonald Holbein, 1900, Short story
The Sacred Fount, 1901, Novel
The Wings of the Dove, 1902 Novel
Flickerbridge, 1902, Story
The Story in It, 1902, Story
The Ambassadors, 1903, Novel
The Beast in the Jungle, 1903, Story
The Birthplace, 1903, Story
The Golden Bowl, 1904, Novel
Fordham Castle, 1904, Short story
English Hours, 1905, Non-fiction
The American Scene, 1907, Non-fiction
The High Bid, 1908, Play, from the story 'Covering End' of 1895
Julia Bride, 1908, Short story
The Jolly Corner, 1908, Short story
The Velvet Glove, 1909, Short Story
The Bench of Desolation, 1909, Short Story
Crapy Cornelia, 1909, Short story
Mora Montravers, 1909, Short story
The Outcry, 1909, Play
Italian Hours, 1909, Non-fiction
A Small Boy and Others, 1913, Autobiography
Notes of a Son and Brother, 1914, Autobiography
Posthumously published:
    The Middle Years, 1917, Autobiography
    The Ivory Tower, 1917, Novel
    The Sense of the Past, 1917, Novel

William James
The Principles of Psychology, 1890
The Will to Believe and Other Essays, 1897
Human Immortality, 1898
Talks to Teachers on Psychology and to Students on some of Life's Ideals, 1899
Varieties of Religious Experience, 1902
Pragmatism, 1907
A Pluralistic Universe, 1909
The Meaning of Truth, 1909
Posthumously published:
Some Problems in Philosophy, 1911

Howard Sturgis
Tim, 1891
All That was Possible, 1895
Belchamber, 1904

Julian Sturgis *(a selected list)*
An Accomplished Gentleman, 1879
John Maidment, 1885
Comedy of a Country House, 1889
The Folly of Pen Harrington, 1897
Stephen Calinari, 1901

Hugh Walpole
The Wooden Horse, 1909
Maradick at Forty, 1910
Mr Perrin and Mr Traill, 1911
The Prelude to Adventure, 1912
Fortitude, 1913
The Duchess of Wrexe, 1914
The Golden Scarecrow, 1915
The Dark Forest, 1916
Joseph Conrad, 1916

H. G. Wells
The Time Machine, 1895, Novel
The Wonderful Visit, 1905
The Stolen Bacillus, and Other Incidents, 1895
The Island of Dr Moreau, 1896
The Wheels of Chance, 1896
The Plattner Story, and Others, 1897
The Invisible Man, 1897
Certain Personal Matters: A Collection of Material, Mainly Autobiographical, 1897
The War of the Worlds, 1898
When the Sleeper Wakes: A Story of Years to Come, 1899
Tales of Space and Time, 1899
Love and Mr Lewisham, 1900
The First Men in the Moon, 1901
Anticipations of the Reaction of Mechanical and Scientific Progress upon Human Life and Thought, 1901
The Discovery of the Future, 1902
The Sea Lady: A Tissue of Moonshine, 1902
Mankind in the Making, 1903
Twelve Stories and a Dream, 1903
The Food of the Gods, and How It Came to Earth, 1904
A Modern Utopia, 1905

Kipps: The Story of a Simple Soul, 1905
In the Days of the Comet, 1906
The Future in America: A Search after Realities, 1906
This Misery of Boots, 1907
New Worlds for Old, 1908
The War in the Air, and Particularly How Mr Bert Smallways Fared While It
    Lasted, 1908
First and Last Things: A Confession of Faith and Rule of Life, 1908
Tono-Bungay, 1909
Ann Veronica, 1909
The History of Mr Polly, 1910
The New Machiavelli, 1911
The Country of the Blind and Other Stories, 1911
Floor Games, 1911
Marriage, 1912
Little Wars: A Game for Boys from Twelve Years of Age to One Hundred and
    Fifty and for That More Intelligent Sort of Girls Who Like Boys' Games, 1913
The Passionate Friends, 1913
An Englishman Looks at the World, 1914
The World Set Free, 1914
The Wife of Sir Isaac Harman, 1914
The War that Will End War, 1914
Boon, the Mind of the Race, the Wild Asses of the Devil, and the Last Trump,
    Being a First Selection from the Literary Remains of George Boon, Appropriate
    to the Times, 1915
Bealby: A Holiday, 1915
The Research Magnificent, 1915
Mr Britling Sees it Through, 1916

Edith Wharton
The Decoration of Houses (with Ogden Codman, Jr.), New York, 1897
The Greater Inclination, New York, 1899
The Touchstone, New York, 1900. Published in England as A Gift from the
    Grave, London, 1900
Crucial Instances, New York, 1901
The Valley of Decision, 1902. 2 vols.
Sanctuary, New York, 1903
The Descent of Man, and Other Stories, New York, 1904. One additional
    story, The Letter, is in the English publication of 1904
Italian Villas and Their Gardens, New York, 1904
Italian Backgrounds, New York, 1905
Madame de Treymes, New York, 1907
The Fruit of the Tree, New York, 1907
A Motor-Flight through France, New York, 1908
The Hermit and the Wild Woman and Other Stories, New York, 1908
Artemis to Actaeon and Other Verse, New York, 1909
Tales of Men and Ghosts, New York, 1910

WORKS WRITTEN BY THE AUTHORS, *1895–1915*

Ethan Frome, New York, 1911
The Reef, New York, 1912
The Custom of the Country, New York, 1913
Fighting France, from Dunkerque to Belfort, New York, 1915

INDEX

INDEX